Arthur Biddle, George Biddle

A Treatise on the Law of Stock Brokers

Arthur Biddle, George Biddle

A Treatise on the Law of Stock Brokers

ISBN/EAN: 9783743315174

Manufactured in Europe, USA, Canada, Australia, Japa

Cover: Foto ©ninafisch / pixelio.de

Manufactured and distributed by brebook publishing software (www.brebook.com)

Arthur Biddle, George Biddle

A Treatise on the Law of Stock Brokers

A TREATISE

ON THE LAW OF

STOCK BROKERS.

BY
ARTHUR BIDDLE AND GEORGE BIDDLE,
OF THE PHILADELPHIA BAR.

PHILADELPHIA:
J. B. LIPPINCOTT & CO.
1882.

Copyright, 1881, by J. B. LIPPINCOTT & Co.

TO

GEORGE W. BIDDLE,

THIS BOOK IS AFFECTIONATELY DEDICATED,

BY THE AUTHORS.

PREFACE.

The transactions growing out of the sale and hypothecation of the securities dealt in at the Stock Exchange already form, both in their number and magnitude, one of the most important branches of business carried on in great commercial centres, and the questions arising out of them are subjects upon which the lawyer is almost daily called upon to advise.

Several excellent works have been written on kindred subjects, which, however, have been devoted rather to the character of such securities, and the obligations they impose upon the corporations issuing them, than to the law governing the parties buying and selling them. In the present work the authors have attempted to discuss the law relating to the agents in these transactions,—stock brokers and their customers,—and the character of the thing sold, so far as it relates to questions arising out of sales of it.

ARTHUR BIDDLE,
221 South Sixth Street, Philadelphia.

GEORGE BIDDLE,
208 South Fifth Street, Philadelphia.

TABLE OF CONTENTS.

PART I.

THE STOCK BROKER.

CHAPTER I.
                                                                          PAGE

DESCRIPTION OF THE STOCK BROKER 33

CHAPTER II.

THE STOCK BROKER AND THE STOCK EXCHANGE 43
    Section I.—Description of the Constitution and Nature of the
        Stock Exchange 43
        § 1. The London Stock Exchange 44
        § 2. The American Stock Exchange 49
    Section II.—The Clearing House 55
       " III.—Effect of the Rules of the Stock Exchange . . 65
       " IV.—Terms of the Trade used on the Stock Exchange . 69

CHAPTER III.

THE STOCK BROKER AND HIS PRINCIPAL 75
    Section I.—Creation of the Agency 75
       " II.—Scope of the Stock Broker's Authority to Act . 85
       " III.—Execution of Authority 100
        § 1. General Rules 100
        § 2. Liability of the Stock Broker to his Principal . . 106

		PAGE
§ 3. Liability of the Principal to the Stock Broker	. .	107
1. General Rules	. .	107
2. Advances and Disbursements .	. . .	110
3. Commissions	. .	116
§ 4. Stock Broker's Lien . . .	. . .	118
Section IV.—Dissolution of the Stock Broker's Agency	. .	122
1. By the Broker	. .	122
2. By the Principal . . .	. .	123
3. By the Mere Operation of Law .	. .	123

CHAPTER IV.

RELATION OF THE STOCK BROKER TO THIRD PARTIES . . . 129
    Section I.—Stock Broker's Relation to Third Parties, ordinarily 129
    " II.—Stock Brokers and Stock Jobbers 132

PART II.

THE SALE.

CHAPTER I.

THE THING SOLD AT THE STOCK EXCHANGE. 139
    Section I.—Under what Species of Property Securities Sold at the Stock Exchange are Classed 140
    Section II.—Negotiability of these Securities 148
    " III.—Incidents attached to the Thing Sold . . . 174

CHAPTER II.

THE CONTRACT OF SALE. 182
    Section I.—The Necessary Ownership by the Parties in the Thing Sold 182
    Section II.—The Mutual Assent of the Parties to the Contract 190
    " III.—The Price 193

CHAPTER III.

EFFECT OF THE 17TH SECTION OF THE STATUTE OF FRAUDS ON THE CONTRACT 194

Section I.—What Contracts are within the 17th Section of the Statute 195
Section II.—What Securities are "Goods, Wares, and Merchandises" within the meaning of the 17th Section . . 197
Section III.—Earnest, Payment, and Acceptance . . . 204
" IV.—What is a Sufficient Memorandum in Writing . 205
" V.—Who is an Agent duly Authorized . . . 206

CHAPTER IV.

EFFECT OF THE STATUTE OF MORTMAIN ON THE CONTRACT . . 207

CHAPTER V.

EFFECT OF THE FOURTH SECTION OF THE STATUTE OF FRAUDS ON THE CONTRACT 214

CHAPTER VI.

EFFECT OF THE USAGE OF TRADE ON THE CONTRACT . . . 215

CHAPTER VII.

RELATION OF THE VENDOR AND VENDEE AFTER THE CONTRACT . 230
Section I.—Relation of Vendor and Vendee after an Executed and Executory Contract of Sale 230
Section II.—Specific Performance 234
§ 1. English Cases 235
§ 2. American Cases 247

CHAPTER VIII.

COMPLETION OF THE CONTRACT, OR THE DELIVERY OF THE THING SOLD 258
Section I.—The Vendor 260
§ 1. What the Vendor must Deliver 261
§ 2. The Implied Condition attached to the Delivery by the Vendor 262
§ 3. The Manner of Effecting the Delivery . . . 266
Section II.—The Vendee 281
§ 1. Acceptance and Payment 281
§ 2. Registration 283

CHAPTER IX.

	PAGE
AVOIDANCE OF THE CONTRACT	287
Section I.—Avoidance of the Contract by Fraud, etc. . .	288
§ 1. Fraud	288
§ 2. Mistake	288
§ 3. Failure of Consideration	289
Section II.—Avoidance of the Contract by Illegality . .	290
§ 1. Contracts Illegal at Common Law because in Restraint of Trade	290
§ 2. Contracts Illegal because in the Nature of Wagers .	296
I. Where the vendor, at the formation of the contract, has not the goods in his possession, nor a reasonable expectation of getting them, but contemplates an actual unconditional delivery .	302
II. Where the vendor, at the formation of the contract, contemplates a symbolical, but not a manual, unconditional delivery . . .	302
III. Where the parties, at the formation of the contract, contemplate an actual delivery, but conditional as to time	309
IV. Where the parties, at the formation of the contract, contemplate no actual delivery, but reserve the option to do so or not . . .	310
V. Where the parties, at the formation of the contract, contemplate no delivery at all, but only a settlement of the difference in prices . .	313

PART III.

THE PLEDGE.

CHAPTER I.

FORMATION OF THE PLEDGE	322
Section I.—Who may Pledge	322
" II.—The Subject-Matter of the Pledge	337
" III.—Manner of Effecting the Pledge	338

CHAPTER II.

EFFECT OF THE PLEDGE. 339
   Section I.—The Pledgee's Title in the Pledge 340
   " II.—The Pledgee's Right to Enjoy the Use of the Thing
        Pledged 342
     § 1. Pledgee's Right to Vote, collect Dividends, Coupons,
        etc. 342
     § 2. Pledgee's Right to Sell the Pledge 343
     § 3. Pledgee's Right to Sub-Pledge or Rehypothecate . 353
       I. When securities have been deposited as collateral for the payment of a debt, with the right on the part of the pawnee to sell or otherwise dispose of the same in the event of the non-payment of the debt, and the pawnee repledges the securities to a third party for an advance to himself, can the original pawnor, the debt remaining unpaid, treat the contract of pawn between himself and the first pawnee as at an end, so as to bring an action of detinue or trover against the second pawnee, without tendering the amount of the debt, for which the security has been given? 354
       II. If the contract of pawn between the first pawnee and the original pawnor is not at an end in the event of the former thus rehypothecating the security deposited with him for a debt of his own, is it, at all events, such a breach of the contract of pawn that an action for damages will lie against the first pawnee, at the hands of the first pawnor, and can the original pawnor, on tendering the amount of his own debt to the second pawnee, obtain possession of the subject of the pawn? 364

CHAPTER III.

AVOIDANCE OF THE CONTRACT OF PLEDGE 370

PART IV.

REMEDIES OF THE PARTIES FOR A BREACH OF THE CONTRACT OF SALE.

CHAPTER I.

REMEDIES OF THE PARTIES AGAINST EACH OTHER, OF CREDITORS AGAINST THE THING ITSELF, AND OF THE PARTIES AGAINST THE CORPORATION FOR REFUSING TO TRANSFER STOCK ON ITS TRANSFER BOOKS 388
    Section I.—Remedies of the Parties against Each Other . . 389
    " II.—Remedies of Creditors against the Thing itself . 391
    " III.—Remedies of the Parties against a Corporation for not Transferring Stock on its Transfer Books . 393
        1. Where the company acts on a forged transfer, and issues a certificate which a *bona fide* purchaser subsequently buys . . . 405
        2. Where the transferee purchases stock, and takes a forged power to transfer to the company, and gets certificates issued to him by reason of the forged power . . . 407
        3. Where the transferee bargains for stock, and refuses to take the certificates till registered in his name, and the company issues certificates on the faith of a forged power of transfer presented by the seller 410

CHAPTER II.

MEASURE OF DAMAGE FOR THE BREACH OF THE CONTRACT OF SALE AND PLEDGE 413
    Section I.—Measure of Damages where no Consideration has passed 414
    Section II.—Measure of Damages where the Consideration has passed 416

TABLE OF CASES.

A.

	PAGE
A. & T. Co. v. Commonwealth	180
Abinger, Bulteel v.	334, 336
Ackerman v. Emott	84
Ackley, McDowell v.	67
Acraman v. Cooper	146, 391
Adams, Brown v.	376
Adams, Hunt v.	273
Adams, N. P. R. R. Co. v.	174
Adams, Thompson v.	52, 69
Albrecht, Duncuft v.	146, 199, 239
Alexander v. Brame	213, 336
Alexander, Dunmore v.	191
Alford, Knapp v.	128
Allaire v. Hartshorne	373
Allen v. Dykers	103, 363, 419
Allen v. Hearn	298
Allen, Hyatt v.	179
Allen v. Kinyon	424
Allen v. Pegram	145
Alley v. Hotson	128
Allison v. Wilson's Ex.	213
Alton & S. R. R. Co., Ryder v.	176
Alvord v. Smith	298
Ammant v. N. Alex. Turnpike Co.	392
Amory, Harvard College v.	84
Anderson, Hodson v.	128
Androscoggin R. R. Co. v. Bank	342
Anglo-American Tel. Co., Simm v.	157, 407, 411, 412
Appleby, Pickering v.	146, 198
Archer, Upton v.	274
Arents v. Commonwealth	168
Arey, Hinkle v.	34
Argenti, Hyatt v.	353
Armistead, De Beguis v.	115
Armstrong v. Toler	107, 112, 113, 114
Arnold v. Bank	393
Arnold, Chauncey v.	277
Arnold v. Ruggles	146
Arnott v. Pittston	295
Arthurs, Cramer v.	213
Ashby v. Blackwell	410
Ashe v. Johnson	250
Ashford, Home v.	296

	PAGE
Ashhurst v. Given	333
Ashton v. Atlantic Bank	324
Ashton v. Dakin	303
Ashton v. Lord Langdale	210, 213
Aspinwall, Commissioners v.	165
Aston, In re	105
Atkins, Kemble v.	34, 40, 91
Atkinson v. Atkinson	269, 273
Atkinson v. Brooks	373
Atkinson, Magee v.	46, 96, 131
Attorney-General v. Bouwens	159
Atty.-Genl., Marsh v.	213
Aucompte, Cockerell v.	88
Aurora City v. West	168
Austin v. Curtis	373
Austin v. Gillaspie	250
Ayres v. Harness	274

B.

	PAGE
Babcock, Stephens v.	100
Babcock v. Thompson	298
Badger, Prickett v.	116
Bahia & San Francisco Ry. Co., In matter of	405, 416
Baker v. Drake	353, 419, 420
Baker, Glynn v.	158
Baker, Mack v.	372
Baker, Tarlton v.	298
Baldwin, Bryan v.	351
Baldwin v. Commonwealth	250
Baldwin v. Williams	146
Ball v. Dunsterville	82
Ball v. Gilbert	298
Ball, Paul v.	142
Bullard v. Burgett	360
Bank, Androscoggin R. R. Co. v.	342
Bank, Arnold v.	393
Bank, Ashton v.	324
Bank, Bank of Kentucky v.	399, 401
Bank, Bayard v.	323, 331
Bank v. Boyd	428
Bank v. Brays	180

14 TABLE OF CASES.

	PAGE
Bank, Bullard v.	177
Bank v. Burr	266
Bank v. Carrington	372
Bank v. Chambers	373
Bank, Coles v.	393
Bank, Conant v.	178
Bank v. Cook	338, 342
Bank, Cross v.	271
Bank, Davis v.	393
Bank v. Dubuque R. R. Co.	348
Bank, Dutton v.	376
Bank v. Evans Charities	395, 404
Bank, Fisher v.	375
Bank, Foster v.	393
Bank, Grant v.	178
Bank v. Hall	277, 328
Bank v. Hammond	278
Bank, Hutchins v.	145, 147
Bank, In re, etc.	242
Bank v. Kortright	156, 178, 276, 393, 419
Bank, Laird v.	177
Bank v. Lanier	154, 177
Bank v. Leavenworth	373
Bank, Lee v.	374
Bank, Leggett v.	178
Bank, Lockwood v.	177
Bank v. Lowry	328
Bank v. McCleod	85, 90
Bank v. McDougall	302
Bank v. McElrath	374
Bank, McNeil v.	359, 362, 374
Bank, Mathews v.	153, 155, 156
Bank v. Minot	348
Bank, Moodie v.	155
Bank v. New England Bank	95
Bank v. N. Y. & N. H. R. R. Co.	149, 396
Bank of Commerce's Appeal	375, 401
Bank, Phelps v.	179
Bank, Plymouth Bank v.	178
Bank, Pollock v.	248, 410
Bank, Pratt v.	410
Bank, Presbyterian Congregation v.	178
Bank, Purchase v.	249
Bank v. R. R. Co.	156, 168, 277, 372, 374
Bank v. Reese	417, 419
Bank, Reese v.	178
Bank, Rex v.	83, 393
Bank, Robinson v.	242
Bank, Rogers v.	177, 179
Bank, Royer v.	373
Bank, Sabin v.	179
Bank v. Schuylkill Bank	399
Bank v. Smalley	178
Bank, State v.	174, 176, 180
Bank, Stevens v.	351
Bank, Stracy v.	393

	PAGE
Bank, Torrey v.	348
Bank v. Trenholm	94, 105, 364
Bank, Vansands v.	178
Bank, Wallis v.	123
Bank v. Waltham	142
Bank v. Welch	373
Bank v. Williams	376
Bank v. Wilson	266
Barclay, Hamonds v.	118
Barclay Coal Co., Morris Run Coal Co. v.	291, 295
Baring v. Corrie	34
Barkman, Bertrand v.	373
Barnet, Van Hook v.	273
Barnewell, Henderson v.	34, 95, 206
Barnum v. Munn	267
Barr v. Schroeder	128
Bartholomew, Drybutter v.	144
Bartlett v. Drew	179
Bartlett, Walker v.	172, 269, 284
Bassett, Granger v.	180
Basten v. Butler	112
Bates v. Ins. Co.	176
Bates v. Wiles	423
Baud v. Fardell	84
Bay, Coddington v.	373
Bayard v. Bank	323, 331
Bayley v. Wilkins	111, 218
Bayliffe v. Butterworth	94, 224
Bean, Jenners v.	373
Beckendorff, Musgrave v.	419
Beeker v. Vrooman	112
Beers v. Crowell	200
Beetston v. Beetston	113
Belfield, Bradford v.	333
Bell, Bowlby v.	199, 283
Bell, Catlin v.	85, 96, 100
Bell, Mocatia v.	107, 131
Bellas v. McCarty	329
Belote v. White	336
Beltzhoover v. Darragh	330
Bemis, Howe v.	350
Benedict, Bigelow v.	311, 318
Bennett v. Hull	197, 369, 382, 417
Bennett, Work v.	362, 382, 417
Benoit v. Conway	128
Bentley, N. A. Col. As. Co. v.	393
Bercich v. Marye	424
Berger v. Duff	334, 336
Berger, Stahl v.	275
Bernard, Coggs v.	356
Bertram v. Godfrey	87
Bertrand v. Barkman	373
Betterbee v. Davis	282
Beverley v. Lincoln Gas Co.	83
Bianchi v. Nash	286
Biederman v. Stone	109
Bigelow v. Benedict	311, 318

TABLE OF CASES.

	PAGE
Bigelow, Orr v.	178
Biggs, Rex v.	82
Birch, Walker v.	122
Bird, Meadows v.	373
Blackburn v. Scholes	123
Blackmore v. Shelby	187
Blackstone v. Buttermore	128
Blackwell, Ashby v.	410
Blake, Cole v.	286
Blanchard v. Stevens	372
Blane, Grizewood v.	314
Blane, Sayles v.	285
Bligh v. Brent	142
Blood v. Goodrich	276
Bloodgood, Kane v.	180
" Blyth v. Carpenter	387
Boardman v. Gore	278
Bodenhammer, Newsom v.	388
Bohlen's Estate	336
Bond, Clough v.	330
Bond, Conkey v.	90
Bonsall, Kirkpatrick v.	312
Booth v. Fielding	95
Boston, King v.	112
Boston Water-Power Co., Sewall v.	410
" Bourne v. Seymour	89
Bouvier, Smith v.	302
Bouwens, Attorney-General v.	159
Bowden, Goodwin v.	128
Bower v. Jones	116
Bowlby v. Bell	199, 283
Boyd, Bank v.	423
Boylan v. Huguet	146, 386, 387, 391, 423
Boyson v. Coles	90
Bradford v. Belfield	333
Bradley v. Holdsworth	142, 199
Bragg v. Fessenden	272
Brainerd v. N. Y. & N. H. R. R. Co.	168
Brainerd, Sewall v.	174
Brame, Alexander v.	213
Brancker, Parker v.	120
Brandt, Sharman v.	96, 97
Brass v. Worth	345
Brays, Bank v.	180
Breedlove v. Johnson	278
Brenizer, Morrow v.	213
Brent, Bligh v.	142
Breton v. Pierce	372
Brewster v. Hartley	338
Bridge Co., Ellis v.	266
Briggs, Oriental Steam Co. v.	245
Brightwell v. Mallory	174
Brinley, Jones v.	140
Bristoe, Coles v.	47, 48, 133, 134, 222
Bristowe, Grissell v.	41, 48, 134, 222
Brockway, Chappell v.	293
Bromley v. Coxwell	100

	PAGE
Bronson's Ex., Newton v.	336
Brookman, Rothschild v.	90
Brooks, Atkinson v.	373
Brooks v. Martin	114
Brooks, Watts v.	118
Brown v. Adams	376
Brown v. Coal & Nav. Co.	180
Brown v. Croft	118
Brown v. Duncan	112
Brown, Fisher v.	423
Brown v. Johnson	280
Brown v. Leeson	297
Brown v. McGran	86, 120
Brown v. Speyers	302
Brown v. Thompson	298
Brown v. Turner	72, 298
Brown v. Ward	346
Brown v. Williamson's Ex.	333
Brua's Appeal	298, 305, 309, 317
Brundage v. Brundage	179
Bryan v. Baldwin	351
Bryan v. Lewis	185, 186, 302, 351
Bryce, Canaan v.	107, 112, 115
Buckeridge v. Ingram	144
Budd v. Hiler	386
Bullard v. Bank	177
Bulteel v. Abinger	334, 336
Bunn v. Riker	298
Bunting, Somerby v.	202
Burgett, Ballard v.	360
Burns v. Lynde	273
Burr, Bank v.	266
Burroughs v. Richmond	174
Burslem, Pidgeon v.	118
Burt, Durant v.	114
Burt v. Dutcher	419
Busk, Pickering v.	84, 94, 262
Butler v. Basten	112
Buttermore, Blackstone v.	128
Butterworth, Bayliffe v.	94, 224, 343
Butterworth v. Kennedy	343
Buttrick v. Holden	332
Byers v. McClanahan	274
Byrne, Ward v.	295

C.

C. R. & B. Co. v. A. & G. R. R. Co.	424
Calais Steamboat v. Van Pelt	332
Caldwell, Nauman v.	419
Caldwell, Weightman v.	200
Cambers, Knight v.	118
Cameron v. Durkheim	304
Campanari v. Woodbury	128
Campbell, Cockran v.	94
Campbell, Pym v.	319
Canaan v. Bryce	107, 112, 115

TABLE OF CASES.

	PAGE		PAGE
Capp v. Topham	110	Clough v. Bond	330
Capper, Reeves v.	383	Coal & Nav. Co. v. Brown	180
Capper, Rex v.	142	Cobb v. Doyle	372
Cappur v. Harris	236	Cochran v. Retberg	280
Carlisle, Commonwealth v.	294	Cockerell v. Aucompte	88
Carpenter, Blyth v.	387	Cockran v. Campbell	94
Carpenter v. R. R. Co.	180	Cockran v. Irlam	94, 95
Carpenter, Sea v.	116	Coddington v. Bay	373
Carriger v. Whittington	128	Coddington v. Paleologo	280
Carrington, Bank v.	372	Cofield v. Clark	424
Carroll, Gaiusford v.	414	Coggs v. Bernard	356
Carter, Whitwell v.	298	Coker, Hitchcock v.	291, 296
Cartwright v. McCook	424	Colburn, Long v.	81
Cason v. Cheely	197	Cole v. Blake	286
Cassard v. Hinman	302	Cole, Ins. Co. v.	146, 203
Cassiday v. McKenzie	124	Cole v. Milmine	302
Cassily, Cummins v.	272	Cole, Olivierson v.	72, 298
Catlin v. Bell	85, 96, 100	Cole, Young v.	85, 93, 264
Caulk, Moody v.	422	Coles v. Bank	393
Cauty, Stewart v.	217	Coles, Boyson v.	90
Cease, Pickering v.	318	Coles v. Bristowe	47, 48, 133, 222
Cedar County, Clapp v.	168	Coles v. Trecothick	95
Chambers, Bank v.	373	Coles, Wells v.	142
Chapin v. First Univ. Soc.	333, 335	Colket v. Ellis	66
Chapman v. Morton	286	Collamer v. Day	298
Chapman v. Shepherd	108	Collinson v. Lister	329
Chapman, White v.	112	Colt v. Netterville	198, 236
Chappell v. Brockway	293	Colvin v. Williams	200
Charlaron v. McFarlane	278	Combe's Case	336
Churmley v. Winstanly	123	Commander, Gourdin v.	278
Chase v. Westmore	121	Commercial, etc. Co., Treasurer v.	251
Chauncey v. Arnold	277	Commissioners v. Aspinwall	165
Cheely, Cason v.	197	Commissioners v. Clark	167
Chester Glass Co. v. Dewey	266, 269	Commonwealth, A. & T. Co. v.	180
Child v. Morley	46	Commonwealth, Arents v.	168
Chitty, Fulkeron v.	142	Commonwealth, Baldwin v.	250
City v. Lamson	168	Commonwealth v. Carlisle	294
City of Dubuque, Gelpcke v.	167, 174	Commonwealth v. Hunt	296
City of New London, Society for Savings v.	168	Comstock, Willoughby v.	346, 350, 352
		Conant v. Bank	178
City of Ohio v. R. R. Co.	180	Conham, Mores v.	356
Clapp v. Cedar County	168	Conkey v. Bond	90
Clark, Cofield v.	424	Conner, Gibson v.	373
Clark, Commissioners v.	167	Conway, Benoit v.	123
Clark v. Flint	247	Cook, Bank v.	338
Clark v. Foss	302, 318	Cook, Cropper v.	91
Clark v. Gibson	297	Cook v. Helms	373
Clark v. Lee Co.	168	Cook, Merchants' Bank v.	342
Clark v. Mfg. Co.	168	Cooke v. Davis	312
Clark, Petrie v.	373	Cooke, Freeman v.	403
Clark v. Pinney	415	Cooke, Mussell v.	198, 201, 205
Clark, Tainter v.	336	Cookson, Duke of Somerset v.	234
Clarke, Dixon v.	282	Cooper, Acraman v.	146, 391
Clarke v. Iowa City	174	Cooper, Davidson v.	270
Clarke v. Janesville	168	Cooper v. Phibbs	289
Clarke, Smith v.	168	Cooper v. Ray	383
Clegg v. Townshend	100, 110	Copeland v. Ins. Co.	90
Clendaniel v. Hastings	275	Corrie, Baring v.	34

TABLE OF CASES.

	PAGE		PAGE
Cortelyou v. Lansing	419	Davis, Owen v.	114
Cottle, Hammon v.	100	Dawson, Pothonier v.	121
County, Johnson v.	168	Day, Collamer v.	298
Couturier, Hastie v.	188	Day v. Holmes	227, 273
Covill v. Hill	360	Day v. Swift	383
Cowell, R. R. Co. v.	180	De Begnis v. Armistead	115
Cowles v. Whitman	249	De Berenger, Rex v.	296
Cowling v. Cowling	140, 141	De Bernardy v. Harding	116
Coxwell, Bromley v.	100	De Haven, Ruchizky v.	61, 115, 307
Craig v. Vicksburg	168		317, 383
Cramer v. Arthurs	213	De Haven v. Williams	330
Credit Foncier Co., Crouch v.	148, 156	De Medina, Stephen v.	283
	158, 160, 170	De Pass's Case	172
Creed, Lightfoot v.	109, 111	De Tastet, Webster v.	100
Crocker, Smith v.	272	Dean v. James	282
Croft, Brown v.	118	Deares, Heger v.	336
Cropper v. Cook	91	Deas, Thorne v.	122
Cross v. Eglin	88	Debouchout v. Goldsmid	90, 92
Cross v. State Bank	271	Deere v. Lewis	424
Crouch v. Credit Foncier Co.	148, 156	Delafield, State v.	91, 168
	158, 160, 170	Delamater's Estate	140
Crowell, Beers v.	200	Dennison, Ex parte	385
Cruikshank v. Duffin	324	Dennison, Wilson v.	336
Crull v. Dodson	198, 201, 205	Denny v. Hamilton	391
Crutcher, Williams v.	278	Denny, Lyon v.	275
Cud v. Rutter	235	Denton v. Livingston	391
Cummins v. Cassily	272	Derby v. Gallup	424
Curran v. State	179	Derby, Ryerson v.	298
Curry v. Woodward	180	Devin v. Himer	277
Curtis, Austin v.	373	Devisme, Nightingal v.	140
Cushman v. Hayes	350	Devoss v. Richmond	168
Cushman v. Jewelry Co.	353	Dewees v. Miller	297
Cushman v. Thayer Mfg. Co.	156, 249	Dewey v. Chester Glass Co.	266, 269
		Dexter, Johnson v.	344
		Diamond v. Lawrence Co.	164, 166
D.		Dick v. Page	126
		Dickinson, Fletcher v.	344
Da Costa v. Jones	297	Dickinson v. Lilwall	128
Dails v. Lloyd	110	Dickinson, Smith v.	274
Dakin, Ashton v.	308	Dickson v. Hamer	273
Dalbiac, Railway Co. v.	393	Dickson's Executor v. Thomas	61, 115
Dalrymple, Ins. Co. v.	346, 347, 350		306, 317, 383
Dane, C. & G. E. R. R. Co. v.	310	Diggle v. Higgs	298
Daniell, Gwillim v.	89	Dixon v. Clarke	282
Darragh, Beltzhoover v.	330	Dixon v. Ewart	124
Dartmouth, Howe v.	84	Dixon v. Yates	232, 259
Daubigny v. Duval	355	Dodge v. Tileston	112, 116
Davenport v. Sleight	273	Dodson, Crull v.	198, 201, 205
Davenport, Telegraph Co. v.	340	Doloret v. Rothschild	237, 246
Davidson v. Cooper	270	Donald v. Suckling	354, 357, 361, 364,
Davidson, Way v.	383		369
Davies, McCombie v.	355	Doolittle, King v.	373
Davis v. Bank	393	Dorriens v. Hutchinson	48
Davis, Betterbee v.	282	Dotterell, Gosden v.	140, 141
Davis, Cook v.	312	Douglass, Hunt v.	336
Davis, Entwhistle v.	212, 218	Downes v. Ross	197
Davis v. Funk	352	Downing v. Potts	175
Davis v. Haycock	390	Dowson v. Gaskoin	141

2

TABLE OF CASES.

	PAGE
Doxey v. Miller	298
Doyle, Cobb v.	372
Drake, Baker v.	353, 419, 420
Drew, Bartlett v.	179
Drew v. Munn	126
Drury v. Foster	278
Drybutter v. Bartholomew	144
Dryer v. Lewis	424
Dubuque, Gelpcke v.	167, 174
Dubuque R. R. Co., Bank v.	348
Duff, Berger v.	334, 336
Duffin, Cruikshank v.	324
Duguid v. Edwards	90
Duke of Somerset v. Cookson	234
Duncan, Brown v.	112
Duncan v. Hill	215
Duncan v. Hodges	278
Duncan v. Jaudon	332
Duncuft v. Albrecht	146, 199, 289
Dunkley, Goswell v.	95
Dunmore v. Alexander	191
Dunsterville, Ball v.	82
Durant v. Burt	114, 168
Durant v. Iowa Co.	168
Durkee v. Stringham	117, 212
Durkee v. Vt. Ct. Ry. Co.	117
Durkheim, Cameron v.	304
Dutcher v. Burt	419
Dutton v. Connecticut Bank	376
Duval, Daubigny v.	355
Dwight, Thayer v.	383
Dykers, Allen v.	103, 363, 419

E.

	PAGE
Eagle Ins. Co., McCulloch v.	191
Eagleton v. Gutteridge	270
East India Co. v. Hensley	92
Eaton, Mewburn v.	48, 136, 318
Eaton, Perkins v.	298
Eckstein v. Reynolds	282
Edminston v. Wright	110
Edwards, Duguid v.	90
Edwards v. Hall	213
Edwards v. R. R. Co.	197
Edwards, Robins v.	96, 97
Ege, Miller v.	329
Egerton, McIlvaine v.	302
Eglin, Cross v.	87
Eickel v. Meyer	116
Elliott, Good v.	297
Elliott v. Merryman	329
Elliott, Payne v.	146, 391
Elliott, Tenant v.	113
Ellis v. Bridge Co.	266
Ellis, Colket v.	66

	PAGE
Ellis, Eyles v.	282
Ellis, Wilkes v.	34
Ellis's Appeal	325
Elsee v. Gatward	122
Elwes, Forrest v.	416
Ely v. Sprague	180
Emott, Ackerman v.	84
English, Huntington R. R. Co. v.	415, 417
Entwhistle v. Davis	212, 213
Essex & C. Co., Sargeant v.	178
Evans v. Hudson Bay Co.	178
Evans, Legg v.	355
Evans, Texira v.	270
Evans v. Waln	53, 91, 228
Evans v. Wister	53, 68, 215
Evans v. Wood	244
Evans Charities, Bank v.	395, 404
Ewart, Dixon v.	124
Ex parte Dennison	385
Ex parte Kerwen	276
Ex parte Marnham	314
Ex parte Mather	112
Ex parte Mathew	178
Ex parte Pyke	113
Ex parte Willcocks	342
Ex parte Young	316, 318
Eyles v. Ellis	282

F.

	PAGE
Fairlie v. Fenton	96
Fairmaner, Webb v.	280
Fall, Johnson v.	297
Fancourt v. Thorne	353
Fardell, Baud v.	84
Fareira v. Gabell	107, 115, 308, 317, 383
Farnsworth v. Garrard	112
Fay v. Wheeler	204
Featherstonehough, Hill v.	118
Fellows v. Harris	373
Fenouille v. Hamilton	373
Fenton, Fairlie v.	96
Ferguson v. Paschall	251
Ferree, Mt. Holly Co. v.	156
Fessenden, Bragg v.	272
Field v. Kinnear	415
Field v. Sawyer	118
Fielding, Booth v.	95
First Univ. Soc., Chapin v.	338, 335
Fisher v. Brown	423
Fisher v. Essex Bank	375
Fisher v. Fisher	353
Fisher, Leavitt v.	156
Fisher v. Marsh	96
Fisher, People v.	295

TABLE OF CASES.

	PAGE
Fisher, Shaw v.	239
Fisher v. Taylor	333
Fitch, Knight v.	113
Fitch, Sewall v.	197
Fitzsimmons v. Woodruff	286
Fletcher v. Dickinson	344
Fletcher v. Marshall	106
Fletcher, Volans v.	168
Flint, Clark v.	247
Fobes, Leach v.	248
Foll's Appeal	252
Forrest v. Elwes	416
Forrest, North v.	203
Forshaw, Haines v.	325
Foss, Clark v.	302, 318
Foster v. Bank	393
Foster, Drury v.	278
Fowler v. Hollins	34, 35
Fox v. Mackreath	85, 90
Frampton, Percival v.	372
Franklin Ins. Co., Sargeant v.	175
Frazier v. Hilliard	187
Freedm. Sav. & Trust Co., Talty v.	361
Freeman v. Cooke	403
Freeman, Ry. Co. v.	168
French v. Ramge	424
Friend, Wheeler v.	297
Frontino, etc., Gold Co., Hart v.	406, 411
Frost, Gibbs v.	278
Fulkeron v. Chitty	142
Fuller, Pierce v.	293
Fulvey v. O. & H. R. R. Co.	423
Funk, Davis v.	352
Furness, Paine v.	372

G.

Gabell, Fareira v.	107, 115, 308, 317, 383
Gainsford v. Carroll	414
Gale v. Reed	291
Gallup, Derby v.	424
Gardener v. Pullen et al.	236
Gardner v. Gardner	82
Garrard, Farnsworth v.	112
Garrard v. P. & C. R. R. Co.	329
Garwood, Moore v.	168
Gascoyne, Langford v.	330
Gaskoin, Dowson v.	141
Gatward, Elsee v.	122
Gauger, Gilbert v.	309
Gaussen v. Morton	128
Geisse, Walker v.	373
Gelpcke v. City of Dubuque	167, 174
Gennett, State Ins. Co. v.	374
German Ass. Co. v. Sendmeyer	276
Gething, Mumford v.	296

	PAGE
Gibbs v. Frost	278
Gibbs, Whittemore v.	200
Gibson, Clark v.	297
Gibson v. Conner	373
Gilbert, Ball v.	298
Gilbert v. Gauger	309
Gilbert v. Iron Co.	175
Gillan, Phené v.	387
Gillaspie, Austin v.	250
Gillett v. Peppercorne	84, 90
Gilmore v. Woodcock	298
Gilmour v. Supple	232
Gilpin v. Howell	102, 104, 385, 386, 387
Ginter, Kent v.	422
Given, Ashhurst v.	333
Girard, McCulloch v.	319
Glyn v. Baker	158
Glynn, Morris v.	211, 212
Godfrey, Bertram v.	87
Goldner, Hammick v.	267
Goldsmid, Debouchout v.	90
Gooch v. Holmes	204
Gooch, Nicholson v.	68, 215, 298
Good v. Elliott	297
Goodfellow, Ins. Co. v.	178
Goodrich, Blood v.	276
Goodwin v. Bowden	128
Goodwin v. Hardy	179
Goodwin v. Robarts	97, 162, 169, 171, 172
Gordon v. Strange	282
Gore, Boardman v.	278
Gorgier v. Mieville	159, 160, 169
Gosden v. Dotterell	140, 141
Goswell v. Dunkley	95
Gouldsbury, Hudleston v.	140
Gourdin v. Commander	278
Gowen, Pancoast v.	53
Graham v. Holt	273
Graham, Maddox v.	168
Graham v. Ogle	275
Granger v. Bassett	180
Granger, Hudson v.	124
Grant v. Bank	178
Gratz v. Redd	179
Graves, Horner v.	292
Gray, Hinde v.	296
Green v. Price	293
Green, Storm v.	424
Greening v. Wilkinson	416
Greenlow v. King	348
Greenough v. Wells	336
Gregg, Morgan v.	419
Grenaux v. Wheeler	373
Griffen, Vawter v.	200
Grissell v. Bristowe	41, 48, 118, 184, 222
Grizewood v. Blane	314

TABLE OF CASES.

	PAGE
Guerriere v. Peile	193
Gutteridge, Eagleton v.	270
Gwillim v. Daniell	89

H.

	PAGE
Hackett, Mercer Co. v.	163, 164, 172
Haines v. Forshaw	325
Haines, McKenney v.	423
Hale, Jefferson v.	423
Hall, Camden Bank v.	277
Hall, Edwards v.	213
Hall, Holland v.	112
Hall, In re	393
Hall v. Ins. Co.	178
Hall, Robarts v.	373
Halliday v. Holgate	366
Hallock v. Conn. Ins. Co.	191
Hamer, Dickson v.	273
Hamer v. Hathaway	424
Hamilton, Denny v.	391
Hamilton, Fenouille v.	378
Hammic v. Goldner	267
Hammon v. Cottle	100
Hammond, Bank v.	278
Hamond v. Holiday	116
Hamonds v. Barclay	115
Hanford v. McNair	276
Hannay, Petrie v.	114
Harding, De Bernardy v.	116
Hardy, Goodwin v.	179
Harmstead, Wallace v.	275
Harness, Ayres v.	274
Harris, Cappur v.	236
Harris, Fellows v.	373
Harris v. North Devon Ry. Co.	241
Harris, Tisdale v.	146, 201, 203, 204, 205
Harrison v. Harrison	416
Harrison, Jackson v.	81
Harrison, Sheffield Gas Co. v.	240
Hart v. Frontino, etc., Gold Co.	406, 411
Hart v. Middleton	280
Hartley, Brewster v.	338
Hartley v. Rice	297
Hart's Case, Musgrove &	47, 390
Hartshorne, Allaire v.	373
Harvard College v. Amory	84
Hasbrook v. Vandevoort	342
Hasket v. Wootan	298
Hastie v. Couturier	188
Hastings, Clendaniel v.	275
Hatch, Wicks v.	352
Hathaway, Hamer v.	424
Haven v. Grand Junc. R. R. Co.	168
Hawkins, Jocelyn v.	280
Hawkins v. Kemp	334, 336
Hawkins v. Maltby	48, 136, 222, 245
Hawkins v. Rutt	282
Hawley v. James	334, 336
Haycock, Davis v.	390
Hayes, Cushman v.	350
Hayes v. Riddle	383
Hayes, Stone v.	90
Hayes, Wood v.	362
Hearn, Allen v.	298
Heath, Lambert v.	192, 263, 290
Heath v. Silverthorn	348
Hefferman, Rodriguez v.	90
Heger v. Deares	336
Helm v. Swiggett	178
Helms, Cook v.	373
Hemphill's Appeal	84
Henderson v. Barnwell	34, 95, 206
Henkel v. Pape	191
Hensley, East India Co. v.	92
Hervey, Simms v.	277
Heseltine v. Siggers	168, 188, 199, 231, 233
Hibblewhite v. McMorine	82, 185, 186, 187, 267, 270, 302
Hicks, McKee v.	273
Higgin, Young v.	280
Higgins v. Moore	91
Higgs, Diggle v.	298
Hight v. Ripley	196
Hildreth, Kimball v.	388
Hildyard v. South Sea Co.	157, 410
Hiler, Budd v.	336
Hill, Covill v.	360
Hill, Duncan v.	215
Hill v. Featherstonehough	118
Hill v. Simpson	325
Hilliard, Frazier v.	187
Himer, Devin v.	277
Hinde v. Gray	296
Hinde v. Whitehouse	34
Hinkle v. Arey	84
Hinman, Cassard v.	302
Hinton v. Pinke	142
Hipple, Petillon v.	298
Hitchcock v. Coker	291, 296
Hitchcock, Wood v.	286
Hoag, Sawyer v.	179
Hodge, Hoit v.	298
Hodges, Duncan v.	278
Hodgkinson v. Kelly	218
Hodgson v. Anderson	128
Hoit v. Hodge	298
Holbrook v. New Jersey Zinc Co.	394
Holcomb v. Holcomb	333
Holden, Buttrick v.	332
Holdship v. Patterson	333
Holdsworth, Bradley v.	142, 179
Holgate, Halliday v.	366

TABLE OF CASES. 21

	PAGE
Holiday, Hamond v.	116
Holland v. Hall	112
Holland, Savings Institution v.	878
Holland, Shaw v.	414
Hollins, Fowler v.	34, 85
Holmes, Day v.	227, 273
Holmes, Gooch v.	204
Holmes, Spooner v.	168
Holt, Graham v.	273
Home v. Ashford	296
Horner v. Graves	292
Hotchkiss v. Oliver	187
Hotson, Alley v.	128
Houghtaling v. Marvin	128
Howard v. Tucker	110
Howarth, Mixer v.	196
Howe v. Bemis	350
Howe v. Dartmouth	84
Howe v. Starkweather	144, 391, 392
Howell, Gilpin v. 102, 104, 385, 386, 387	
Howell v. R. R. Co.	180
Hubbersty v. Ry. Co.	393
Huddell & Seitzinger, In re	872
Hudleston v. Gouldsbury	140
Hudson v. Granger	124
Hudson, Winfield v.	68
Hudson Bay Co., Evans v.	178
Hughes, Rann v.	81
Hughes, Whittlesay v.	386
Huguet, Boylan v.	146, 386, 387, 391, 423
Hull, Preston v.	274
Humble v. Langston	267, 270, 284
Humble v. Mitchell	146, 199, 269
Hunt v. Adams	273, 296
Hunt, Commonwealth v.	296
Hunt v. Douglass	386
Hunt v. Rousmanier	117, 128
Huntington R. R. Co. v. English	415, 417
Huntress, Inhab. of So. Berw. v.	277
Hurley, Robinson v.	343, 347
Hutchins v. Bank	145, 147
Hutchinson, Dorriens v.	48
Hyatt v. Allen	179
Hyatt v. Argenti	858
Hyde v. Woods	43, 50, 69
Hynes v. Redington	84

I.

In re Aston	105
In re Hall	393
In re Huddell & Seitzinger	372
In re London, etc., Bank	242, 244
In re Marquis of Hertford	181
In re Mercantile Credit Association Co.	105

	PAGE
In the matter of the Bahia & San Francisco Ry. Co.	405, 416
Indiana v. Sprague	164
Ingram, Buckeridge v.	144
Ingram v. Little	272
Inhabitants of S. Berw. v. Huntress	277
Ins. Co., Bates v.	176
Ins. Co. v. Cole	146, 208
Ins. Co., Copeland v.	90
Ins. Co. v. Dalrymple	346, 347, 350
Ins. Co. v. Gennett	374
Ins. Co. v. Goodfellow	178
Ins. Co., Hall v.	178
Ins. Co., Hallock v.	191
Ins. Co. v. Ins. Co.	90
Ins. Co., Isaacs v.	280
Ins. Co. v. Le Roy	180
Ins. Co., Luling v.	176, 180
Ins. Co., McCulloch v.	191
Ins. Co., Rogers v.	374
Ins. Co., Rudolph v.	393
Ins. Co., Sargeant v.	266
Ins. Co., Shipman v.	179, 876
Ins. Co., Tayloe v.	191
Iowa Co., Clarke v.	174
Iowa Co., Durant v.	168
Irlam, Cockran v.	94, 95
Iron Co., Gilbert v.	175
Iron Co., Isham v.	144
Iron Co., Newberry v.	374
Irwin, Seiple v.	91
Isaacs v. Ins. Co.	280
Ish v. Crane	126
Isham v. Iron Co.	144
Isherwood v. Whitmore	282
Ives, Phillips v.	297, 298

J.

Jackson v. Harrison	81
Jackson v. Plank Road Co.	180
Jackson, Richardson v.	286
Jackson, Roberts v.	116
Jackson, Sinclair v.	333, 334, 335, 336
James, Dean v.	282
James, Hawley v.	334, 336
Jamison, Pearson v.	334, 336
Janesville, Clarke v.	168
Jarvis v. Rogers	122, 360, 361
Jaudon, Duncan v.	382
Jaudon, Markham v.	225, 338, 353, 379, 419, 420, 422
Jefferson v. Hale	428
Jefferson, Mills v.	134
Jeffries, Montriou v.	112
Jenners v. Bean	373

TABLE OF CASES.

	PAGE
Jessop v. Lutwyche	118
Jessop, Powell v.	199
Jewelry Co., Cushman v.	353
Jocelyn v. Hawkins	280
Johns v. Johns	145
Johnson, Ashe v.	250
Johnson, Breedlove v.	278
Johnson, Brown v.	280
Johnson v. County	168
Johnson v. Dexter	344
Johnson v. Fall	297
Johnson v. Mulry	197, 206
Johnson, Shepherd v.	416
Johnson v. Stear	356
Johnson v. Underhill	341
Johnson v. Wilcox	128
Johnston v. Usborne	217, 341
Jones, Bower v.	116
Jones v. Brinley	140
Jones, Da Costa v.	297
Jones v. Littledale	96
Jones v. Powel	118
Jones v. R. R. Co.	176, 180
Jones, Reddick v.	373
Jones v. Smith	332
Jones v. Williams	332
Josephs v. Pebrer	112, 117
Judges, State v.	228

K.

	PAGE
Kane v. Bloodgood	180
Karnes v. R. R. Co.	179, 180
Keating v. Wilson	390
Keeler v. Taylor	294
Kelly, Hodgkinson v.	218
Kelly, Neiler v.	102, 146, 350, 385, 387, 391, 417, 418
Kemble v. Atkins	34, 40, 91
Kemmil v. Wilson	319
Kemp, Hawkins v.	334, 336
Kempson v. Saunders	290
Kennedy, Butterworth v.	343
Kent v. Ginter	422
Kentish, Sanders v.	416
Kerwen, Ex parte	276
Keyser's Appeal	333
Kid v. Mitchell	424
Kilner, Tempest v.	193, 199
Kimball v. Hildreth	383
King v. Boston	112
King v. Doolittle	373
King, Greenlow v.	348
King v. Paterson	180
King, Stapleton v.	424
King v. Wilson	168

	PAGE
Kinnear, Field v.	415
Kinyon, Allen v.	424
Kirkpatrick v. Bonsall	312
Kitchen, Robinson v.	106
Knapp v. Alford	128
Knight v. Cambers	113
Knight v. Fitch	113
Knipe, Ogle v.	140
Knowles, Lawrence v.	283
Kortright, Bank v.	156, 178, 276, 393, 419
Kost, Wheeler v.	341
Kuhn v. McAllister	146, 391

L.

	PAGE
Laird, Union Bank v.	177
Laishley, Steers v.	106
Lambert v. Heath	192, 263, 290
Lamberton v. Windom	344
Lamson, City v.	168
Lane v. Melville	197
Lane, San Antonio v.	168
Lang v. Smyth	160, 171
Langdale, Ashton v.	210
Langford v. Gascoyne	330
Langston, Humble v.	267, 270, 284
Langton v. Waite	90, 91, 101, 104, 131, 384
Lanier, Bank v.	154, 177
Lansing, Cortelyou v.	419
Lardner, Murray v.	168, 338
Laussatt v. Lippincott	95
Law, Sloo v.	333
Lawrence v. Knowles	283
Lawrence Co., Diamond v.	164, 166, 242
Lawson, City v.	168
Laytin, Osgood v.	179
Le Roy v. Globe Ins. Co.	180
Leach v. Fobes	248
Leavenworth, Bank v.	373
Leavitt v. Fisher	156
Lee v. Bank	374
Lee v. Smead	373
Lee Co., Clark v.	168
Lee Co., Thompson v.	168
Leeson, Brown v.	297
Legg v. Evans	355
Leggett v. Bank	178
Lehman v. Strassberger	113
Leonard v. N. Y. Co.	191
Levan, Sigfried v.	275
Levitt, Raymond v.	294
Lewis, Bryan v.	185, 186, 302
Lewis, Deere v.	424
Lewis, Dryer v.	424

TABLE OF CASES.

Case	Page
Lewis v. Littlefield	298
Lewis, Morris Canal Co. v.	168, 340
Lewis v. Mott	360, 361
Life Ins. Co., Rossiter v.	94
Lightfoot v. Creed	109, 111
Lightner's Appeal	340
Lilwall, Dickinson v.	123
Lincoln Gas Co., Beverley v.	83
Lindo, Smith v.	118
Linley, Taylor v.	213
Lippincott, Laussatt v.	95
Lister, Collinson v.	329
Littell, Wallis v.	319
Little, Ingram v.	272
Little, Williams v.	373
Little, Wilson v.	176, 350
Littledale, Jones v.	96
Littlefield, Lewis v.	298
Littlefield, Williams v.	121
Livingston, Denton v.	391
Livingston, Miller v.	116
Lloyd, Dails v.	110
Lobdell v. Stowell	419
Lockwood v. Mer. Nat. Bank	177
Logan v. Musick	309
London, etc., In re	242, 244
Long v. Colburn	81
Lorymer v. Smith	186, 302
Lowe v. Thomas	140, 141
Lowe, Torrington v.	131, 136
Lowry v. Commercial Bank	328, 335
Lowther v. Lowther	90
Ludwick, Reitenbaugh v.	419
Luling v. Atlantic Ins. Co.	176, 180
Lutwyche, Jessop v.	118
Lyman, Naglee v.	373
Lynde, Burns v.	273
Lyon v. Denny	275

M.

MacDowell v. Ackley	67
Macgruder, Riggs v.	204
Mack v. Baker	372
Mackreath, Fox v.	85, 90
McAllister, Kuhn v.	146, 391
McArthur v. Seaforth	416
McCallan, Mortimer v.	130, 137, 186, 302
McCarty, Bellas v.	329
McClanahan, Byers v.	274
McCleod, Bank v.	85, 90
McClellan, Rozet v.	353
McClure, Manning v.	373
McCollum, Porter v.	168
McCombie v. Davies	355
McConnell v. Murphy	89
McCook, Cartwright v.	424
McCulloch v. Eagle Ins. Co.	191
McCulloch, Girard v.	319
McCullough, Piatt v.	336
McCullough, Rankin v.	345
McDaniels v. Manf. Co.	343
McDonald, Stalker v.	373
McDonald, Startup v.	281
McDougall, Bank v.	302
McElrath, Broadway Bank v.	374
McFarlane, Charlaron v.	278
McIlvaine v. Egerton	302
McGran, Brown v.	86, 120
McKee v. Hicks	273
McKeen, Vicksburg R. R. Co. v.	178
McKenney v. Haines	428
McKenzie, Cassiday v.	124
McKinnel v. Robinson	107, 112
McMorine, Hibblewhite v.	82, 185, 186, 267, 270, 302
McNair, Hanford v.	276
McNeil v. Tenth Nat. Bank	153, 359, 362, 874
Maddox v. Graham	168
Magee v. Atkinson	46, 131
Mallan v. May	293
Mallory, Brightwell v.	174
Maltby, Hawkins v.	48, 136, 222, 245
Manly, Thayer v.	419
Manning v. McClure	373
Manf. Co., Clark v.	168
Manf. Co., McDaniels v.	343
Manf. Co., Warren v.	112
Marblehead Ins. Co., Quiner v.	273
Marblehead, Quiner v.	269
Margitson, Simpson v.	280
Markham v. Jaudon	225, 338, 353, 377, 379, 419, 420, 422
Marnham, Ex parte	314
Marquis of Hertford, In re	181
Marsh v. Atty.-Genl.	213
Marsh, Fisher v.	96
Marsh, Stearns v.	350
Marshall, Fletcher v.	106
Marshall v. Rutton	78
Martin, Brooks v.	114
Martin v. Terrell	298
Martin, Warner v.	94
Marvin, Houghtaling v.	128
Marye, Bercich v.	424
Mason, Valette v.	373
Master v. Miller	270
Mather, Ex parte	112
Mathew, Ex parte	178
Mathews v. Bank	155, 166, 172
Maus v. Worthing	272
Maxted v. Paine	41, 136, 223

TABLE OF CASES.

	PAGE
May, Mallan v.	293
May v. Quimby	373
Mayor v. Reynolds	88
Mayor v. Till	88
Meadows v. Bird	373
Mearns, Robinson v.	298
Melville, Lane v.	197
Mercantile Credit Association Co., *In re*	105
Mercer Co. v. Hacket	163, 164, 172
Merchants' Bank v. Cook	342
Merry, Nickall v.	47, 136
Merryman, Elliott v.	329
Messick, Roxborough v.	373
Mewburn v. Eaton	48, 136, 318
Meyer, Eickel v.	116
Meyer v. Muscatine	168
Meyers v. Perigal	209
Meyers v. R. R. Co.	168
Miami Co., Moran v.	168
Middleton, Hart v.	280
Middleton, Poole v.	243
Mieville, Gorgier v.	159, 160, 169
Miller, Dewees v.	297
Miller, Doxey v.	298
Miller v. Ege	329
Miller v. Livingston	116
Miller, Master v.	270
Miller v. R. & W. R. R. Co.	168, 174
Miller v. Race	148, 164
Mills v. Jefferson	174
Milmine, Cole v.	302
Milne, Walker v.	209, 211
Minot, Middlesex Bank v.	348
Minot v. Paine	179
Mitchell, Humble v.	146, 199, 269
Mitchell, Kid v.	424
Mitchell v. Newhall	192, 218, 263
Mitchell, Pray v.	203
Mitchell v. Reynolds	291
Mixer v. Howarth	196
Mocatta v. Bell	107, 131
Mollett v. Robinson	91, 96, 97
Montriou v. Jeffries	112
Moody v. Bank	155
Moody v. Caulk	422
Moore v. Garwood	168
Moore, Higgins v.	91
Moore, Wiley v.	275
Moore, Wilson v.	325
Moran v. Miami Co.	168
Mores v. Conham	356
Morgan v. Gregg	419
Morgan, Scarfe v.	119
Morley, Child v.	46
Morris, Duffin v.	324
Morris v. Glynn	211, 212
Morris, Poirier v.	372

	PAGE
Morris, Tyrrell v.	324
Morris v. Wallace	84
Morris Canal Co. v. Lewis	168, 340
Morris Run Coal Co. v. Barclay Coal Co.	291, 295
Morrow v. Brenizer	218
Morse v. Royal	90
Mortimer v. McCallan	130, 137, 186, 302
Morton, Chapman v.	286
Morton, Gaussen v.	128
Morton v. Perry	142
Morton, Williamson v.	324
Mosby v. State	274
Mott, Lewis v.	360, 361
Moulton, Wheelock v.	145
Mount, Ry. Co. v.	398
Mount, Woolcott v.	424
Mt. Holly Co. v. Ferree	156
Moxey's Appeal	53, 67
Mulry, Johnson v.	197, 206
Mumford v. Gething	296
Munn v. Barnum	276
Munn, Worrell v.	81, 276
Murphy, McConnell v.	89
Murphy, Sheppard v.	222
Murray v. Lardner	168, 338
Muscatine, Meyer v.	168
Musgrave v. Beckendorff	419
Musgrove & Hart's Case	47, 390
Musick, Logan v.	309
Mussell v. Cooke	198, 201, 205
Myers v. Y. & C. R. R. Co.	168

N.

	PAGE
N. A. Col. Ass. Co. v. Bentley	398
N. B. A. Co., Swan v.	370
N. Y. Co., Leonard v.	191
N. Y. & N. H. R. R. Co., Brainerd v.	168
N. Y. & N. H. R. R. Co., Mechanics' Bank v.	149, 396
Naglee v. Lyman	373
Naglee v. Wharf Co.	376
Nash, Bianchi v.	286
Nauman v. Caldwell	419
Neiler v. Kelly	102, 146, 162, 350, 385, 387, 391, 417, 418
Nelson, United States v.	278
Nelson v. Wellington	344
Netterville, Colt v.	198, 236, 276
New Alex. Turnpike Co., Ammant v.	392
New Jersey Zinc. Co., Holbrook v.	394
Newberry v. Iron Co.	374

TABLE OF CASES.

	PAGE
Newbold v. Pritchett	142
Newbould, Wheeler v.	344
Newhall, Mitchell v.	192, 218, 263
Newsom, Bodenhammer v.	383
Newton v. Bronson's Ex.	336
Nicholls v. Rosewarne	181, 372, 392
Nicholson v. Gooch	68, 215, 298
Nicholson, Stuart v.	291
Nickall v. Merry	47, 136
Nightingal v. Devisme	140
Noakes, Warwick v.	283
North v. Forrest	203
North v. Phillips	305, 317, 383, 415, 417
Northrup v. Shook	33, 38, 376
Nourse v. Prime	102
Noyes, Pitkin v.	197
Nunn, Drew v.	126
Nutter v. Stover	373
Nutter, Winchester v.	297
Nutting, Wellman v.	107
Nyce's Estate	84

O.

	PAGE
Ocmulgee Mills, Phillips v.	302
Ogle, Graham v.	275
Ogle v. Knipe	140
Oliver, Hotchkiss v.	187
Olivierson v. Cole	72, 298
Organ, People v.	272
Oriental Steam Co. v. Briggs	245
Orr v. Bigelow	178
Osgood v. Laytin	179
Overseers of the Poor v. Sears	175
Owen v. Davis	114
Owen v. Perry	277
Owen v. Routh	416

P.

	PAGE
Page, Dick v.	126
Paine v. Furness	372
Paine, Maxted v.	41, 136, 223
Paine, Minot v.	179
Palmer, Parker v.	286
Pancoast v. Gowen	53
Pape, Henkle v.	191
Parke, Vaux v.	333
Parker v. Branker	120
Parker v. Palmer	286
Parker, Sparling v.	207
Parsons v. Webb	90

	PAGE
Paschall, Ferguson v.	251
Paterson, King v.	180
Patterson, Holdship v.	333
Paul v. Ball	142
Payne v. Elliott	146, 391
Pearson v. Jamison	336
Pebrer, Josephs v.	112, 117
Pegram, Allen v.	145
Peile, Guerriere v.	193
Pennock, Wilson v.	336
People v. Fisher	295
People v. Organ	272
Peppercorne, Gillett v.	84, 90
Percival v. Frampton	372
Perigal, Meyers v.	209
Perkins v. Eaton	298
Perry, Morton v.	142
Perry, Owen v.	277
Persh v. Quiggle	419
Peters, Swift v.	372
Peterson, King v.	180
Peterson, Wagner v.	419
Petillon v. Hipple	298
Petrie v. Clark	373
Petrie v. Hannay	114
Phelps v. Bank	179
Phené v. Gillan	387
Phibbs, Cooper v.	289
Phillips v. Ives	297, 298
Phillips, North v.	305, 317, 383, 415, 417
Phillips v. Ocmulgee Mills	302
Piatt v. McCullough	336
Pickard v. Sears	403
Pickering v. Appleby	146, 198
Pickering v. Busk	84, 94, 262
Pickering, Cease v.	198, 318
Pidgeon v. Burslem	118
Pierce v. Breton	372
Pierce v. Fuller	293
Pinto v. Santos	100
Pinke, Hinton v.	142
Pinkerton v. R. R. Co.	423
Pinney, Clark v.	415
Pitkin v. Noyes	197
Pittston, Arnott v.	295
Plaice v. Russell	324
Plank Road Co., Jackson v.	180
Plumer, Taylor v.	83
Poirier v. Morris	372, 410
Pollock v. National Bank	248, 410
Poole v. Middleton	243
Porter v. McCollum	168
Porter v. Viets	315, 319
Porter, Wells v.	186, 302
Pothonier v. Dawson	121
Pott v. Turner	88
Potts, Downing v.	175

TABLE OF CASES.

	PAGE
Powell v. Jessop	199
Powell, Jones v.	118
Prall v. Tilt	155, 328
Pratt v. Machinists' Bank	410
Pray v. Mitchell	203
Prentice v. Zane	373
Presbyterian Congregation v. Bank	178
Preston v. Hull	270, 274
Price, Green v.	293
Price v. Price's Heirs	142
Prichard v. Prichard	142
Prichett, Newhold v.	142
Prickett v. Badger	116
Prime, Nourse v.	102
Pullen, Gardener v.	236
Purchase v. Bank	249
Pyke, Ex parte	113
Pym v. Campbell	319

Q.

Quiggle, Persh v.	419
Quimby, May v.	373
Quiner v. Marblehead Ins. Co.	269, 273

R.

Race, Miller v.	148, 164
Ramge, French v.	424
Rankin v. McCullough	345
Rann v. Hughes	81
Ray, Cooper v.	383
Raymond v. Levitt	294
R. R. Co. v. Adams	174
R. R. Co. v. Bank	342
R. R. Co., Brainerd v.	168
R. R. Co., Bridgeport Bank v.	156, 277
R. R. Co., C. R. & B. Co. v.	424
R. R. Co., Carpenter v.	180
R. R. Co., City of Ohio v.	180
R. R. Co. v. Cowell	180
R. R. Co. v. Dane	310
R. R. Co., Edwards v.	197
R. R. Co. v. English	415, 417
R. R. Co. v. Fulvey	423
R. R. Co., Garrard v.	329
R. R. Co., Haven v.	168
R. R. Co., Howell v.	180
R. R. Co., Jones v.	176, 180
R. R. Co., Karnes v.	179
R. R. Co. v. McKeen	178
R. R. Co., Mechanics' Bank v.	149, 396, 403
R. R. Co., Miller v.	168, 174

	PAGE
R. R. Co., Myers v.	168
R. R. Co., Nat. Bank v.	168, 372, 374
R. R. Co., Pinkerton v.	423
R. R. Co., Ross v.	251
R. R. Co., Ryder v.	176, 180
R. R. Co. v. Schuyler	151, 374, 398, 401
R. R. Co., State v.	180
R. R. Co., Ward v.	410
R. R. Co., White v.	168
R. R. Co., Willis v.	400, 403
Railway Co. v. Dalbiac	393
Ry. Co., Durkee v.	117
Ry. Co. v. Freeman	168
Ry. Co., Harris v.	241
Ry. Co., Hubbersty v.	393
Ry. Co. v. Mount	393
Ry. Co., White v.	166
Redd, Gratz v.	179
Reddick v. Jones	373
Redington, Hynes v.	84
Reed v. Gale	291
Reed v. Warner	90
Reese v. Bank	178
Reese, Bank of Montgomery v.	417, 419
Reeves v. Capper	383
Reitenbaugh v. Ludwick	419
Retberg, Cochran v.	280
Rex v. Bank	83, 393
Rex v. Biggs	82
Rex v. Cappur	142
Rex v. De Berenger	296
Reynolds, Eckstein v.	282
Reynolds, Mayor v.	83
Reynolds, Mitchell v.	291
Reynolds, Treadwell v.	286
Rice, Hartley v.	297
Richardson v. Jackson	286
Richmond, Burroughs v.	174
Richmond, Devoss v.	168
Rickey v. TenBroeck	424
Riddle, Hays v.	383
Riggs v. Macgruder	204
Riker, Bunn v.	298
Ripley, Hight v.	196
Robarts, Goodwin v.	97, 162, 169, 170, 171
Roberts v. Hall	373
Roberts's Appeal	340
Roberts v. Jackson	116
Robins v. Edwards	96, 97
Robinson v. Chartered Bank	242
Robinson v. Hurley	343, 347
Robinson v. Kitchen	106
Robinson, McKinnel v.	107, 112
Robinson v. Mearns	298
Robinson, Mollett v.	91, 96, 97
Robinson v. Smith	373

TABLE OF CASES. 27

	PAGE
Rodriguez v. Hefferman	90
Rogers v. Huntingdon Bank	177
Rogers v. Ins. Co.	374
Rogers, Jarvis v.	122, 360, 361
Romaine v. Van Allen	419
Rosewarne, Nicholls v.	181, 392
Ross, Downes v.	197
Ross v. Union Pacific R. R. Co.	251, 253
Rossiter v. Life Ass. Co.	94
Rothschild v. Brookman	90
Rothschild, Doloret v.	237, 246
Rousmanier, Hunt v.	117, 128
Routh, Owen v.	416
Rowley, Shaw v.	268
Roxborough v. Messick	373
Roy, Cooper v.	383
Royal, Morse v.	90
Royer v. Bank	373
Rozet v. McClellan	353
Ruchizky v. De Haven	61, 115, 307, 317, 383
Rudolph v. Ins. Co.	393
Ruggles, Arnold v.	146
Russell, Plaice v.	324
Russell, Stray v.	49, 136
Rutt, Hawkins v.	282
Rutter, Cud v.	235
Rutton, Marshall v.	78
Ryan, Turbeville v.	274
Ryder v. Alton & S. R. R. Co.	176
Ryerson v. Derby	298

S.

	PAGE
Sabin v. Bank	179
Safferty, Tompkins v.	68, 132, 229
Salmon, Taylor v.	90
Sampson v. Shaw	294, 298
San Antonio v. Lane	168
Sanders v. Kentish	416
Sanderson v. Walker	90
Santos, Pinto v.	100
Sargeant v. Essex & C. Co.	178
Sargeant v. Franklin Ins. Co.	175, 266
Saunders, Kempson v.	290
Saunders, Smart v.	121
Saunders, Walpole v.	297
Saunders v. Weber	336
Savings Institution v. Holland	373
Sawyer, Field v.	118
Sawyer v. Hoag	179
Sawyer v. Taggart	303, 318
Sawyer & Hamilton v. Taggart	303
Sayles v. Blane	285
Scarfe v. Morgan	119

	PAGE
Scholes, Blackburn v.	123
Schroeder, Barr v.	128
Schuyler, N. Y. & N. H. Co. v.	151, 374, 398, 401
Schuyler, White v.	249
Sea v. Carpenter	116
Seaforth, McArthur v.	416
Sears, Overseers of the Poor v.	175
Sears, Pickard v.	403
Seiple v. Irwin	91
Sendmeyer, German Ass. Co. v.	276
Sewall v. Boston Water-Power Co.	156, 410
Sewall v. Brainerd	174
Sewall v. Fitch	197
Seymour, Bourne v.	89
Shankland's Appeal	333
Sharman v. Brandt	96, 97
Shaw v. Fisher	239
Shaw v. Holland	414
Shaw v. Rowley	268
Shaw, Sampson v.	294, 298
Shaw v. Spencer	154, 227, 331
Sheffield Gas Co. v. Harrison	240
Shepherd, Chapman v.	108
Shepherd v. Johnson	416
Sheppard v. Murphy	222
Shetucket, Stoddard v.	180
Shipman v. Ætna Ins. Co.	179, 376
Shook, Northrup v.	33, 38, 376
Sigfried v. Levan	275
Siggers, Heseltine v.	160, 168, 188, 199, 231, 233
Silverthorn, Heath v.	343
Simm v. Anglo-American Tel. Co.	155, 157, 407, 410, 411, 412
Simms v. Hervey	277
Simpson, Hill v.	325
Simpson v. Margitson	280
Sims, Wiltshire v.	91, 193
Sinclair v. Jackson	333, 334, 335, 336
Sleight, Davenport v.	273
Sloo v. Law	333
Small, Stanton v.	302
Smalley, Bank v.	178
Smart v. Saunders	121
Smead, Lee v.	373
Smith, Alvord v.	298
Smith v. Bouvier	302
Smith v. Clarke	168
Smith v. Crocker	272
Smith v. Dickinson	274
Smith, Jones v.	332
Smith v. Lindo	118
Smith, Lorymer v.	186
Smith, Robinson v.	302
Smith v. Thomas	61, 115
Smith v. Tracy	94, 262

TABLE OF CASES.

	PAGE
Smyth, Lang v.	160, 171
Society of Savings v. City of New London	168
Solomon, Westrop v.	225, 264, 290
Somerby v. Bunting	202
South Sea Co., Hilyard v.	157, 410
Southard v. Steele	272
Sparling v. Parker	207
Speake v. United States	278
Spencer, Shaw v.	154, 227, 331
Speyers, Brown v.	302
Spooner v. Holmes	168
Sprague, Ely v.	180
Sprague, Indiana v.	164
Spratley, Watson v.	199, 211, 214
Stahl v. Berger	275
Stalker v. McDonald	373
Stanton v. Small	302
Stapleton v. King	424
Starkweather, Howe v.	144, 391, 392
Startup v. McDonald	281
State v. Bank	174, 176, 180, 271
State, Curran v.	179
State v. Delafield	91, 92, 168
State, Mosby v.	274
State v. R. R. Co.	180
State v. The Judges	278
Stear, Johnson v.	356
Stearns v. Marsh	350
Steele, Southard v.	272
Steers v. Laishley	106
Stephen v. De Medina	283
Stephens v. Babcock	100
Stevens v. Bank	351
Stevens, Blanchard v.	372
Stewart v. Cauty	217
Stockholm v. Stockholm	191
Stoddard v. Shetucket	180
Stone, Biederman v.	109
Stone v. Hayes	90
Storm v. Green	424
Stover, Nutter v.	373
Stowell, Lobdell v.	419
Stracy v. Bank	393
Strange, Gordon v.	282
Strassberger, Lehman v.	113
Stray v. Russell	49, 136
Stray, Taylor v.	49, 92, 111, 117
Stringham, Durkee v.	212
Stuart v. Nicholson	291
Suckling, Donald v.	354, 357, 364, 369
Supple, Gilmour v.	282
Sutton v. Tatham	42, 86, 216, 225
Swan v. N. B. H. Co.	270
Swift, Day v.	383
Swift v. Peters	372
Swift v. Tyson	372
Swiggett, Helm v.	178

T.

	PAGE
Taft, Todd v.	247
Taggart, Sawyer et al. v.	303, 318
Tainter v. Clark	336
Talty v. Freedm. Savings & Trust Co.	361
Tarlton v. Baker	298
Tatham, Sutton v.	42, 86, 216, 225
Tayloe v. Fire Ins. Co.	191
Taylor, Fisher v.	333
Taylor, Keeler v.	294
Taylor v. Linley	213
Taylor v. Plumer	33
Taylor v. Salmon	90
Taylor v. Stray	49, 92, 111, 117
Telegraph Co. v. Davenport	340
Telegraph Co., Simm v.	175
Tempest v. Kilner	198, 199
Tenant v. Elliott	118
TenBroeck, Rickey v.	424
Terrell, Martin v.	298
Texira v. Evans	270
Thayer v. Dwight	383
Thayer Manf. Co., Cushman v.	156, 249
Thayer v. Manly	419
Thomas, Dickson's Exec. v.	61, 115, 306, 317, 388
Thomas, Lowe v.	140, 141
Thomas, Smith v.	61, 115
Thompson v. Adams	52, 69
Thompson, Babcock v.	298
Thompson, Brown v.	298
Thompson v. Lee Co.	168
Thorne v. Deas	122
Thorne, Fancourt v.	353
Tileston, Dodge v.	112, 116
Till, Mayor v.	83
Tilson v. Warwick	83
Tilt, Prall v.	155, 328
Tippetts v. Walker	142
Tisdale v. Harris	146, 201, 204, 205
Todd v. Taft	247
Toler, Armstrong v.	107, 112, 113, 114
Tomlinson v. Tomlinson	207, 209
Tompkins v. Safferty	68, 132, 229
Topham, Capp v.	110
Torrey v. Bunk	348
Torrington v. Lowe	131, 136
Tourne, Vance v.	416
Tousley, Wilkinson v.	298
Townshend, Clegg v.	100, 110
Tracy, Smith v.	94, 262
Treadwell v. Reynolds	286
Treasurer v. Commercial Coal Co.	251
Trecothick, Coles v.	95
Trenholm, Bank v.	94, 105, 364
Trevor v. Wood	191, 192
Trye, Williams v.	298

TABLE OF CASES.

	PAGE
Tucker, Howard v.	110
Turbeville v. Ryan	274
Turner, Brown v.	72, 298
Turner, Pott v.	33
Tyrrell v. Morris	824
Tyson, Swift v.	872

U.

	PAGE
Underhill, Johnson v.	841
Union Pacific R. R. Co., Ross v.	251
United States v. Nelson	278
United States, Speake v.	278
Upton v. Archer	274
Usborne, Johnston v.	217

V.

	PAGE
Valette v. Mason	873
Van Allen, Romaine v.	419
Van Hook v. Barnet	273
Van Pelt, Calais Steamboat Co. v.	332
Vance v. Tourne	416
Vandever's Appeal	333, 385
Vandevoort, Hasbrook v.	342
Vanduzer, Ward v.	112
Vansands v. Bank	178
Vaux v. Parke	383
Vawter v. Griffen	200
Vicksburg, Craig v.	168
Viets, Porter v.	315, 319
Volans v. Fletcher	168
Vrooman, Beeker v.	112

W.

	PAGE
Wagner v. Peterson	419
Waite, Langton v.	90, 91, 101, 104, 131, 383, 386
Walker v. Bartlett	172, 269, 284
Walker v. Birch	122
Walker v. Geisse	873
Walker v. Milne	209, 211
Walker, Sanderson v.	90
Walker, Taylor v.	90
Walker, Tippetts v.	142
Wallace v. Harmstead	275
Wallace, Morris v.	84
Wallis v. Littell	319
Wallis v. Manhattan Bank	128

	PAGE
Waln, Evans v.	91, 128, 228
Walpole v. Saunders	297
Walsh v. Whitcomb	128
Waltham, Bank v.	142
Ward, Brown v.	846
Ward v. Byrne	295
Ward v. R. R. Co.	410
Ward v. Vanduzer	112
Warner v. Martin	94
Warner, Reed v.	90
Warren v. Manf. Co.	112
Warwick v. Noakes	283
Warwick, Tilson v.	83
Water-Power Co., Sewall v.	156, 410
Watson v. Spratley	199, 211, 214
Watts v. Brooks	118
Way v. Davidson	388
Webb v. Fairmaner	280
Webb, Parsons v.	90
Weber, Saunders v.	336
Webster v. De Tastet	100
Weightman v. Caldwell	200
Welch, Bridgeport Bank v.	878
Wellington, Nelson v.	844
Wellman v. Nutting	107
Wells v. Coles	142
Wells, Greenough v.	336
Wells v. Porter	186, 862
Wentworth, West v.	419
West, Aurora City v.	168
West v. Wentworth	419
Westmore, Chase v.	121
Westropp v. Solomon	225, 264, 290
Wharf Co., Naglee v.	876
Wheeler, Fay v.	204
Wheeler v. Friend	297
Wheeler, Grenaux v.	873
Wheeler v. Kost	341
Wheeler v. Newbould	844
Wheelock v. Moulton	145
Whitaker, Wilson v.	415
Whitcomb, Walsh v.	128
White, Belote v.	336
White v. Chapman	112
White v. Ry. Co.	166
White v. Schuyler	249
White v. V. & M. R. R. Co.	168
Whitehouse, Hinde v.	84
Whitman, Cowles v.	249
Whitmore, Isherwood v.	282
Whittemore v. Gibbs	200
Whittington, Carriger v.	128
Whittlesay v. Hughes	336
Whitwell v. Carter	298
Wicks v. Hatch	352
Wilcox, Johnson v.	128
Wildman v. Wildman	142
Wiles, Bates v.	423

	PAGE		PAGE
Wiley v. Moor	275	Wister, Evans v.	53, 68, 215
Wilkes v. Ellis	84	Wood, Evans v.	244
Wilkins, Bayley v.	111, 218	Wood v. Hayes	362
Wilkinson, Greening v.	416	Wood v. Hitchcock	286
Wilkinson v. Tousley	298	Wood, Trevor v.	191, 192
Willcocks, Ex parte	362	Woodburn, Campanari v	128
Williams, Baldwin v.	146	Woodcock, Gilmore v.	298
Williams v. Bank	376	Woodruff, Fitzsimmons v.	286
Williams, Calvin v.	200	Woods, Hyde v.	48, 50, 69
Williams v. Crutcher	278	Wood's Appeal	326, 361
Williams, De Haven v.	330	Woodward, Curry v.	180
Williams, Jones v.	332	Woolcott v. Mount	424
Williams v. Little	373	Wootan, Hasket v.	298
Williams v. Littlefield	121	Work v. Bennett	362, 369, 382, 417
Williams v. Trye	298	Worrell v. Munn	81, 276
Williamson v. Morton	324	Worth, Brass v.	345
Williamson's Ex., Brown v.	383	Worthing, Maus v.	272
Willis v. Darby R. R. Co.	400, 408	Wright, Edminston v.	110
Willoughby v. Comstock	346, 350		
Wilson, Bank v.	266		
Wilson v. Dennison	336		
Wilson v. Keating	319		
Wilson v. Kemmil v.	319	Y.	
Wilson, King v.	168		
Wilson v. Little	176, 350	Yates, Dixon v.	232, 259
Wilson v. Moore	325	Young v. Cole	85, 98, 264
Wilson v. Pennock	336	Young, Ex parte	316
Wilson v. Whitaker	415	Young v. Higgins	280
Wilson's Ex., Morris v.	213		
Wiltshire v. Sims	91, 193		
Winchester v. Nutter	297		
Windom, Lamberton v.	344	Z.	
Winfield v. Hudson	168		
Winstanly, Charmley v.	123	Zane, Prentice v.	373

STOCK BROKERS.

STOCK BROKERS.

PART I.

THE STOCK BROKER.

CHAPTER I.

DESCRIPTION OF THE STOCK BROKER.

	PAGE		PAGE
Definition of a stock broker	33	Remarks of Brett, J.	35
Brokers primarily	34	Remarks of Woodruff, J.	38
Additional functions of stock brokers	34	Brokers of city of London	39
		Stock brokers in the United States	40
Remarks of Mr. Bell	34	The Stock Exchange	40
Broker cannot be agent of both parties to the contract	34	Effect of the rules of the Stock Exchange on non-members	41
Distinction between stock and other brokers	35	Division of Part I.	42

A STOCK BROKER[1] is an agent who, usually in his own name, makes a contract on behalf of his principal for the purchase or sale of stocks, scrip, debentures, bonds, and other like securities, receiving a compensation in money therefor.[2]

Definition of a stock broker.

Strictly speaking, a broker is a mere negotiator,[3] who brings the parties together to make bargains and

---

[1] He is a trader within the Bankrupt Act, Tayler v. Plumer, 3 M. & S. 562.

[2] See the definition of a broker, by Tindal, C. J., in Pott v. Turner, 6 Bingham, 702; see, also, Story on Agency, § 28.

[3] See Northrop v. Shook, 10 Blatchford C. C. R. 243.

sales in matters of trade and commerce,[1] and is for many purposes treated as the agent of both parties.[2] But gradually the broker has by commercial usage come frequently to undertake the further office of making and executing the contract in his employer's,[3] and even in his own name, to the buyer.[4] In this latter instance he is entrusted with the possession and disposition of his employer's property, and is thus enabled by his own agency to give a good title in it to the buyer. Perhaps it would be more accurate in such a case to call the agent a factor instead of a broker, for he more nearly resembles the former than the latter. Indeed, as has been remarked,[5] "the character of fac- "tor and broker is frequently combined; the broker "having possession of what he is employed to sell, or "being empowered to obtain possession of what he is "employed to purchase. Properly speaking, in these "cases he is a factor." The stock broker comes under this latter class of brokers,[6] having generally confided to him the control of the securities he is about to sell for his employer, as well as having imposed upon him the duty of accepting the delivery of those he has purchased for him, and being the only person known to third parties in the transaction.[7] The broker is never the agent of more than one of the parties, unless notice to that effect be given.[8]

A broker, primarily, is simply a mere negotiator or middle man.

Stock brokers have additional functions added to their business.

Remarks of Mr. Bell.

Stock broker cannot be agent of both parties to the contract.

---

[1] See Fowler v. Hollins, 7 L. R., Q. B. C. 628.

[2] See Hinde v. Whitehouse, 7 East, 558; Hinkle v. Arey, 27 Maine, 362; Henderson v. Barnwell, 1 Young & Jarvis, 387; Benjamin on Sales, p. 208.

[3] Baring v. Corrie, 2 B. & Ald. 137; Kemble v. Atkins, 7 Taunton,

260.

[4] Fowler v. Hollins.

[5] By Mr. Bell, in his Commentaries, 1 Bell Com. 366, § 409 (4 ed.).

[6] An auctioneer is not a broker, Wilkes v. Ellis, 2 H. Bl. 555.

[7] Lloyd's Paley on Agency, 18; Pickering v. Busk, 15 East, 38.

[8] Story on Agency, § 31.

CHAP. I.] DESCRIPTION OF THE STOCK BROKER. 35

It is essential to an exposition of the questions and cases arising out of the transactions on the Stock Exchange, to understand the difference between the characteristics of an ordinary mercantile broker, who is a mere negotiator, and a stock broker. The latter is indeed a broker; but under the usages of business in England and in this country, and probably everywhere, where Stock Exchanges exist, he is something besides. As between him and his principal, he acts in the relation of agent, and, as such agent, may receive the property purchased, or, in case of a sale, he may make the delivery of the property sold. He may take the formal title of the property purchased and convey that formal title to a purchaser, without his principal's ever being known in the transaction, to third parties. And in all transactions conducted through the medium of the Stock Exchange, the stock broker becomes, as regards third parties and those dealing with him in the Exchange, a principal purely. His character of agent, so far as his own liability in the transaction is concerned, is not recognized, and he is bound on all such contracts made by him as though he were, in fact, the principal himself; and he may be sued either at law or in equity as if he were the actual owner of the property he contracts to sell or the ultimate purchaser of what he intends to buy, which is, of course, not the case with mercantile brokers. An excellent exposition of the character of a broker, simply, is given in Fowler *v.* Hollins.[1] *Distinction between a stock broker and an ordinary broker.*

Fowler v. Hollins.

"Properly speaking," said Mr. Justice Brett, "a broker is a mere negotiator between the other parties. *Remarks of Mr. Justice Brett.*

[1] L. R., 7 Q. B. C. 616.

"If the contract which the broker makes between the
"parties be a contract of purchase and sale, the prop-
"erty in the goods, even if they belong to the supposed
"seller, may or may not pass by the contract. The
"property may pass by the contract at once, or may
"not pass until a subsequent appropriation of goods
"has been made by the seller and has been assented
"to by the buyer. Whatever may be the effect of the
"contract as between the principals, in either case no
"effect goes out of the broker. If he sign the contract,
"his signature has no effect as his; but only because it
"is in contemplation of law the signature of one or
"both of the principals: no effect passes out of the
"broker to change the property in the goods. The
"property changes either by a contract which is not
"his, or by an appropriation and assent, neither of
"which is his. In modern times, in England, the
"broker has undertaken a further duty with regard to
"the contract of purchase and sale of goods. If the
"goods be in existence, the broker frequently passes a
"delivery order to the vendor to be signed, and on its
"being signed, he passes it to the vendee. In so doing
"he still does no more than act as a mere intervener be-
"tween the principals. He himself, considered as only
"a broker, has no possession of the goods, no power
"actual or legal of determining the destination of the
"goods, no power or authority to determine whether
"the goods belong to the buyer or seller, or either; no
"powers, legal or actual, to determine whether the
"goods shall be delivered to the one or be kept by the
"other. He is throughout merely the negotiator be-
"tween the parties. And therefore by the civil law

"brokers were not treated as ordinarily incurring any
"personal liability by their intervention, unless, per-
"haps, there was some fraud on their part:" Story on
"Agency, § 30. "And if all a broker has done, be
"what I have hitherto described, I apprehend it to be
"clear that he would have incurred no personal liability
"to any one according to English law. He could not
"be sued by either party to the contract for any breach
"of it. He could not sue any one in any action in
"which it was necessary to assert that he was the owner
"of the goods. He is dealing only with the making
"of a contract, which may or may not be fulfilled, and
"making himself the intermediary passer on, or carrier,
"of a document, which may or may not be obeyed
"without any liability thereby attaching to him towards
"either party to the contract. * * * If goods have
"been delivered under a contract so made and a de-
"livery order so passed, still he has had no power,
"actual or legal, of control, either as to the delivery or
"non-delivery, and probably no knowledge of the de-
"livery, and he has not had possession of goods. * * *
"But then in some cases a broker, although acting as
"an agent for a principal, makes the contract of pur-
"chase and sale in his own name. In such case *he
"may be sued by the party with whom he has made
"such contract* for a non-fulfilment of it. But so also
"may his undisclosed principal. And although the
"agent may be liable upon the contract, yet I appre-
"hend nothing passes to him by the contract. The
"goods do not become his. He could not hold them,
"even if they were delivered to him, as against his
"principal. He could not, as it seems to me, in the

"absence of anything to give him a special property in them, maintain any action in which it was necessary to assert that he was the owner of the goods. The goods would be the property of his principal. And although two persons, it is said, may be liable on the same contract, each as sole contractor, yet it is impossible that two persons can each be the sole owner of the same goods; although the agent may be held liable as a contractor on the contract, he is still only an agent and has acted only as an agent."

The difference between a person who acts simply as a broker and one who conducts the business of stock brokerage, as now conducted, is fully stated in Northrop v. Shook.[1]

Northrop v. Shook.

Remarks of Judge Woodruff.

"I have," said Judge Woodruff, "said on a former occasion, cited to me on this trial, that, in such transactions as these, the actor is not a mere broker. I think so still. It is not a part of the duty or authority of the mere broker to make the purchase and sale in his own name. He is but a go-between or negotiator between two principals. It is not a part of his duty or office, as a mere broker, to pay the price, or to assume any liability therefor. He binds his principal, or, oftentimes, both of the principals in the transaction, by his memorandum. He is, in short, a mere agent, acting by authority of another. And these same observations are true of other agents. It is, however, equally clear, that agents may make themselves liable on the contracts which they in fact make for others, either voluntarily or by not disclosing their agency. It would, nevertheless, be

[1] 10 Blatchford C. C. R. 243.

CHAP. I.]   DESCRIPTION OF THE STOCK BROKER.   39

"true, that their act of purchase and sale would be
"in execution of their authority as agent, and their
"principal would and must so treat it. They do not
"cease to be agents therein, because they go further
"than, as agents, they were bound to go, and add their
"personal liability, in order to aid in the transaction.
"As between them and their principal they act in the
"relation of agents. So, they may, by express au-
"thority, or, it may be, by authority implied from the
"usages of trade (when such usages exist), receive the
"property purchased, and be themselves the instru-
"ments of making delivery, when they make sales;
"and, by consent of the principal, they may take formal
"title and convey that formal title to the purchaser,
"and may even convert the transaction, as between
"them, into an agreement for a speculation in stock in
"the name of the agent, for the account of his prin-
"cipal. While all these may be superadded to the
"duty and authority of a mere agent to buy and sell,
"there still remains the substantive fact, that, whatever
"effect these other attending circumstances may have,
"between him and his principal, as the result of the
"payment by himself, or of his taking title, the actual
"agency for his principal is not withdrawn from the
"transaction."

The calling of a stock broker is a licensed vocation open to all persons not laboring under any legal disability; in short, any one capable of making and enforcing a legal contract may become one. *Brokerage, a licensed vocation open to all.*

Brokers of the city of London, up to the year 1870, were under the control of the city corporation, and a series of acts were passed defining and regulating their *Brokers of the city of London.*

conduct.[1] By them, brokers were required to give a bond and take an oath, the form of which, prior to the year 1818, is given in Kemble *v.* Atkins,[2] and the new regulations imposed in that year can be seen in "Russell on Factors and Brokers," in the Appendix.[3] But by the London Relief Act of 1870, most of these powers were taken away, the rules and regulations being no longer enforced by the corporation, and the bond no longer required; and brokers are now only required to be admitted by the corporation, while a list of brokers is kept from which any one may be expelled for certain offences in the mode pointed out by the act.[4]

Stock brokers in the United States.

In the United States, stock brokers are governed to some extent in the exercise of their calling by various statutes in the different States,[5] relating to them; but chiefly by regulations of their own making, in the following manner:

It has been customary for stock brokers, in large commercial centres, to establish associations called, in Great Britain and the United States, Stock Exchanges, with a convenient place for carrying on the business of brokerage, under regulations made by themselves. These associations have proved of such commercial value, and the Stock Exchange is so convenient and useful an institution, that it has become the almost sole medium for the purchase and sale of stocks, govern-

The Stock Exchange.

Stock Exchange is the usual medium for the

---

[1] See Statutes of 6 Anne, c. 16; 10 Anne, c. 19, s. 121; 57 George III., c. 60.

[2] 7 Taunton, 260.

[3] See, also, Cavanagh on the Law of Money Securities.

[4] See Benjamin on Sales, pp. 273 –275.

[5] See 1 Purdon's Digest, pp. 179–182; II. Revised Statutes of New York, 1004 (Banks & Bros'. 6th ed.); General Laws of California, p. 904, art. iii. §§ 6273, 6274, sec. 5 (Hittell).

CHAP. I.]   DESCRIPTION OF THE STOCK BROKER.   41

ment and railway bonds, debentures, scrip, etc., and the quotations of its sales are considered as marking the market value of these securities. *sale of stocks, bonds, and the like securities.*

Any one, *sui juris*, on paying a license can, by conforming to the regulations imposed by the State, exercise the calling of a broker. But such a person does not necessarily become a member of any Stock Exchange; though in that case he may either employ members of the Stock Exchange to transact his business there for him, or carry on his operations outside of it altogether, with non-members. Such persons, though governed in their dealings by the law of the land relating to stock brokers, are not necessarily affected by the regulations or usages of the Stock Exchange to a greater degree than any other class of non-members of that body. But where a person employs as his broker a member of the Stock Exchange, he is presumed in law to be affected with knowledge of all the usages of the Exchange, so far as they are reasonable, and he is, in any questions between himself and third parties, growing out of his broker's contracts in the Stock Exchange, on his account, bound by them.[1] Hence a non-member of the Stock Exchange, who deals through a member, is affected with knowledge of its regulations. Moreover, the rules of the Stock Exchange have, in many cases, from its being the sole medium of stock transactions, passed into general commercial usages, and have so come to possess the binding force of general commercial custom. And hence, even as between a principal and his

A stock broker not necessarily a member of a Stock Exchange.

Effect of the Stock Exchange usages on brokers, non-members thereof.

Customs of the Stock Exchange are often evidence of commercial usage.

---

[1] Grissell *v.* Bristowe, L. R., 4 C. P. 37; Maxted *v.* Paine, L. R., 6 Exch. 132.

broker, the reasonable regulations of the Stock Exchange may, as commercial customs, be binding upon both, though the principal have no actual notice of them.[1] What is "reasonable" cannot be determined or defined by any legal rule, but is a matter for the determination of the court, having regard to the general effect of the custom in question, upon the mercantile community.

A stock broker is obviously governed in his transaction by his obligations to his employer and third parties, as well as by the regulations of the Stock Exchange. He may therefore be conveniently considered,—

I. With reference to the Stock Exchange.
II. With reference to his customer or principal.
III. With reference to third parties.

[1] Sutton *v.* Tatham, 10 Adol. & Ellis, 27 [1839].

CHAPTER II.

THE STOCK BROKER AND THE STOCK EXCHANGE.

	PAGE		PAGE
SECTION I.—CONSTITUTION AND NATURE OF STOCK EXCHANGE.		Cases discussed	50
		Method of dealing on American Exchanges	53
Definition	43	Ordinary sales and special bargains	54
Its establishment in London	44		
Its nature and constitution	44		
Sales thereon	45		
Account days	46	SECTION II.—THE CLEARING HOUSE.	
Method of dealing	46		
Jobbers	46	Definition	56
Passing a name	47	Its *modus operandi*	57–61
Tickets passed	47	Legality of deliveries at	61
Buying in; selling out	48		
Continuing shares	48	SECTION III.—EFFECT OF RULES OF THE STOCK EXCHANGE.	
Backwardation and contango	48		
Non-current securities	48	On non-members	67
American Exchanges	49	Cases discussed	67
Philadelphia Board of Brokers	49		
Membership or seat on the American Exchanges	49	SECTION IV.—TERMS OF THE TRADE.	

SECTION I.—DESCRIPTION OF THE CONSTITUTION AND NATURE OF THE STOCK EXCHANGE.

THE Stock Exchange, in its present form in England and the United States, may be defined to be a voluntary business association or club, formed by its members for the purpose of buying and selling stocks, etc., among each other, either as principals in their transactions, or as agents acting for outsiders of the association, and having a code of laws regulating the admission, conduct, and expulsion of its members.[1]

Definition of the Stock Exchange.

The idea which is at present conveyed by the words

[1] See the definition in Paterson on the Stock Exchange, p. 26; also that of Miller, J., in Hyde *v.* Woods, 4 Otto, p. 523.

Establishment of Stock Exchanges the result of circumstances.

"Stock Exchange" was not conceived at any one distinct period, but has been the result of circumstances and business necessity; and Stock Exchanges have been the gradual growth of upwards of a century in England and America. We shall first examine as briefly as possible the nature and constitution of the London Stock Exchange, and then that of those in this country.

§ 1. *The London Stock Exchange.*

The origin of the London Stock Exchange.

In London, when dealings in stocks began to be considered an important part of mercantile transactions, the stock brokers, who had hitherto met each other in the streets or wherever they could, began to meet regularly in an apartment of the Bank of England, and removed subsequently to a house hired by them for the special purpose of dealing in securities, and a small admission fee was paid by each stock broker. It became, however, impossible to carry on successfully such an institution, for numbers of persons became members who were of doubtful reputation. In 1801 a number of brokers formed the conception of the present association, and organized themselves into a business club, an entrance and an annual fee being paid by each member, whose admission was carefully scrutinized by a committee, and having a set of rules drawn up to regulate the business conduct of each person while a member of the association.

Constitution of the London Stock Exchange.

The London Stock Exchange, says Mr. Cavanagh in his work on the Law of Money Securities,[1] now consists of two distinct bodies: 1. The shareholders or proprietors, who own the building where business is

---

[1] See p. 515.

CHAP. II.] STOCK BROKER AND STOCK EXCHANGE. 45

transacted, and who are interested as members of a joint stock undertaking; and, 2. The subscribers, or persons generally described as members of the Stock Exchange, or of the house, who transact business. A person desirous of being elected as a subscriber or member, is obliged, before his application for election can be entertained, to give security, three existing members becoming his sureties, in a limited amount, for the meeting of his engagements during three years, and then an election for his admission is held by ballot. Every year a re-election takes place, though almost always the member, if his character is not doubtful, is re-elected. When elected, a member pays an entrance fee and an annual subscription, but has no vested interest in his membership beyond the right of exercising his employment, etc., during his membership, and cannot dispose of it on leaving the association. A regular list is kept of the securities commonly sold at the London Stock Exchange, while particular rules govern the production of any new securities put on the market. Two kinds of established securities are quoted on the official list,—the current and the non-current; the former being those for which there is an active market, and the latter, for which the market is not active. Admission to the Stock Exchange.

List of the securities on the market.

In both the active and non-active securities the sales are made "for money," or "for the account." In the former case, the broker pays the money down and gets an immediate delivery or transfer of stock. In the latter case, the contract is for a future delivery, which is made on a subsequent day, called the "settling" or "account" day, when the contract is completed. If no Sales made for "money" or the "account."

time is mentioned, it is understood that the delivery is to be on the account day. For government Consols there is one account day in each month, and two account days for other English and foreign stocks and shares; and where a new security is put on the market, an account day is arranged upon for it.

Account days.

The method of dealing followed in the London Stock Exchange differs from the system pursued in America or the continent of Europe. In all operations in stocks, the members dealing divide themselves into two classes of operators, known as jobbers or dealers, and brokers. The former class are intermediaries between the buying and selling brokers, acting on their own account, while the latter act as the agents of their respective principals in the transactions, but deal with the jobbers in the ordinary relation of seller and purchaser. Both are actually members of the Stock Exchange, and technically speaking stock brokers, but dividing themselves into these two classes for each stock transaction. After the transaction is completed, the jobber may then act as a broker in another operation, and *vice versa;* but a stock broker cannot act in both capacities in the same transaction. The transaction is executed as follows. A broker desirous of executing a commission goes to a jobber, and asks him to name a price. The jobber, if assenting, will name two prices, one at which he binds himself to sell, and one at which he binds himself to buy. The broker then discloses his intention of buying or selling, as the case may be, and usually does not disclose his principal.[1] A memorandum is then made of

Method of dealing on the Stock Exchange in London.

Jobbers.

Illustration of dealings.

---

[1] See Child *v.* Morley, 8 Term Reports, 610; Magee *v.* Atkinson, 2 M. & W. 440.

the sale by each party in his book, and usually a bought and sold note is given by each to the other. The jobber is then at liberty to resell the shares if he has purchased, or buy shares from some other broker or jobber to complete the contract if he has sold, and frequently the original number of shares sold by a broker is split up into smaller lots before the shares are finally all taken up by one or several brokers.[1] The contract of sale remains *in statu quo* till the "name day" or "ticket day," which is the day before "settling day," when the buying broker is obliged to "pass a name," which may be either that of his principal or of some one else put forward by him, to the jobber. This is done by his giving the jobber a ticket bearing the name of the ultimate transferee intended, and the price at which the sales were effected, together with the broker's name. The ticket or tickets are then passed on till the selling broker gets them, who is bound to accept the names offered, unless he can show some good reason why he should not, as, for example, fraud, or where the name of the transferee is not that of a person *sui juris*, etc.[2] The broker passing on the name is bound to pay the purchase-money to the original seller.[3] A contract is thus constituted between the original seller and the ultimate buyer, enforcible at law.[4] It makes no difference whether the price on the ticket differs from that at which the shares were originally sold, the difference being paid or received by the "jobber" in the transaction, and this is a mere adjust-

Name day or ticket day.

Passing a name.

Tickets passed.

[1] See Coles *v.* Bristowe, 4 L. R., C. A. 3.
[2] See Nickalls *v.* Merry, 7 L. R., E. & G., App. 530.
[3] See Rules of London Stock Exchange.
[4] Musgrove and Hart's Case, 5 L. R., Eq. 193.

ment of prices which does not affect the original seller.[1] On "settling day" the seller gives up his stock to be transferred, and ten days are allowed by the rules of the Stock Exchange for this. If the shares are not given up, the purchasing member may "buy in" shares to the amount of the contract, which is done publicly on the Stock Exchange, and the member, through whose default this has become necessary, is compelled to make good any increase in the price paid on such purchase, together with the commission of the broker buying in.

Buying in.

Similarly, if the price be not paid to the holder of the shares, he may "sell out" and claim from the defaulting buyer the difference or diminution in price caused by his neglect, besides a commission for selling out.[2]

Selling out.

It often happens that the broker desires to "continue shares," or to postpone the day of payment or delivery, and this may be done by the payment of a premium, called in the seller's case "backwardation," and in the buyer's "contango." When the name is passed, the jobber is released from any liability in the matter.[3] Sometimes the broker comes to an understanding without the aid of the jobber, and in the case of foreign or provincial stock the broker has to seek out one who deals in it.

Continuing shares.

Backwardation and contango.

In the transactions in securities that are non-current the broker usually applies to the jobber, who, however, does not make an offer till he has found some one who is willing to buy or sell.

Sales of non-current securities.

---

[1] See Newburn *v.* Eaton, 20 L. T. 449.

[2] See Dorriens *v.* Hutchinson, 1 Smith, 420.

[3] Grissell *v.* Bristowe, L. R., 4 C. P. 36; Coles *v.* Bristowe, L. R., 3 Eq. 257, 3, c. 388; Hawkins *v.* Maltby, L. R., 4 Ch., App. 200.

CHAP. II.]   STOCK BROKER AND STOCK EXCHANGE.   49

When the price is paid or ready to be paid, the selling broker hands over to the buying broker or brokers, genuine transfers and certificates, with the rights and interests which they convey; but it is not considered to be the duty of the vendor's broker to procure a registration of the transfers, which devolves on the purchaser, who, however, might have the right to call on the vendor to get him to concur in the purchase.[1]

§ 2. *The American Stock Exchange.*

The Stock Exchange in the United States had much the same origin as that in London; as, for example, in Philadelphia, about the beginning of the present century, "the first place of meeting appears to have "been in the Exchange Coffee House in Second Street, "where, in one corner of a room, used by merchants "and others as a common rendezvous at certain hours "of the day, the brokers met to deal in stocks, bills "of exchange, and promissory notes." The scene of operations was then changed from one place to another, till the occupation of the present building of the Stock Exchange. *Origin of the Stock Exchange in America. The Philadelphia Stock Exchange.*

The Stock Exchanges in America are entitled the Stock Exchange,[2] or Stock and Exchange Boards,[3] and are unincorporated associations, whose real estate and other property are usually vested in trustees selected by the members.

The membership is somewhat different from that in London. A person desiring to become a member[4] *The membership.*

---

[1] Taylor *v.* Stray, 2 C. B., N. S. 175; Stray *v.* Russell, 1 Ellis & Ellis, 888.

[2] See Constitution and By-Laws of Philadelphia and New York Stock Exchange.

[3] See Constitution and By-Laws of San Francisco Board.

[4] The applicant must be of legal age.

makes his application to the proper officers of the Stock Exchange, and an election, usually by ballot, is held for his admission, if there be a vacancy in the membership, which is often exclusively in the charge of an elective committee. In the event of his being elected, a fixed initiation fee is then paid. His membership is termed a "seat," which, as the membership is limited, has a moneyed value. In case there is no vacancy, he may purchase a seat from some member desirous of quitting the Stock Exchange. But he does not, by the purchase, acquire any right to membership in the Exchange until he is duly elected, when he pays a small initiation fee. An outgoing member of good financial standing may dispose of his membership, for its market value, to any one desirous of entering the association, subject to the nominee's election as a member. Upon the death of a member his seat is sold, and the proceeds, after his debts to members are paid, pass to his executors; and upon the insolvency of a member his seat may be ordered to be sold by the Stock Exchange, when the proceeds are first applied to satisfying his debts to members of that institution. The member thus has a vested interest in his seat, but holds it always subject to his debts to the association and to his fellow-members. The following cases are illustrations of the legal nature of a "seat" on the Stock Exchange in the United States.

Admission by purchase of seat.

The "seat," or membership.

Hyde v. Woods.

In Hyde v. Woods[1] the nature of membership in the Stock Exchange was discussed at some length by Miller, J., in the Supreme Court of the United States. Art. 15 of the Constitution of the Stock Exchange

[1] 4 Otto, 523.

CHAP. II.]   STOCK BROKER AND STOCK EXCHANGE.   51

of San Francisco provided that "in sales of seats for "account of delinquent members, the proceeds shall be "applied to the benefit of the members of this Board "exclusive of outside creditors, unless there shall be a "balance after payment of the claims of members in "full." A member became bankrupt, and assigned his seat to be sold and to have the proceeds distributed among his creditors in the Board. His creditors outside of the Exchange contended that such a distribution of the proceeds constituted a preference under the Bankrupt Act, and was void. The question here arose, whether the stipulations in the by-laws of the Stock Exchange, making the "seat" first liable to creditors inside of the Stock Exchange, were valid as against outside creditors, and whether it constituted property subject to attachment and execution at the suit of any creditor, whether a member of the Stock Exchange or not.

In deciding the distribution among the creditors in the Exchange to be valid, Justice Miller said, "There "is no reason why the Stock Board should not make "membership subject to the rule in question, unless it "be that it is a violation of some statute, or of some "principle of public policy. It does not violate the "provision of the bankrupt law against preference of "creditors, for such a preference is only void when "made within four months previous to the commence-"ment of the bankrupt proceedings. Neither the "bankrupt law nor any principle of morals is vio-"lated by this provision, so far as we can see. A "seat in this Board is not a matter of absolute pur-"chase. Though we have said it is property, it is

Remarks of Miller, J.

"encumbered with conditions when purchased, without "which it could not be obtained. * * * It never was "free from the conditions of Article 15. * * * That "rule entered into and became an incident of the "property when it was created, and remains a part of "it into whose hands soever it may come. As the "creators of this right—this property—took nothing "from any man's creditors when they created it, no "wrong was done to any creditor by the imposition of "this condition. * * * It is said that it is against the "policy of the bankrupt law, against public policy, to "permit a man to make in this or any other manner a "standing or perpetual appropriation of his property "to the prejudice of his general creditors; and it is to "this point that the numerous authorities are cited. "They all, however, relate to cases where a man has "done this with property which was his own,—prop-"erty on which he himself imposed the direction, or "the encumbrance, which impeded creditors. It is "quite different where a man takes property, by pur-"chase or otherwise, which is subject to that direction "or disposition when he receives it."

Thompson v. Adams.

In Thompson v. Adams,[1] a similar rule existed in the Philadelphia Stock Exchange, and a member purchased a seat with money advanced to him by C., his partner's brother, for the purpose, but without notifying the Stock Exchange that he had not paid for it out of his own money, or that he was not the real owner thereof. Upon the dissolution of the partnership, he gave C. a bill of sale of the seat, also without notifying the Board thereof. At his death, he was indebted to members of the Stock

[1] 7 Weekly Notes of Cases (Phila.), 281.

CHAP. II.] STOCK BROKER AND STOCK EXCHANGE. 53

Exchange, and the proceeds of the sale of the seat were claimed by them, and by C., who held the bill of sale for it.

The Supreme Court of Pennsylvania held that the constitution and articles of a voluntary association such as the Stock Exchange were a law unto its members, and that C.'s claim, as equitable owner of the seat, against the members, could not be supported, as he was a stranger to the association, while the legal owner, as a member, was subject to its regulations. "The seat "was not property," said the court, "in the eye of the "law, * * * but was the mere creature of the Board, "and of course was to be held and enjoyed with all the "limitations and restrictions which the constitution of "the Board chose to put upon it." Substantially the same question was decided by the same court in Pancoast v. Gowen,[1] and later in Moxey's Appeal,[2] and in Wister v. Evans.[3] It may therefore be considered as established that a "seat" is held subject to the restrictions placed upon it by the Stock Exchange creating it.

Pancoast v. Gowen et al. Moxey's Appeal. Wister v. Evans.

There is in many of the American Stock Exchanges a trust or insurance fund established, out of which the family or legal representatives of each member are, on his death, entitled to receive a fixed sum.[4] The rules of the Exchanges regulate the admission of members, the assessments to which they are subject, the rate of their remuneration, and their expulsion in case of insolvency.

The method of dealing in the American Stock Ex-

---

[1] 5 Weekly Notes of Cases (Phila.), 36.
[2] 9 ibid. 441. [3] 1 ibid. 182.
[4] See Gratuity Fund of Philadelphia Exchange in book of Rules; Trust Fund in books of Rules of New York and San Francisco Exchanges.

changes is much less complicated than in England. Certain hours are set apart for the transaction of business, and the day often divided into sessions or sittings of the Board. A "regular list" of stocks and bonds, etc., active in the market, is called once or oftener at each session, and during the calling, the shares or securities are bought or sold. There is also frequently, as in New York, another list, with certain stocks upon it, called, and the lists may be re-called, according to the rules of the association. Certain rules regulate the placing or "listing" new stocks or securities on the regular list of the Exchange, which, however, vary in the different Stock Exchanges.

During the calling of the stocks at the sessions of the Board, a member, desirous of executing a contract, makes a bid, or an offer to either buy or sell, as the case may be, certain shares of stock, or bonds, etc., and if any one desires to close with him, he accepts the offer and the bargain is made. A bought or sold note containing a memorandum of the sale may then be exchanged, and often by the rules of the Exchange the sale is recorded in books of the Stock Exchange. The sales are for "cash" or "regular way," or "on time," or in some cases for "the account." Sales for cash need no explanation, as the thing is paid for and delivered in a short time. In sales "regular way," or in the absence of any special agreement, the security is deliverable the next day, at or before a designated hour, unless the day be a holiday, when the delivery takes place on the following day. In sales on time, or by a special agreement, the security is deliverable at the time specified, unless that

CHAP. II.]   STOCK BROKER AND STOCK EXCHANGE.   55

be a Sunday or a holiday, and then the delivery is on the preceding day; usually, in Philadelphia and New York, the time does not exceed sixty days, and in San Francisco, it does not exceed ninety days.

In New York, there is under certain circumstances an account day fixed for sales in government securities, which is the fifteenth and thirtieth of each month.[1] *Sales for the account.*

In general, the delivery is effected either by the vendor handing the vendee broker a stock certificate, or other evidence of the security, with a power of attorney irrevocable, to transfer, executed in blank by the person in whose name the security is legally registered; and in certain cases the selling broker is compelled, by the rules of the Exchange, to guarantee the power of attorney, as in Philadelphia; or else to cause an actual transfer to the vendee broker to be made.[2] In the New York Stock Exchange, the buyer may demand an actual transfer on the books of the company; and in Philadelphia, either party may do so; and usually where the delivery is by certificate and blank power of attorney, the buyer may insist on having the certificates in not more than one hundred shares each.[3] *Delivery.*

SECTION II.—THE CLEARING HOUSE.

Much of the business of stock brokers in respect to the delivery of shares of stock is carried on through the instrumentality of an institution which is termed the Clearing House. In order, therefore, to have a *The Clearing House.*

---

[1] See Rules of New York Stock Exchange, p. 66.
[2] For deliveries when the transfer books are closed, see Rules of the different Stock Exchanges.
[3] See Rules of New York and Philadelphia Stock Exchanges.

thorough and accurate knowledge of their business, it will be necessary to clearly understand the operation and effect of the Clearing House with respect to stock transactions. We shall give a detailed account of the Clearing House, the more so, as questions concerning the Clearing House and its legality have lately arisen in Pennsylvania, and it is manifest from the language used by the court in passing on those questions that they have failed to comprehend its effect or *modus operandi*. In considering the Clearing House we shall endeavor, first, to define it, as briefly as we can; and then, to describe somewhat more at length its *modus operandi*.

Definition of the Clearing House.

The Clearing House may be defined to be a bureau or agency, established by the members of the Stock Exchange for those stock brokers who are members of it, and who may choose to avail themselves of its use; where a sheet containing the account of the purchases and sales of stock and the prices thereof, made by each of such stock brokers, and maturing during that day, is sent, and which, by the mutual assent of the buying and selling stock brokers, is elected and authorized by them to act as the common agent of each, both in balancing their respective accounts in their several transactions in stock maturing during that day, and the prices for the same, and also in accepting and making for each, a symbolical, actual and legal delivery of the shares of stock sold by each respectively, together with

Explanation of the *modus operandi* of the Clearing House.

the payment therefor: by setting off the number of shares of stock due to and from each stock broker, as shown by their respective accounts. Where a sheet of each such stock broker balances exactly, that is to say, where the number of bought shares equals the number of sold shares, as well as the prices therefor, then the delivery is complete and the account is closed up; but where the total number of bought shares exceeds the total number of sold shares, or *vice versa*, then the account is balanced by the Clearing House as far as possible, and the balance of stock due to him from it, or from him to it, is either paid to him by some other stock broker, directed thereto by the Clearing House, acting as his receiving agent, or by him to some other broker, being directed similarly by the Clearing House, acting as the agent of that other broker; and the balance in money resulting from the different prices of stock is paid over by the different parties in the same way.

Though the idea of the Clearing House is nothing new, since it has been used for a long time both by the banks in respect to their cheques, and also by railroad companies, who have a sort of Clearing House, where the different exchange tickets over each other's lines, which are sold by them severally, are cleared, it will be best, perhaps, in order to comprehend clearly the nature and legal effect of this institution, in regard to transactions in stocks, to describe its *modus operandi* somewhat at length and to give an actual illustration.

Idea of the Clearing House not new.

ACCOUNT OF A. & CO. WITH THE CLEARING HOUSE.

PENNA. R. R. CO. SHARES.

Chart of Clearing House

No. of Shares.	From Whom.	Amount.	Certification.	No. of Shares.	To Whom.	Amount.	Certification.
200	V. & Co.	13,300	V. & Co.	100	L. & Co.	6,650	L. & Co.
500	X. & Co.	33,250	X. & Co.	100	M. & Co.	6,650	M. & Co.
300	Y. & Co.	19,800	Y. & Co.	500	N. & Co.	33,250	N. & Co.
200	Z. & Co.	13,200	Z. & Co.	700	R. & Co.	46,225.67	R. & Co.
200	Balance.	13,400			Due C. H.	174.33	
1400		92,950		1400		92,950	

The above chart is a Clearing House sheet, and the meaning of it is as follows:

Suppose A. & Co., being stock brokers and members of the Stock Exchange, are employed by B. & Co., C. & Co., D. & Co., and E. & Co. to sell 1400 shares of stock,—100 for B. & Co., 100 for C. & Co., 500 for D. & Co., and 700 for E. & Co.,—and suppose A. & Co. are handed by these parties respectively the number of shares which each is desirous of selling. At the same time S. & Co. desire A. & Co. to buy 200 shares of the same stock for them, T. & Co. desire A. & Co. to buy 500 shares of the same stock, Q. & Co. desire A. & Co. to buy 300 shares of the same stock, and R. & Co. desire the same parties to buy 200 shares of the same stock for them.

Now it will be observed here that, ordinarily, A. & Co. would have eight distinct transactions in stock at the least to execute, 1400 shares of stock having to be sold for different parties by them, and 1200 shares of stock having to be bought for different parties by them. Ordinarily, this would therefore necessitate at least eight deliveries of stock to be made in these transactions (and possibly many more), as well as payments of large amounts of money for these deliveries. Assuming the stock to be that of the Pennsylvania Railroad Company, which is probably worth $65 or $66 a share,[1] nearly $200,000, or its equivalent, thereabouts, would have to be used in these transactions made by this one firm alone, and 2600 shares of stock would also be required to effect the various deliveries. Now by using the agency of the Clearing House all these

[1] October, 1881.

transactions between the brokers may be accomplished by about 200 shares of stock and by the employment of about $175. Therefore in transactions ordinarily amounting in number with regard to shares of stock to 2800, and with regard to money to $200,000, the actual money used by the brokers among each other is reduced to less than $200, and the actual shares of stock also to less than the same figures.

Before the Clearing House was established in Philadelphia, stock brokers made use of a system of due bills, which economized money and stock to a certain extent, as is done now in New York.

As soon as the aforesaid firm of A. & Co. have bought and sold these shares at the Stock Exchange, they make up what is called the Clearing House sheet as shown above. The figures on the extreme left under the words "number of shares" indicate, with the exception of the last line, the numbers of shares they have bought for their customers. The letters in the column immediately on the right of the aforesaid figures represent the brokers from whom they have bought them at the Stock Exchange. The figures under the word "amount," again, to the right of this column, represent the amounts of money severally paid for the purchase of the above shares. The letters under the word "certification" represent the signatures or certificates of the brokers from whom they have purchased, to the effect that the transactions are correctly stated on the Clearing House sheet. The remaining half of the Clearing House sheet represents, on the other hand, the sales for their customers, and is arranged in the same manner as the purchases. It will be observed that A. & Co. have sold 200 shares more than they have purchased, therefore the sheet does not balance on both sides, and in order to make it balance, they add 200 shares to the number of shares purchased, making the purchased and sold shares thus balance. In adding this balance they will of course have to add the price to the several amounts of the purchased shares. Now probably the different lots of these shares have been sold at different prices, so that A. & Co. cannot choose any particular price which will be equal to the prices paid for each of them respectively; therefore a price is selected as near as possible to the average price of the market value of the shares sold during that day. We have said that this price is selected; but it would be more proper to say that every day there is a fictitious price fixed upon by the Clearing House as near as possible to the probable opening value, in even numbers, of the stock to be sold or maturing during that day. This value is fixed upon by the Clearing House for each stock at or just after the opening sales. Now this fictitious value may be either more or less than the market value; therefore, as A. & Co. have charged the Clearing House with 200 shares to balance their sheet, the same firm must either pay to or receive from the Clearing House the difference between the total amount of the various sums of money received as the product of all the actual sales on this Clearing House sheet made by them, and the total amount of money paid by them for the shares they have actually purchased, plus the amount they have charged the Clearing House with as the price of the

CHAP. II.] STOCK BROKER AND STOCK EXCHANGE. 61

200 shares balance. In the example given this difference will be found to be $174.33, and this is added to the amount of money they have received for their sales. The number of shares bought, now balance with the number of sold shares, as well as the prices. This sheet is received by the Clearing House, and as far as the bought and sold shares balance, they are set off against each other, and the balance of the 200 shares is directed by the Clearing House, as the agent of some buying broker, to be delivered by A. & Co. to him; and A. & Co. pay the Clearing House $174.33, which is the difference aforesaid.

The legality of deliveries through the agency of the Clearing House has been questioned in Pennsylvania, and the Supreme Court of that State have held that such deliveries are fictitious transactions and void by the common law of Pennsylvania, being a mere settlement of differences.[1] If, however, we examine the relation of the Clearing House to the buying and selling brokers carefully, it will not be difficult to see the untenability and fallacy of such a proposition, and moreover it is clear from the language used by the Supreme Court, in passing on this question, that it failed entirely to understand the nature and *modus operandi* of the Clearing House.

Legality of Clearing House deliveries.

The Clearing House is the agent of both of the parties, and where a selling broker sends to it his account of sold shares, the Clearing House in such a case is authorized by the buying broker to accept such shares, and if such an account were to contain nothing

---

[1] See Ruchizky *v.* De Haven *et al.*, 10 Weekly Notes of Cases (Phila.), 109; Smith *v.* Thomas, 10 *ibid.* 112.

but sold shares, the Clearing House, as the agent of a buying broker, would simply direct the selling broker to deliver the shares to his (the Clearing House's) principal; but where the account contains bought as well as sold shares, the Clearing House then, acting as agent of both of the brokers, sets off one transaction against the other. This the principals themselves might, perfectly legally, do, and, consequently, it is obvious that their agents may do the same. In fact, the sheets sent to the Clearing House by the different brokers are substantially nothing but bills of sale made by them, and made to them, and sent to their common agent the Clearing House. When the transactions balance, there is but little difficulty; and the question in regard to the illegality of these transactions of the Clearing House seems generally to have arisen, in the minds of some people at least, where the bought and sold shares do not balance in the respective sheets of the different brokers. It has been fallaciously argued that *here* is a proof that the whole transaction is a mere settlement of differences, since the brokers themselves do not receive or deliver any stock or money, with the exception of the before-mentioned small amount of stock they deliver, and the small amount of money which they pay. But this difficulty is at once removed by a very cursory examination of the position of the brokers delivering or receiving the aforesaid balance of money and stock. The broker delivering, thus, the balance, is acting under the direction of the Clearing House, which acts as the agent of the receiving broker, or *vice versa*. For instance, where the accounts of any two stock brokers at the Clearing

House show 200 shares purchased by one of the other, and 100 shares sold, *vice versa*, there is a balance of 100 shares. The Clearing House then says to the vendor of the 200 shares, "We accept on behalf of "the vendee of the 100 shares his 100 shares, we set "off the 100 shares he is to receive against the 100 "shares he has sold you, and so far the transaction is "complete: now you have purchased of him another "100 shares, and we, as your agent, will then direct "the same broker, as vendor, to hand them over to you, "and the payment will be made in the same way. As "his agent, we have accepted the 100 shares you have "sold him; as your agent, we have accepted the 200 "shares he has sold you; 100 shares have been set off, "and now we tell him to deliver the other 100 to you, "the payments when not balancing being similarly "made." Such a transaction is eminently legal and real. Suppose there had been no Clearing House in this last case, but that the buying and selling brokers had come to each other, after the close of the business day, and one said to the other, "You owe me 200 "shares of stock; I owe you 100 shares of stock, "which may or may not have been sold at different "prices. Now instead of your sending to me 200 "shares and my sending to you 100 shares, simply "send to me 100 shares, the rest of our transactions "balancing, and if in balancing there is a difference "in the prices, we will adjust that difference.".

No one will deny that such a transaction is perfectly legal, and if such a transaction is perfectly legal if done by principals, it is certainly legal if performed by their agents, or if performed by their common agent, as in this instance, viz., the Clearing House.

One word with regard to the customers of the brokers. They are not in any way affected by the Clearing House. The Clearing House simplifies merely the transactions of the brokers as between each other. In the case supposed, A. & Co., for instance, might deliver the 1200 shares to their customers out of the 1400 shares they have received from their other customers, and deliver the 200 balance to the broker whom the Clearing House points out. And they might deliver the price or value received for the shares to be purchased, in payment, as far as possible to their other customers; and this would economize money and stock, viz., since 1400 shares of stock and $100,000 of money would be used by brokers and customers, instead (without the Clearing House's aid) of $200,000 of money and 2600 shares of stock, at least; and if the shares were frequently resold, it would be necessary to use hundreds of thousands of dollars. As one share is equivalent to and as good as another, this can very readily be done, and saves the loss of allowing a large number of shares to lie at the office of some company waiting for registration, and money drawing no interest. It will be observed also that shares can only be cleared at the Clearing House because one share is as good as another. Where a hundred brokers have sent in their respective sheets, the Clearing House may possibly direct a delivery of the balance to be made from one broker to another, with whom the former has had no transaction. But this is perfectly legal. The Clearing House has accepted all the shares the selling broker has sent to it on his Clearing House sheet, or bill of sale, as the agent of the buying broker or original vendee, and requests the former, the vendor, to deliver the balance to some other vendee, the shares having been subsequently resold by the original vendee to a sub-vendee; and so, if the price or payment of the difference in money is given, to a broker whose sheet shows him entitled to it.

The term, settlement of differences, is an incorrect expression, used with reference to the Clearing House delivery. It can never be a settlement of differences. And it may be said that all the transactions effected through its instrumentality must be valid, for it is obvious, if a single incorrect or invalid sheet is sent in to it, it will render incorrect all other sheets which are in any way connected with the sheet this particular broker has sent in.

Sometimes the broker may use shares of his own, to make deliveries before he gets those of his customer; but where a broker uses his own shares in completing the transaction, he loans them temporarily to the vendor, for he can never use them for his customer's transactions, as his own; not being allowed to sell or buy as sole agent between the two parties to the sale; and so with the purchase money.

SECTION III.—EFFECT OF THE RULES OF THE STOCK EXCHANGE.

As members of the Stock Exchange expressly agree, on their entering it, to conform to and abide by its rules, they are legally bound by them, so far as they are not against public policy; but where the interests *Effect of rules on members.*

of non-members, such as principals or creditors, are concerned, somewhat difficult questions may arise. The law merchant in most cases assumes, as already stated, that one dealing with a stock broker is bound by the current mode of dealing, that is to say, in making his contract with the broker, he does so, subject to all existing reasonable rules and usages of the trade.[1] When, therefore, an outsider employs, as his broker, a member of the Stock Exchange, he contracts with him subject to the known and reasonable usage of the trade prevailing at that place, as well as subject to the reasonable rules of the Stock Exchange, and that, probably, whether he himself is aware of the rules or not. With regard to the case of creditors, non-members, it follows that as the broker is governed by the rules of the Stock Exchange, the broker's creditors, in other transactions with the broker, are affected also by them; the rules to bind, however, must always be valid and reasonable. A few cases will best illustrate the principles of law on this subject, and what have been considered valid rules.

Colket v. Ellis.

The following case of Colket v. Ellis[2] is an illustration of a custom that is binding on brokers where both are cognizant of a usage.

Here the Court of Common Pleas at Philadelphia, held that a custom among brokers to sell stock deposited as collateral security for a call loan, at the Board of Brokers (*i.e.*, Stock Exchange), on the failure of the borrower to pay on the day, on which the demand was made, was not illegal, as between the parties familiar with that mode of dealing, the custom not being invalid *in se*.

---

[1] See Story on Agency, § 60, etc.   [2] 32 Leg. Int. (Phila.), 82 [1881].

CHAP. II.] STOCK BROKER AND STOCK EXCHANGE. 67

As illustrations of rules binding on non-members, where there is a relationship of debtor and creditor existing between them and the stock broker, in consequence of transactions other than sales at the Stock Exchange, the cases of Moxey's Appeal,[1] and MacDowell v. Ackley,[2] may be cited.

Effect of rules on non-members.

Moxey's Appeal. MacDowell v. Ackley.

In Moxey's Appeal,[3] it was held that the constitution and articles of the Stock Exchange of Philadelphia were a law unto its members, and that it was perfectly competent for such an association to make a regulation to the effect, that if a suspended member failed to comply with all his contracts his seat should be sold, and the proceeds distributed among his creditors, members of the association; and that though such a regulation gave the members of the association an advantage over other creditors, they had a right to stipulate for it.

Moxey's Appeal.

In MacDowell v. Ackley,[4] in 1865, plaintiff became a member of the Stock Exchange. In 1875 the Exchange passed an amendment to its constitution, providing for a gratuity fund, from which a sum of $2000 was to be paid to the representatives of every full member on his decease; and a full member was to be one owning a seat, whether suspended or not. M. paid up certain assessments for the formation of the fund. Subsequently it was provided that any suspended member, who should fail for three months to pay certain dues and assessments on account of the fund, should cease to be a full member for this purpose. There was no evidence to show whether M. knew of this amendment

MacDowell v. Ackley.

---

[1] 9 Weekly Notes of Cases (Phila.), 441.
[2] 8 ibid., 464.
[3] 9 Weekly Notes of Cases (Phila.), 441.
[4] 8 Weekly Notes (1880), 464.

or not. M., having been in arrears, was suspended, and the court held, that having subscribed to the constitution and by-laws he was bound by them.

Evans v. Wister.

In Evans *v.* Wister,[1] the court held, that a seat in the Philadelphia Board of Brokers was a mere license, created merely and existing by the rules made in respect to it, to which each entering member subscribes, and not subject to attachment at the hands of outside creditors of that body.

In these cases, we thus see, that the courts have held, that the sale of a seat on the Stock Exchange being a mere license, on the bankruptcy or insolvency of a member, a distribution of the proceeds, according to the rules of that body, among his creditors, members of the Stock Exchange, in preference to his outside creditors, is not an invalid preference within the meaning of the Bankrupt Acts.

But suppose a rule of the Exchange authorized the officers of that body to take possession of the other property of a bankrupt or insolvent, and distribute it among his Exchange creditors before any of it was distributed among his outside creditors, in other transactions, not connected with the Stock Exchange.

Nicholson v. Gooch.

The question arose in Nicholson *v.* Gooch,[2] but the case turned on another point.

Tompkins v. Safferty.

In Tompkins *v.* Safferty,[3] however, the question was decided. Here C., a member of the Stock Exchange, being unable to meet his engagements, notified the secretary. By the rules of that association the defaulter ceases to be a member and his estate is distributed by

---

[1] Weekly Notes (Phila.), 181.
[2] 5 El. & Black, 999.
[3] L. R., 3 App. Cas. 213.

CHAP. II.]   STOCK BROKER AND STOCK EXCHANGE.   69

the official assignees of the Exchange. C., becoming insolvent, handed over possession of his estate, £5000, to them, stating that he had no other creditors excepting those in the Stock Exchange. In an action by the assignee in bankruptcy to recover this sum of money so paid, the court held, that what C. had done was an act of bankruptcy, a *cessio bonorum*, and that the money so paid created an invalid preference over his other creditors, and that such a rule of the Stock Exchange was only an honorary regulation, and not binding on outsiders.

The reader is referred further to the cases of Hyde v. Woods and Thompson v. Adams, quoted on a former page, as illustrations of the same principle. Hyde v. Woods. Thompson v. Adams.

SECTION IV.—TERMS OF THE TRADE USED ON THE STOCK EXCHANGE.

There are, as in all professions, a peculiar set of terms used by stock brokers in their dealings, which it is necessary to insert in the description of the Stock Exchange, for it would be impossible fully to comprehend the cases relating to the subject, without understanding the terms used in the transactions of stock brokers. Terms of the trade.

ACCOUNT, THE, consists of three days, viz.: contango day, the name day, and the settling day.

ACCOUNT, SALE FOR. A sale for the account is a contract of sale to be performed on a future day, called the account day.

ACCOUNT DAY, is the regular day or days in each month, on which, in England, established securities are to be received and paid for. In England there is one account day in each month for government stock, and two for other English and foreign stock and shares.

ALLOTMENT, consists of a certain specific amount of scrip, or number of shares. Allotments may be issued of scrip, before the company is formed, and of scrip and shares after it is formed.

BACKWARDATION, is the seller's postponement to deliver shares, with the consent of the buyer, upon a payment of a premium to the latter.

BEAR, is one who contracts to sell securities for future delivery, expecting to profit by a fall in the market.

BLIND POOL. See POOL.

BONUS, is a premium or fee given to do, or to omit to do, something.

BULL, is one who buys with a view of gaining by a rise in the market.

BUYER'S OPTION. See OPTION.

BUYING IN. In the London Stock Exchange, if shares sold are not within a certain time transferred, the buyer may "buy in" the shares or securities from other dealers in the Exchange, up to the amount of his bargain, and claim the difference or loss, if any, from his seller.

CALL, is an option to claim stock at a fixed price on a certain day.

CALLS, are assessments on shares of stock, usually for unpaid instalments of the subscription thereto.

CARRYING STOCK. Where a broker purchases and holds shares of stock, in his own, or his principal's name, and on behalf of his principal, before the principal advances him the money with which to do it, he is said to be carrying the stock for his principal.

CONTANGO, is the postponement of payment by the buyer of stock on the payment of a premium to the seller.

CONTANGO DAY, is the day to which contracts for contango are postponed.

CONTINUATION, is the agreement to postpone a settlement until the next settling day.

DEALER. See JOBBER.

FLAT, without interest. Where stocks are borrowed by a broker to make his deliveries, he usually deposits the market value of the stock with the lender, who ordinarily allows the current rate of interest on the deposit until the stock is returned. Where the stock is scarce and its use is valuable, or where for any other reason the lender refuses to allow interest on the deposit, the stock is said to be borrowed " flat."

JOBBER, is the intermediary acting between brokers on the Stock Exchange. The term is probably peculiar to the London Exchange.

LAME DUCK, is one who is unable to meet his contracts in the Exchange,—an insolvent.

LONG, TO BE, is to own stock, or to hold contracts for the purchase of stock, bought to sell at an advance.

MAKING A PRICE, is the jobber's naming two prices to the broker, at one of which he binds himself to sell, and at the other to buy.

MAN OF STRAW. See NAME.

MARGIN, is a collateral security, usually in money, deposited with a broker to secure him from loss on contracts entered into by him on behalf of his principal.

MONEY, SELLING FOR, is a contract of sale, where

the money is paid down and the stock delivered at once.

NAME, PASSING A, is the forwarding of a name by the buying broker to a jobber, of a person agreeing to sell or take shares of stock as the ultimate buyer. The transferee of shares, on which unpaid calls are still due, is personally liable for their amount. A broker or jobber may therefore refuse to deliver such shares to a person not *sui juris* or to an insolvent, because in such case the liability of the seller for the calls would still remain.

Where the buying broker forwards a name of a person not responsible, as that of the purchaser of the shares, in order to avoid personal responsibility for unpaid calls, such a name is said to be that of a "MAN OF STRAW."

NAME DAY, is the day preceding settling day.

NOVATION, is the substitution of one contract for another.

OMNIUM, is stock; see Olivierison *v.* Coles, 1 Starkie's Reports, 496; Brown *v.* Turner, 7 Term Reports, 630.

OPTION, signifies, in America, a right or privilege to receive or deliver a certain number of shares of a specified stock on a certain day at a certain price, with or without interest.

In England, it signifies the right to buy or sell at a future day at a certain price, or to do neither.

OPTION ACCOUNT DAY, is the day before account day or name day.

OPTION MONEY, is booked at the time the transaction is effected, and paid on settling day. If the price be the same at the expiration of the option time as that

CHAP. II.] STOCK BROKER AND STOCK EXCHANGE. 73

originally fixed, the person paying has the right to declare whether he buys or sells, or does nothing.

POOL, is a copartnership temporarily formed for stock operations, usually in some specific stock.

PUT, is an option to deliver stock or not on a certain day at a certain price.

PUT AND CALL, is an option to claim or to deliver a certain stock at a certain day and price.

REGULAR WAY (in America), is a sale with delivery and payment on the following day.

SCRIP, is an agreement by a company to pay interest or dividends, or to issue stock or bonds. The word is usually applied to the certificate, in which the agreement is contained.

SELLER'S OPTION. See OPTION.

SELLING FOR MONEY. See MONEY.

SELLING OUT, is the right the holder of shares contracted to be sold has, if he is not paid on a certain day, to sell them out in the Exchange, and claim any loss or difference from the buyer.

SETTLING DAY, is the day on which the accounts are settled up and the contract completed.

SHARE, is a certain proportion of interest of the capital or stock of an incorporated company, being the smallest fraction into which the stock is divided, and entitles the holder to receive dividends when declared, and to the other privileges that appertain to a corporator.

SHARE WARRANTS. By the Companies Act of 1867, 30 and 31 Vict. c. 131, sections 27–36, companies, whose capital consists of stock, or fully paid-up shares, are authorized to issue, under certain conditions, share warrants, transferable by delivery if drawn to bearer, or, if not, by endorsement and delivery.

SHAVE, is a premium paid for an extension of the time of delivery or payment, or for the right to vary a stock contract in any particular.

SHORT, SELLING, is making a contract to deliver stock, one does not own.

SPREAD EAGLE, is where a broker buys a certain stock at seller's option, and sells the same at seller's option within a certain time, on the chance that both contracts may run the full time and he gain the difference.

STRADDLE, is a put and call.

TICKET, is the slip containing the ultimate buyer's name, which is issued by the purchasing broker, or the broker for whom he is acting, and duly passed on, on name day, to the seller.

TICKET DAY, is the name day.

ULTIMATE BUYER OR PURCHASER, is the name of the person actually buying or selling stock which is forwarded on the ticket.

WASH. Where a broker receives an order to buy and also an order to sell the same number of shares of the same stock, he is bound to execute both orders separately to the best advantage of each principal. Where, however, he simply transfers the stock from one to the other principal and retains the difference, the operation is said to be a "wash," which is invalid.

CHAPTER III.

THE STOCK BROKER AND HIS PRINCIPAL.

	PAGE
SECTION I.—CREATION OF AGENCY.	
Preliminary remarks	75
Who may be stock brokers	76
Married women, lunatics, etc.	76
Any man *sui juris* may be principal	78
Married women at common law	78
By statute. *Feme sole* traders.	79
Infants, lunatics, drunkards	80
Appointment of agent by natural persons	81
Appointment by artificial persons	82
Corporations	82
Municipal corporations	83
Trustees	84
SECTION II.—SCOPE OF AUTHORITY TO ACT.	
Cases discussed	85
Ambiguous terms	87
Meaning of "about," "more or less," etc.	87
Adverse interests of stock broker to principal	89
Washing	90
Pledge	90
Statute in Pennsylvania	91
Sale	91
Payment	91
Price	92
Condition of genuineness in sale	92
Warranty in sale	94

	PAGE
Delegation of authority	94
Deviation	96
Liability to third parties	96
Public agents	97
Illegal transactions	100
SECTION III.—EXECUTION OF AUTHORITY.	
I. General rules	100
Skill and diligence	100
Accounts	100
Pledge, return of identical shares	100
Cases discussed	101
Penal act in Pennsylvania	104
II. Liability of the stock broker to his principal	106
III. Liability of the principal to the stock broker	107
1. General rules	107
2. Advances and disbursements	110
Cases discussed	111
3. Commissions	116
Cases discussed	117
IV. Stock broker's lien	118
SECTION IV.—DISSOLUTION OF AGENCY.	
1. By stock broker	122
2. By principal	123
3. By mere operation of law.	123
By death	124
At common law	124
At civil law	124
Cases discussed	124

SECTION I.—CREATION OF THE AGENCY.

A MEMBER of the Stock Exchange, when acting as a broker, has been defined to be an agent,[1] and it is proposed in this chapter to define the position occu-

Preliminary remarks.

---
[1] See *supra*, page 38.

pied by him to his principal, or, as it is usually termed, his customer.

A member of the Stock Exchange, when acting as a broker, makes a contract for the purchase or sale of securities for a principal. It is obvious, then, that no one not *sui juris*, or able to make a legal contract, can be a stock broker. Thus, neither married women, as a general rule, infants, nor lunatics can exercise this calling; but beyond this legal disability, every one may become one. As already stated, however, a stock broker is not necessarily a member of any Stock Exchange, but can only become so on being duly elected into such a body. Any man of good character and *sui juris* is generally eligible for membership of the Stock Exchange, unless its membership be full, or some other rule of that body prove an obstacle. If elected, he may, in America, continue his membership so long as he conforms to the rules. The Stock Exchange, however, may, as it is a voluntary association, impose, by rules, restrictions on the eligibility of applicants,[1] and thus, as to future members, upon the terms of membership itself.

There is no legal reason to prevent women, if *sui juris*, from acting as stock brokers; but it has not yet ever been customary to admit them to any Stock Exchange. A married woman could not, of course, unless constituted a *feme sole* trader, act as an agent.

A *feme sole* trader was a term originally applied to

---

[1] See Rules and Regulations of London Stock Exchange, p. 18; Constitution and By-Laws of the Philadelphia Stock Exchange, p. 24; Constitution and By-Laws of the San Francisco Stock Exchange, p. 10; Constitution and By-Laws of the New York Stock Exchange, p. 13.

the wives of mariners who by an old custom of the English law were allowed to make binding contracts notwithstanding their coverture. But the power of married women to enter into business and to make binding contracts of a general character, notwithstanding their coverture, has been greatly extended in America by the statutes of the various States, as for instance in New York and Pennsylvania. Under the act of May 4, 1855,[1] in Pennsylvania, as well as under similar statutes in most of the States, a married woman may enter into any business and make all contracts appertaining to such business, and in New York she may hold, convey, sue and be sued for, her separate property as if *feme sole*.[2] How far, if cohabitation should still exist, in most of the States the consent of the husband would be necessary to a married woman's carrying on a separate business, is, perhaps, a point of some doubt, since it does not seem specifically provided for by any statute. But if a married woman should, with the consent of her husband, or in case of desertion or any of the other categories pointed out by the statutes, without his consent, choose to carry on the business of a broker, and qualify herself to do so in the manner required by the *feme sole* trader statutes, she would undoubtedly be able to make all contracts appertaining to that business, and to bind herself, as well as her principal, by her agencies.

It does not, however, follow that even a *feme sole* trader can always bind herself or her principal by *any* contracts she might make. It has been held in some

---

[1] Acts of 1855, p. 430. [2] Rev. Stat. N. Y., vol. 8 (6th ed.), p. 159, art. 6.

How far a feme sole trader can contract.

States that a *feme sole* can only validly contract in or about the business carried on by her, and that a promissory note given by her, outside of, or not connected with, that business, is void. Unless therefore stock brokerage was the business specially carried on by a *feme sole*, she might be legally incapacitated from binding herself or her principal in a stock contract, or one arising out of a stock transaction. Of course in those cases where the contract of the *feme sole* is valid,[1] she may sue and be sued with regard to her separate estate as though *sui juris*, though the name of the husband is usually joined in the action, to conform to pre-existing usage.

Who may be principals, or customers.

Any one capable of making a legal contract may do so by an agent;[2] and therefore any one *sui juris* may become the principal or customer of the broker, and sue or be sued both on the contract made through his broker with third parties, as well as on the contract between himself and the broker.

Married women at common law.

At the common law the contract of a married woman is absolutely void, and the only redress is an appeal to her husband's sense of right;[3] nor is the contract one which can be ratified at her husband's death, but is void *ab initio*.[4] In England and America, however, of late years a series of statutes have greatly enlarged her powers of making contracts when living separate from her husband, and even, in some States, when living with him, with regard to her separate estate, as in New York. How far, then, married women may become

---

[1] See Rev. Stat. N. Y., vol. 3 (3d ed.), p. 159.

[2] Story on Agency, § 6.

[3] 2 Marshall *v.* Rutton, 8 T. R. 545.

[4] See Benjamin on Sales, Book I., chap. ii., American and English Notes.

the *principals* in stock transactions, depends upon the general principles just laid down.

In his work on Agency, Section 6, Judge Story says, "But where a married woman is capable of doing "an act, or of transferring property or rights with the "assent of her husband, then, perhaps, she may, with "the assent of her husband, appoint an agent or at-"torney to do the same. So with regard to her sepa-"rate property, she may perhaps be entitled to dispose "of it, or to encumber it through an agent or attorney; "because in relation to such separate property she is "generally treated as a *feme sole.* I say perhaps, for "it may admit of question." *Remarks of Judge Story.*

Where a married woman may, by recent statutes, contract with the assent of her husband, she may with his assent authorize an agent to do any administrative act. But where she has authority by statute to do an act, as, for instance, to sell personal property, while she herself can, of course, make a valid transfer of it, and thus complete an executed sale, it by no means follows that she can bind herself by an executory contract, to sell it. This would involve a general power on her part to bind her separate estate by contract, which, we have just seen, has been questioned. It follows, therefore, that it is doubtful whether she can authorize an agent to make an executory contract for her, as, for example, to sell securities. Such a *contract*, as well as one to purchase, would probably be at the broker's risk. *Married women by statute.*

But a married woman, with her husband's assent, may employ a broker to sell her own securities at a stipulated price, or to invest her own money by the purchase of securities. And where the securities or money are furnished to the broker, he would probably run no risk in selling them. In some of the United States, as in Pennsylvania, there are various acts (see Act of 29th February, 1872, Section 1, 1st April, 1874, Section 1, 18th March, 1875, Section 1) permitting a married woman to "sell and transfer" certain securities without the consent of her husband and as if a *feme sole*. The words of all these acts are "sell and transfer." It is probable, however, that these words only allow a married woman to make an executed sale, but not to make an executory contract to sell which would be enforced. If this view be correct, a married woman in Pennsylvania cannot be a principal in a stock transaction, unless where the same is an executed one,—that is to say, where the broker is merely employed to complete the sale. In other words, it is always at the broker's risk if she act independently as a principal in any stock transaction.

Feme sole traders.

With regard to *feme sole* traders it is probable that in most of the United States the same rule applies. A *feme sole* may undoubtedly make a binding contract in regard to any business which she is carrying on. But unless it can be shown conclusively that the stock transaction in which she undertakes to act as principal, is in fact incident to the business carried on by her, it will not follow that she possessed the legal capacity to make it. And to ascertain whether, in fact, the transaction was incident to her business, would involve a question of law in every case. *Prima facie*, therefore, a broker would have to act at his own risk also if his principal were a *feme sole* trader. With regard to

CHAP. III.]   STOCK BROKER AND HIS PRINCIPAL.   81

infants, their liability is somewhat different from that of married women, as their contracts are voidable only and may be ratified when they come of age, and is substantially the same as other persons' not *sui juris*.[1] Infants, lunatics, drunkards.

The agency of the stock broker may be created either by a direct contract in writing, as by deed, or otherwise, or verbally, without any writing;[2] or it may arise indirectly by implication.[3] It has indeed been often asserted that the creation of an agent should be directly by deed; but such a rule, if it ever existed, is now obsolete.[4] Where, however, the stock broker is required to execute a sealed instrument, his agency must be created by an instrument equally solemn.[5] The usual method of transferring stocks, etc., in America, is for the principal to give the stock broker an irrevocable power of attorney in blank to transfer the same, so that this question is not of such moment as it might otherwise have been.

Appointment of agency.

By natural persons.

Authority to execute sealed instruments.

It arises, however, where a broker has been verbally instructed to purchase stocks which are carried by him in his own name. When a principal directs the sale of such securities, it is usually by parol, and in the absence of any decision it may be inferred from the nature of the transaction, that a verbal instruction to sell stock belonging to the customer and allowed by him to stand in the broker's name, is valid, since it is undoubtedly valid as to third parties on the doctrine of estoppel.

The question as to how far a stock broker can fill up

---

[1] Benjamin on Sales, chap. ii.
[2] Long *v.* Colburn, 11 Mass. 97.
[3] Rann *v.* Hughes, 7 Term Rep. 350.
[4] See the two preceding cases in notes.
[5] Coke Litt. 40 *b*; Worrall *v.* Munn, 1 Selden, 229; Harrison *v.* Jackson, 7 Term Rep. 207.

6

Power of attorney.

a power of attorney in blank will be discussed later.[1] But the stock broker may sign any unsealed instrument though the creation of his agency was by parol,

Authority to execute unsealed instruments.

as, for instance, where the Statute of Frauds requires the instrument to be in writing to bind the party, the agent may be authorized to sign without any writing, unless the statute expressly says the authority must also be in writing.[2] The question as to how far an instrument, bad as a deed, may be held valid as a simple instrument, is treated of by Judge Story in his work on Agency, section 49 of the text, and in the notes thereto. When the principal is present when the deed is signed by the stock broker, and cognizant of its import, it would probably be looked upon as if the principal had signed it himself.[3]

Appointment by artificial persons.

By the old rule of the common law, the agent of a corporation received his appointment through the instrumentality of an instrument under seal, on the ground that no creation of agency by a corporation was binding, which was not evidenced by an instrument under the seal of the corporation. But latterly this rule has been considerably relaxed, and now an agent or stock broker may receive his authority to act on behalf of a corporation, by either direct authority, or indirectly by implication[4] when his acts are ratified by the corporation, and the stock broker's acts are the acts of the corporation, for the breach of which an action will lie on the implied promise.[5]

---

[1] See *infra*, in chapter, on the completion of the contract.

[2] See Story on Agency, § 50.

[3] Ball *v.* Dunsterville, 4 Term Rep. 313; Hibblewhite *v.* McMorine, 6 M. & W. 200; Gardner *v.* Gardner, 5 Cush. (Mass.) 483.

[4] See Dillon on Municipal Corporations, §§ 459–461; Green's Brice's *Ultra Vires*, p. 356; Story on Agency, §§ 52, 53, notes.

[5] See Rex *v.* Biggs, 3 P. Wil-

Thus, corporations acting within the scope of their authority have substantially the same liability to action as natural persons, and may be sued as principals either on their express or implied contract for breaches of contract to their agents. When, however, a corporation acts *ultra vires* the power of the corporation, it has been questioned whether the agent can recover for advances made to it, or as compensation for his services in any way. Where money has been advanced to the corporation for its exigencies, the rule appears to be that the corporation cannot avoid payment by denying the authority to contract the loan.[1] So it would seem that a stock broker could recover compensation for his trouble where the corporation had not authority to employ him, though his remedy would be an action on the *quantum valebat*, or *quantum meruit*, and not on the express contract. With regard to municipal corporations who are themselves agents, the rule is very strict, and they cannot even ratify the acts of their agents when beyond the scope of their authority.[2]

Corporations acting ultra vires.

Municipal corporations.

The general rule in the United States courts, at least, seems to be that all express contracts, *ultra vires*, are void. (See Thomas *v.* The Railroad Company, 11 Otto, 84.)

Thomas v. Railroad Co.

The chief difficulty, however, is to ascertain in the case of a stock transaction whether power to make the contract can or cannot be implied on the general powers of the corporation. Here a distinction may

Implied power of corporation to contract.

liams, 419; Rex *v.* Bank, Douglass' Rep. 524; Mayor *v.* Till, 4 Bingham, 75; Tilson *v.* Warwick & Co., 4 B. & C. 963; Beverley *v.* Lincoln Gas Co., 6 A. & E. 829.

[1] See Notes by Green to Brice's *Ultra Vires*, p. 623.
[2] Mayor *v.* Reynolds, 20 Maryd. 1. See Dillon on Municipal Corporations; Story on Agency, § 53, notes.

arise, between a power to sell and a power to contract the purchase. Almost any corporation may make a valid contract for the sale of securities actually owned by it, unless subject to some trust. But it does not follow that a corporation would have authority to buy, or to make contracts to buy securities generally. This power can only be implied from the character of the business which the corporation was chartered to carry on, and a broker in making contracts of purchase for a corporation would act at his own risk, unless he could show, that its charter clearly conferred the right upon the directors to bind it in a contract of such nature.

Trustees. In England,[1] and in several of the United States,[2] trustees, who are themselves agents for others, are not allowed to invest the money of the *cestuis que trustent* in the shares of private and trading corporations, but they are limited in their choice of investment to certain public securities, such as government loans, in the United States,[3] and government loans and Bank of England stock,[4] in England, which, as a rule, do not vary greatly in value, and consequently a trustee *prima facie* is not permitted to invest in shares of stock unless he is specially allowed by the trust deed to do so. The broker, therefore, in accepting an order from a trustee must find out the exact authority the trustee has delegated to him, otherwise if he executes such an order he does so at his own risk.[5]

---

[1] Howe *v.* Dartmouth, 7 Vesey, 150; Hynes *v.* Redington, 1 Jones & Lat. 589; Baud *v.* Fardell, 7 De G. M. & G. 628.

[2] Nyce's Estate, 5 W. & S. 254; Hemphill's App., 18 Penn. 303; Ackerman *v.* Emott, 4 Barb. N. Y.

626; Morris *v.* Wallace, 3 Barr, Pa. 319.

[3] See *supra*, note 2.

[4] 22 & 23 Vict. c. 35; otherwise in Massachusetts, Harvard College *v.* Amory, 9 Pick. 446.

[5] Gillett *v.* Peppercorne, 3 Beav.

CHAP. III.] STOCK BROKER AND HIS PRINCIPAL. 85

The subject of trustees will be discussed further on, in Part III.

SECTION II.—SCOPE OF THE STOCK BROKER'S AUTHORITY TO ACT.

The stock broker is obliged to act strictly in accordance with his principal's instructions, and if he deviates from them he will be responsible,[1] even though he thereby intended to benefit his principal.[2] A stock broker is, however, always employed with reference to the existing and reasonable usages of the trade, or Stock Exchange, and it does not make any difference, whether the principal was aware of them at the time or not, or even, if he secretly makes another arrangement.

Thus, in Young v. Cole,[3] certain Guatemala bonds were placed, by the defendant, in the hands of the plaintiff to sell, who thereupon sold them to B. and received therefor the market value. A few days after the sale, B., discovering that the bonds were not stamped, and in consequence would not be recognized by the government by whom they purported to have been issued, returned them to the plaintiff. It appeared that the understanding of the Stock Exchange was, that Guatemala bonds meant Guatemala bonds duly stamped, and that in dealing in foreign funds stock brokers act as principals, and are liable to be expelled, if they do not make good their differences; and the plaintiff refunded B.'s money. The court held that the defendant was bound by the rules of the Stock

Young v. Cole.

78; Bank v. MacCleod, 7 Moo. P. C. C. 35; Fox v. Mackreath, 1 L. C. Eq. 140 (3d ed.); see, also, 12 Cent. Law Journal, p. 266.

[1] Catlin v. Bell, 4 Campb. 183.
[2] Idem.
[3] 4 Scott, 489.

Exchange, and that he was liable to the plaintiff for the money repaid to B., and that the plaintiff was competent to rescind the contract without applying to him.

<small>Sutton v. Tatham.</small>

So in Sutton v. Tatham,[1] a broker on the Stock Exchange, being employed to sell shares, was by mistake directed to sell 250 instead of 50. The shareholder called the next day, and, informing the broker of the mistake, asked him if he could remedy it, who said "no," and then the shareholder told him to do the best he could. By the rules of the Stock Exchange, brokers on sales of this description do not name any principal, and if the vendor is not prepared to complete the sale, the purchaser buys the requisite number of shares, and holds the vendor liable for the difference. The broker paid the difference, being unable to make good the contract, the purchaser having made up the shares at a loss, and the court held, the shareholder was liable to the broker for such difference. Lord Denman said, he thought a person who employed one who is notoriously a broker was bound to authorize his acting in obedience to the rules of the Stock Exchange; and Littledale, J., said, "A person who employs a broker must be supposed to give him authority to act as other brokers do. It does not matter whether or not he himself is acquainted with the rules by which brokers are governed."

<small>Remarks of Littledale, J.</small>

<small>Instructions of the broker.</small>

It not infrequently happens that the instructions of the principal are couched in doubtful and ambiguous language, and in such cases, where the broker is misled he will be excused.[2]

---

[1] 10 A. & E. 27.
[2] See Story on Agency, § 74; Brown v. McGran, 14 Peters' Rep. 480.

CHAP. III.]   STOCK BROKER AND HIS PRINCIPAL.   87

The rule of the interpretation of written instruments, where their language is doubtful, is that that meaning most adverse to the writer is to be received. Usually, however, such letters of instruction are construed liberally, because, as Judge Story observes, in his work on Agency, they are given in a loose and inartificial manner, and much is to be gathered from the custom of the trade; but if on the whole the sense is plain, the agent is bound to act correctly. *Ambiguous instructions.*

As, for instance, where in Bertram *v.* Godfrey[1] the agent was ordered to sell some of the funds, "if they "should be at 85, or above that price," the court held that the broker was bound to sell when that figure was reached. *Bertram v. Godfrey.*

The quantity of securities to be bought or sold is indicated occasionally by such ambiguous words as "about," "more or less," etc. In some of the Stock Exchanges, as, for example, in New York, there is a special by-law providing for the construction of certain ambiguous terms. Thus, Article VI. of the by-laws of the New York Stock Exchange prescribes that "in all contracts where the term 'about' is used, either "as to the time, or number of shares, the variation "of the former shall not be more than three days, nor "the latter more than ten per cent." Where, however, there are no such provisions, it would not be inappropriate to refer to a few cases as illustrations of what construction the courts have put on such terms, and which have been collected by Mr. Benjamin in his valuable work on Sales, page 569. *Meaning of words "about," "more or less."*
Meaning of word "about" in the New York Stock Exchange.

[1] 1 Knapp, 381.

Cross v. Eglin.

In Cross *v.* Eglin,[1] the purchase was of "about 300 "quarters (more or less) of foreign rye * * * shipped "on board the 'Queen Elizabeth,' etc., also, about 50 "quarters of foreign red wheat," etc. The vessel arrived, having on board 345 quarters of rye and 91 of wheat. The plaintiffs, the buyers, had paid by bill of exchange for 50 quarters of wheat and 300 quarters of rye; but the defendants, making no dispute about the wheat, insisted that the plaintiffs should take the whole 345 quarters of rye, and refused to deliver any unless they would accept all. The plaintiffs thereupon, after making a formal demand of 300 quarters of rye and 50 of wheat, abandoned the contract, and sued for the amount of the bill of exchange which they had paid. Evidence was offered (and rejected), to show that it was contrary to the custom of merchants to require a buyer to receive so large an excess as was offered to the plaintiffs, under the expression "more "or less." The plaintiffs had a verdict, and the court refused to disturb it, Lord Tenterden, C. J., and Littledale, J., both thinking that the excess was too great to be covered by the words "more or less," Park and Patteson, JJ., expressing a doubt on that point, but holding, that the expressions being obscure, the burthen of proof lay on the vendors, who were seeking to enforce the contract, and that they had failed to show clearly what was the meaning of the parties.

Cockerell v. Aucompte.

In Cockerell *v.* Aucompte,[2] the court refused to give consideration to an objection against paying for 127 tons of coal, on a contract to deliver 100 tons "more

[1] 2 B. & Ad. 106. [2] 2 C. B., N. S. 440.

CHAP. III.] STOCK BROKER AND HIS PRINCIPAL. 89

"or less;" but the coals had been supplied, and there was no offer to return them.

In Bourne *v.* Seymour,[1] there was a contract for the sale of "about" 500 tons of nitrate of soda, but the terms of the written contract made out by the brokers were so obscure that the case is of no value as a precedent. Cresswell, J., said that he did not think the parties understood the contract. *Bourne v. Seymour.*

In McConnell *v.* Murphy,[2] decided in the Privy Council in April, 1873, where the sale was of "all of "the spars manufactured by A., say about 600, aver-"aging 16 inches; the above spars will be out of the "lot manufactured by T. B." The court held that a tender of 496 spars, which were all of the specified lot that averaged 16 inches, was a substantial performance of the contract by the vendor. These words "say about 600" were held to be words of expectation and estimate only, not amounting to an understanding that the quantity should be 600. The case of Gwillim *v.* Daniell (2 C. M. & R. 61; 5 Tyr. 644) was approved and followed; and the effect of the word "say," when prefixed to the word "about," was considered as emphatically marking the vendor's purpose to guard himself against being supposed to have made an absolute promise as to quantity. *McConnell v. Murphy.*

Frequently the meaning of such terms is left to the jury to determine, from the circumstances of the case at issue. *Meaning of doubtful terms often left to the jury.*

In the execution of his contract, the broker must not have interests adverse to those of his employer, for *Stock broker cannot have interests ad-*

[1] 16 C. B. 337.   [2] 21 W. R. 609.

verse to his principal.

then he can hardly fairly carry out his contract.[1] The stock broker, therefore, cannot be the agent of both the buyer and the seller; and if he does, in such a case the transaction may be set aside.[2] Nor can he purchase for himself, when employed to sell.[3] And it is not necessary that the broker should have made any profit in the transaction.[4]

Washing.

The system known among stock brokers as "washing stock,"[5] which is, substantially, where the broker acts for both the buyer and the seller, is therefore illegal.

It will be hardly necessary to add that all profits made by the broker in a transaction belong to his principal.[6]

Power to pledge.

A broker's authority to sell does not give him any right to pledge his principal's securities for advances made to him on any other account than that of his principal.[7] The authority, express or implied, of the broker to hypothecate securities handed to him by his principal for sale, for advances on the latter's account, and how far the broker himself has a lien for such advances on the principal's securities, is treated of

---

[1] Stone v. Hayes, 3 Denio, 575; Duguid v. Edwards, 50 Barb. 288; Taylor v. Salmon, 4 M. & W. 139; Conkey v. Bond, 34 Barb. 276.

[2] Ins. Co. v. Ins. Co., 20 Barb. 470; see, also, Rothschild v. Brookman, 5 Bligh, N. S. 165; Gillett v. Peppercorne, 3 Beav. 78; Bank v. MacCleod, 7 Moo. P. & C. C. 35; Fox v. MacKreath, 1 L. C. Eq. 146 (3d ed.)

[3] Copeland v. Ins. Co., 6 Pick. (Mass.) 198; Reed v. Warner, 5 Paige (N. Y.), 650; Lowther v.

Lowther, 13 Vesey, 95; Taylor v. Salmon, 4 M. & W. 139.

[4] Sanderson v. Walker, 13 Vesey, 601; Morse v. Royal, 12 Vesey, 355; Langton v. Waite, L. R., 6 Eq. 165.

[5] See definition of this term.

[6] Paley on Agency (Lloyd), 37; Story on Agency, § 214, note.

[7] Parsons v. Webb, 8 Greenl. 38; Debouchout v. Goldsmid, 5 Vesey, 211; Rodriguez v. Hefferman, 5 John. Ch. 429; Boyson v. Coles, 6 M. & Sel. 14.

separately hereafter.[1] But no usage or custom of trade will authorize the broker to pledge the property of his principal to secure his own debt, or to apply its proceeds directly or indirectly to the payment of his own debt. Nor, where the broker employs another member of the Exchange, to sell the principal's securities, can the latter retain out of their proceeds a debt due him from the broker.[2] There is in Pennsylvania a penal statute[3] forbidding any re-hypothecation of securities by the broker at all, though up to this time there are no decisions upon it.[4] *Penal statute in Pennsylvania.*

It is the broker's duty to sell for cash, and not on credit,[5] and it is the usual custom of the Stock Exchange for a stock broker to sell for an undisclosed principal.[6] It may be assumed, that the authority given a stock broker to buy or sell securities, will also give him an implied authority to pay or receive payment for the same. It is true that originally an ordinary broker could not receive payment,[7] but if there is a usage of the trade to the effect, that it is part of the duty of a stock broker in the trade usually to receive payment, it would probably be upheld, if known to both parties;[8] and probably the principal would be *Sale.*

Payment.

---

[1] See Part III., Pledge; see, also, Langton v. Waite, L. R., 6 Eq. 165.
[2] See Evans v. Waln, 71 Pa. 75.
[3] Act of May 21, 1878; but see supplement to this Act, 10th June, 1881, P. L. 1881, p. 107, which excepts the hypothecation of stock, not fully paid for and carried by the broker, from the effect of this act.

[4] *I.e.*, September, 1881.
[5] Wiltshire v. Sims, 1 Campb. 268; State v. Delafield, 8 Paige (N. Y.), 527.
[6] Kemble v. Atkins, 7 Taunton, 260.
[7] Higgins v. Moore, 34 N. Y. 417; Seiple v. Irwin, 30 Pa. 513.
[8] See Cropper v. Cook, L. R., 8 C. P. 194; Mollett v. Robinson, L. R., 5 C. P. 646.

bound by the broker's paying over money for shares, according to the rules of the Stock Exchange.

Taylor v. Stray.

Thus, for example, in Taylor v. Stray,[1] the court held, that where certain persons had directed their brokers to purchase shares for them, they necessarily gave them the authority to pay for them according to the rules of the Stock Exchange.

The stock broker must sell for cash, and not on credit, unless authorized.

State v. Delafield.

In State v. Delafield,[2] a public agent for a State was held to have exceeded his authority in selling on credit, though evidence was given of a usage of the trade for private agents to do so.

Price.

Frequently, by the rules of the Stock Exchange, as, for instance, those of London and New York,[3] there is a particular medium of exchange designated, as that, in which the broker must receive and make payment, and this is always money. Where there is no such regulation of the Stock Exchange, undoubtedly it is the broker's duty to take nothing but *money* in payment, unless specially authorized by his principal to do otherwise.

The stock broker, usually, is told to buy or sell at a certain price, and then he must necessarily sell at that price, but when he has authority to sell generally, he can bind his principal by any reasonable price at which he may honestly sell.[4]

Condition of genuineness.

In every sale at the Stock Exchange there is always an implied condition that the article sold is genuine,

---

[1] 2 C. B., N. S. 197.
[2] 8 Paige (N. Y.), 527.
[3] See rules of those institutions.
[4] See Story on Agency, § 109; East India Co. v. Hensley, 1 Esp. 111.

or is what it purports to be; that is to say, is what is known and available at the Stock Exchange as such. This, it will be observed, is not a warranty, nor at all analogous to one, but is merely an inherent condition in the sale, that the purchaser gets what he bargains for, and what is known at the Stock Exchange as such. It by no means implies that the thing sold has any intrinsic or inherent value beyond, indeed, being salable at the time of the sale on the Stock Exchange.

The following case is an illustration of the principle.

In Young v. Cole,[1] A. purchased from a stock broker certain securities termed Guatemala bonds, which, on discovering that they had no stamp, he returned to the stock broker and demanded back the purchase money, alleging, that being unstamped they were therefore useless. Evidence was offered to show that what were known at the Stock Exchange as Guatemala bonds were stamped bonds. Tindall, C. J., said the "money was delivered upon the faith "and understanding, that the bonds the plaintiff had "received from the defendant were genuine and avail- "able Guatemala bonds, and salable on the Stock "Exchange. It seems, therefore, that the considera- "tion on which the money was paid has failed as com- "pletely, as if the defendant had contracted to sell "foreign gold coin, and had handed over counters "instead. *This is not a case of warranty*, but the "question is whether the defendant has not delivered "something which, though resembling the article con- "tracted to be sold, is of no value. I am of the "opinion that he has."

Young v. Cole.

[1] 4 Scott, 489.

Warranty.

But it is not the custom of the brokers on the Stock Exchange to sell with a warranty;[1] and as the power of agents to act is to be gathered, either from their express authority, or from an implied usage of the trade,[2] a broker will not be authorized to bind his principal by a warranty unless specially authorized to do so.

Smith v. Tracy.

The case of Smith *v.* Tracy[3] is a good illustration. There A. had purchased a lot of bank stock, the agent authorized to sell representing that the bank was safe, and the investment a good one. The owner of the stock had given a receipt for the purchase money, though ignorant of the warranty. The court held that the power to sell did not imply the power to warrant, there being no usage of trade to that effect in like transactions, and that the fact of the owner of the stock having given a receipt for the purchase money did not affect the case, as he was ignorant of the collateral warranty of his agent.

Delegation of authority.

A special personal trust is imposed on the stock broker, and he cannot therefore delegate his authority to a clerk or other agent to act for him without an arrangement with his principal to that effect.

Cockran v. Irlam.

Thus, in Cockran *v.* Irlam,[4] Lord Ellenborough said, "A principal employs a broker from the opinion he "entertains of his personal skill and integrity; and a "broker has no right without notice to turn his prin- "cipal over to another, of whom he knows nothing."[5]

---

[1] Smith *v.* Tracy, 36 N. Y. 79.
[2] Bayliffe *v.* Butterworth, 1 Exch. 425; Pickering *v.* Busk, 15 East, 38.
[3] 36 N. Y. 79.
[4] *Per* Lord Ellenborough, in Cockran *v.* Campbell, 2 M. & S. 301; see, also, Bank *v.* Trenholm, 12 Tenn. 520.
[5] See, also, Warner *v.* Martin, 11 Howard, 209; Rossiter *v.* Life Ass. Co., 27 Beav. 377, note in 12 Cent. Law Jour. 266.

But where the authority is purely ministerial and not in any way discretionary, the authority may be delegated. *Delegation of authority in ministerial acts.*

There are, however, perhaps certain exceptions to this rule; as, where an order given to a stock broker is to be executed in a foreign town, or on the floor of another association, of which he could not be, or was not, a member. *Delegation of a power by implication.*

Thus, in Laussatt v. Lippincott,[1] where a person ordered his goods to be sold by an agent at public auction, and the sale could only be made by a licensed auctioneer, the authority to substitute him in the agency, so far as the sale was concerned, was held by the court to be implied. So it is possible, if there was a well-known usage of the trade, that stock brokers on the Stock Exchange could substitute other members in transactions, such a usage might be upheld by the courts; though this is not probable. In any case where the acts of the sub-agent are ratified by the principal, this is of course sufficient.[2] When a sub-agent is properly employed by the stock broker, as where the principal gave an express authority to employ one, the original broker will not be liable for the errors or negligence of the sub-agent, unless where the original broker was either guilty of fraud in the substitution,[3] or did not use due diligence in his selection.[4] Where a broker, not being in London, employs a second broker to operate for *Laussatt v. Lippincott.*

---

[1] 6 Serg. & Rawle (Pa.), 386; see, also, Bank v. New England Bank, 1 Cush. (Mass.) 177.

[2] Coles v. Trecothick, 7 Vesey, 236; see Henderson v. Barnwell, 1 Y. & J. 387. The sub-agent would have no privity with the principal of the original broker, Booth v. Fielding, 1 W. R. 245.

[3] Story on Agency, § 201.

[4] Goswell v. Dunkley, 1 Strange, 680; Cockran v. Irlam, 2 M. & S. 301, note.

him, there is no privity between the principal and the second broker.[1]

Deviation. A stock broker cannot, as we have seen, in any case deviate from his strict instructions, and only when acting within the scope of his authority is his principal bound by his acts, and is he enabled to bind his principal.[2]

It has been remarked above that stock brokers frequently, nay, generally, contract in their own names, and the question then arises, whether stock brokers are personally liable on their contracts.

Broker's liability to third parties. The general rule is, that where a broker describes himself as acting for a principal he cannot be bound personally;[3] and probably he would not be bound personally, though he did not disclose his principal, as the description of the existence of the agency alone would be sufficient to put the parties dealing with him on their guard;[4] though if there is a known usage of the trade by which a broker is usually held personally in such a case, he would probably be personally liable. But, in the absence of a usage to the contrary, if the broker contract in his own name, even though he be a recognized professional agent or middle man by trade, and though he be known in the particular transaction to be such, he is liable and bound by the contract.[5] And where the broker, in reality a principal, describes himself as a broker or agent, though perhaps, in the

---

[1] Robins v. Edwards, 5 W. R. 1065.
[2] Catlin v. Bell, 4 Campb. 183.
[3] Fairlie v. Fenton, L. R., 5 Ex. 169; Fisher v. Marsh, 6 B. & S. 416.
[4] See, on this point, Sharman v.

Brandt, L. R., 6 Q. B. 720; Mollett v. Robinson, L. R., 5 C. P. 646; 7 C. P. 84.
[5] Jones v. Littledale, 6 A. & E. 486; see, also, Magee v. Atkinson, 2 M. & W. 440.

CHAP. III.] STOCK BROKER AND HIS PRINCIPAL. 97

absence of a usage of the trade, he would not be able to sue on the contract, nor bind the other party,[1] yet on the Stock Exchange, where nearly all brokers usually act as agents, and are known so to act, and, by the rules of the Exchange and usage of the trade, are treated as principals *qua* each other, such a broker would probably be personally liable on the contract.[2]

With regard to bankers or brokers, of great resources and capital, acting as public agents, who undertake to float government loans, the rule of their liability differs somewhat from that of private agents.

Public agents.

In Goodwin *v.* Robarts,[3] the London and Paris Houses of de Rothschild & Co. floated some scrip of the Russian and Austro-Hungarian governments. On the argument of the case in the Exchequer Chamber, it was contended that these firms were to be looked upon as principals in the transaction. Cockburn, C. J., said, "We entirely dissent from the contention, that the contract in question is one in which the Messrs. de Rothschild can be looked upon as principals. And though our decision on that head may not be essential to the conclusion we have arrived at on the case, we think it desirable, in a matter in which the public are so much interested, that our view should be made known. It is plain on the face of the document that the Messrs. de Rothschild only profess to be acting as the agents of the foreign governments. The law on this subject is correctly laid down in Story on Agency, in the chapter on the Liabilities of

Goodwin v. Robarts.

Remarks of Cockburn, C. J.

---

[1] Sharman *v.* Brandt, L. R., 6 Q. B. 720.
[2] See Robins *v.* Edwards, 15 W. R. 1065; see, also, the case of Mollett *v.* Robinson, *supra*, on this general point.
[3] L. R., 10 Ex. 337.

Story on Agency quoted by Cockburn, C. J.

"Public Agents, s. 302. Collecting the English and
"American authorities in a note, the learned jurist
"writes as follows: 'In the ordinary course of things,
"an agent, contracting on behalf of the government,
"or of the public, is not personally bound by such a
"contract, even though he would be by the terms of
"the contract, if it were an agency of a private nature.
"The reason of the distinction is, that it is not to be
"presumed, either that the public agent means to bind
"himself personally in acting as a functionary of the
"government, or, that the party dealing with him in
"his public character, means to rely on his individual
"responsibility. On the contrary, the natural presump-
"tion in such cases is that the contract was made upon
"the credit and responsibility of the government itself,
"as possessing an entire ability to fulfil all its just con-
"tracts, far beyond that of any private man, and that
"it is ready to fulfil them not only with good faith,
"but with punctilious promptitude, and in a spirit of
"liberal courtesy. Great public inconvenience would
"result from a different doctrine, considering the vari-
"ous public functionaries which the government must
"employ in order to transact its ordinary business
"and operations; and many persons would be deterred
"from accepting of many offices of trust under the
"government, if they were held personally liable upon
"all their official contracts. This principle not only
"applies to simple contracts, both parol and written,
"but also to instruments under seal which are executed
"by agents of the government in their own name, and
"purport to be made by them on behalf of the gov-
"ernment; for the like presumption prevails in such

CHAP. III.] STOCK BROKER AND HIS PRINCIPAL.

'cases, that the parties contract not personally, but merely officially within the sphere of their appropriate duties.'

"Chancellor Kent lays down the law to the like effect (2d Commentaries, p. 810, 7th ed.): 'There is a distinction in the books between public and private agents on the point of personal responsibility. If an agent on behalf of the government makes a contract, and describes himself as such, he is not personally bound, even though the terms of the contract be such as might, in a case of a private nature, involve him in a personal obligation. The reason of the distinction is, that it is not to be presumed that a public agent meant to bind himself individually for the government, and the party who deals with him in that character is justly supposed to rely upon the good faith and undoubted ability of the government. But the agent in behalf of the public may still bind himself by an express engagement, and the distinction terminates in a question of evidence. The inquiry in all the cases is, to whom was the credit, in the contemplation of the parties, intended to be given. This is the general inference to be drawn from all the cases, and it is expressly declared in some of them.' *Kent's Commentaries quoted.*

"It is true these authors are speaking of persons acting as agents for their own governments; but the reasoning applies equally to persons acting as agents for a foreign government, and the same presumption must arise in both cases. Nor can we suppose that the persons taking this scrip did so otherwise than through their faith in the honor of the foreign government, just as they would have had to trust to it on

" their afterwards receiving the bonds in lieu of the
" scrip. They would then be equally without legal re-
" dress against the foreign government, and must have
" trusted to its honor in the fulfilment of its engage-
" ments."

Illegal transactions.

When the broker is ordered by his principal to commit an illegal transaction, he is not liable for refusing to do it.[1]

SECTION III.—EXECUTION OF AUTHORITY.

§ 1. *General Rules.*

Skill and diligence.

A principal has a right to expect from the stock broker a reasonable amount of skill as well as due diligence in the execution of his contracts;[2] and when securities are deposited with a broker, he is bound to use a reasonable amount of care in keeping them, or in putting them in a place of safety.[3] Also the broker

Unnecessary expense.

must avoid all unnecessary expense in carrying on his principal's transactions.[4] The broker should keep ac-

Accounts.

counts with his principal of payments and disbursements, and when he employs a sub-agent the latter is accountable to the first agent.[5]

Return of identical shares of pledged stock.

When a purchase of stocks has been effected by a broker for his principal, or when shares of stock have been deposited with a broker, as security, the question has been several times raised, whether he would be bound to return the identical shares of stock, or

---

[1] Catlin *v.* Bell, 4 Campb. 183; Webster *v.* De Tastet, 7 Term Rep. 157; and see *infra*.
[2] Story on Agency, §§ 182, 183.
[3] Bromley *v.* Coxwell, 2 B. & P. 438; Hammon *v.* Cottle, 6 S. & R. (Pa.) 290; Story on Agency,

§ 200.
[4] Clegg *v.* Townshend, 16 L. T. 180.
[5] Pinto *v.* Santos, 5 Taunton, 447; Stephens *v.* Babcock, 3 B. & A. 354.

whether any shares of the same kind would be a sufficient tender of the deposit to the bailor.

In Langton v. Waite,[1] A. & B., stock brokers, borrowed for the plaintiff a sum of money, for a term of three months, from the defendants, who were also stock brokers, upon the security of certain railway shares, which were transferred by the plaintiff to the name of the defendant firm. In the mean time the plaintiff contracted to sell the stock, and tendered the amount of the loan to the defendants with interest in full for the loan, and demanded the stock before the expiration of the term. The defendants refused to deliver it back, in consequence of which the plaintiff was obliged to go into the market and get stock for his purchase at a loss. At the expiration of the term the loan was repaid with interest, and the defendants, who, pending the loan, had sold the plaintiff's stock and purchased other stock of the same kind, retransferred it to the plaintiff, who claimed, however, the amount of the profits the defendants had realized from the sale of the stock.

There was a rule of the London Stock Exchange offered in evidence, to the effect that "in all cases of "loans on the deposit of security, the lender is bound "to return the *identical securities deposited*, unless it "be otherwise stipulated," etc.; and the court held, that the plaintiff was entitled to recover the amount of his claim, as the terms of the rule were very explicit, and forbade the pledgee to deal with the stock loaned.

It will be observed that this case, however, being decided in consequence of an express rule of the

[1] L. R., 6 Eq. 165.

Stock Exchange on the subject, is not an authority where no such rule existed; and in Gilpin *v.* Howell,[1] where there was no evidence of any such rule or custom, the court seemed to be of a different opinion, and we shall quote selections from the opinion of Bell, J., on the point. The judge in the court below charged the jury, that the plaintiff could recover, if the defendants, the holders of stock of the Girard Bank as collateral security from the plaintiff, had "either parted with "the Girard Bank stock pledged to them, *or thrown it* "*undistinguished into the general mass of their own* "*stock, or that of other persons in their custody,* so as to "be unable to discriminate the identical shares of stock "originally purchased for the plaintiff. * * * It is, in "general, true, that where the pledge is distinctive in "its character, and therefore capable of being recog-"nized among other things of a like nature, or where a "mark is set upon it with a view to its discrimination, "the pledgee is bound to redeliver the identical article "pledged, and cannot substitute something of a like "kind, unless so authorized by the contract. But I "think there is a manifest difference, *ex necessitate,* "where the thing pledged, from its very nature, is "incapable, in itself, of identification, if once mingled "with other things of the same kind. In such case, "it is the duty of the pledgeor to put a mark upon it "by which it may be distinguished; for, as is said in "Nourse *v.* Prime *et al.*,[2] if a person will suffer his "property to go into a common mass without making "some provision for its identification, he has no right

Gilpin v. Howell.

Remarks of Bell, J.

Nourse v. Prime referred to.

---

[1] 5 Barr (Pa.), 41; see also Neiler *v.* Kelly, 69 Pa. 409.

[2] 4 John. Ch. Rep. 490.

"to ask more than that the quantity he put in should "*always be there and ready for him.* By a just fiction "of law, that *residuum* shall be presumed to be the "portion he put in. The good sense of these remarks, "made in immediate reference to a pledge of shares of "bank stock, recommend them to our adoption. They "are repeated by Chancellor Kent, in the S. C., re-"ported in 7 Johns. Ch. Rep. 69, and noticed with "approbation by Nelson, C. J., in Allen *v.* Dykers.[1] "Speaking of Nourse *v.* Prime, he says, '*as it appeared* "*the defendants always had on hand the requisite* "*quantity of shares,* the law will presume the shares "so on hand, from time to time, were the shares de-"posited, *because the parties have not reduced the* "*shares to any more certainty.*' It may be, that even "in a pledge of stock, which frequently passes from "hand to hand with almost as little ear-mark as money "itself, the pledgeor may identify and stipulate for a "return of the very same stock, by handing his cer-"tificate to the pledgee with a blank power to transfer, "not to be used except on a failure to redeem, or in "some other mode devised for the same purpose. But "where, as here, the shares pledged never stood in the "name of the pledgeor, but passed at once from the "former owner to the pledgee, without anything done "by the former to set them apart from other like shares "of the latter, or even a request proffered to this effect, "it is not perceived how, with any show of reason, it "can be made the subject of complaint, that the pledge "necessarily was mingled with the other similar stock "of the pawnee. * * * As already intimated, under

Remarks of Nelson, J., in Allen *v.* Dykers quoted.

[1] 3 Hill (N. Y.), 593.

"the circumstances of this case, nothing further was in-
"cumbent on the defendants than to have at all times
"under their control the requisite number of shares,
"ready to be transferred to the plaintiff when legally
"demanded, unless, indeed, it was the agreement and
"understanding of the parties, that the defendants,
"until the money borrowed was repaid, should deal
"with the pledged stock as if it was their own. In such
"case it would be within the power of the pledgees to
"sell or otherwise dispose of it pending the loan. * * *
"If it be found that this was the understanding of the
"parties, then no more can be required at the hand of
"the defendants than a readiness to redeliver the requi-
"site number of shares of the same stock when the
"loan was repaid."

Langton v. Waite not inconsistent with Gilpin v. Howell.

It will be observed that the case of Langton v. Waite[1] turned on the construction of the rule of the Stock Exchange; but had there been no such rule, according to the principles enunciated by Bell, J., in the preceding case, the defendants would still have been liable, since they had disposed of the plaintiff's stock, without apparently keeping a like amount of a similar security on hand, and were not ready to return the pledge, on demand, on the tender of the payment of the loan, by the plaintiff, in full with the interest; so that Langton v. Waite[2] cannot be taken to militate against the principles of the opinion delivered in Gilpin v. Howell.[3]

Penal act and supplement with regard

In Pennsylvania, however, there is an act on the subject, which forbids all re-hypothecation, and makes

---

[1] *Supra*, page 101.
[2] *Supra*, page 101.
[3] *Supra*, page 102.

it a penal offence.¹ A supplement has been since passed restricting somewhat its application.² As yet there are no decisions on either the act or the supplement. *to re-hypothecation of shares, etc., in Pennsylvania.*

In Tennessee, in Bank *v.* Trenholm,³ it was held, that a contract of pledge by a factor, of the goods of his principal for debts of his own, is absolutely void, and the pledgee took no title, even though ignorant of the factor's character as such; and that the pledge would not even be good up to the extent of the factor's charges thereon, where he has made no demand for them. *Bank v. Trenholm.*

The communications of a stock broker with his principal have been held not to be privileged, and in certain cases he will be compelled to disclose his principals. *Broker's communications.*

Thus, in *In re* Mercantile Credit Association Co.,⁴ where, in the winding up of a company, the liquidator desired to substitute the name of the transferor for that of the transferee, on the books of the company, it was held, that the broker would be compelled to give evidence. *In re Mercantile Credit Association Co.*

So, in *In re* Aston,⁵ it was held by Sir John Romilly, M. R., that a stock broker would be compelled to disclose the names of the persons for whom he had purchased shares in a joint stock company, which had neither been incorporated, chartered, nor registered, and which was regulated by no deed of settlement, and whose shares passed by delivery; and the court further held, that when a broker objected to answer questions on the ground that he might subject himself to penalties, though he would in many instances be the only

---

¹ Act May 25, 1878, Purdon's Digest, 2107.
² Act of June 10, 1881, P. L. 1881, p. 107.
³ 12 Tenn. 520.
⁴ 37 L. J., Ch. 295.
⁵ 27 Beavan, 474.

one to determine his own liability, yet when the facts disclosed raised a point of law as to his liability, the court must decide it.

§ 2. *Liability of the Stock Broker to his Principal.*

The stock broker will be held liable to his principal for the violation of any of his duties, or for an act of negligence in the performance of them; and what such a violation of duty is will frequently be a question of fact for the jury. In such cases he will be required to make good the loss to his principal. It was held in Robinson *v.* Kitchen,[1] that a broker could not, after assuming to be a broker, deny the fact and refuse to account, because he was not properly entitled to act.

But it must be borne in mind that a broker does not usually agree absolutely to procure shares or scrip, etc., for his employer, but generally only engages not to omit getting them if an occasion presents itself. He is only bound to use due and reasonable diligence in endeavoring to procure them. A broker is not liable to his principal, however, for refusing to execute an illegal transaction.

Thus, in Steers *v.* Laishley,[2] a broker, having paid certain stock jobbing losses, drew a bill of exchange for the amount on the defendant, and, after its acceptance, endorsed it to a person, who knew of the illegal transaction out of which it arose. The court held, that such endorsee could not recover, the maxim of the law in such cases being, *Ex turpi causa non oritur actio*, nor could he have recovered it from the prin-

Robinson v. Kitchen.

Steers v. Laishley.

---

[1] 25 L. J., Ch. 441, *per* Parke, B., in Fletcher *v.* Marshall, 15 M. & W. 762.

[2] 6 Term Reports, 61.

cipal, if he had primarily advanced the money for such illegal transactions.

So, in Armstrong *v.* Toler,[1] the reader will find the same principles enunciated, and the question elaborately discussed.[2] The late Pennsylvania decisions on this subject, being somewhat peculiar, will be discussed later, under the Avoidance of the Contract.

Armstrong v. Toler.

§ 3. *Liability of the Principal to the Stock Broker.*

1. The principal is likewise liable to a broker, for any fault of his own, whereby the broker is prevented from, or impeded in, the execution of his contract, as, for example, where the principal is guilty of bad faith or of negligence, or does not comply with a reasonable existing custom of the trade.

General rules.

Thus, in Mocatta *v.* Bell,[3] the defendant employed a stock broker to obtain a loan on the security of bonds transferable by delivery. The broker, accordingly, borrowed a sum from the plaintiff, a part of which he wrongfully applied to his own use, and being unable to redeem the bonds, the defendant, knowing the facts, promised to call and give the broker his cheque for the deficiency on receiving back the bonds. The broker, acting on the faith of his promise, gave a crossed cheque to the plaintiff, and redeemed the bonds, and on the same day the defendant by a trick obtained possession of the bonds without giving up his cheque, and the broker's cheque being in consequence returned, the broker became a defaulter. The court held, that the

Mocatta v. Bell.

---

[1] 11 Wheaton, 258.
[2] See, also, Fareira *v.* Gabell, 89 Pa. St. 89; Canaan *v.* Bryce, 8 B. & A. 179; Wellman *v.* Nutting, 4 Mass. 484; McKinnel *v.* Robinson, 8 M. & W. 484.
[3] 24 Beavan, 585.

defendant was responsible to the plaintiff for the fraud, and that the bonds in his hands were still liable to repay the plaintiff his debt.

Chapman v. Shepherd.

In Chapman *v.* Shepherd,[1] the plaintiff, a broker at Nottingham, and not a member of the London Stock Exchange, instructed by the defendant in April to buy for his account shares in " Overend & Co.," purchased of X. & S., brokers in London and members of the Stock Exchange, the shares, and an account was sent by them to the defendant. The shares, not being resalable at the price reserved by the defendant, were carried over two or three settling days, ultimately to the 11th May, by C. & S., who paid the differences. On 10th May, Overend & Co. suspended, and on 11th May, a petition was presented for winding up, but no order was made till June, and C. & S. were compelled to pay the price of the shares to the person from whom they had bought them, according to the regulations of the Stock Exchange. The plaintiff repaid Messrs. C. & S., and sued the defendant for the money. The defendant contended, *inter alia*, that the whole transaction was void by the 153d section of the Companies Act, 1862, and that the brokers having knowledge of the fact ought not to have made any payments, after the petition for winding up had been presented; but the court held, the action lay, and that the legislature had not intended the act to avoid a contract. Willes, J.,

Remarks of Willes, J.

said, "The plaintiffs, having done everything that they "were bound to do, having purchased the shares in "obedience to the instructions of their principals, and "having been compelled by virtue of the rules and

[1] L. R., 2 C. P. 228.

"regulations of the Stock Exchange to pay the price to
"the persons from whom they bought them, seek to be
"reimbursed the moneys they so paid; and they are
"met by an objection that the whole transaction was
"rendered void by the 153d section of the Companies
"Act, 1862, and consequently that they, having notice
"of that fact, ought not to have made the payments.
"If the Act of Parliament had annulled the trans-
"actions, it might have been necessary to consider if
"the practice of brokers on the Stock Exchange could
"make any difference. Now, it is familiar law that a
"principal who employs an agent to purchase goods for
"him in a particular market, is to be taken cognizant
"of, and is bound by, the rules which regulate deal-
"ings therein; and the agent is entitled to be indem-
"nified by his principal for all he does in accordance
"with those rules. Here, however, we must first in-
"quire whether the foundation of the argument has any
"validity, whether the 153d section of the statute did
"avoid the contract. I think it did not. * * * The
"agent was, I think, clearly entitled in each case to be
"reimbursed by his principal. If it were necessary
"to consider the matter, I must own I cannot conceive
"that there is any injustice in the regulation of the
"Stock Exchange which makes the buying broker re-
"sponsible personally for the price of the stock or
"shares. A broker, however, who receives only a
"small commission on the purchase, should not in
"fairness be subjected to such a risk as that which
"is sought to be cast upon him in this case."[1]

[1] See, also, Biederman *v.* Stone, L. R., 2 C. P. 504; also, Light- foot *v.* Creed, 8 Taunton, 268.

Advances and disbursements.

2. The principal is also liable to the broker for all advances and disbursements made by him on the principal's behalf,[1] and if the broker in delivering his account to his principal has omitted to make a charge due, this does not preclude him from setting it off in an action by the principal for the balance of the account.[2] It is scarcely necessary to add that the principal is so liable when he expressly requests a disbursement to be made, but also when he gives such orders as will necessitate an outlay of money by the agent, or when he orders the broker to act in a market in which he may be compelled to make an outlay of money by the usage of the trade of that place. But it must always appear that such advancements or disbursements were reasonably made, and in good faith.[3] And if the broker incurs any unnecessary or unauthorized expense on his principal's behalf, he is liable personally; as where, acting on supposed instructions, he defended a suit which was undefended virtually, and sued for the costs, he was non-suited,[4] and where the stock broker has officiously or without his principal's authority made them, he will not be bound to reimburse him.[5] No difficulty can arise where the principal actually orders the disbursements, but when the broker does so by an implied authority, the application of the principle is not so clear. These disbursements for, the most part occur where the broker is compelled by a usage of trade to make them. We

---

[1] See two preceding cases; also, Story on Agency, § 335.
[2] Dails v. Lloyd, 12 C. B. 531.
[3] Capp v. Topham, 6 East, 392.
[4] Clegg v. Townshend, 16 L. T. 180.
[5] Howard v. Tucker, 1 B. & A. 712; Edminston v. Wright, 1 Campb. 88.

CHAP. III.]   STOCK BROKER AND HIS PRINCIPAL.   111

shall cite here a few illustrations, and refer the reader for further examples to the chapter on Usage of Trade.

In Taylor *v.* Stray,[1] the defendant had directed his stock brokers to purchase some shares in a bank company for him, which they accordingly did for a settling day from a jobber. In the mean time the bank stopped payment, and the defendant notified his brokers that he would not complete the contract, and that they were not to pay for the shares. By the deed of settlement, no transfers could be made without the directors' consent, and on the settling day they refused to permit the transfer; but transfers were made by the holder to the defendant, and the brokers were compelled by the rules of the Stock Exchange to pay for them. The court held, that the defendant was bound to repay the brokers, notwithstanding the stoppage of the bank and refusal of the directors.

Taylor v. Stray.

In Bayley *v.* Wilkins,[2] the court held, that the broker could recover from their principal certain differences, which they had been compelled to pay in consequence of the principals having on the day of settlement made default in the completion of the contract of sale, there being a rule of the Stock Exchange, that brokers are responsible to each other for their engagements.

Bayley v. Wilkins.

In Lightfoot *v.* Creed,[3] though an action of a like character was held not to lie, the chief justice, who heard the case on appeal, intimated that it would have lain in another form, but that the pleadings were defective. An agent cannot recover from his principal,

Lightfoot v. Creed.

---

[1] 2 C. B., N. S. 174. [3] 8 Taunton, 268.
[2] 7 C. B. 886.

if he be guilty of negligence, and so if the broker be guilty of negligence he cannot recover for expenses incurred for his principal.

Farnsworth v. Garrard. In Farnsworth *v.* Garrard,[1] Lord Ellenborough said he had a conference with the judges on the subject, and that, in an action for services, the plaintiff's negligence may be proved against him to reduce the amount of the demand, and if no good service, no pay.

Montriou v. Jeffries. In Montriou *v.* Jeffries,[2] it was held that an attorney could not recover for expenses incurred by his own inadvertence and negligence.

White v. Chapman. In White *v.* Chapman,[3] it was determined that a factor guilty of gross negligence or misconduct in selling the goods of his principal, could make no detention for his commissions.

An agent is never called upon to perform an illegal act, and if he does one in behalf of his principal and makes advances therefor, he cannot recover.[4] There is no distinction at present recognized in the courts *Mala prohibita and mala in se.* between *mala prohibita* and *mala in se*, and an agent knowingly advancing money for either cannot recover; as, where he advances money for gaming,[5] or illegal stock-jobbing, or illegal insurances.[6]

A distinction is, however, to be made where the money is advanced knowingly in furtherance of the

---

[1] 1 Campb. 38.
[2] 2 Car. & Payne, 113.
[3] 1 Stark, Rep. 91; see also King *v.* Boston, 2 Com. Contr. 363; Beeker *v.* Vrooman, 13 John. R. 302; Basten *v.* Butter, 7 East, 479; Dodge *v.* Tileston, 12 Pick. 328.
[4] Josephs *v.* Pebrer, 3 B. & C. 639; Holland *v.* Hall, 1 B. & Ald. 53; Armstrong *v.* Toler, 11 Wheat. 258.
[5] McKinnel *v.* Robinson, 3 M. & W. 434.
[6] Ward *v.* Vanduzer, 2 Hall, 162; *Ex parte* Mather, 3 Vesey, Jr., 373; Canaan *v.* Bryce, 3 B. & Ald. 179; Brown *v.* Duncan, 10 B. & C. 98.

CHAP. III.]   STOCK BROKER AND HIS PRINCIPAL.   113

illegal scheme, and where it is advanced in a transaction collateral to it, as, for instance, in Tenant v. Elliott.[1] Where money is paid to an agent for his principal arising out of an illegal transaction, the principal has a right of action against the agent for it. And on this subject the law is elaborately discussed in the case of Armstrong v. Toler[2] by Marshall, C. J. Where the agent advances money to pay for an illegal transaction, the agent may recover if he himself has not been connected with the transaction. *Tenant v. Elliott.*

Thus, in Beetston v. Beetston,[3] the court held, that the plaintiff could recover on a cheque, given by the defendant to the plaintiff, for moneys received by the defendant for winnings on bets made by the defendant with third persons, as agent for the plaintiff. *Beetston v. Beetston.*

And so, though contracts for the purchase and sale of stock within the wagering acts of 8 & 9 Vict. c. 109, may be voidable, that section cannot be pleaded to an action by a broker for money paid at the request of the principal.[4]

In Ex parte Pyke,[5] it was held, that money lent to pay gambling debts was not within the act, though knowingly lent. *Ex parte Pyke.*

In Lehman v. Strassberger,[6] A., by a factor, contracted with B. for the purchase of cotton for a future delivery, but not intending to actually make any delivery, but that the contract should be settled by a payment of differences only, and the court held, that a note given by S. to the factor advanced by him to pay *Lehman v. Strassberger.*

---

[1] 1 Bos. & Pull. 3 ; Warren v. Manf. Co., 13 Pick. 518.
[2] 11 Wheat. 258.
[3] L. R., 1 Ex. D. 13.
[4] Knight v. Fitch, 15 C. B. 566; Knight v. Cambers, 15 C. B. 562.
[5] L. R., 8 Ch. D. 754.
[6] 2 Woods, C. C. 554.

8

Remarks of Woods, J.

the losses on such contracts, and for his commissions in making the same, was a valid obligation. Woods, Cir. J.,[1] said, "when therefore they (the plaintiffs) sue "Strassberger to recover money paid by them for him, "on such contracts, and their compensation for their "services, the court is not called upon to enforce a "contract against the law between the parties to that "contract, but simply to enforce the collection of a "note, the consideration of which is money advanced "and services performed by agents for their principal.

"If Strassberger was suing the parties with whom "he contracted, either to buy or sell cotton for the dif- "ference between the contract and the market price, "then the case would approach more nearly to what "is forbidden by the New York statute. It is the case, "to put it in its strongest light for the defendants, of "an agent who advances money to his principal to pay "losses incurred in an illegal transaction, and takes his "note for the money so advanced. In such case the "contract between the principal and agent, made after "the illegal transactions are closed, although it may "spring from them and be the result of them, is a "binding contract.[2] * * * It has even been held, that "partners who have been engaged in illegal transac- "tions shall be held to account to each other for "profits of such transactions.[3] * * * The fact that the "agent includes in a note given for money, paid by him "for losses in an illegal transaction, compensation as "for his services, does not taint the note. Such com-

---

[1] Now, Associate Justice of the Supreme Court of the United States.
[2] Durant v. Burt, 98 Mass. 161; Petrie v. Hannay, 3 Term, 418; Owen v. Davis, 1 Bailey, 315; Armstrong v. Toler, 11 Wheaton, 258.
[3] Brooks v. Martin, 2 Wall. 78.

"missions would not avoid the note unless given for "services as agent in a transaction which is not merely "*malum prohibitum*, but *malum in se.*"[1]

It will be observed that Woods, J., takes a distinction in money advanced for a void contract and one voidable only, and in regard to money advanced to complete them after their formation; and the distinction is obvious. With regard to the latter, as the borrower may fulfil the contract, not being void, the agent may recover from him for advancing; but in the former case, where the contract is void, as the borrower can never fulfil it, the money is lent on a void consideration, and cannot be recovered by the lender.

The Pennsylvania cases alone oppose the universal doctrine, and hold that money so advanced may not be recovered by the agent, as in the cases of Fareira *v.* Gabell,[2] Smith, Exc. *v.* Thomas,[3] Ruchizky *v.* De Haven;[4] and these cases are the more remarkable, because in Fareira *v.* Gabell something very like a binding charge was given to the jury to find the contract a gambling one, and in the other two cases the jury found both the contracts *bona fide*, and the Supreme Court, only, held them to be gambling, on an apparent misconception of the real facts.

Cases in Pennsylvania opposed to the universal doctrine.
Fareira v. Gabell.
Smith v. Thomas.
Ruchizky v. De Haven.

In the case of Ruchizky *v.* De Haven *et al.*, it is to be noticed that the court laid down the somewhat singular proposition that, where a stock broker carries stock for his principal, the broker is the real principal in the transaction, and the speculation is in the collat-

Principles enunciated in Ruchizky v. De Haven.

---

[1] See De Begnis *v.* Armistead, 10 Bing. 107; Canaan *v.* Bryce, 3 B. & A. 179.
[2] 8 Norris (Pa.), 89.
[3] 10 W. N. C. (Pa.) 112.
[4] 10 W. N. C. (Pa.) 109.

eral security or margin, and not in the original transaction at all; and, therefore, all such transactions being invalid, the agent is engaged in a wagering contract on his own behalf as principal, and cannot recover from his accomplice (ordinarily his real principal) the money advanced him.

Commissions. 3. The broker is also entitled to a commission, or such reasonable compensation as either the rules and customs of the trade, or express agreements with his principal, may have fixed upon, as an equivalent to the principal, for his services,[1] and it may be said that where the Stock Exchange has fixed a certain rate of compensation, that will be considered as *prima facie* the rate agreed upon. Perhaps where there is no rule on the subject, or no agreement, the court may arrange what is the proper compensation for the broker to receive.[2] But to entitle the broker to his commissions, he must have performed faithfully and fully the whole contract,[3] except where he is prevented from so doing by his principal's fault;[4] for if he has been guilty of great negligence, or gross misconduct, or unskilfulness in the performance of his duties, he cannot recover his commissions, but will even become liable to his principal for the amount he has lost by his bad conduct.[5]

Where a broker has received an order, which is subsequently countermanded by his principal, and which having already executed in part, the non-exe-

---

[1] Eickel v. Meyer, 3 Campb. 412; Roberts v. Jackson, 2 Stark. 199.
[2] See Bower v. Jones, 8 Bing. 65; Miller v. Livingston, 1 Caine, Rep. 349.
[3] Sea v. Carpenter, 16 Ohio, 412.
[4] See De Bernardy v. Harding, 8 Exch. 822; Prickett v. Badger, 1 J. Scott (N. S.), 296.
[5] Hamond v. Holiday, 1 C. & P. 384; Dodge v. Tileston, 12 Pick. 328.

cution of it would be of great damage to him, the rule of law would probably be, that he would have the right to go on and charge his principal for the whole contract, plus his commissions, as in the case, for instance, of Taylor *v.* Stray,[1] we have recently referred to. *Taylor v. Stray.*

Perhaps the rule of law on the subject may be thus stated: when the broker has performed part, and is placed in such a position that he will suffer injury if he do not go on, he may recover a commission for the whole, and where he can stop and claim a part commission without any detriment to himself, and his principal rescinds his order, his duty is to stop; or, in other words, where the broker acquires a power coupled with an interest in the transaction, his principal must pay for the whole.[2]

The opinion of the court in Durkee *v.* The Central Railway Company of Vermont,[3] was to the effect, that a broker is not entitled to a full commission, where he has not performed the full service required of him; but he is entitled to compensation, by way of a *quantum meruit*, in proportion for his services rendered, where the order is countermanded, unless the party employing him reserved the right to recall his order, or there is some well-known usage of the trade to that effect, which the court will not, however, assume to be so until it is so notorious as to be universally recognized. It is perhaps hardly necessary to add, that where the contract is illegal the broker cannot get his commissions, as where, in the case of Josephs *v.* Pebrer,[4] *Durkee v. Vt. Ct. Ry. Co.*

Josephs v. Pebrer.

---

[1] 2 C. B., N. S. 197.
[2] See the reasoning in the great case of Hunt *v.* Rousmanier, 2 Mason, 244; 8 Wheaton, 174; 1 Peters, 1.
[3] 29 Vermont Rep. 127.
[4] 3 B. & C. 639.

the broker was employed to sell the stock of an illegal association.

For fraud to his principal, in any transaction, the stock broker forfeits all his commissions.[1]

Field v. Sawyer.

Watts v. Brooks.

Jessop v. Lutwyche.

In England, in the case of Field *v.* Sawyer[2] the court held, that a broker could not recover his commissions unless he be a sworn broker, though in Watts *v.* Brooks[3] they said that if the broker had actually made disbursements he could recover them, whether he were a sworn broker or not. In Jessop *v.* Lutwyche[4] the court held, on demurrer, that a plea to the effect that the broker was unlicensed, was bad. Where a broker is an executor, it has been held, that he cannot charge double commissions, both as executor and as broker.[5]

§ 4. *Stock Brokers' Lien.*

Definition of lien by Grose, J.

A lien of personal property has been defined by Grose, J., in Hamonds *v.* Barclay,[6] to be "a right in "one man to retain that which is in his possession "belonging to another, till certain demands of him, "the person in possession, are satisfied." It is not our intention, here, to go at great length into the history and law of liens. That belongs more appropriately to the author of a book on agency, and the reader is referred to the work of Story on Agency, for an elaborate discussion on the subject, in chapter xiv.

We shall here give an outline of the law of the lien

---

[1] Brown *v.* Croft, 6 C. & P. 16, note; Hill *v.* Featherstonehough, 7 Bing. 569.

[2] 5 C. B. 844, note A.

[3] 3 Vesey, Jr., 612.

[4] 10 Exch. 614; see, also, Pidgeon *v.* Burslem, 3 Exch. 470; Smith *v.* Lindo, 5 C. B., N. S. 587.

[5] Jones *v.* Powel, 6 Beavan, 488.

[6] 2 East, 235.

of brokers on the goods or securities of their principals. It is to be borne in mind that, as the trade of stock brokers is carried on chiefly by the deposits of margin, or collateral security, by the principal, it is not so necessary to discuss at length the law of liens, since the right of lien is usually settled by express contract, or by implication from the custom of the trade,[1] which latter is usually the case, and that part of a broker's business will be discussed later, under the head of Pledge, Part III.

Ordinarily a lien is the mere right of detention of the goods till the price, or advances and disbursements, are paid, and factors and brokers have a lien on goods, when purchased, for the moneys paid and liability incurred by them in respect to such purchase; and, unless the usage of trade or the particular agreement or course of dealing between the parties varies this right, they are not bound to part with the possession of the goods, or to deliver them, or to ship them subject to the absolute control of the principal, until they are reimbursed or secured for such advances and liabilities.[2] Frequently an important question arises how far a stock broker or factor can sell the goods, after notice to his principal, for advances and disbursements; for it is to be remembered that, though ordinarily the lien, unlike the pledge, cannot be sold by agents, yet factors constitute one of the exceptions to the rule, and it is also to be borne in mind that as a stock broker is not a broker in the ordinary sense, but rather a factor, being the consignee of securities, which generally in the United

Lien ordinarily.

---

[1] See remarks of Alderson, B., in Scarfe v. Morgan, 4 M. & W. 270.
[2] Story on Agency, § 874.

States have been known as merchandise: *Merx quicquid vendi potest,* and usually having all the indicia of ownership, and being never able, without an understanding, to be the agent of both parties, he therefore may be considered to be rather governed by the general common law regulating factors.[1]

Remarks of Story, J., in Brown v. McGran.

With regard to factors, Story, J., in Brown *v.* McGran,[2] said, "Wherever a consignment is made to a "factor for sale, the consignor has a right, generally, to "control the sale thereof, according to his own pleasure, "from time to time, if no advances have been made "or liabilities incurred on account thereof; and the "factor is bound to obey his orders. This arises from "the ordinary relation of principal and agent. If, "however, the factor makes advances, or incurs liabili-"ties on account of the consignment, by which he ac-"quires a special property therein, then the factor has "a right to sell so much of the consignment as may be "necessary to reimburse such advances or meet such "liabilities; unless there is some existing agreement, "between himself and the consignor, which controls or "varies this right; * * * and in no case will a factor "be at liberty to sell the consignment contrary to the "orders of the consignor, although he has made ad-"vances, or incurred liabilities thereon; if the con-"signor stands ready, and offers to reimburse and "discharge such advances and liabilities."

Parker v. Brancker.

In the case of Parker *v.* Brancker,[3] the court held the same principle, and said, a factor could sell, for advances

---

[1] A stock broker is not probably a factor, within the meaning of the various factors' acts passed in England, and in the United States, unless mentioned specifically.
[2] 14 Peters, 494.
[3] 22 Pick. (Mass.) 40.

made, the goods, at a fair market price, though below that at which the consignor gave instructions to sell.

In England the contrary doctrine has been held,[1] but Gibbs, C. J., made[2] an exception, where goods deposited as collateral security were concerned. "Undoubtedly," said he, "as a general proposition, a right of lien gives no right to sell the goods. But where "goods are deposited, by way of security, to indemnify "a party against a loan of money, it is more than a "pledge. The lender's rights are more extensive than "such as accrue under an ordinary lien in the way of "trade. These goods were deposited to secure a loan. "* * * I think, therefore, the defendant had a right "to sell." The factor, it has been said, however, cannot retain or sell more than sufficient to meet his expenses, when demanded by the principal, though, perhaps, he might retain the whole till his debt was paid. But, be this as it may, the owner can always dispose of the property subject to the lien, and this is a personal privilege of the party himself, who is entitled to it, and cannot be set up by any third person, against the principal, either as a defence or as a right of action.[3] *Contrary rule in England. Exception made by Gibbs, C. J.*

No lien can arise, where the right of lien would be inconsistent with the contract made by the agent with his principal, as where the goods or securities were to be delivered and payment made on a future day,[4] or held subject to the order of a third party, or given as *Lien must be consistent with the contract with the principal.*

---

[1] Smart v. Saunders, 5 M. G. & S. 895.
[2] Pothonier v. Dawson, Holt's N. P. 383.
[3] Story on Agency, § 372.
[4] Chase v. Westmore, 5 M. & S. 180; Williams v. Littlefield, 12 Wend. 362.

security for another debt.¹ A person cannot, of course, acquire a lien on goods, founded on an unlawful contract, or upon his own misconduct or fraud.²

Liens can only attach on liquidated demand.

Usually a lien can only attach to certain and liquidated demands, and not to those which are only ascertainable through the action of a jury.³

Stock broker sometimes a banker.

It not unfrequently happens that a stock broker performs to a very considerable extent the duties and functions of a banker, and in such cases, his rights to lien will be governed by the laws relating to bankers on this subject.⁴

The broker's right over securities deposited with him as collateral, will be considered hereafter, under Pledge, Part III.

SECTION IV.—DISSOLUTION OF THE STOCK BROKER'S AGENCY.

The authority of the broker to act may be terminated, by the stock broker, by the principal, or by the mere operation of law.

Dissolution of agency by the stock broker.

1. The stock broker may dissolve the agency by renunciation, and this may take place either when he has not executed any of the conditions of the contract, or only a part of them. In consequence of this the principal may receive some injury, and in such a case the broker is liable in damages to him for what he has suffered, provided the agency was undertaken for a valuable consideration.⁵ If, however, it was merely

---

¹ Jarvis v. Rogers, 15 Mass. 389; Walker v. Birch, 6 T. R. 258.
² Story on Agency, § 860.
³ Chitty on Com. and Manf. 548.
⁴ See Story on Agency, §§ 380-81.
⁵ Thorne v. Deas, 4 John. 84; Elsee v. Gatward, 5 T. R. 143.

gratuitous, the principal cannot recover damages for a non-performance, unless the contract was in part executed by the broker, and the principal has been injured by the broker's not going on.[1]

2. Again, the broker's agency may be terminated by the act of the principal in revoking the agency. In this case, as we have remarked under the head of commissions, the principal is liable to the broker in damages for the loss the broker may have sustained by the breach of the contract, and where the contract is coupled with an interest the principal cannot repudiate the agency, but the broker's power is irrevocable.[2] *By the principal.*

3. Finally, the agency of the broker may be concluded by the mere operation of law, as, for example, where the terms of the contract of agency are fulfilled, or where the period for completion of the contract has expired.[3] Also it may be concluded by a change in the legal status of the parties, for since the agent only acts at all by an authority delegated from the principal, his power to act must cease as soon as the capacity of the principal to delegate his authority ceases. Thus, for example, where the principal becomes insane, as in the case of Wallis v. Manhattan Bank,[4] the agent's authority to act is suspended or terminated, or where, as in the case of Charmley v. Winstanly,[5] a woman by her marriage revoked her powers to act. So, of course, the agency would be terminated by the agent's marriage or insanity. *By the mere operation of law.* *Wallis v. Manhattan Bank.* *Charmley v. Winstanly.*

---

[1] See Story on Agency, on Bail, §§ 164–172.
[2] Campb. 341; Benoit v. Conway, 10 Allen, 528.
[3] *Supra*, page 117.
[4] 2 Hall, 495.
[5] 5 East, 266.
[6] See Dickinson v. Lilwall, 4 Campb. 279; Blackburn v. Scholes,

Bankruptcy. Also, the bankruptcy of the principal, with respect to those things that pass by operation of the bankrupt law, revokes the agency, but the authority of the agent will not be revoked with respect to those rights that do not pass by the bankrupt law, but remain in the bankrupt's hands, as trustee or guardian,[1] and it may be said that the agent's bankruptcy will be governed by the same rule, though it would not suspend the agent's right to act merely ministerially or formally,[2] but perhaps it might revoke the agent's right to receive money for the principal.[3]

Agency terminated by death.
Agency generally revoked by death by the common law of England and America.
And the death of either party also generally concludes the agency.[4] We have said that the agency is *generally* revoked by the death of either party, because, although this is a correct statement of the common law of England and of most of the States of the North American Confederation, some of the States have somewhat altered or modified the principle of the common law, and have inclined towards the rule adopted by the civilians in Scotland, France, and in such countries where the civil law exists; that the death of the principal does not necessarily instantaneously revoke the agency, but that third parties who have engaged in *bona fide* transactions, after the principal's death, and innocently, will be protected.

Otherwise by the civil law, as in Scotland and France.

Missouri, Ohio, and Pennsylvania incline towards the civil law.
The States that seem to have abandoned the rigorous rule of the common law are Pennsylvania, Missouri, and Ohio.

Cassiday v. McKenzie.
Thus, in Pennsylvania, in Cassiday *v.* McKenzie,[5] it

---

[1] Chitty on Com. and Manf. 223. 27.
[2] Dixon *v.* Ewart, 8 Merivale, 322.
[3] Hudson *v.* Granger, 5 B. & A.
[4] See Story on Agency, §§ 487–488.
[5] 4 W. & S. (Pa.) 282.

was held, that the acts of an agent or attorney, done after the death of his principal, are binding on the parties, when he was ignorant of his death. Rogers, J., said, "It is conceded that the death of the principal is "*ipso facto* a revocation of a letter of attorney. But "does it avoid all the acts of the attorney intermediate "between the death of the principal and notice of it? "* * * But, if this doctrine applies, why does it not "apply to the case of factors, foreign or domestic, to "commission merchants, to supercargoes, and masters of "ships, and to various other agencies which the neces-"sities of commerce may require? In the case of a "foreign factor, for example, has it been supposed "that his acts, after this implied revocation of au-"thority, are void? Cases of this kind must often "have occurred, and it would astonish the mercantile "world to be informed that the factor was liable on a "contract made in the name of his principal, because "he was dead, a fact of which he was ignorant, and of "which he could not by any possibility be informed, "or that the merchant who was trusting his goods on "the credit of the principal was to be cast on him who "may have been of doubtful solvency, for payment. "Can it be, that a payment, made to an agent from a "foreign country, and from one of our cities to the "Western States, employed for the special payment of "collecting debts, is void, because his principal may "have died the very day before the actual receipt of "the money? That a payment may be good to-day "or bad to-morrow from the accidental circumstance of "the death of the principal, which he did not know, "and which by no possibility could he know? It

Remarks of Rogers, J.

"would be unjust to the agent and unjust to the debtor. In the civil law, the acts of the agent, done *bona fide* in ignorance of the death of his principal, are held valid and binding upon the heirs of the latter. The same rule holds in the Scottish law; and I cannot believe the common law is so unreasonable, notwithstanding the doubts expressed by Chancellor Kent in the second volume of his Commentaries, 646."

Dick v. Page.

In Missouri, in Dick *v.* Page,[1] in speaking of the hardships of the rule of the common law, Scott, J., said, "To hold that this transaction is void would shock the sense of justice of every man, and we cannot be persuaded that a principle which would produce such a result should be applied to the facts which exist in this case."

Remarks of Scott, J.

Ish v. Crane. Holding of Sutliffe, J.

And in Ohio, in Ish *v.* Crane,[2] Sutliffe, C. J., after a very copious review of the authorities, held, that, though generally the death of the principal was a revocation, *ipso facto*, of the agency by operation of law, yet a *bona fide* transaction done by an agent, and not necessarily in the name of the principal, after the death of the principal, but in ignorance of the event, and within the scope of his authority, was valid and binding on the representatives of the principal. It will be seen that in this case a distinction was taken between the case where the act was necessarily done in the principal's name, and where it was required only to be done in that of the agent alone.

Distinction between acts necessarily done in principal's name, and in that of agent, made in Ish v. Crane.

Drew v. Nunn.

In England, in the late case of Drew *v.* Nunn,[3] however, Brett, L. J., seemed inclined to modify the strict

---

[1] 17 Mo. 234.   [2] 8 Ohio, N. S. 521.
[3] 19 Amer. Law Reg. 98.

English rule, though the point was not decided there by him, but was merely *obiter*. He said, "Sup- *Remarks of Brett, L. J.* "posing * * * a principal holds out a person to be "his agent, and then of his own accord withdraws the "agency. As between the principal and the agent "the right to bind the principal has ceased, and then "the agent does a wrongful act by acting with a third "person as though the authority continued; neverthe- "less, if the agent has been held out as having author- "ity to the third person, and the latter acts with the "agent before he has received any notice of the au- "thority having ceased, the principal is still bound, "upon the ground that he made representations upon "which the third person had a right to act, and can- "not retract from the consequences of those represen- "tations. * * * Therefore, in my opinion, although "the lunatic recovers his reason, he cannot, after his "recovery, any more than if he had never been a "lunatic, say that an innocent person, who acted on "representations made before lunacy, had not a right "to do so. A difficulty, no doubt, arises in stating a "general principle applicable to such cases as these, "but, for my own part, although it is not necessary to "decide the question to-day, I should think that the "same rule would apply in the case of the principal's "death as of his lunacy; and that if representations "made by a person during life were acted upon after "his death by an innocent third party, without any "knowledge of the death, the principal's executors "would be bound."

It may, in conclusion, be remarked, that in England there are several statutes relating to the revocation of

Old English rule modified by statute somewhat. agency by death, which greatly modify the old English rule; as, for instance, the act of 22 & 23 Vict. ch. 35, s. 26.

And so the Indian Contract Act of 1872, 208, Illustration (C.), may be referred to.

And by the death of the grantor, a power of attorney to transfer stock in the Bank of England is not revoked, but it still binds the executors and administrators of the deceased, unless the bank have written notice, as respects the bank.

It must, however, be remembered that these cases do not apply where there exists a power coupled with an interest, but only where the power is merely naked.

Agency not ipso facto revoked by death, where there is a power coupled with an interest. And where there is a power coupled with an interest, the agency is not *ipso facto* revoked by the change in the legal status of the parties. The reason of this is obvious, since, as the broker shares the interest with the principal, he may execute the transaction as well as the principal. In short, he is a partner in interest, and is his own, as well as his principal's agent.[1]

---

[1] See Alley *v.* Hotson, 4 Campb. 325; Hunt *v.* Rousmanier, 8 Wheat. 174; Walsh *v.* Whitcomb, 2 Esp. 565; Hodgson *v.* Anderson, 3 B. & C. 842; Houghtaling *v.* Marvin, 7 Barb. 412; Carriger *v.* Whittington, 26 Mo. 313; Johnson *v.* Wilcox, 25 Ind. 182; Campanari *v.* Woodburn, 15 C. B. 400; Goodwin *v.* Bowden, 54 Me. 424; Knapp *v.* Alford, 10 Paige, 205; Barr *v.* Schroeder, 32 Cal. 609; Gaussen *v.* Morton, 10 B. & C. 731; Blackstone *v.* Buttermore, 53 Pa. 266.

CHAPTER IV.

RELATION OF STOCK BROKER TO THIRD PARTIES.

	PAGE		PAGE
SECTION I.—STOCK BROKER'S RELATION TO THIRD PARTIES, ORDINARILY.		Cases discussed	130
		SECTION II.—JOBBERS.	
Preliminary remarks	129	Cases, defining their relation to brokers, discussed	133
Stock broker's relation, that of an ordinary agent	129		

WE have now discussed the relation of the stock broker to the Stock Exchange, or the place where his functions are principally exercised, as well as his relation to his customer, or principal; in the remainder of this book we shall occupy ourselves with his relation to the thing he deals in, or to a description of the law of the sale, pledge, etc., of the securities dealt in by the stock broker, in which are implied his chief relations to third parties. Before, however, entering upon that, it will perhaps not be amiss to say a word particularly, about his relations to parties other than his principal.

Preliminary remarks.

SECTION I.—STOCK BROKER'S RELATION TO THIRD PARTIES, ORDINARILY.

The relations of the stock broker to third parties are not unlike those of any other agent, except where some peculiar custom of his trade renders them different, as, for instance, where the customs of the Stock Exchange have raised up peculiar relations with the jobbers. We shall cite a few cases, as illustrations of

Relations to third parties ordinarily like those of any other agent.

what attempts have been made to introduce rules of the Exchange or customs of the trade to alter his relations towards third parties, and then say a word about the stock broker's relation with that peculiar dealer on the English Stock Exchange, known as the jobber.

Thus, it has been attempted in various places to hold the brokers primarily liable to each other, for contracts made on the Stock Exchange, and the following cases are illustrations of that doctrine, and the courts' opinions upon it.

Mortimer v. McCallan.

In Mortimer *v.* McCallan,[1] one T., a stock broker, had applied to the plaintiff, a stock jobber, for the purchase of stock for the defendant. The plaintiff, not having any stock on hand, applied to one W., who agreed to transfer, and did transfer, stock standing in his name, to the defendant. Evidence was given that it was the usage on the Stock Exchange to credit the broker, even though the principal were disclosed, though credit was sometimes given the principal and his cheque taken, where the broker's credit was not sufficient. The judge left it to the jury to say whether credit in the case was given the broker or the broker and principal.

Remarks of Lord Chief Baron Abinger.

On appeal, Lord Abinger, C. B., said, "I have no "doubt myself, from the long experience I have had in "matters of this description, that there is an under-"standing between the parties on the Stock Exchange "that *inter se* they hold the broker liable. I do not "say that understanding would not have a very great "influence on the question in individual cases; but it

[1] 6 M. & W. 58.

"is admitted in this case, that there was evidence which
"showed that it was doubtful, whether the party meant
"to hold the broker only responsible, or to have also
"the security of the principal. I do not apprehend
"the rules of the Stock Exchange would make any
"difference as to the right of a party who sells stock,
"to choose to what person credit shall be given if he
"thinks proper, and the evidence shows that it was the
"case sometimes to look to the principal. That, then,
"brings it to a question in this particular case, whether
"or not the plaintiff meant to take the credit of Tay-
"lor only, and give up that of the defendant, or whether
"he insisted on the credit of the defendant. Now that
"was a question for the jury."

In Mocatta v. Bell,[1] the court held, that a third party would not be compelled to treat a broker as a principal, owing to the account subsisting between the broker and principal.

Mocatta v. Bell.

In Langton v. Waite,[2] Sir Richard Malins said "the "law is clearly settled that a principal may sue upon "a contract entered into on his behalf by an agent, "although his name was wholly concealed at the time "of the contract."

Langton v. Waite.

In Magee v. Atkinson,[3] A. being employed by B. to sell certain shares for him, agreed with C., D.'s broker, to sell him the shares, of which A. afterwards informed his clerk, who entered it as a sale from A. to C., and a contract note was sent to C. A. subsequently saw the entry, and altered it by putting the name of B. as seller,

Magee v. Atkinson.

[1] 27 L. J. 237; see, also, Torrington v. Lowe, 19 L. T., N. S. 816.
[2] L. R., 6 Eq. 165.
[3] 2 M. & W. 441.

and directed another note to be sent to C. with B.'s name as seller, which was accordingly done, and C. received both together. D. brought an action against A. for not completing the sale, and it was left to the jury to say whether the second note was only a correction of the first, and instructed them, that if the defendant entered a written contract in his own name he could not afterwards say he was merely a broker. And the court on appeal held this to be a proper direction, and that evidence, that it was the custom at Liverpool to send brokers' notes without disclosing the principal's name, was properly rejected; Alderson, B., saying that

Remarks of Alderson, B. "the custom offered to be proved is a custom to violate "the common law of England."

Tompkins v. Safferty. Tompkins v. Safferty[1] is an illustration of where the courts would not allow a rule of the Stock Exchange to vary a stock broker's relation of debtor and creditor to outside parties. The court said here, that a rule by which, in the event of the stock broker's bankruptcy, the assets of the broker were to be distributed by official assignees, as they think proper, was honorary only, and, when the distribution was invalid and against the intent of the bankrupt law, it would not be upheld. Lord Blackburn said the laws of the Stock Exchange were only an honorary agreement, that the members would keep, on joining that body, but not enforceable at law, when the interests of outsiders were affected.

SECTION II.—STOCK BROKERS AND JOBBERS.

There is an anomalous character on the English Stock Exchange known by the name of jobber. He

[1] L. R., 3 A. C. 213.

CHAP. IV.] RELATION TO THIRD PARTIES.   133

is, as we have seen,[1] a stock broker, and acts as intermediary between the purchasing and selling stock brokers, taking up the shares of the latter and supplying the wants of the former, and expecting to make a profit in the fall or rise of the market. His method of dealing has been described before.[2] The custom of the Stock Exchange is that the selling broker effects a sale to a jobber, who agrees to take the shares, and at settling day hands in the name of the transferee to the selling broker.

Jobbers are intermediaries between buying and selling brokers.

It has been more than once attempted to hold that a contract between the vendor and ultimate vendee is not a real contract, but that the jobbers were liable on the contract after the transferee's name was by them handed to the selling broker.

In Coles *v.* Bristowe,[3] Malins, V. C., held, that the jobber was liable, even after he had handed in the transferee's name to the seller, and the shares were paid for; but on appeal this was reversed, and the liability of the jobber to the vendor was there clearly defined.[4] The court said the contract or liability of a jobber on the Stock Exchange, who has purchased shares for the next settling day, is, that on that day he will either take the shares himself and bind himself to accept and register a transfer and indemnify the vendor against future calls, or give the name of one or more transferees to whom no reasonable objection exists, and who will take and pay for the shares, and when he takes the latter course, and the names are accepted by the vendor, and transfers are executed to,

Coles v. Bristowe.

---

[1] See *supra*, Chapter II.
[2] See *supra*, Chapter II.
[3] L. R., 6 Eq. Cas. 149.
[4] L. R., 4 Ch. App. Cas. 3.

and paid for by, the transferees, or their broker, the liability to indemnify the vendor is shifted from the jobber to the transferees. But, on the other hand, the jobber's liability continues clear and unbroken until an acceptance of the transfers by the transferees or their brokers, and the jobbers are not discharged by merely agreeing to pay the price, or giving a name that may turn out to be objectionable.

<small>Grissell v. Bristowe.</small>

The same result was reached by the court in Grissell v. Bristowe,[1] in which, again, the opinion of the lower court was reversed, Cockburn, C. J., giving an exhaustive opinion on the subject, to the effect that the custom on the Stock Exchange for a jobber to be relieved of all liability in the transaction, after he had substituted a person to whom the vendor could not reasonably object, and the vendor had accepted the name and received the purchase money, was not an unreasonable custom. In this case, Kelly, C. B., remarked, "I am desirous of adding a few words to the "judgment of the Lord Chief Justice, in every part "of which I entirely concur. The observation I wish "to make is that when the practical effect of this usage "or mode of dealing on the Stock Exchange comes to "be considered, it will be found that there is no hard-"ship or injustice in it as regards the interests of the "public, but the contrary. In the great majority of "transactions which occur, the solvency or responsibil-"ity of the nominee or ultimate buyer is a matter of "indifference to the seller; for, when the settling day "arrives, the seller transfers, and the buyer pays the "price, or, if he makes default, it is at once paid by the

<small>Remarks of Kelly, C. B.</small>

[1] L. R., 4 C. P. 36.

"jobber or the purchaser's broker, and the transaction "is closed. It is only upon a sale of shares in a joint "stock company with an unpaid-up capital, and of "which the solvency is doubtful, or which (as was the "case with Overend, Gurney & Co., at the time of the "contract in question) has actually stopped payment, "that it concerns the seller to ascertain that the ul-"timate buyer is a responsible man. This he has "an opportunity of doing under the regulations of "the Stock Exchange; and surely there is nothing "unreasonable or unjust in subjecting to whatever de-"gree of trouble and risk may attend such a transac-"tion, the seller of shares, which are often worse than "valueless, which he is glad to part with at an almost "nominal price, or at a premium paid to the buyer for "taking them, and which have become the symbols, "not of a title to profits and dividends, but of a lia-"bility to losses and calls. On the other hand, this "practice affords to the public the very great advantage "of being enabled, by means of a stock broker and a "jobber, to buy or to sell at any moment any quantity "of stock or any number of any description of shares "at the market-price of the day ; * * * whereas, with-"out such a practice, every one having any given "amount of stock, English, foreign, or colonial, or of "debentures or shares in railways, or other joint stock "companies, to buy or to sell, must wait until a seller "or a buyer could be found, to sell or to buy the exact "quantity of stock or of shares, which is to be parted "with or acquired—a state of things which in this "country, where some hundreds of these purchases "and sales are effected every day, would be found in-

"tolerable, and would speedily demand a remedy, than "which no better could be devised than this practice "so long established, and which has never until now "been called in question." Bramwell, Channell, and Pigott, BB., concurred.[1]

Principal not affected by differences paid by jobber.

The courts have also held, that the vendor has nothing to do with the differences in payment made by the jobber,[2] and that money paid by one broker to another jobber cannot be recovered by the principal.[3]

Name passed by jobber must be of one sui juris.

It must, however, be remembered that the name put forward as that of the ultimate purchaser by the jobber, must be that of a person *sui juris*, or else the jobber is still liable to the vendor.[4] This is eminently reasonable, for otherwise the jobber would be relieved from his contract to the vendor, when the vendor could have no hold against the ultimate vendee.

"Man of straw" put forward by jobber.

On the other hand, it has been held, that if the vendor make no objection to the name of the transferee, and he is *sui juris*, he will be bound by him, even though such transferee be not a responsible man.

Maxted v. Paine.

As, for example, in Maxted *v.* Paine,[5] it was held, that the jobber was released when he had put forward a "man of straw," as that of the transferee.

Jobbers usually credit brokers, but a contrary intention may be shown.

By the rules of the Exchange, the jobbers usually give credit to the brokers, and they are *inter se* liable on their contracts; but where it clearly appears that the jobber trusted to the principal for payment, instead of the broker, the custom of the Stock Exchange does not apply.

---

[1] See, also, Torrington *v.* Lowe, L. R., 4 C. P. 26; Hawkins *v.* Maltby, L. R., 6 Eq. 505.
[2] Mewburn *v.* Eaton, 20 L. T. 449.
[3] Stray *v.* Russell, 1 E. & E. 888.
[4] Nickall *v.* Merry, L. R., 7 Eng. & Irish App. 530.
[5] L. R., 6 Exch. 132.

Thus, in Mortimer *v.* McCallan,[1] T., a broker, applied to a jobber for the purchase of stock, and the latter applied to W., who transferred it to the defendant. In an action by the jobber against the defendant, it appeared that in such transactions, credit is usually given to the broker, by the custom of the Exchange, though sometimes to the principal when the former's credit is not thought sufficient; and it was held, that under these circumstances the court was right in leaving the question to the jury to say whether, in the case, credit had been given to the principal or not.

Mortimer v. McCallan.

[1] 6 M. & W. 58.

PART II.

THE SALE.

INTRODUCTION.

IN this part of our work, we intend to examine particularly the law relating to the sale of the securities usually dealt in by stock brokers on the Stock Exchange, and we shall divide the subject as follows, viz.:

<small>Division of subject.</small>

Chapter I. The Nature of the Thing sold at the Stock Exchange.

Chapter II. The Contract of Sale.

Chapter III. The Effect of the 17th Section of the Statute of Frauds on the Contract.

Chapter IV. The Effect of the Statute of Mortmain on the Contract.

Chapter V. The Effect of the 4th Section of the Statute of Frauds on the Contract.

Chapter VI. The Effect of the Usage of Trade on the Contract.

Chapter VII. The Relation of the Vendor and Vendee after the Contract.

Chapter VIII. The Completion of the Contract; and

Chapter IX. The Avoidance of the Contract.

CHAPTER I.

THE THING SOLD AT THE STOCK EXCHANGE.

	PAGE		PAGE
Division of chapter	139	In America, bonds payable to bearer are negotiable	164
SECTION I.—UNDER WHAT SPECIES OF PROPERTY THESE SECURITIES ARE CLASSED.		Diamond v. Lawrence Co.	164
		Mercer Co. v. Hacket	164
		Coupons	168
Shares of stock	140	Scrip bonds negotiable	169
Not money	140	Goodwin v. Robarts	169
Nor, generally, real estate	142	Scrip of stock doubtful	171
Usually choses in action	145	Remarks of Cockburn, C. J., on negotiability	173
Preferred stock	146		
Scrip, bonds, debentures	147		
SECTION II.—NEGOTIABILITY OF THESE SECURITIES.		SECTION III.—INCIDENTS ATTACHED TO THE THING SOLD.	
Shares of stock not negotiable	148	Bonds, coupons	174
Nor, ordinarily, bonds	157	Sale or transfer	174
In England, certain bonds are negotiable	158	Calls, dividends, pledge, etc.	175
		Lien on stock and dividends	176
Cases reviewed	158	Stock subject to execution, etc.	181

THE sales at the Stock Exchange are usually confined to certain well-defined classes of securities, such as shares of stock, registered and coupon bonds, scrip, debentures, and the like. In order, then, to comprehend the law relating to stock brokers with regard to the things sold at the Stock Exchange, it will be necessary to have a slight insight into the nature and incidents of these securities. The subject may be conveniently examined by ascertaining, first, under what species of property these securities can be classed; secondly, their negotiability; and, thirdly, the incidents that are attached to, and attendant upon them.

Sales at Stock Exchange confined to certain securities.

Division of chapter.

SECTION I.—UNDER WHAT SPECIES OF PROPERTY SECURITIES SOLD AT THE STOCK EXCHANGE ARE CLASSED.

Shares of Stock.

And, first, what are shares of stock?[1]

Shares of stock defined.

The capital of a company is usually divided into shares of stock, which, ordinarily, may be defined to be, a certain proportion or interest in the capital or stock of a corporation or company. At one time it was attempted to treat stock as money, and in the old case of Nightingal *v.* Devisme,[2] where the declaration was for money had and received, etc., when shares of stock had been transferred to the defendant, the action was held not to lie, Lord Mansfield saying,

Nightingal *v.* Devisme.

Remarks of Lord Mansfield.

"This is a new species of property, arisen within the "compass of a few years. It is *not money*. We do "not say that an action *cannot be framed* so as to come "at justice in this case; but we are all of the opinion "that this action for *money had and received to the use* "*of the plaintiffs* * * * will not lie in the present "case, where *no money was had and received.*" This case was followed somewhat later by Jones *v.* Brinley,[3] where stock was declared positively not to be money; and the later cases are to the same effect.[4]

Stock not money.

Jones *v.* Brinley.

It is true that sometimes a bequest of money has

---

[1] In England, usually, "stock" refers to government securities, and "shares" to securities not governmental. This distinction is not usually observed in America.

[2] 5 Burrows, 2589.

[3] 1 East, 1.

[4] Ogle *v.* Knipe, 38 L. J., Ch. 692; Gosden *v.* Dotterell, 1 M. & K. 56; Hudleston *v.* Gouldsbury, 10 Beav. 547; Lowe *v.* Thomas, 5 De G. M. & G. 815; Cowling *v.* Cowling, 26 Beav. 449; Delamater's Estate, 1 Wharton (Pa.), 362.

CHAP. I.] THE THING SOLD AT STOCK EXCHANGE. 141

been held to pass stock, but in such cases the courts have always held, that the context must clearly show that such was the intention of the testator.

Thus, in Dowson v. Gaskoin,[1] the testatrix gave pecuniary legacies and £200 each to her executors, "and whatever remained of moneys" to the five children of E. D., and this was held to pass the stock.

Dowson v. Gaskoin.

The case of Gosden v. Dotterell[2] is difficult to reconcile with Dowson v. Gaskoin, in which former case the testator ordered "the rest of my *money*" to be equally divided between his brother and niece, and these latter words were held not to pass Consols. Sir John Leach said of it, there was no doubt a clear intention to pass the stock under the term "moneys," "but if the term money shall not pass stock unless there "be some explanation in the will, I fear the testator's "intention will not be carried out. I doubt very much "whether any rule can be laid down. It would seem "difficult to justify this conclusion, that if sufficient be "found in a will to show that the testator intended the "stock to pass, still that the word should not be suffi- "cient to effectuate that intention without explanatory "context."

Gosden v. Dotterell. Dowson v. Gaskoin.

Remarks of Sir John Leach.

In Cowling v. Cowling,[3] the words "all my moneys "and notes" did not pass stock, and the Master of the Rolls said, that what confirmed him in his opinion was that the testator mentioned three classes of things specifically; 1, "my goods and furniture," 2, "all my plate and linen," and 3, "all my moneys and notes," and that therefore he did not mean to pass the

Cowling v. Cowling.

[1] 2 Keen, 14.
[2] 1 Myl. & K. 56.
[3] 26 Beav. 449; see, also, Lowe v. Thomas, 5 De G. M. & G. 815.

stock.¹ Stocks not being money, the question has frequently arisen whether they are ever real property, and in a few cases, as in Wells *v.* Coles,² and Price *v.* Price's Heirs,³ they have been held an interest in real estate.

Wells v. Coles.
Price v. Price's Heirs.

The Cape Sable stock was made real estate by statute.⁴ But as a rule, both in England and in the United States, the courts have generally held shares of stock to be personal property.⁵

Cape Sable stock made real estate by statute.
Stock usually personal property.

In Bradley *v.* Holdsworth⁶ there was indeed a statute on the subject, but the court were of the opinion that without the statute they would have considered them personal property.

Bradley v. Holdsworth.

In Bligh *v.* Brent,⁷ after an extended hearing, Alderson, B., gave a clear and elaborate opinion on the question. In this case the court held, that shares in the Chelsea Water Works Company were personal property, and would pass in a will not executed according to the provisions of the Statute of Frauds, on the grounds of vesting in the executor, the usage of transferring them as personal property, and the general nature of the shares. Alderson, B., said, "Now, in "the first place, we have a corporation to whose "management the joint stock of money subscribed by "its individual corporators is entrusted. They have

Bligh v. Brent.

Remarks of Alderson, B.

---

¹ See, also, Prichard *v.* Ib., L. R., 11 Eq. 282; Newbold *v.* Prichett, 2 Wharton, 46; Fulkeron *v.* Chitty, 4 Jones, Eq. 244; Morton *v.* Perry, 1 Metc. 446; Paul *v.* Ball, 31 Texas, 10; Hinton *v.* Pinke, 1 P. W., Notes, 548.

² 2 Conn. 567; later made personalty by statute, 2 Conn. Stat.; 1, 1818, May, c. 10.

³ 6 Dana, 107.

⁴ 3 Bland, 606.

⁵ See, also, Tippetts *v.* Walker, 4 Mass. 595; Thompson on Stockholders, § 210; Bank *v.* Waltham, 10 Metc. 334; Rex *v.* Capper, 5 Price, 217; Wildman *v.* Ib., 9 Vesey, 174.

⁶ 3 M. & W. 422.

⁷ 2 Y. & C. Exch. 268.

CHAP. I.] THE THING SOLD AT STOCK EXCHANGE. 143

" power of vesting it at their pleasure in real estate,
" or in personal estate, limited only as to amount, and
" of altering from time to time the species of property
" which they may choose to hold; and, in order to
" give them greater facilities and advantages, certain
" powers are entrusted to the undertakers by the legis-
" lature, and that even before they were constituted a
" body corporate, of laying down pipes, and thereby
" occupying land for the purposes of their under-
" taking. These powers render the use of joint stock
" by the body corporate more profitable, but they
" form no part of the joint stock itself; and one
" decided test of this is, that they belong inalienably
" to the corporation, whereas all the joint stock is
" capable expressly of being sold, exchanged, varied,
" or disposed of at the pleasure of the corporate body.
" * * * The property is money—the subscriptions
" of individual corporators. In order to make that
" profitable, it is entrusted to a corporation who have
" an unlimited power of converting part of it into
" land, part into goods; and of changing and dis-
" posing of each from time to time; and the purpose
" of all this is, the obtaining a clear surplus profit
" from the use and disposal of this capital for the
" individual contributors. It is this surplus profit
" alone which is divisible among the individual cor-
" porators. The land or chattels are only the instru-
" ments (and those varying and temporary instru-
" ments) whereby the joint stock of money is made
" to produce profit. * * * This case varies most
" materially from those * * * where the individual
" corporators have the property" and "the corpora-

"tion have only the management." Lord Abinger, C. B., and Parke, B., concurred.

<small>Land owned individually by stockholders is not personal property.</small>

Where, however, as was suggested by Alderson, B., the land owned by a corporation is vested individually in its stockholders, and the corporation only manage it, there, no doubt, the shares would be real property.

<small>Drybutter v. Bartholomew.</small>

As, for instance, in Drybutter v. Bartholomew,[1] where the husband was seised in right of his wife of a share of the New River Water, and both made a mortgage by way of a lease for 1000 years by deed without fine, reserving a pepper-corn rent, it was held, the wife could not be barred *sans* fine.

<small>Buckeridge v. Ingram.</small>

So, in the case of Buckeridge v. Ingram,[2] where it was expressly ordained that "the share of a party "dying shall descend and go to the heirs and assigns "of the party so dying," and from the usage and general understanding between the proprietors, the Master decided the shares to be in the nature of realty, though there the undertakers do not appear to have been a corporation.

A distinction has been drawn between railway and canal companies' shares, and those of a bank or manufacturing corporation, but this distinction is the result of a superficial view of the subject; for it is plain that in each case the land is held in the same way by the corporation, and in each case the shares only give a right to the ultimate profits of the company to the shareholder, while the land is only in one case more intimately connected with the objects of the corporation than in the other.[3] In short, the rule may be

---

[1] 2 P. W. 127.
[2] 2 Vesey, Jr. 652.
[3] See Howe v. Starkweather, 17 Mass. 240; Isham v. Iron Co., 19

CHAP. I.] THE THING SOLD AT STOCK EXCHANGE. 145

thus stated: that where, as in ordinary cases, the company becomes a trustee and holds the lands in trust for the individuals, then the shares are personal property, but where each individual shareholder has a distinct vested right in the land of the company as such, and the company merely manage it as an agent, in that case the shares would be in the nature of realty.

But frequently the character of such property is regulated by statute; and the reader is referred to Angell & Ames on Corporations, § 559, note 2. *Reader referred to Angell & Ames on Corporations.*

Shares of stock, being usually personal property, and not actual money, may be termed choses in action, as indeed all this class of securities virtually are. "If," said Shaw, C. J., in Hutchins *v.* State Bank,[1] "a share in a bank is not a chose in action, it "is in the nature of a chose in action; and, what is "more to the purpose, it is personal property. A "State bond or note, a certificate of a sum due from "the State or the United States and ordinarily called "'stock,' is a chose in action, and an evidence of "debt, though no action lies for it. So a certificate "of bank shares is proof of a definite aliquot part of "a money fund, created for a particular purpose, and "placed under the management of a corporation regu-"lated by it. And a certificate of stock is a muni-"ment of title of the same nature with the note or "bond of a private person, ordinarily called a 'chose "in action,' or of a State or United States bond, note, "or certificate of debt."[2] And so Lord Denman, C. *Shares of stock are virtually choses in action.*

Hutchins v. State Bank. Remarks of Shaw, C. J.

Vt. 230; Johns *v.* Johns, 1 Ohio St. 350; Wheelock *v.* Moulton, 15 Vt. 519.

[1] 12 Metc. (Mass.) 421.

[2] See definition of Mr. Williams, noticed by Dillon, D. J., in Allen *v.* Pegram, 16 Iowa, 173.

10

Humble v. Mitchell.

Arnold v. Ruggles.

J., in Humble *v.* Mitchell,[1] said, "shares in a joint "company like this are mere choses in action, in-"capable of delivery,"[2] and are, as Durfee, C. J., remarked in Arnold *v.* Ruggles, "an ideal thing."[3]

The question has been frequently agitated as to whether government bonds and shares are goods, wares, and merchandises under the Statute of Frauds; and though in England[4] the courts have held they were not, yet generally in the United States a different conclusion has been reached.[5] This subject will be further treated of in Chapter III., Part II., on the Statute of Frauds. Shares of stock are the subject of larceny, felony, and generally of execution,[6] on which latter subject there are, in England and America, various statutes, giving and regulating the remedy and method of procedure.

Preferred shares of stock.

Frequently companies issue *preferred shares of stock*, or what are called preference shares of stock, or preferred shares, which are shares, whose dividends are payable in priority to those of ordinary shares.[7] In order to issue such stock, an express power must be given in the charter of the company, or by a legisla-

---

[1] 11 A. & E. 205.

[2] The action of trover does not usually lie for stock as such. Acraman *v.* Cooper, 10 M. & W. 585; Neiler *v.* Kelly, 19 Sm. (Pa.) 403; but see, *contra*, Boylan *v.* Huguet, 8 Nev. 345; Kubn *v.* McAllister, 1 Utah, 273; Payne *v.* Elliott, Reporter, May 26, 1880, p. 678.

[3] 1 R. I. 165.

[4] Humble *v.* Mitchell, 11 A. & E. 205; Pickering *v.* Appleby, 1 Comyns, 353; Duncuft *v.* Albrecht, 12 Simons, 189.

[5] Tisdale *v.* Harris, 20 Pick. (Mass.) 9; Baldwin *v.* Williams, 3 Metc. 365. In New York the statute employs the words "things in action"; Rev. Stat., Edmonds's edition, 140; and in Florida and Mississippi the words "and personal property" are added. See Ins. Co. *v.* Cole, 4 Fla. 359; Rev. Code, c. 60, Art. 1, of Miss.

[6] Paterson on the Stock Exchange, p. 22.

[7] See Green's Brice's *Ultra Vires*, p. 145.

CHAP. I.]   THE THING SOLD AT STOCK EXCHANGE.   147

tive enactment. The power to issue preference stock has also been claimed to exist from the power of a corporation to borrow money, and to secure such borrowed money by a certain pledge of income, it being contended, that the issuing of preferred stock is in theory, as in practice, a mode of borrowing money, as distinguished from the ordinary hazard attendant upon ordinary shares of stock.[1]

Scrip is merely the evidence of an agreement to issue shares or stock, and may be classed within the same category as stock, and is a chose in action.[2] It is often issued by projectors of companies, and entitles the holder to become a co-proprietor of the future company, and his liability will depend principally on the engagements he has entered into with the projectors. And sometimes it is issued, after the company is formed, instead of allotment of shares; though what such a contract is, is not clearly understood. It must presumably be determined by the terms under which the scrip is issued, read in connection with the constating instrument of the corporation.[3] Scrip.

Bonds, whether coupon or registered, are also choses in action, and are direct obligations in writing, signed and under seal, to pay certain sums of money, at a certain time and out of a designated or specific fund, and with a penalty attached in case of non-payment.[4] Bonds.

Debentures are written and usually sealed obligations to pay a certain sum out of the assets of Debentures.

---

[1] Green's Brice's *Ultra Vires*, p. 147, note.
[2] See opinion of Shaw, P. J., in Hutchins v. Bank, 12 Metc. (Mass.)
[3] 426.
See Green's Brice's *Ultra Vires*, p. 149.
[4] See Hutchins v. Bank, *supra*.

property, or out of a specified part of them, and creating a lien or charge on them.[1]

SECTION II.—NEGOTIABILITY OF THESE SECURITIES.

It is important to see whether, or, if so, how far, any of these securities may be negotiable, or pass from hand to hand freed from the equities of the former holder, for of course the fact of their negotiability would greatly enhance their commercial or market value. In the notes to Miller *v.* Race, quoted by Blackburn, J., in Crouch *v.* Credit Foncier Co.,[2] a safe test with regard to the negotiability of such instruments is laid down. "It may," said he, "there-"fore be laid down as a safe rule, that where an "instrument is by the custom of trade transferable, "like cash, by delivery, and is also capable of being "sued upon by the person holding *pro tempore*, then "it is entitled to the name of a *negotiable instrument*, "and the property in it passes to a *bona fide* transferee "for value, though the transfer may not have taken "place in market overt. But that if either of the "above requisites be wanting, *i.e.*, if it be either not "accustomably transferable, or though it be accus-"tomably transferable, yet if its nature be such as "to render it incapable of being put in suit by the "party holding it *pro tempore*, it is not a negotiable "instrument, nor will delivery of it pass the property "of it to a vendee, however *bona fide*, if the transferor "have not a good title to it, and the transfer be made "out of market overt."

Notes to Miller v. Race, quoted by Blackburn, J., in Crouch v. Credit Foncier Co.

---

[1] See *ante*, note 3, page 147.   [2] L. R., 8 Q. B. Cas. 374.

CHAP. I.] THE THING SOLD AT STOCK EXCHANGE. 149

In England, shares of stock, as we shall see,[1] do not pass from owner to owner by a delivery of the certificate with a power of attorney annexed;[2] so that the question which we are about to discuss must be confined to the American cases.

Negotiability of certificates of shares of stock.

In Mechanics' Bank v. New York & New Haven R. R. Co.,[3] it appeared that the company was required by its by-laws to transfer stock on its books, and to require the former certificate of ownership to be surrendered prior to the making of such transfer, and the issue of a new certificate. The company established a transfer agency, making its president the agent, with the proper powers. He, however, fraudulently gave to one Kyle a certificate in the usual form for eighty-five shares, when the latter owned no stock, nor had any standing on the company's books in his name, nor had surrendered any certificate. The plaintiffs, relying on these certificates as valid, made a loan to Kyle, taking the certificates, with a power of attorney to transfer, as security.

Mechanics' Bank v. New York & New Haven R. R. Co.

The corporation subsequently refused to transfer, and in an action against them, the court held, that, the certificates not being negotiable, the plaintiffs did not acquire any rights against the company, the certificates being void. Comstock, J., in a learned opinion, said, "It seems to me, therefore, that we are brought "directly to the question, whether certificates of stock "in the defendant's corporation are to be regarded as "negotiable instruments, in the sense of the commer- "cial law, so that by their endorsement and delivery

Remarks of Comstock, J.

---

[1] See following pages.
[2] See 12 Amer. Law Register, N. S. p. 699.
[3] 3 Kernan (N. Y.), 599.

"to a purchaser in good faith, a title to the stock they
"profess to represent may be acquired, although in
"the hands of the vendor they are spurious and void,
"and although the company itself has never recog-
"nized the transfer. This question, I think, must be
"answered in the negative. They contain, in the
"first place, no words of negotiability. They de-
"clare, simply, that the person named, is entitled to
"certain shares of stock. They do not, like nego-
"tiable instruments, run to the bearer or to the order
"of the party to whom they are given. They com-
"mence, it is true, with the words, 'be it known,' but
"such words have no tendency to show that they
"possess the quality claimed for them; a phraseology
"quite similar may be found in bonds and other in-
"struments which no one ever thought to be nego-
"tiable. But, aside from the absence of any language
"of these certificates which can impart to them a ne-
"gotiable character, both the laws of the corporation
"and the certificates themselves contain special re-
"strictions, which seem to me to put this question at
"rest. I do not suppose that a corporation, without
"something extraordinary in its charter, can place
"such restraints upon the sale of its stock, that the
"individual holder may not transfer as good a title
"in equity as he himself possesses by any mode of
"assurance good upon general principles of law. But
"if a natural person has an undoubted right so to
"express the terms of his obligation that it shall not
"be negotiable in the commercial sense, or in any
"sense which can give to the purchaser a title superior
"to that of his vendor, I see no reason to doubt that

"corporations possess the same right. Has the de-
"fendant so expressed it in these certificates of stock?
"I think it has. It has distinctly declared, both in
"its by-laws and on the face of the certificates, that
"shares can be transferred only on the books, and on
"the surrender of the evidence of the owner's previous
"title. If an illustration were wanted of the value
"of such a restriction, it is furnished in the present
"case. But, whatever its value, the restraint is lawful
"in itself, and one which the corporation had an un-
"doubted right to impose. I do not say that it pre-
"vents the owner of stock from selling his shares by
"an outside transfer, so that the vendee will acquire
"in equity his own rights; but to say that the holder
"of a false and fraudulent certificate, by endorsing
"and delivering it to another person, can create a
"title hostile to the corporation itself, would be to
"deny to the restriction any meaning or effect what-
"ever." After an elaborate review of the cases, the
learned judge concluded he was supported by them.

In New York & New Haven R. R. Co. *v.* Schuyler,[1] the by-laws of the corporation were substantially to the same effect as in the previous case, and an issue of spurious stock was had by persons held out as their agent by the company.

One of the principal questions in the case was, whether certain persons, who, holding genuine certificates of stock, which had been, however, held to be worthless because of a subsequent transfer, at the company's agency, to *bona fide* purchasers of the same shares of stock, by the party to whose credit it

R. R. Co. *v.* Schuyler.

[1] 34 N. Y. 30.

stood on the books, had a title superior to those subsequent *bona fide* purchasers; and, if so, whether the company are liable to them for allowing the transfers on their books without demanding a surrender of the outstanding certificates.

<small>Opinion of the court.</small>

With regard to this the court said, "Where the "stock of a corporation is by the terms of its charter "or by-laws transferable only on its books, the pur- "chaser, who receives a certificate with the power of "attorney, gets the entire title, legal and equitable, as "between himself and his seller, with all the rights "the latter possessed; but as between himself and "the corporation, he acquires only an equitable title, "which they are bound to recognize and permit to be "ripened into a legal title, when he presents himself, "before any effective transfer on the books has been "made, to do the acts required by the charter or by- "laws, in order to make a transfer. Until those acts "be done, he is not a stockholder, and has no claim "to act as such; but possesses as between himself and "the corporation, by virtue of the certificate and "power of attorney, the right to make himself, or "whomsoever he chooses, a stockholder. * * * The "stock not having passed by delivery of the certifi- "cate and power of attorney, the legal title remains "in the seller so far as affects the company and sub- "sequent *bona fide* purchasers, who take by transfer "duly made on the books, and hence a buyer in good "faith, who takes a transfer in conformity to the "charter and by-laws, permitted to be made by the "authorized officer of the corporation, becomes vested "with a complete title to the stock, and gets all the

"rights and equities of the holder of the certificate of
"the stock itself. What other rights and equities he
"may possess is another question; but if the trans-
"feree has taken in good faith and for value, the stock
"is gone, and beyond his reach, and beyond recall by
"the corporation. * * * The non-production and sur-
"render of the certificates at the time of the transfer,
"is not fatal to the title of the transferee," etc.

In McNeil v. Tenth National Bank,[1] the plaintiff, owning certain shares of stock, delivered the certificates with an assignment in blank, and power of attorney, to certain persons, as security for a loan, who without any authority sold it to a *bona fide* purchaser for value, and the question was whether he could hold out against the original owner, and it was held the original owner could not dispute the title of the purchaser. Rapallo, J., said, "It must be conceded, "that as a general rule applicable to property other "than negotiable securities, the vendor or pledgeor "can convey no greater right or title than he has. "But this is a truism predicable of a simple transfer "from one party to another where no other element "intervenes. It does not interfere with the well-"established principle that where the true owner "holds out another, or allows him to appear as the "owner of, or as having full power of disposition "over, the property, and innocent third parties are "thus led into dealing with such apparent owner, "they will be protected. Their rights do not depend "upon the actual title or authority of the party with "whom they deal directly, but are derived from the

McNeil v. National Bank.

Remarks of Rapallo, J.

[1] 1 Sickles (N. Y.), 825.

"act of the real owner, which precludes him from "disputing, as against them, the existence of the title "or power, which through negligence or mistaken "confidence he allowed to appear to be vested in the "party making the conveyance. * * * The true point "of inquiry in this case is, whether the plaintiff did "confer upon his broker such an apparent title * * * "as will thus estop him from asserting his own title "as against parties who took *bona fide*."[1]

Shaw v. Spencer.

In Shaw *v.* Spencer,[2] it was held, that, where a certificate of stock in a corporation in the name of A. B., as trustee, is by him fraudulently pledged for his own debt, and accepted without inquiry, and the pledgee, after notice, voluntarily pays an assessment on the stock to one of the *cestuis que trustent*, as treasurer of the corporation, in the presence of the other, the *cestuis que trustent* are not estopped from recovering the value of the stock; and Foster, J., in speaking of the habit of brokers to transfer stock

Remarks of Foster, J.

with powers of attorney in blank, said, "The fact "that it is usual for dealers in stock to take certificates "with blank transfers upon them and to fill them up "with the names of the purchasers, was wholly im-"material. Such a practice, as we have already "observed, does not make the shares negotiable, and "the purchaser whose name is written into the trans-"fer must always derive his title immediately and "solely from the stockholder of record."

Bank v. Lanier.

In the Supreme Court of the United States, in Bank *v.* Lanier,[3] Davis, J., said, "It is in obedience

---

[1] See, also, 29 Sickles, 223.   [3] 11 Wallace, 377.
[2] 100 Mass. 382.

CHAP. I.] THE THING SOLD AT STOCK EXCHANGE. 155

"to this requirement (*i.e.*, of transferring) that stock "certificates of all kinds have been constructed in a "way to invite the confidence of business men, so "that they have become the basis of commercial "transactions in all the large cities of the country, "and are sold in open market the same as other "securities. Although neither in form nor character "negotiable paper, they approximate to it as nearly "as practicable."

Remarks of Davis, J.

In Mathews *v.* National Bank,[1] the bank loaned money to one C. upon the security of a certificate of really two shares of stock in a railway company, altered, however, by the debtor so as to read two hundred, after C. had procured it from the company to be assigned to the bank as collateral security. Upon the payment of the debt the cashier of the bank signed a blank assignment on the back of the certificate, supposing it to be genuine, and C. subsequently conveyed it to the plaintiff as collateral. The court held, that the latter, as a *bona fide* purchaser for value, could compel the company to compensate him for damages.[2]

Mathews v. National Bank.

In Pennsylvania and New Jersey the same rule is recognized.

Thus, in Moodie *v.* Bank,[3] and in Prall *v.* Tilt,[4] it was held, though the securities were not negotiable, yet an innocent purchaser from one who had all the muniments of title in him, should not suffer, though

Moodie v. Bank. Prall v. Tilt.

---

[1] 14 Amer. Law Reg. 153.
[2] See also Simm *v.* Telegraph Co., 20 Amer. Law Register, 159; see, also, note of Redfield, J., to case in text.
[3] 3 W. N. C., Phila., 118.
[4] 28 Eq. Rep. (N. J.) 479.

such person had wrongfully parted with the certificates of stock.

The reader is also referred to the following cases in the note.[1]

The principle derived from a perusal of these cases, is that in no case have certificates of stock, with an assignment in blank and power of attorney to transfer, been regarded by any of the courts as negotiable instruments,—that is to say, in the same sense as bills or notes; but that where a man puts these securities into another's hands, and gives him the complete indicia of ownership over them, then such a person will be estopped subsequently from disputing the title, which he has either imprudently or negligently placed in the power of another.

Mathews v. Bank.

It has indeed been thought by a few persons, that the decision in Mathews v. Bank has extended to an alarming extent the doctrine of the negotiability of these securities; and Judge Redfield, in a somewhat singular note to that case in the American Law Register,[2] and Mr. Lewis, in his book on the Law of the Stock Exchange, in which he sympathizes with Judge Redfield, lament the extent to which the doctrine of negotiability has been carried in Mathews v. Bank, and consider the decision in the case as untenable, Judge Redfield even going so far as to assure the reader, in the opening paragraphs of his

---

[1] Mt. Holly Co. v. Ferree, 2 Green (N. J.), 117; Crouch v. Credit Foncier, etc., L. R., 8 Q. B. 374; Bridgeport Bank v. R. R. Co. 30 Conn. 231; Leavitt v. Fisher, 4 Duer, 1; Bank v. Kortright, 22 Wend. 348; Cushman v. Thayer Manf. Co., 76 N. Y. 365; Sewall v. Water-Power Co., 4 Allen, 277.

[2] 14 A. L. R., note 162.

note, that it would be "difficult to maintain the ar-"gument in its application to the facts of the case, "without recognizing certificates of stock endorsed "in blank, or with powers to transfer, as negotiable "paper in the fullest sense." We are, however, of the opinion, that Judge Redfield's and Mr. Lewis's apprehensions are not justified by the judgment in the case, for the opinion of the court in Mathews *v.* Bank has not at all extended the negotiability of certificates of stock with blank assignments, beyond that maintained by any of the cases cited in the text. The principle decided by Mathews *v.* Bank is that a corporation which has accepted and acted upon a forged transfer of its shares, and issued a new certificate, or filled up a blank assignment on a forged certificate, which a *bona fide* purchaser subsequently buys, is liable to such purchaser, either by way of estoppel, or otherwise, for the value of his shares, as the purchaser acts, not upon the faith of the forged transfer, but on that of their certificate. This principle is fully settled in America,[1] where the delivery of stock by a power of attorney in blank to transfer, with the certificate, is looked favorably upon as well as in England, when the assignment is properly executed.[2]

Bonds, known simply as such, as, for example, ordinary or registered, are not by the common law or by law merchant negotiable instruments, and *debentures* viewed in the "light of choses in action," says Mr. Brice, in his treatise on *Ultra Vires*, page 163,

<small>Bonds.</small>

<small>Debentures.</small>

<small>Brice on Ultra Vires.</small>

---

[1] See 37 Georgia, 515, and the preceding cases in the text.
[2] Hildyard *v.* South Sea Co., 2 P. W. 76; Simm *v.* Anglo-American Tel. Co., 20 A. L. R. 159, and note by Mr. Bennett.

are non-negotiable, and therefore assignable in chancery only, and taken subject to equities.[1]

But of late years it has become customary to issue peculiar kinds of bonds, as coupon bonds, and debenture bonds payable to bearer, or order; and the question is, how far these may be negotiable instruments.

Glyn v. Baker.

In England, in the case of Glyn *v.* Baker,[2] says Blackburn, J., in Crouch *v.* Credit Foncier Co.,[3] "the "form of the East India bond was that the East "India Company acknowledged to have received of "W. G. Sibley 100*l.*, which the Company promised "to repay to Sibley, his executors, or assigns, by en- "dorsement. It was, therefore, in form a promissory "note for value received, payable to order, and, had "it been signed as such by an agent of the East India "Company, would have been negotiable. But it was "a bond under the seal of the East India Company,

Holding of Le Blanc, J.

"and Le Blanc, J., said, 'It is clear that no action "could have been brought on this bond but by Sib- "ley the obligee, or in his name; or, if he died, in "the name of his executors.' There was no evidence "in the case that such bonds were negotiable.

"The alarm occasioned by this decision was so great "that within a month afterwards an act (51 Geo. III. c. "64) was passed to make East India bonds negotiable "like promissory notes. It seems not to have oc- "curred to any one that it could have been said that "this was already done by virtue of the Statute of "Anne, the promise in writing being signed by the "East India Company's seal. This seems a strong

---

[1] Green's Brice's *Ultra Vires*, pp. 123–129.
[2] 18 East, 509.
[3] L. R., 8 Q. B. C. 381.

CHAP. I.] THE THING SOLD AT STOCK EXCHANGE. 159

"authority for saying that instruments under the seal of a body corporate are not exceptions from the general rule laid down in Byles on Bills, p. 67, n., 10th ed., that 'at common law bills of exchange and promissory notes, being simple contracts, cannot be under seal, at least so as to retain their negotiable qualities.' And it certainly is very desirable that it should not be left doubtful on the face of an instrument whether it is a covenant or a promise."

In Attorney-General v. Bouwens,[1] it was found in the special verdict, as to Russian, Danish, and Dutch bonds, that those securities have always been dealt with as transferable within England by delivery only, that it was not necessary to do any act out of England to render such a transfer valid, and that the bearers of the bonds have always been treated and dealt with by the agents of the three sovereigns as entitled to the money payable under the bonds, and the court held the bonds transferable in England, so as to render the executors of the holder liable to probate duty in respect of them. *Attorney-General v. Bouwens.*

In Gorgier v. Mieville,[2] where the King of Prussia caused bonds to be issued whereby he declared himself and his successors bound *to every person who should for the time being be the holder of the bond,* for the payment of the principal and interest in the manner there pointed out, and which were proved to have been sold generally on the market, and passing from hand to hand, like exchequer bills, at a variable price, according to the state of the market, the bonds were held to be negotiable instruments. So in Hesel- *Gorgier v. Mieville.*

[1] 4 M. & W. 171. [2] 8 B. & C. 45.

tine v. Siggers,[1] Spanish bonds were treated as passing by delivery.

Lang v. Smyth.

In Lang v. Smyth,[2] the plaintiff placed in the hands of his agents certain Neapolitan bonds, with coupons, or receipts for half-yearly interest, payable to the bearer of the coupons, the coupons referring to a certificate, which gave the holder the option of converting his bonds into the funded debt. The interest on these coupons was paid to the holder of them, without the production of the certificate, though the bonds were never sold without the certificate on the market. The plaintiff having the certificates, his agent pledged the bonds fraudulently to the defendant as security for a debt, and the lower court left it to the jury to say whether the bonds without the certificates were negotiable, and, the jury finding they were not, the court on appeal upheld their verdict.

Gorgier v. Mieville, quoted by Blackburn in Crouch v. Credit Foncier Co.

Blackburn, J.,[3] observed, in criticising Gorgier v. Mieville, "We have no intention to throw the least "doubt on this decision; but we do not think it "applicable to an English instrument made in Eng-"land; and we express no opinion as to what might "be the law as to obligations made by subjects abroad, "which, by the law of the country where they were "made, are negotiable in that country."

Crouch v. Credit Foncier Co.

Crouch v. The Credit Foncier of England,[4] as reported, is as follows. In May, 1869, the defendants, a limited company, registered under the act of 1862, sold to M. a document under the seal of the company

---

[1] 1 Exch. 856.
[2] 7 Bingham, 284.
[3] Crouch v. Credit Foncier, L. R., 8 Ex. Q. B. C.
[4] See preceding note.

and signed by two directors and the secretary. It was numbered and headed with the name of the company, and called "Debenture," and proceeded, "the company hereby promise, subject to the con-"ditions endorsed in this debenture, to pay to the "bearer £100 on the 1st of May, 1872, or upon any "earlier day upon which this Bond shall be entitled "to be paid off according to the conditions, and in-"terest at 8 per cent., on the 1st of November and "the 1st of May in each year; and also a further "sum of £10 by way of interest or bonus, at the "same time the principal sum is paid off." By the conditions endorsed, a certain number of the bonds were to be drawn for twenty-one days before the days for the payment of the half-yearly interest, and any bond drawn was to be advertised and paid off with the interest and bonus due, the bond being given up, and no further interest being payable. In July, 1869, the bond was stolen from M., and in October, 1871, the number of the bond was drawn. At the end of 1871 the plaintiff purchased the debenture from S., who had since absconded. The defendants, having notice of the robbery, refused to pay the debenture to the plaintiff, and he brought an action, alleging that he was the lawful bearer of the debenture. It was admitted on the trial that similar documents had been treated as negotiable, and also that the plaintiff had taken his title from the thief, and the jury found that the plaintiff had given value for the debenture without notice. The court held, Blackburn, J., delivering the opinion, that the contract contained in the conditions prevented the debenture from being a promissory note, even if it had been under hand only, and that it was not competent for the defendants to attach the incident of negotiability to such instrument, contrary to the general law, and that though the custom was to treat them as negotiable, it was of recent origin and not the law merchant, and that made no difference, since such a custom, even though general, could not attach an incident to a contract contrary to the general law. From this last case Mr. Brice, in his work on "Ultra Vires," edited by Mr. Green, on page 164, though he admits the cases are conflicting, concludes that it is substantially settled that debentures are not negotiable at law in England.

Goodwin v. Robarts. Remarks of Cockburn, C. J.

In criticising this case, however, in Goodwin v. Robarts,[1] Sir Alexander Cockburn, C. J., said that the reporter assumed from the notes of the judge, that evidence of the fact that similar instruments had been considered negotiable by usage had been offered on the trial, whereas that was not so, nor was any express admission to that effect made; "but it was "said that these instruments being only of recent "introduction, it followed that such custom, to what-"ever extent it had gone, must have been recent too. "Under these circumstances the court held, that while "it was incompetent to the defendants, as an in-"dividual company, to give that, which was not a "negotiable instrument at law, the character of ne-"gotiability by making it payable to bearer, the "custom could not have that effect, because, being "recent, it formed no part of the ancient law mer-

[1] See *infra*, page 169.

CHAP. L.] THE THING SOLD AT STOCK EXCHANGE. 163

"chant. * * * We cannot, however, concur in think-
"ing the latter ground conclusive. While we quite
"agree that the greater or less time during which
"a custom has existed may be material in deter-
"mining how far it has generally prevailed, we cannot
"think that, if a usage is once shown to be universal,
"it is the less entitled to prevail because it may not
"have formed part of the law merchant as pre-
"viously known and adopted by the courts. * * *
"The judgment in Crouch v. The Credit Foncier
"may well be supported on the ground that in that
"case there was substantially no proof whatever of
"general usage. We cannot concur in thinking that
"if proof of general usage had been established, it
"would have been a sufficient ground for refusing to
"give effect to it, that it did not form part of what
"is called the 'ancient law merchant.'" *Crouch v. Credit Foncier.*

It may be remarked that the American courts, as for instance the opinion of Grier, J., in Mercer Co. v. Hacket, *infra*,[1] shows, place their decisions on this subject chiefly on the ground of usage and the "law merchant." *Opinion of Grier, J., in Mercer Co. v. Hacket.*

In conclusion, we cannot therefore absolutely say that in England the courts have resolved these securities to be at law non-negotiable as yet.

"The weight of authority must, however," as Mr. Brice observes, "now be considered to be in favor of "the proposition that such instruments are in equity, "at least, negotiable free from the equities primarily "attaching to them," and the reader is referred to his work for the authorities on that point.[2] *These securities negotiable at equity in England.*

---

[1] Page 165.   [2] Green's Brice's *Ultra Vires.*

Negotiable at law in America.

In America the subject may be considered by a number of decisions as settled, and the following rule adopted, viz.:[1] that any obligations properly issued, either by any public or private corporation, and made payable to "bearer" or "order," or otherwise having the properties of negotiability, and passing by delivery, are negotiable, even though under seal. And this conclusion seems to have been reached by the courts, chiefly, because they considered that the necessities of mercantile and commercial methods of dealing demanded that such instruments should be treated as negotiable.

Diamond v. Lawrence Co.

In Diamond v. Lawrence County,[2] however, the Supreme Court of Pennsylvania held that such coupon bonds had not the quality of commercial paper in that State, but the purchaser took them subject to equities, and the coupons subject to the same equities.

It may be remarked that the court added, they differed from all the decisions, on this subject, but were resolved to stand alone on this point; and the reasoning of the learned judge, Woodward, J., who delivered the opinion of the court, is not very convincing or clear.[3]

Mercer Co. v. Hacket.

In Mercer County v. Hacket,[4] on an appeal from the decision of the Supreme Court of Pennsylvania, the Supreme Court of the United States refused to follow the decision in Diamond v. Lawrence Co., but held such coupon bonds, payable to bearer, negotiable, and that the corporate seal upon them made no difference. Grier, J., said, "We have decided

Diamond v. Lawrence Co. not followed.

---

[1] Indiana v. Sprague, 13 Cent. Law Jour. 127.
[2] 37 Pa. 353.
[3] See this case referred to in notes to Miller v. Race, 1 Smith's Leading Cases, 7th Amer. ed., 808.
[4] 1 Wallace, 83.

CHAP. I.] THE THING SOLD AT STOCK EXCHANGE. 165

"in the case of Commissioners of Knox County *v.* Commissioners *v.* Aspinwall quoted.
"Aspinwall,[1] that where the bonds on their face im-
"port a compliance with the law under which they Remarks of Grier, J.
"were issued, the purchaser is not bound to look
"further. The decision of the Board of Commis-
"sioners may not be conclusive in a direct proceeding
"to inquire into the facts before the rights and in-
"terests of other parties had attached; but *after* the
"authority has been executed, the stock subscribed,
"and the bonds issued and in the hands of innocent
"holders, it would be too late, even in a direct pro-
"ceeding, to call it in question. * * * This species of
"bonds (coupon bonds payable to bearer) is a modern
"invention, intended to pass by manual delivery, and
"to have the qualities of negotiable paper; and their
"value depends mainly upon this character. Being
"issued by States and corporations, they are necessa-
"rily under seal. But there is nothing immoral, or
"contrary to good policy, in making them negotiable,
"if the necessities of commerce require that they
"should be so. A mere technical dogma of the courts
"or the common law cannot prevent the commercial
"world from inventing or using any species of secu-
"rity not known in the last century. Usages of trade
"and commerce are acknowledged by courts as part
"of the common law, although they may have been
"unknown to Bracton or Blackstone, and this mal-
"leability to suit the necessities and usages of the
"mercantile and commercial world is one of the most
"valuable characteristics of the common law. When
"a corporation covenants to pay to bearer, and gives

[1] 21 Howard, 545.

"a bond with negotiable qualities, and by this means obtains funds for the accomplishment of the useful enterprises of the day, it cannot be allowed to evade the payment, by parading some obsolete judicial decision, that a bond, for some technical reason, cannot be made payable to bearer. That these securities are treated as negotiable by the commercial usages of the whole civilized world, and have received the sanctions of judicial recognition, not only in this court,[1] but of nearly every State in the Union, is well known and admitted.

Diamond v. Lawrence Co. opposed to all the authorities.

"But we have been referred to the case of Diamond v. Lawrence County for a single decision to the contrary. The learned judge who delivered the opinion of the court in that case says, 'We will not treat these bonds as negotiable securities. *On this ground we stand. All the courts, American and English, are against us.* We know the history of these municipal and county bonds; how grand jurors and county commissioners and city officers were moulded to the purpose of speculators; how reckless railroad officers abused the overwrought confidence of the public, and what burdens of debt and taxation have resulted to the people. A moneyed security was thrown upon the market by the paroxysm of the public mind.'

"If this decision of that learned court was founded on the construction of the constitution or statute law of the State, or the peculiar law of Pennsylvania as to titles to land, we would have felt bound to follow it. But we have often decided that on ques-

[1] White *v.* Ry. Co., 21 Howard, 575.

CHAP. I.] THE THING SOLD AT STOCK EXCHANGE. 167

"tions of mercantile or commercial law, or usages "which are not peculiar to any place, we do not feel "bound to yield our own judgment, especially if it "be fortified by the decisions of 'all other English "and American courts.' These securities are not "peculiar to Pennsylvania. * * * Although we doubt "not the facts stated as to the atrocious frauds which "have been practised, in some counties, in issuing "and obtaining these bonds, we cannot agree to over- "rule our own decisions and change the law to suit "hard cases. The epidemic insanity of the people, "the folly of railroad 'speculations,' are pleas which "might have just weight in an application to restrain "the issue or negotiation of these bonds, but cannot "prevail to authorize their repudiation, after they "have been negotiated, and have come into the pos- "session of *bona fide* holders."

In Gelpcke *v.* City of Dubuque,[1] the Supreme Court of the United States again held, that municipal bonds, with coupons payable to "bearer," have, by universal usage and consent, all the qualities of commercial paper, and will entitle the party recovering on the coupons, to the amount on them, with interest and exchange at the place where by their terms they are made payable.

Gelpcke v. Dubuque.

And, finally, in Commissioners *v.* Clark,[2] the principles of the foregoing cases were again affirmed.

Commissioners v. Clark.

These decisions, then, seem to establish without doubt the negotiability in the Federal courts of these kinds of bonds, to the same extent as promissory notes and bills of exchange; and the reader is re-

[1] 1 Wallace, 175.   [2] 94 U. S. Rep. 278.

168   THE STOCK BROKER.   [PART II.

ferred to the cases in the note, which are to the same effect.[1]

Coupons.

The following propositions with regard to coupons have been laid down by Mr. Ashbel Green in his note to Brice's *Ultra Vires*, page 179, viz.:

1. That coupons may be dissevered from the bonds and be sued upon as separate instruments by the holder, although he be not the holder of the bonds.[2]

2. That coupons thus dissevered have the like qualities of commercial paper as the bonds to which they are attached. See the cases to note 2.

Scrip.

Certificates of scrip in England and America are issued by public and private associations, which are publicly sold in the open market, and, usually, pass by mere delivery[3] from hand to hand, and do not require any formal transfer or stamp.[4] Sometimes these

---

[1] Myers v. York & Cumberland R. R. Co., 43 Me. 232; White v. V. & M. R. R. Co., 21 Howard, 575; Moran v. Miami Co., 2 Black. 722; Meyer v. Muscatine, 1 Wallace, 384; Thompson v. Lee Co., 3 Wall. 327; Aurora City v. West, 7 Wall. 82; Clark v. Lee Co., 20 Wall. 583; Durant v. Iowa Co., 1 Woolw. 72; King v. Wilson, 1 Dillon, C. C. R. 555; Miller v. R. & W. R. R. Co., 40 Vt. 399; Bank v. R. R. Co., 8 R. I. 375; Haven v. Grand Junc. R. R. Co., 109 Mass. 88; Society for Savings v. City of New London, 29 Conn. 174; State v. Delafield, 8 Paige, 527; Brainerd v. N. Y. & H. R. R. Co., 25 N. Y. 496; Morris Canal Co. v. Lewis, 1 Beasley, 323; Winfield v. Hudson, 4 Dutch. 255; Craig v. Vicksburg, 31 Miss. 217; Porter v. McCollum, 15 Ga. 528; Clark v Mfg. Co., 15 Wend. 256; Smith v. Clarke, 54 Mo. 58; Clarke v. Janesville, 10 Wisc. 136; Clapp v. Cedar County, 5 Cl. (Iowa) 15; Maddox v. Graham, 2 Metc. (Ky.) 56; Devoss v. Richmond, 18 Gratt. (Va.) 338.

[2] Bank v. R. R. Co., 8 R. I. 375; Spooner v. Holmes, 102 Mass. 503; Murray v. Lardner, 2 Wall. 110; Thompson v. Lee, 3 Wall. 327; City v. Lamson, 9 Wall. 477; San Antonio v. Lane, 32 Texas, 405; Johnson v. County, 24 Ill. 75; but see Meyers v. R. R. Co., 43 Me. 232; Arents v. Com., 18 Gratt. 750.

[3] See the cases referred to in the preceding note, and in the note to Green's Brice's *Ultra Vires*, p. 177.

[4] See Ry. Co. v. Freeman, 2 Man. & Gran. 606; Heseltine v. Siggers, 1 Exch. 856; Volans v. Fletcher, 1 Exch. 20; Moore v. Garwood, 4 Exch. 681.

CHAP. I.] THE THING SOLD AT STOCK EXCHANGE. 169

certificates are agreements to give, under certain circumstances, stock, or bonds, and sometimes mere shares of stock. Possibly certificates of scrip for shares of stock are not negotiable at present; but where the agreement by the association on the certificate is to give bonds to the holders, and the certificates pass by delivery by a general custom of the market, there is no doubt that they would be negotiable instruments, certainly in the United States, in analogy to the cases above cited, relative to debentures. *[margin: Certificates of scrip for bonds usually negotiable.]*

In England, in the case of Goodwin v. Robarts,[1] Sir Alexander Cockburn, C. J., in a very able opinion, held, that scrip, issued by the Russian government, by the agent in England, by the terms of which the holder was to be entitled, on payment in full of the instalments due from him, to delivery by the agent of definitive bonds of that government, on their arrival in England, and which, by the usage of bankers and brokers, was transferred by mere delivery, passed a good title to a *bona fide* holder for value without title, and was negotiable. It may be added that in this case all the instalments were actually paid up to give a good title before the present holder got the scrip. It was contended in a very able argument by Mr. Benjamin, Q. C., that a promise to pay money was distinguishable from a promise, like this, to give a bond only, and therefore the case was not governed by Gorgier v. Mieville,[2] which was merely a promise to pay money; but the House of Lords held the distinction, though ingenious, not to be sound. *[margin: Goodwin v. Robarts.]* *[margin: Goodwin v. Robarts not distinguishable from Gorgier v. Mieville.]*

[1] L. R., 10 Exch. Cas. 337; L. R., 1 A. C. 476.   [2] *Supra*, p. 159.

Remarks of Lord Hatherly affirming Goodwin v. Robarts.

Lord Hatherly said, in affirmance of the judgment of Cockburn, C. J., in the Exchequer Chamber, the only difference from Gorgier v. Mieville, is that "in "that case the court had to deal with the bonds them-"selves on which the Prussian government was bound "to make payment; in this case we have to deal with "an instrument which entitles its holder to receive "those bonds, all the payments having been made at "the time when it was handed over. Can there be "any rational distinction between these two docu-"ments? or, as Mr. Baron Bramwell put the question, "if a broker was alike to go into the market with a "portion of this scrip in one hand and a bond in the "other, and sold both, could you hold that there was "a substantial or rational distinction to be drawn "between the right of a person who so acquired, "according to the practice of the Stock Exchange, "the one document, and the right of a person who "in the same way acquired the other?"

It has been stated that the instalments were fully paid up; but had that not been so, the case might also have been decided in the same way, and Lord Selborne remarked that even in that event he would have had no doubt of the matter.

It will be remembered that all the English cases we have cited, in which the question of negotiability at law of bonds or scrip was involved, have been *Crouch v. Credit Foncier Co.* cases of foreign bonds or scrip, except that of Crouch v. Credit Foncier,[1] where it will be remembered that *Distinction of Blackburn, J.* Blackburn, J., took a distinction between "English "instruments made by an English company in Eng-

---

[1] See p. 160, *supra.*

CHAP. I.] THE THING SOLD AT STOCK EXCHANGE. 171

"land," and "a public debt created by a foreign or "colonial government, the title to portions of which "is by them made to depend on the possession of "bonds expressed to be transferable to the bearer or "holder, on which there cannot properly be said to be "any right of action at all, though the holder has "a claim on a foreign government." But of these cases, coming within the latter category, the judges, both in the Exchequer Chamber and on appeal, have said, in Goodwin v. Robarts, that it made no difference whether the contract be considered a foreign or English contract, since if it exists at all it must "not "depend on what might be its negotiability by the "foreign law, but on how far the universal usage of "the monetary world has given it that character here." "The question," says Tindal, C. J., in Lang v. Smyth, "is not so much what is the usage in the country "whence the instrument comes, as in the country "where it passed."[1]

Goodwin v. Robarts.

Remarks of Tindal, C. J., in Lang v. Smyth, quoted in Goodwin v. Robarts.

Where the certificates of scrip are for shares instead of bonds, as, for instance, railroad scrip, we believe there are no decisions directly on the question of their negotiability, and it is perhaps doubtful if such certificates could be held to be negotiable; scrip for bonds is a mere agreement to give a security for money to bearer, and cannot logically, as we have seen, be distinguished from the security itself; but certificates of scrip for shares are but agreements to give a thing, not specific or certain in value, not in itself negotiable; and it might be asked, how then can the agreement to give it be negotiable?

[1] Goodwin v. Robarts, p. 169, *supra*.

With regard to shares, it has been held that every holder of a share, where the name was left in blank, though he omitted to register as a shareholder, became, by the mere act of purchasing the shares and holding the scrip certificates, liable for calls, and bound to indemnify the former holder.[1] The mere fact, too, of passing by delivery cannot serve to make them negotiable, like bills of lading, and they are only *quasi* negotiable. Still, if it could be proved that there was a universal usage to consider them as negotiable, it would be, in our opinion, difficult to say why they should not be so considered, according to the principles of Mercer Co. *v.* Hacket, and Goodwin *v.* Robarts. And again, there is another strong argument in favor of the negotiability of certificates of scrip "to bearer," which is that the first purchaser, taking them to bearer, would be estopped from saying they were not so, as he bought and sold, knowing they passed "to bearer," and could consequently not invoke equities against a subsequent holder.

Mercer Co. v. Hacket.
Goodwin v. Robarts.

In concluding this subject, we must observe that we cannot agree with those lawyers who, like the judges of the Supreme Court of Pennsylvania, and Redfield, C. J.,[2] of Rhode Island, would restrain the negotiability of these instruments in the face of the necessities of trade, and think that the enlarging the negotiability of commercial instruments would be greatly to the detriment of either the security or honesty of the community, and we will end by quoting

---

[1] See Walker *v.* Bartlett, 18 C. B. 845; De Pass's case, 4 De G. & J. 544.

[2] See his curious note to Matthews *v.* Massachusetts Bank, in 14 Amer. Law Register, p. 153.

the remarks of Cockburn, C. J., in Goodwin *v.* Robarts, on this subject. "The universality of a usage "adopted between buyers and sellers is conclusive "proof of its being in accordance with public conve- "nience; and there can be no doubt that by holding "this species of security to be incapable of being "transferred by delivery, and as requiring some more "cumbrous method of assignment, we should mate- "rially hamper the transactions of the money market "with respect to it, and cause great public incon- "venience. No doubt there is an evil arising from "the facility of transfer by delivery, namely, that it "occasionally gives rise to the theft or misappropri- "ation of the security to the loss of the true owner. "But this is an evil common to the whole body of "negotiable securities. It is one which may be in a "great degree prevented by prudence and care. It "is one which is counterbalanced by the general con- "venience arising from facility to transfer, or the "usage would never have become general to make "scrip available to bearer, and to treat it as trans- "ferable by delivery. It is obvious that no injustice "is done to one who has been fraudulently dispos- "sessed of scrip through his own misplaced confi- "dence, in holding that the property in it has passed "to a *bona fide* holder for value, seeing that he him- "self must have known that it purported, on the face "of it, to be available to bearer, and must be pre- "sumed to have been aware of the usage prevalent "with respect to it in the market in which he pur- "chased it. Lastly, it is to be observed that the "tendency of the courts, except only in the time of

Remarks of Cockburn, C. J., in Goodwin v. Robarts.

"Lord Holt, has been to give effect to mercantile "usage in respect to securities for money, and that "where legal difficulties have arisen, the legislature "has been prompt to give the necessary remedy, as "in the case of promissory notes and of the East "India bonds."

SECTION III.—INCIDENTS ATTACHED TO THE THING SOLD.

With regard to *bonds* or *debentures,* being simple obligations to pay money, there is little peculiar, and nothing need be said.

Coupons. With respect to *coupons,* we may say that, when detached from the bonds, they are still liens, and that, whether the holders are entitled to payment in the order the coupons fall due, or to a *pro rata* *Interest.* distribution,[1] and also that they bear interest from the date of demand of payment and refusal.[2]

Transfer of bonds. *Coupons* and *bonds* may be transferred either to bearer, when negotiable, as we have seen, or, when not, subject to the equities of the former holders.

One of the most important incidents attached to shares of stock in a trading or mining company is *Transferability of shares of stock.* their transferability, or the right of the owner to transfer them to some one else freely at the market value.[3] For one of the peculiarities of these securities is that the owner may transfer to whoever he likes, as no election to membership is necessary.

[1] Miller v. R. & W. R. R. Co., 40 Vt. 399; Sewall v. Brainerd, 38 Vt., 364.
[2] Clarke v. Iowa City, 20 Wall. 583; Gelpcke v. Dubuque, 1 Wall. 175; Burroughs v. Richmond, 65 N. C. 234; N. P. R. R. Co. v. Adams, 54 Pa. 94; Mills v. Jefferson, 20 Wisc. 50.
[3] Brightwell v. Mallory, 10 Yerger, 196; State v. Bank, 10 Ohio, 91.

Thus, in Overseers of the Poor *v.* Sears,[1] Shaw, C. J., said, "In all bridge, railroad, and turnpike "companies, in all banks, insurance companies, manu- "facturing companies, and generally in corporations "having a capital stock and looking to profits, mem- "bership is constituted by a transfer of shares, accord- "ing to the by-laws, without any election on the part "of the corporation itself." Remarks of Shaw, C. J.

The method of transfer will be treated of *infra*, in Chapter VIII., in the chapter on the Completion of the Contract.

The owner of a share has also the privilege of *voting* at the elections of officers held by the corporation, and this also passes to his transferee, not being a personal privilege. Since, as no election to membership in public or trading corporations is necessary, the transferee of stock must of course be entitled to all the privileges of the transferor.[2] Voting.

The owner or his transferee of the shares, it also may be said, is liable to assessments or calls, when it is proper for the company to make them. We shall not go into this subject or that of subscriptions here, as that does not, except indirectly, affect stock brokers, whose duty is *prima facie* only to sell, and who may never own a share of stock; but it concerns rather their customers, and for this subject the reader is referred to Green's Brice's *Ultra Vires*, or Angell & Ames on Corporations. Calls.

The owner or his transferee has also a right to Dividends.

---

[1] 22 Pick. (Mass.) 122.
[2] See Gilbert *v.* Iron Co., 11 Wend. 627; Sargeant *v.* Franklin Ins. Co., 8 Pick. 90; Downing *v.* Potts, 3 N. J. 66.

dividends on his shares, which are the general division, among the shareholders, of the profits of the company in proportionate shares, and which can only be so declared.[1] The declaration of dividends is discretionary with the directors, and while they act in good faith the courts will rarely interfere.[2]

Declaration of dividends.

Pledge.

In analogy to the sale of stock, the owner or his transferee may also pledge it, and the transfer of the legal title is not inconsistent with a pledge of it.[3] The subject of Pledge will be considered hereafter under that head.[4]

Lien of corporations on shares.

A word may be said with regard to the liens that may be held on these securities. A joint stock corporation has no implied lien upon the shares of stock of a shareholder, which may have been transferred by him as security for any demand against him, and consequently, though they may have a demand against one, they are compelled, notwithstanding such indebtedness, to enter on their books such a transfer of the stock, or become liable to an assignee for a refusal to do so; unless, indeed, there may be a provision in the charter respecting such a transfer or indebtedness.

Bates v. Ins. Co.

Thus, in Bates *v.* Ins. Co.,[5] the company refused to transfer unless the assignee would pay the debts of the assignor, and the court held, that the assignee could recover the money, since the corporation were not authorized to make such a demand.

---

[1] Jones *v.* R. R. Co., 29 Barb. 353; Ryder *v.* Alton & Say. R. R. Co., 13 Ill. 516.

[2] State *v.* Bank, 6 La. 745; Luling *v.* Ins. Co., 45 Barb. 510.

[3] See Wilson *v.* Little, 2 Comst. (N. Y.) 443.

[4] See Part III.

[5] 3 John. Cas. 238.

CHAP. I.] THE THING SOLD AT STOCK EXCHANGE. 177

But where there is a provision in the charter that the corporation may make such a lien, the above rule would not hold.

Thus, in Rogers *v.* Huntingdon Bank,[1] it was enacted that "no stockholder indebted to the bank, shall "be authorized to make a transfer, or receive a dividend, till such debt shall have been discharged," or security to the satisfaction of the directors given therefor. A shareholder, indebted to the bank on a discounted note and an instalment on the stock, gave one power of attorney to receive dividends in his own name, and another to transfer the stock to the plaintiff, who had placed in the hands of an attorney a sum to pay the instalment. The instalment was paid. The court held, that the plaintiff was not entitled to a transfer of the stock, nor to a return of the instalment. Tilghman, C. J., said, "The words" of the act "embrace all debts, and "there is good reason for extending them to all. "When the directors discount a note of a stockholder, they know that his stock is liable, and, "therefore, may be less attentive to the sufficiency of "the endorsers. The endorsers, too, have an interest "in the lien of the bank, and it may be presumed "that many persons have been induced to endorse, on "the strength of this lien."[2]

Rogers v. Huntingdon Bank.

Remarks of Tilghman, C. J.

There must, however, appear an express and clear provision of their rights to this lien.

Thus, in Bullard *v.* Bank,[3] and in Bank *v.* Lanier,[4]

Bullard v. Bank.

---

[1] 12 S. & R. (Pa.) 73.
[2] See, also, Union Bank *v.* Laird, 2 Wheat. (U. S.) 390.
[3] 18 Wall. 589.
[4] 11 Wall. 369; but see Lockwood *v.* Mer. Nat. Bank, J. R. 308.

12

Bank v. Lanier.

it was held, that a national bank, though having a power to regulate the transfer of its stock, could not create a lien by a by-law on the stock.

Vansands v. Bank.

But in Vansands v. Bank,[1] where a certificate declared the holder entitled to a certain number of shares "transferable at said bank only by him or his "attorney on the surrender of this certificate, subject, "nevertheless, to his indebtedness and liability at the "bank, according to the charter and by-laws of said "bank," the court held, that the last clause referred only to the mode of transfer, and did not mean that the lien must be one provided for by the charter and by-laws; but that the bank had a lien on the stock, though none was expressly given by any by-law, and the charter provided that the stockholders might establish by-laws and regulations for the well ordering of the concerns of the bank, and made the stock transferable according to the rules so prescribed.[2]

To discuss the interpretations that the courts have placed on the various charters, or by-laws, with regard to their right of lien, would not be appropriate here, and would be a mere recital of a voluminous list of cases, and the reader is referred to some work on stock and stockholders for that, as well as to the following cases.[3]

---

[1] 26 Conn. 144.

[2] See Vicksburg R. R. Co. v. McKeen, 14 La. An. 724; Conant v. Bank, 1 Ohio St. 298; Helm v. Swiggett, 12 Ind. 194.

[3] Hall v. Ins. Co., 5 Gill, 484; Reese v. Bank, 14 Md. 271; Grant v. Bank, 15 S. & R. 140; Ins. Co. v. Goodfellow, 9 Mo. 149; Leggett v. Bank, 25 Barb. 326; Presbyterian Congregation v. Bank, 5 Barr, 345; Evans v. Hudson Bay Co., 7 Vin. Abr. 125, pl. 2; 1 Strange, 645; Plymouth Bk. v. Bank, 10 Pick. 454; Bank v. Smalley, 2 Cowen, 770; Bank v. Kortright, 22 Wend. 348; Ex parte Mathew, 5 De G. M. & G. 837; Orr v. Bigelow, 20 Barb. 21; Sargeant v. Essex & C. Co., 9 Pick.

CHAP. I.] THE THING SOLD AT STOCK EXCHANGE. 179

It would seem that though a corporation may have no lien on the shares of stock of a shareholder, unless specially permitted by proper authority, yet it may have one on dividends, if they have notice of a transfer, when the dividends are already declared. But in Rogers v. Huntingdon Bank, cited above,[1] the company were held obliged to make the transfer when the last instalment was paid, and the assignee to be entitled to the dividends thereafter made.

Lien of corporations on dividends.

Rogers v. Bank.

With regard to creditors' and shareholders' lien, Mr. Green remarks in his note to Brice's *Ultra Vires*, page 139, "Dividends improperly declared and paid "may be recovered back. The assets of a corporation "are a trust fund for the payment of its debts, and "its creditors have a lien thereon and the right to "priority of payment over its stockholders. Where "property of a corporation has been divided among "stockholders, before its debts have been paid, a judg- "ment creditor, after return of execution unsatisfied, "may maintain an action in the nature of a creditor's "bill against a stockholder to reach what was so re- "ceived by him. It is immaterial whether he got it "by fair agreement or by a wrongful act."[2]

Lien of creditors of corporation. Remarks of Mr. Green in note to Brice's Ultra Vires.

A shareholder in a corporation has no legal title to the property or profits of the corporation until a division is made or a dividend actually declared.[3] But

202; Sabin v. Bank, 21 Vt. 353; Shipman v. Ætna Ins. Co., 29 Conn. 245.
[1] See page 177.
[2] Bartlett v. Drew, 57 N. Y. 587; see, also, Osgood v. Laytin, 8 Keys, 521; Gratz v. Redd, 4 B. Mon. 178; Curran v. State, 15 How. 304;

Sawyer v. Hoag, 17 Wall. 610.
[3] Goodwin v. Hardy, 57 Me. 143; Minot v. Paine, 99 Mass. 101; Phelps v. Bank, 26 Conn. 269; Karnes v. R. R. Co., 4 Abb. Pr., N. S. 107; Hyatt v. Allen, 56 N. Y. 553; Brundage v. Ib., 1 N. Y. Supr. Ct. (T. & C.) 82;

a dividend declared of the earnings of the company becomes thereupon the individual property of the stockholder, to be received by him on demand. It is a severance from the common fund of the company of so much for the use and benefit of each corporator in his individual right, which may be demanded by him, and if refused become the subject of an action for money had and received to his use. A dividend declared, becoming the individual right of the stockholder, is thereafter held as a trust fund that cannot be devoted to other objects; and, accordingly, the action of assumpsit lies to recover the dividends as a debt due from the corporation to the individual stockholder, after demand of payment.[1] The dividends must be general, so that each stockholder will receive his proportionate share, and the directors have no authority to declare a dividend on any other principle.[2]

The declaration of dividends is discretionary with the directors of the corporation, and so long as they act in good faith the courts will not interfere, even though they may deem their judgment erroneous.[3]

Curry v. Woodward, 44 Ala. 305.

[1] Granger v. Bassett, 98 Mass. 462; Stoddard v. Shetucket, 34 Conn. 542; Kane v. Bloodgood, 7 John. Ch. 90; Carpenter v. R. R. Co., 5 Abb. Pr. 277; Jones v. R. R. Co., 29 Barb. 353; Howell v. R. R. Co., 51 Barb. 578; King v. Paterson, 5 Dutch. 82; Jackson v. Plank Road Co., 2 Vroom, 277; Brown v. Coal & Nav. Co., 9 Pa. 207; R. R. Co. v. Cowell, 28 Pa. 329; Bank v. Brays, 4 H. & J. 358; State v. R. R. Co., 6 Gill, 363; City of Ohio v. R. R. Co., 6 Ohio St. 489; and in

Le Roy v. Globe Ins. Co., 2 Edw. Ch. 657, the Vice-Chancellor was of opinion that a bill in equity would lie to recover possession of the money as a trust fund.

[2] Jones v. R. R. Co., 29 Barb. 353; Luling v. Atlantic Ins. Co., 45 Barb. 510; A. & T. Co. v. Commonwealth, 3 Brews. 366; State v. R. R. Co., 6 Gill, 363; Ryder v. R. R. Co., 13 Ill. 516.

[3] State v. Bank, 6 La. 745; Ely v. Sprague, Clarke, Ch. 351; Karnes v. R. R. Co., 4 Abb. Pr., N. S. 107; Luling v. Ins. Co., 45 Barb. 510.

In England stock may now be charged with judgment debts[1] and taken in execution,[2] and its transfer may be stopped by a stop order[3] and restraining order,[4] and a distringas.[5] And in America various statutes have been passed with reference to the modes by which stock may be reached by judgment and other creditors.

Stock subject to execution, by statute.

[1] 1 & 2 Vict. 110, §§ 14, 15. See Nicholls v. Rosewarne, 6 C. B., N. S. 480.
[2] 1 & 2 Vict. 110, § 12.
[3] Daniell's Chancery Prac., c. 37.
[4] 5 Vict. c. 5, s. 4.
[5] 5 Vict. c. 5, 525; In re Marquis of Hertford, 1 Hare, 584.

CHAPTER II.

THE CONTRACT OF SALE.

	PAGE		PAGE
Parties to the contract	182	Contracts are for a thing *in esse.*	188
SECTION I.—THE NECESSARY OWNERSHIP BY THE PARTIES IN THE THING SOLD.		SECTION II.—THE MUTUAL ASSENT OF THE PARTIES TO THE CONTRACT.	
Stock brokers may make a valid sale	183	Illustrations of this principle. Contracts by post-office	190 190
Contract of sale not for a specific article	183	Contracts by telegraph Mutual assent with reference to thing contracted for	191 191
Contracts for future delivery	185	SECTION III.—THE PRICE.	

Parties to the contract.

IN all the sales at the Stock Exchange, the parties to the contract of sale are either principals represented by stock brokers, or are such brokers, themselves acting in the capacity of principals; and as, under the head of principal and stock broker, we have examined the necessary qualifications that each of such parties must possess to make a valid contract, it will not be needful here to consider the legal status of the parties to the contract. In this chapter, then, we shall consider, first, the necessary ownership of, or dominion over, the thing sold by the parties to the contract; secondly, their mutual assent to the contract; and, thirdly, the price.

SECTION I.—THE NECESSARY OWNERSHIP BY THE PARTIES IN THE THING SOLD.

Rule as to ownership at common law.

The rule of the common law is, that nobody but the legal owner or his representative can make a valid con-

CHAP. II.] THE CONTRACT OF SALE. 183

tract of sale.[1] There are, however, certain exceptions to this rule, as in the case, in England, of sales made in market overt, and in the sales of negotiable securities, which pass by delivery;[2] and so factors, stock brokers, pawnees, and public officers,[3] may give a good title to the thing sold, although they have no legal ownership in it, but hold it only in their custody, subject to their principal's orders. Where, then, the authority of the stock broker to sell is legally constituted, he is enabled to make a valid contract, and to pass a legal title to the purchaser in the thing sold.

Stock brokers may make a valid sale.

Some few of the contracts of sale at the Stock Exchange are immediately followed by a delivery of the article contracted for, and the whole transaction executed on the spot; and of such a transaction nothing need be said. But the great majority of contracts of sale at the Stock Exchange, both in England and in the United States, are made for a future delivery; and this kind of contract demands considerable attention.

The great majority of the contracts of sale at the Stock Exchange are for a future delivery.

It is to be observed that the contract of sale at the Stock Exchange is never, or very rarely, a contract for the sale of a particular article, or specific chattel, but merely for one of a designated class of articles, and that any one of the class will satisfy the conditions of the contract.

Contract of sale not for a specific article.

Thus, in Heseltine v. Siggers,[4] where the declaration stated that the plaintiff "bargained with the defendant "to buy, and *then bought* from him, and the defend- "ant then agreed to sell, *and then sold*, to the plaintiff, "certain foreign stock, to wit, 28,000 Spanish stock,"

Heseltine v. Siggers.

---

[1] Benjamin on Sales, p. 7.
[2] Ibid., p. 12.
[3] Ibid., p. 14.
[4] 1 Exch. Rep. 856.

etc., the defendant refused to deliver the bonds, and the plaintiff, who, after his purchase, had sold the stock to another person, was in consequence obliged to purchase the bonds at a loss. The plaintiff offered in evidence a stamped sold note, but there was no evidence of any bought note. The defendant contended that the declaration being formed on an agreement to deliver bonds, the plaintiff was bound to prove that property in the specific bonds had passed to the plaintiff.

<small>Judgment of Parke, B., and Pollock, C. B.</small>

But the court, Parke, B., and Pollock, C. B., held, that the words "bought" and "sold" must be construed with reference to the subject-matter of the contract, and as meaning an *agreement* to buy and sell; and that a contract for the sale of stock, exchequer bills, and securities of that description, in which the property passes by delivery, differs from the sale of a specific chattel, since the delivery of *any* stock, etc., would satisfy the contract.

<small>Distinction between a contract of sale of a specific chattel and stock.</small>

Now, there is this distinction to be observed between a contract of sale of articles of this description, and contracts for the sale of a specific chattel, that, in the latter case, when a bargain has been made, the title of the property may pass at once, as between the vendor and vendee, without any reference to the delivery at all; while in the former, there is nothing but an executory agreement to deliver a specified amount of indefinite parts of a certain class, and which, never becoming definite till some delivery is had, no title can pass to the vendee until the delivery. In the former case, then, as something remains to be done by one of the parties before a title to the thing contracted for

<small>Contract of sale executory.</small>

CHAP. II.] THE CONTRACT OF SALE. 185

can pass, the contract of sale can never be an executed contract until a delivery or setting apart by the vendor.

Sales at the Stock Exchange are, as we have seen above, usually sold for a future delivery, and it frequently happens that at the time of the formation of the contract the thing to be sold is not in the possession of the vendor, but the contract is merely an executory agreement to deliver. *Sales for a future delivery.*

In the well-known case of Bryan *v.* Lewis,[1] Lord Tenterden held, that if goods be sold, to be delivered at a future day, and the seller has not the goods, nor any contract for them, nor any reasonable expectation of receiving them on consignment, but intends to go into the market and buy them, it is not a valid contract, but a wager on the price of the commodity. This severe doctrine of the common law has, however, since been exploded, and a stock broker may legally contract to sell stock, etc., to be delivered at a future day, which is not in his possession nor under his control, and which he may not have any reasonable expectation of getting, at the time of the formation of the contract. *Bryan v. Lewis.*

Thus, in Hibblewhite *v.* McMorine,[2] it was held, that a contract for the sale of fifty shares of the Brighton Railway Company, to be transferred, delivered, and paid for at a future day, the vendor not having the shares in his possession at the time of the contract, nor yet any reasonable expectation of getting them, otherwise than by purchase after the contract had been made, was valid. Parke, B., said, "I have always entertained considerable doubt and suspicion as to the correctness of Lord Tenterden's doctrine in Bryan *v.* *Hibblewhite v. McMorine.* *Remarks of Parke, B. Bryan v. Lewis criticised.*

[1] Ry. & Moo. 386.   [2] 5 M. & W. 462.

"Lewis: it excited a good deal of surprise in my mind "at the time, and, when examined, I think is unten-"able. I cannot see what principle of law is at all "affected by a man's being allowed to contract for the "sale of goods, of which he has not possession at the "time of the bargain, and has no reasonable expectation "of receiving. Such a contract does not amount to a "wager, inasmuch as both the contracting parties are "not cognizant of the fact that the goods are not in the "vendor's possession. * * * There is no indication in "any of the books of such a doctrine having ever "been promulgated from the Bench until the case of "Lorymer *v.* Smith, in the year 1822; and there is no "case which has been since decided on that authority. "Not only, then, was the doubt expressed by Bosanquet, "J., in Wells *v.* Porter, well founded, but the doctrine "is clearly contrary to law."

Lorymer v. Smith.

Wells v. Porter.

Remarks of Alderson, B.

Alderson, B., said that he was of the same opinion, and that such a principle "would put an end to half "the contracts made in the course of trade;" and Maule, B., said, "I have always considered the doctrine laid "down in Bryan *v.* Lewis as contrary to law, and most "inconvenient in practice: and I have often heard it "spoken of with great suspicion, both by lawyers and "mercantile men, upon both grounds,—as against law, "and against all mercantile convenience. It was with "great surprise I heard so accurate a lawyer give utter-"ance to a doctrine so evidently erroneous."

Remarks of Maule, B.

Bryan v. Lewis.

Mortimer v. McCallan. Hibblewhite v. McMorine followed.

So, in Mortimer *v.* McCallan,[1] the court overruled the doctrine laid down in Bryan *v.* Lewis, and followed Hibblewhite *v.* McMorine, holding, that the possession

[1] 6 M. & W. 68.

of the required stock at the time of the *transfer* was quite sufficient, and that the Act of 7 Geo. II. did not apply to such a case, where the party really meant to carry out his contract.

So, in Frazier *v.* Hilliard,[1] it was held, that if a vendor sell a thing, not his own, and subsequently acquire title to it before the contract is repudiated by the vendee, the property vests in the purchaser. And again in Hotchkiss *v.* Oliver,[2] it was decided, that, in a contract of "sale or return," the fact of the vendor having no title at the time of the contract of sale, but only acquiring one afterwards, before the buyer had allowed the time to elapse for returning the goods, could not set up in the defence as failure of consideration in the original contract, in an action for the price. The subject will be further pursued in the chapter on Wagers.

Frazier v. Hilliard.

Hotchkiss v. Oliver.

Having seen that the contracts of sale at the Stock Exchange are usually of an executory character, and that the sale is equally valid, whether the thing contracted for is, or is not, in the possession, or under control, of the vendor, at the time of the formation of the contract, it is important to determine whether the subject of the contract is, or is not, *in esse* at the formation of the contract of sale.

Important to determine whether the contract of sale is for a thing *in esse* or not.

As is well known, the subject-matter of a contract of sale of personal property may be for a thing actually existing, or for a thing that has ceased to exist, or which has not yet come into existence, at the time the contract was formed.

Explanation of executory contracts of sale.

---

[1] 2 Strobh. 309.
[2] 5 Denio, N. Y. 314; see, also, Blackmore *v.* Shelby, 8 Humph. Tenn. 489.

It is not necessary to give an illustration of the first class of contracts, and the case of Hastie *v.* Couturier[1] is an example of the second class. Here a cargo of corn, loaded on a vessel, still on the seas, was sold, and afterwards it was discovered that the corn, becoming heated, had been discharged at an intermediate port: the court held, the sale was properly repudiated by the purchaser.

Examples of the third class are cases where a man sells supplies of milk not yet milked; or cheese not yet made; or different crops not yet sown or grown; or the sale of a mere contingency, like the *venditio spei* of the Romans. Under what class of these executory contracts, then, do the contracts on the Stock Exchange fall?

It is submitted that all the contracts of sale at the Stock Exchange are for a thing existing at the time of the formation of the contract.

The contracts of sale at the Stock Exchange are usually contracts for a future sale of bonds, shares of stock, and scrip. In the sale of bonds and shares of stock, little need be said, for it is obvious that in the case of a bond, the purchaser buys the present right in the vendor of an obligation to be paid money at a future certain day, and as soon as the bond or symbol of the vendor's title to such right is legally delivered to the purchaser, the contract between the parties is at an end. And so the sale of a share of stock, being executed, vests in the vendee the present right the vendor has of a share or proportion of the interest of the concerns of the company, and the contract, the sale being

---

[1] 9 Exch. 102; 5 H. L. C. 673.

legally completed, is then at an end, for there is no further contract of warranty. The only difficulty that could arise in the mind of any one is the contract for a sale of scrip, which some people have supposed to be a contract for a sale of a thing not *in esse*, being, as it is, a sale of a promise to deliver shares or bonds in the future. But this is very clearly a misapprehension of the meaning of the contract, and this is immediately seen, when it is considered *what* is sold. The company, in the first instance, only sell an existing right, or option, or promise, which becomes executed when it is sold and symbolically delivered; and subsequently the same is resold. No executory promise of the sub-vendor is made. He merely sells the interest or title he has in the promise made to him by the company; and, consequently, so soon as such vendor validly completes the sale by delivering up the symbol of the interest or title he has in such a promise, the contract, as between the vendor and vendee, is terminated. Of course the vendee is left to his rights at law or equity against the company, but, in the absence of a guaranty of the vendor, which is never given, he has none against the vendor. The vendor simply sells a promise made to him, and when he has completed the sale of it, has nothing more to do with it. The distinction between a sale of a thing *in esse*, and of a thing not *in esse*, is most important, because, in the former case, the seller of stock or scrip performs his contract by a legal delivery of the certificates or *indicia* of title, while in the latter, the sale could not be completed till the thing contracted for had sprung into existence, and had been delivered.

SECTION II.—THE MUTUAL ASSENT OF THE PARTIES TO THE CONTRACT.

<small>Mutual assent of the parties.</small>

The assent of the parties to the sale, that is to say, of the buyer and seller, must be mutual with regard to the terms of the contract of sale.

<small>The contract must be mutually formed.</small>

In the sales at the Stock Exchange, as in all others, there must be a mutual assent of the parties to the terms of the contract. With respect to contracts that are made by the members of a single Stock Exchange, where the stock brokers deal directly with one another, exchanging bought and sold notes, and, on some Exchanges, even inscribing the terms of each contract in an official registry kept for that purpose, there can be no great danger of the parties to the contract mistaking each other's intentions in regard to the sale; but where a stock broker is given an order to execute on a foreign Stock Exchange, which demands the employment of another stock broker living at a distance, and the necessity of communicating with him by letter or telegraph, the mutual intent of the parties to the contract may not be so clear, and we shall subjoin a few cases, to illustrate the questions that might arise in such cases, and the rulings of the courts upon them.

<small>Contracts effected through the agency of the post.</small>

With regard to contracts effected through the agency of the post-office, the general rule is, that the letter must be received and assent given to its contents before the bargain is struck. The assent may be express, or implied in various ways. The offer is kept open, however, or supposed to be constantly repeated, till the letter, or some other communication, arrives. If the letter is delayed by the sender's fault, the time is extended till its arrival, and the acceptance is complete on the posting of the second letter, notwithstanding delay, if the letter has been not wrongly addressed;[1] but the letter must be placed in the post-office within the proper time.[2]

In Trevor v. Wood,[3] the transmission of the letter was said to be sufficient to make a contract, because an overt act. *Trevor v. Wood.*

In Hallock v. Conn. Ins. Co.,[4] it was decided that the contract arises when any overt act takes place, which may be as various as the terms and form of contracts, and then the acceptor cannot overtake or countermand by telegraph his letter mailed.[5] *Hallock v. Conn. Ins. Co.*

In McCulloch v. Eagle Ins. Co.,[6] the letter recalling the offer to accept was written the day after the acceptance; the first contractor, before he got the second letter, but after the posting of it, agreed to go on, and it was held, no contract. But this is opposed to all the American and English authorities.[7] *McCulloch Eagle Ins. Co.*

In Dunmore v. Alexander,[8] the acceptance and retraction arrived at the same time: held, no contract. *Dunmore v. Alexander.*

Contracts may also be made through the agency of the telegraph, as well as that of the post. There is, however, a difference between the agency of the post-office and a telegraph company; for in the former case, the post is the common agent of both parties, standing *Contracts by telegraph.*

---

[1] Leake on Contracts, 18.
[2] Stockholm v. Ib., 32 Md. 196.
[3] 36 N. Y. 307.
[4] 2 Dutcher (N. J.), 268.
[5] See Henkel v. Pape, L. R., 6 Exch. 7; Leonard v. N. Y. Co., 41 N. Y. 544.
[6] 1 Pick. (Mass.) 288.
[7] Tayloe v. Fire Ins. Co., 9 Howard, 390.
[8] 9 Shaw & Dunlop, 190.

Trevor v. Wood.

in the same relation to each; but in the latter, the telegraph company is only the agent of the party employing him, and in order to make it a valid agency of communication between the parties, there would probably have to be an express or implied agreement by both the parties to the contract to that effect. It was held in Trevor *v.* Wood,[1] that the fact of one of the makers of the bargain using the telegraph raised an implication that that was to be the agency employed.

Mutual assent with reference to thing contracted for.

It is also necessary that the parties should mutually assent with respect to the thing contracted for, and whether there is such assent is a question for the jury.

Lambert v. Heath.

Thus, in Lambert *v.* Heath,[2] the plaintiff instructed his brokers to buy "Kent Coast Railway scrip," and they made a bargain for the purchase, but the scrip was repudiated by the company, who alleged it had been issued by the secretary without authority. In an action by the principal to recover what he had paid the stock brokers, it was held by the court, that the question for the jury was, whether this was the only scrip answering to that name on the market at that time, and not whether it was good scrip or not.

Mitchell v. Newhall.

So, in Mitchell *v.* Newhall,[3] where the stock broker, on being ordered to purchase fifty shares, purchased certain letters of allotment, that passed on the Stock Exchange as shares, there being no *shares* on the market, it was held, the jury might find this a good fulfilment of the contract, it being in evidence that these letters of allotment passed on the Stock Exchange as shares.

[1] 36 N. Y. 307.
[2] 15 M. & W. 486.
[3] 15 M. & W. 308.

In Tempest *v.* Kilner,[1] a contract for the sale of shares in a projected railway company was held to be satisfied by a tender of letters of allotment, where from the circumstances the jury might have inferred that the letters of allotment passed on the Stock Exchange as scrip, and, therefore, that the parties might reasonably have made the contract with reference to such letters, and that consequently there might be a breach of contract before a single share had been really issued.

Tempest v. Kilner.

SECTION III.—THE PRICE.

The agreement with respect to the price, also, must always be mutual, and, as we have already seen, the price of these securities must be money, and the stock broker has no authority to barter or exchange them.[2]

The price.

---

[1] 3 C. B. 249.
[2] Wiltshire *v.* Sims, 1 Campb. 258; Guerriere *v.* Peile, 3 B. & Ald. 616.

CHAPTER III.

EFFECT OF THE 17TH SECTION OF THE STATUTE OF FRAUDS ON THE CONTRACT.

	PAGE		PAGE
Introduction	194	AMERICA ARE GOODS, WARES, AND MERCHANDISES.	
Statute considered only with reference to Stock Exchange securities	195	Cases discussed	197
Division of chapter	195	SECTION III.—EARNEST, PAYMENT, AND ACCEPTANCE.	
SECTION I.—WHAT CONTRACTS ARE WITHIN THE 17TH SECTION.		Cases discussed	204
Stock Exchange securities not within the 17th section of the statute in England	196	SECTION IV.—WHAT IS A SUFFICIENT MEMORANDUM IN WRITING.	
		Cases discussed	205
Rule in America	196	SECTION V.—WHO IS AN AGENT DULY AUTHORIZED.	
SECTION II.—WHAT SECURITIES IN		Cases discussed	206

Statute of 29 Charles II. c. 3. VERBAL contracts for the sale of chattels were much modified by the passage of the statute of 29 Charles II. c. 3, commonly known as the Statute of Frauds, and frequently the question has arisen with regard to the sale of shares, etc., as to whether they are embraced within the 17th section of this statute. This point is especially important to determine, as the Statute of Frauds has not only been enacted in England, but substantially the same statute has also been enacted in the majority of the United States.

The 17th section of the English statute runs as follows:

CHAP. III.]   EFFECT OF STATUTE OF FRAUDS.   195

"And be it enacted, that from and after the said "four and twentieth day of January (A.D. 1677), no "contract for the sale of any goods, wares, or merchan- "dises, for the price of ten pounds sterling,[1] or up- "wards, shall be allowed to be good, except the buyer "shall accept part of the goods so sold, and actually "receive the same, or give something in earnest to bind "the bargain, or in part payment, or that some note or "memorandum in writing of the said bargain be made, "and signed by the parties to be charged by such "contract, or their agents thereunto lawfully author- "ized." *17th section of the Statute of Frauds.*

In our examination of the Statute of Frauds, we do not intend to consider it with reference to its effect on chattels generally, but we simply shall review those cases that have arisen on, and are peculiarly appropriate to, the securities sold at the Stock Exchange. *Statute of Frauds considered with reference to securities sold at the Stock Exchange.*

In our consideration of the statute, it will be convenient to see, *first*, what contracts in securities are within the 17th section; *secondly*, what securities are goods, merchandises, etc.; *thirdly*, what is earnest, payment, acceptance; *fourthly*, what is a sufficient memorandum or note; and, *fifthly*, who is an agent duly authorized. *Division of chapter.*

SECTION I.—WHAT CONTRACTS ARE WITHIN THE 17TH SECTION OF THE STATUTE.

The words of the statute, "contracts for the sale of "any goods," etc., have been variously interpreted in England, and indeed it is perhaps difficult to determine

---

[1] In New Hampshire the value is $33.33; in Maine, $30; in New York, Connecticut, and Massachusetts, and most of the other States where the statute exists, $50; in Vermont, $40. In Pennsylvania and Rhode Island this statute does not exist.

whether they refer to executed contracts of sale or those merely executory. The subject was, however, set at rest in England by the act of Lord Tenterden, known as the Act of 9 Geo. IV. c. 14, s. 7, to the effect that, "the "act shall extend to all contracts for the sale of goods "of the *value* of ten pounds sterling and upwards, not- "withstanding any goods may be intended to be de- "livered at some future time, or may not at the time "of such contract be actually made," etc., and it was decided that this section was to be construed as incorporated within the 17th section of the Statute of Frauds. As, however, the English courts in their later decisions have held, that the securities sold at the Stock Exchange are generally not within the meaning of the 17th section of the Statute of Frauds, it is not necessary to notice this last act further.

In America, where numerous judges have held that bonds, shares, etc., are within the purview of the 17th section of the statute, the courts seem to have reached the conclusion, that the words "contract for sale" mean an executed or executory contract.

In Mixer *v.* Howarth,[1] Shaw, C. J., said, "When "the contract is a contract of sale, either of an article "then existing, or of articles which the vendor usually "has for sale in the course of his business, the statute "applies to the contract, as well as where it is to be "executed at a future time, as where it is to be executed "immediately."

In Hight *v.* Ripley,[2] Shepley, J., said, "It may be "considered as now settled, that the Statute of Frauds

---

[1] 21 Pick. (Mass.) 205.   [2] 19 Maine, 137.

"embraces executory as well as executed contracts for "the sale of goods."[1]

In Johnson v. Mulry,[2] in New York, it was attempted to be shown in the argument that the words of a New York statute, to the effect that a contract for the sale of stock * * * "shall be void, or voidable, "for want of any consideration; or because the non-"payment of any consideration; or because the vendor "at the time of making such contract is not the owner "or possessor of the certificate, or certificates, or other "evidence of such debt, share, or interest," repealed the words of the Statute of Frauds, relative to having such a contract reduced to writing. But the court said, "The statute" (*i.e.*, the one relative to stock) "simply "provides that neither a written or verbal contract "shall be void," for certain reasons, and held, that it did not in any way abrogate the necessity of reducing a contract for the sale of stock to writing.

Johnson v. Mulry.

SECTION II.—WHAT SECURITIES ARE "GOODS, WARES, AND MERCHANDISES" WITHIN THE MEANING OF THE 17TH SECTION.

The decisions are conflicting, as to whether shares, bonds, etc., shall be considered as included within the meaning of the words "goods, wares, and merchan-"dises." We shall first give the English decisions, with those of the American that have adopted the view of the later English cases, and then the cases contra.

---

[1] See Sewall v. Fitch, 8 Cowen, 215; Edwards v. R. R. Co., 48 Maine, 379; Bennett v. Hull, 10 John. 364; Downes v. Ross, 23 Wend. 270; Lane v. Melville, 3 U. C. K. B. 124; Cason v. Cheely, 6 Georgia, 554; Pitkin v. Noyes, 48 N. H. 294.
[2] 4 Robertson, 401.

The earlier English cases were inclined to consider that the words "goods, wares, and merchandises" included shares and bonds, etc.

Mussell v. Cooke.

In Mussell *v.* Cooke[1] (A.D. 1720), A. agreed with the defendant's broker for £5000 of South Sea stock, and the broker, according to the usage, entered this agreement in his pocket-book. It was contended, that this stock was not within the meaning of the statute, as that, at its passing, there was no stock in being but East India stock, and that, for only about £300,000, and lodged in a few hands; and that anyhow this entry was sufficient, on account of the usage, and was also the same as if the party had made it. The Statute of Frauds was pleaded, and, though the case turned on the plea being not sufficient, the Lord Chancellor thought that the plea was well taken.

Crull v. Dodson.

In Crull *v.* Dodson,[2] also, where there was a transaction in South Sea stock, the court held the bargain to be within the statute.

Pickering v. Appleby.

In Pickering *v.* Appleby,[3] the court were equally divided on this subject, six of the judges holding one way, and six the other.

Colt v. Netterville.

In Colt *v.* Netterville,[4] the plea of the statute was overruled, the Chancellor saying that the act of 13 & 14 Car. II. cap. 24, declared that no one should be liable to bankruptcy in respect of their having East India stock, so that stocks, or the dealing in them, would not make a man liable to bankruptcy, nor did they seem to be "wares, goods, or merchandises" within the intent of that act; and, at all events, "the plea is not

---

[1] Precedents in Chancery, 533.
[2] Select Cases in Chancery, 41.
[3] 1 Com. Rep. 354.
[4] 2 P. W. [1725] 307.

"well pleaded, because the bill says that the plaintiff
"did pay 6d. as earnest, and the plea only says, that
"the defendant did not receive or accept it as earnest;
"now it is not material how or in what manner the
"defendant received or accepted it, but how the other
"paid it."

In Humble v. Mitchell,[1] with regard to this subject, Lord Denman, C. J., said, "It appears that no case has "been found directly in point; but it is contended "that the decisions upon reputed ownership are ap- "plicable, and that there is no material distinction be- "tween the words used in the Statute of Frauds, and in "the Bankrupt Act. I think that both the language "and the intentions of the two acts are distinguishable. "* * * Shares in a joint stock company like this are "mere choses in action, incapable of delivery, and not "within the scope of the seventeenth section. A con- "tract in writing was therefore unnecessary."

Humble v. Mitchell. Remarks of Lord Denman, C. J.

This decision was of shares in a joint stock com- pany, and the courts in England have applied its principle to other securities.

Thus, in Heseltine v. Siggers,[2] the court held, that certain Spanish stock or bonds were not within this statute.

Heseltine v. Siggers.

So it was held, in Tempest v. Kilner,[3] in Bowlby v. Bell,[4] in Bradley v. Holdsworth,[5] and in Duncuft v. Albrecht,[6] that a sale of railway shares was not within the meaning of the act.

Tempest v. Kilner. Bowlby v. Bell. Bradley v. Holdsworth. Duncuft v. Albrecht.

And in Watson v. Spratley[7] and Powell v. Jessop,[8]

Watson v. Spratley. Powell v. Jessop.

[1] 11 Ad. & El. 205.
[2] 1 Exch. 856.
[3] 3 C. B. 249.
[4] 3 C. B. 284.
[5] 3 M. & W. 422.
[6] 12 Simons, 189.
[7] 10 Exch. 222.
[8] 18 C. B. 336.

shares in a mining company, on the cost book principle, were held not within the act.

In England, therefore, the law may be considered as settled upon this subject.

In the United States, the different States do not appear to entertain harmonious views.

Beers v. Crowell.

In Beers *et al. v.* Crowell,[1] the court seemed to be inclined to follow the reasoning of the later English cases, and held, that at all events *Treasury cheques* were not within the meaning of the statute.

Vawter v. Griffen.

In Vawter *v.* Griffen *et al.*,[2] the Statute of Frauds of that State omitted the words "wares and merchandises" after the words "goods" of the English statute of Charles II., and the court said that the change in phraseology between the two sections made no difference in the legal effect, for the word "goods" would include "wares and merchandises," and that they would adopt the principles of the present English law, and held promissory notes not to be within the statute, and that, seemingly, bonds, stocks, and shares also were not.

Whittemore v. Gibbs.

In Whittemore *v.* Gibbs,[3] it was held, in New Hampshire, that a promissory note was not goods, wares, or merchandise within the statute.

The following States have laid down, or incline towards, a contrary principle.

Colvin v. Williams.

In Maryland, in Colvin *v.* Williams,[4] in 1810, the court held the sale of bank stock to be within the statute, but gave no opinion.

---

[1] Dudley (Ga.), 28; see, also, Weightman *v.* Caldwell, 4 Wheat. 89, note.
[2] 40 Indiana, 593.
[3] 4 Foster, 484.
[4] 3 H. & J. 38.

CHAP. III.]   EFFECT OF STATUTE OF FRAUDS.   201

In Tisdale *v.* Harris,[1] in 1838, the question came up before the Supreme Court of Massachusetts, as to whether a contract for the sale of shares in a manufacturing company was within the statute. The case was heard before the decision of Lord Tenterden, in Humble *v.* Mitchell, and the Chief Justice, Shaw, considered the question as unsettled in England, and quoted Mussell *v.* Cooke,[2] and Crull *v.* Dodson,[3] approvingly, as the "better opinion," but said, "Supposing this a "new question now for the first time calling for a con-"struction of the statute, the court are of opinion, that "as well as by its terms, as its general policy, stocks "are fairly within its operation. The words 'goods' "and 'merchandise' are both of very large significa-"tion. *Bond*, as used in the civil law, is almost as "extensive as personal property itself, and in many "respects it has nearly as large a signification in the "common law. The word 'merchandise,' also, in-"cluding in general objects of traffic and commerce, "is broad enough to include stocks or shares in incor-"porated companies. There are many cases, indeed, "in which it has been held in England, that buying "and selling stocks did not subject a person to the "operation of the bankrupt laws, and hence it has "been argued that they cannot be considered as mer-"chandise, because bankruptcy extends to persons "using the trade of merchandise. But it must be "recollected that the bankrupt acts were deemed to be "highly penal, and coercive, and tended to deprive a "man in trade of all his property. But most joint

Tisdale v. Harris.

[1] 20 Pick. 9.   [2] Prec. in Ch. 533.
[3] Sel. Cas. in Ch. 41.

"stock companies were founded on the hypothesis, at least, that most of the shareholders took shares as an investment, and not as an object of traffic. * * * These cases, therefore, do not bear much on the general question. The main argument relied upon by those who contend that shares are not within the statute is this, that the statute provides that such contract shall not be good, etc., among other things, except the purchaser shall accept part of the goods. From this it is argued, that, by necessary implication, the statute applies only to goods, of which part may be delivered. This seems, however, to be rather a narrow and forced construction. The provision is general, that no contract for the sale of goods, etc., shall be allowed to be good. The exception is when part are delivered; but if part cannot be delivered, then the exception cannot exist to take the case out of the general doctrine. * * * There is nothing in the nature of stocks or shares in companies, which in reason or sound policy should exempt contracts in respect to them from those reasonable restrictions, designed by the statute to prevent frauds in the sale of other commodities. On the contrary, these companies have become so numerous, so large an amount of the property of the community is now invested in them, and as the ordinary of property, arising from delivery and possession, cannot take place, there seems to be peculiar reason for extending the provisions of this statute to them."

Somerby v. Bunting.

In Somerby *v.* Bunting,[1] the court considered the law in Massachusetts settled, but said, "the words of

[1] 118 Mass. 285 [1874].

CHAP. III.]   EFFECT OF STATUTE OF FRAUDS.   203

"the statute have never yet been extended by any "court beyond securities which are subjects of common "sale and barter, and which have a visible and palpa- "ble form;" and held an oral agreement for the sale of an interest in a patent, before letters were obtained, not to be a contract for the sale of "goods, wares, and "merchandise."

In Alabama,[1] a case arose, in which the Statute of Frauds was involved; the question apparently being whether a promissory note fell within it, being under $200. But the report is nearly unintelligible.

Case in Alabama.

In Connecticut, in North v. Forrest,[2] the question was, whether a discharge from a contract for the sale of stock which had not been in writing, was a sufficient consideration to support a new contract, and the court held, that as the first contract was within the statute, it was a nullity, and was not a good consideration for the second promise.

North v. Forrest.

In Ins. Co. v. Cole,[3] in Florida, the statute included the words "personal property," as well as "goods, "wares, and merchandise," and the court held that the former words included shares of stock, but thought that the latter words did not, following the later English cases.

Ins. Co. v. Cole.

In Pray v. Mitchell,[4] in Maine, the doctrine of Tisdale v. Harris[5] was followed.

Pray v. Mitchell.

In Mississippi, the words "personal property" are included in the act.

In New York,[6] the statute reads "goods, chattels,

---

[1] 29 Ala. 294.
[2] 15 Conn. 400.
[3] 4 Florida, 359.
[4] 60 Maine, 480.
[5] 20 Pick. 9.
[6] 4 Robertson, 401.

and things in action," and shares of stock are considered as included within the act.

Case in Vermont.

In Vermont,[1] apparently, shares of stock come within the purview of the Statute of Frauds.

Riggs v. Macgruder.

In the Federal Court, in Riggs v. Macgruder,[2] in the Circuit Court of the United States, Thurston, J., held, that the sale of notes of a private bank was within the Statute of Frauds.

SECTION III.—EARNEST, PAYMENT, AND ACCEPTANCE.

Tisdale v. Harris.

In Tisdale v. Harris,[3] it was contended by counsel, there was a part performance and part payment, but the court said that, as these occurred since the action had been brought, they could not be relied on to show a cause of action when the action was commenced.

Gooch v. Holmes.

In Gooch v. Holmes,[4] A. agreed with B. to pay him a certain amount for a quantity of bank bills, which were then in C.'s hands subject to D.'s order, and B. procured and delivered to A. the order of D. on C. for the bills. A. got the order, but never presented it, nor received the bills, and the court held, this was not an executed sale, but a contract of sale within the statute. Hathaway, J., said, that the evidence in the case failed to prove a sale and delivery. "According "to the facts presented, the whole matter remained in "contract. It was something *to be* done; nothing was "completed; the bills might have been taken on ex-"ecution as the plaintiff's property. * * * They might "have been presented to the bank and redeemed; they "might have been stolen, or lost, or destroyed, before

---

[1] Fay v. Wheeler, 44 Vt. 292.
[2] 2 Cranch, R. U. S. C. C. 143.
[3] 20 Pick. 9.
[4] 41 Maine, 523.

CHAP. III.]   EFFECT OF STATUTE OF FRAUDS.   205

"the defendant could have presented the order, or
"before he received it."

SECTION IV.—WHAT IS A SUFFICIENT MEMORANDUM
IN WRITING.

In Mussell v. Cooke,[1] A. agreed with B.'s broker for £5000 South Sea stock, and the broker, according to the usage, entered the agreement in his pocket-book. The case turned on the sufficiency of the plea, but the Chancellor thought the memorandum not sufficient within the statute.   *Mussell v. Cooke.*

In Crull v. Dodson,[2] the defendant, a broker, having stock of the plaintiff, was told to sell, when it reached 200, and the broker told the plaintiff he had sold to several parties at that price, and showed entries in his books which looked as if made at a subsequent period, after a rise in the stock. "The court was of opinion "it was a fraudulent transaction, and that on the sale, "if such there was, he should have taken earnest; for "it has been determined here that such a bargain is "within the Statute of Frauds, and without earnest, "only *nudum pactum*."   *Crull v. Dodson.*

In Tisdale v. Harris,[3] the defendant had agreed verbally to transfer shares in a company to the plaintiff, and wrote a letter to an agent to make the transfer to the plaintiff's name, and transmit the certificates to the defendant. The plaintiff's agent signed a memorandum agreeing to pay when the defendant should furnish the certificates. It was held by the court, that the contract was not in writing on the defendant's part.   *Tisdale v. Harris.*

[1] Prec. in Ch. 533. [2] Sel. Cas. in Ch. 41.
[3] 20 Pick. (Mass.) 9.

SECTION V.—WHO IS AN AGENT DULY AUTHORIZED.

Johnson v. Mulry.

In Johnson *v.* Mulry,[1] it was held, that an entry made by the clerk of one of the parties in a book, which the defendant, on seeing, pronounced all right, but which neither party signed, was not sufficient to satisfy the provisions of the statute.

Henderson v. Barnewell.

In Henderson *v.* Barnewell,[2] the parties contracted in presence of the broker's clerk, who brought them together on the Exchange, and one, in the hearing of the other, dictated the terms of the agreement; and it was held in the Court of the Exchequer, that the agency of the clerk was personal, and that neither an entry in the broker's books nor a note signed by him was sufficient, since the agency was personal.

[1] 4 Robertson (N. Y.), 401.   [2] 1 Y. & J. 387.

CHAPTER IV.

EFFECT OF THE STATUTE OF MORTMAIN ON THE CONTRACT.

	PAGE		PAGE
The question in England	207	Rule of Parke, B., in Watson v. Spratley	211
Review of authorities	207	Rule of Sir John Romilly in Norris v. Glynn not followed	212
Rule of Lord St. Leonards in Myer v. Perigal	209		
Rule of Knight Bruce, V. C., in Ashton v. Lord Langdale	210	Rule of Page Wood, V. C., in Entwhistle v. Davis	212

THE question has often been raised in England whether shares of stock fall within the meaning of the Statute of Mortmain.

In Tomlinson *v.* Tomlinson,[1] in 1823, a testator directed certain canal shares to be transferred to certain charitable uses. The shares had been declared to be personal estate by Act of Parliament, and transmissible as such, and Sir John Leach held the charitable bequests of the testator void, and contrary to the Mortmain Act. No opinion in this case is reported.

Tomlinson v. Tomlinson.

In Sparling *v.* Parker,[2] the question was, whether shares in a gas-light and a dock company, which possessed land for the purposes of their undertaking, were within the Mortmain Act of George II., and the court held, they were not. Lord Langdale, M. R., said, "A " shareholder in one of these companies, whether incor- " porated or not, has a right to receive the dividends " payable on his share ; *i.e.*, a right to his just propor-

Sparling v. Parker.

Remarks of Lord Langdale, M. R.

---
[1] 9 Beavan, 459. [2] 9 Beavan, 450.

"tiôn of the profits arising from the employment of
"the joint stock, consisting partly of land; and he has
"a right to assign his share for value; but whilst he
"continues to hold his shares, he has no interest or
"separate right to the land, or any part of it. He is,
"indeed, interested in the employment of the land,
"but he cannot proceed against the land directly, for
"anything which is due him, or make any part of
"the land his own, for the purpose of satisfying any
"demand which he may have as shareholder. He is
"not in the situation of a mortgagee, who has a direct
"interest in the land, which he can make absolutely
"his own by foreclosure, or of a tenant in common, or
"joint tenant, who may make a part of it his own in
"severalty; and if, upon a dissolution or determination
"of the joint concern, he can become an owner of any
"part of the land, it is only upon a new transaction,
"and by acquiring a new title as purchaser. Upon his
"death, nothing descends upon his heir, and his legal
"personal representatives do not acquire any share or
"interest in the land different from that which the
"shareholder possessed. * * * But no case has deter-
"mined, that such as those now in question are within
"the meaning of the act; and on the whole I am of
"opinion that a shareholder in such joint stock com-
"panies as those which are now under my considera-
"tion, is not, in that character or right, entitled to any
"such estate or interest in land, as falls within the
"true intent and meaning and the operation of the
"Mortmain Act of George II."

It is to be noted that, in this case, Lord Langdale said there was no case the other way. Tomlinson *v.*

Tomlinson, the preceding case, was not referred to, and we believe was not at that time reported.

In Walker *v.* Milne,[1] Lord Langdale again laid down the same principles, and even went further, holding that dock and canal shares and bonds secured by an assignment of the rates were not an interest in land within the Statute of Mortmain. He said, that in the decision of the preceding case, he had not been aware of the decision of Sir John Leach in Tomlinson *v.* Tomlinson, but doubted whether that fact would have altered his opinion.

Walker v. Milne.

Tomlinson v. Tomlinson.

In the well-known case of Myers *v.* Perigal,[2] it was held, that a bequest of shares in a bank stock, whose assets, by its deed of settlement, were deemed personal estate, and consisted of freehold and copyhold estates, and money lent on such estates and leasehold hereditaments, was not within the meaning of the Statute of Mortmain.

Myers v. Perigal.

The Lord Chancellor St. Leonards said, "There is " no doubt, that wherever anything savoring of realty " in a will is given to a charity, the legacy is within " the prohibition of the Statute of Mortmain. * * * " The true way to test it would be, to assume that there " is real estate of the company vested in the proper " persons under the provisions of the partnership deed. " Could any of the partners enter upon the lands, or " claim any portion of the real estate for his purpose ? " Or if there was a house upon the land, could any two " or more of the members enter into the occupation of " such house ? I apprehend they clearly could not; " they would have no right to step upon the land ; their

Remarks of Lord St. Leonards.

[1] 11 Beavan, 507. [2] 2 De G. M. & G. 599.

"whole interest in the property of the company is with reference to the shares bought which represent their proportions of the profits. No encumbrancer of any individual member of the company would have any such right. In short, a member has no higher interest in the real estate of the company than that of an ordinary partner seeking his share of the profits out of whatever property those profits might be found to have resulted. If he die at one particular time, he will leave the same interest in the partnership property, although they may consist of real estate at one period and not at another. The quality of the partnership property can neither alter its destination, nor the quantum of a member's interest. Upon all principles, therefore, I think it is perfectly clear that this bequest is not within the statute."

Ashton v. Lord Langdale. In Ashton *v.* Lord Langdale,[1] the same principles were laid down with reference to railway and canal shares, scrip and debentures, not mortgages; but *contra*, as respects mortgages of such companies.

Remarks of Knight Bruce, V. C. The Vice-Chancellor, Knight Bruce, said, "With regard to the mortgages of the undertakings and of the tolls, these interests proceed directly from the corporation, and appear to me to constitute a 'charge or encumbrance affecting lands, tenements, or other hereditaments,' or some estate or interest therein.

"In my opinion they do directly and immediately charge hereditaments, viz., the tolls, if not the land itself, by use of which the tolls are obtained; and if so, they are within the words of the 3d section of the act;" and he said he must overrule the opinion of the

[1] 4 De G. & Sm. 402.

CHAP. IV.] EFFECT OF MORTMAIN ON CONTRACT. 211

Master of the Rolls (Lord Langdale) in Walker *v.* Milne. *(Walker v. Milne overruled.)*

In Morris *v.* Glynn[1] (1859), Sir John Romilly, M.R., held, that shares in the Rhymney Iron Company, formed for the purpose of manufacturing iron, obtained from its own estates, were an interest in land within the act. The Master of the Rolls drew a distinction between the case where the object of the partnership was a dealing with the land itself, and where it deals with other matters, to accomplish which land is held by it, but merely as an accessory to it. But it is doubtful whether his decision is a sound one, or the distinction at all valuable, as the real distinction, evidently, is, whether any shareholder has an interest in any *aliquot portion of the land, or merely in the profits* arising from the land. *(Morris v. Glynn. Rule of Sir John Romilly, M.R. Rule doubtful.)*

Thus, in Watson *v.* Spratley,[2] Baron Parke said, "If the purser of the mine, who had himself the let or "grant of the mine, had the mine, and the machines "and plant, vested in him, in trust to employ the ma- "chinery in working the mine and making the most "profit of it, for the benefit of the coadventurers, who "were to share the profit only, such interest was trans- "ferable by parol, and might be bargained for by "parol. *(Watson v. Spratley. Remarks of Baron Parke.)*

"If he held the mine in trust for himself and the "coadventurers present and future in proportion to "their number of shares, then there was a direct trust "in the realty; for the right to get the minerals was "a real right, and could not be granted without deed, "etc."

---

[1] 27 Beavan, 218. [2] Page 214, *infra.*

The rule laid down by Sir John Romilly is thus seen to be evidently untenable, and was deviated from by Lord Hatherley (then Vice-Chancellor Page Wood) in the following recent case of Entwhistle *v.* Davis[1] (1867). Here, shares in the British Land Company, whose business was to purchase and improve lands, selling and letting them, and in the National Freehold Land Society, established for "raising by subscription "a fund out of which any member should receive the "amount of his share for the erection or purchase of "a dwelling-house, or alter real or leasehold estate," were held not to be within the purview of the mortmain statute of 9 George II. c. 36.

Entwhistle v. Davis.

The Vice-Chancellor, Page Wood, said that he felt compelled to differ from the conclusion reached by the Master of the Rolls in Morris *v.* Glynn,[2] and thought that, as in the case at bar, the shareholders only took the money arising from the profits of the land, and had no direct interest in them further than this, and since there was not a word in the charter of either company giving any shareholder an *aliquot* portion of land, but merely profits, the shares were not within the contemplation of the act.

Rule of Sir John Romilly in Morris v. Glynn not followed.

In Durkee *v.* Stringham,[3] certain parties associated themselves together for the purpose of raising money to be employed for the benefit of the members, in purchasing land, building mills, etc. It was provided in the articles of association that the shares should be transferable by assignment, and should be treated as personalty, and the court held, that each share in such

Durkee v. Stringham.

---

[1] L. R., 4 Eq. Cas. 272.
[2] 27 Beav. 218.
[3] 8 Wisc. 1.

CHAP. IV.] EFFECT OF MORTMAIN ON CONTRACT. 213

a company was an interest in land, but cited no cases in support of its opinion, nor, indeed, did it endeavor at any length to reason the matter out.

The decisions, as will be seen, are somewhat at variance. But we think the reasoning of Lord St. Leonards, in Myers *v.* Perigal, of the Vice-Chancellor, Knight Bruce, in Ashton *v.* Lord Langdale, and of Page Wood, V. C., in Entwhistle *v.* Davis, conclusive, and the rule laid down by Parke, B., in Watson *v.* Spratley, the correct test for these cases.[1]

Myers *v.* Perigal.
Ashton *v.* Langdale.
Entwhistle *v.* Davis.
Watson *v.* Spratley.

[1] See, also, Morrow *v.* Brenizer, 2 Rawle (Pa.), 188; Allison *v.* Wilson's Ex., 13 S. & R. (Pa.) 330; 1 Cramer *v.* Arthurs, 7 Barr, 165; Marsh *v.* Atty. Genl., 2 Johns. & H. 61; Taylor *v.* Linley, 1 Giffard, 67; Edwards *v.* Hall, 6 De G. M. & G. 74; Alexander *v.* Brame, 30 Beav. 153.

CHAPTER V.

EFFECT OF THE 4TH SECTION OF THE STATUTE OF FRAUDS ON THE CONTRACT.

	PAGE		PAGE
Rule settled by cases under former chapter	214	Watson v. Spratley	214

IT would be useless to consider at length, whether the securities sold at the Stock Exchange are an interest in land within the meaning of the 4th section of the Statute of Frauds, as the question is substantially set at rest by the decisions in the preceding cases.

Watson v. Spratley.

We shall, however, refer our readers to the case of Watson v. Spratley,[1] where the question was argued at considerable length, and where it was determined that shares of stock were not an interest in land; Martin, B., giving an elaborate opinion, in which Parke, Alderson, and Platt, BB., concurred.

[1] 10 Exch. 221.

CHAPTER VI.

EFFECT OF THE USAGE OF TRADE ON THE CONTRACT.

	PAGE		PAGE
Customer bound by valid rules of the Stock Exchange	215	Hodgkinson v. Kelly	218
Duncan v. Hill	215	After-made rule not binding	225
Sutton v. Tatham	216	Westropp v. Solomon	225
Semble, principal need know of the existence of the rule	217	Distinction between rules binding on non-members and binding on members	226
Illustrations of valid rules	217	Illustrations of invalid rules	227

THE contracts on the Stock Exchange are, like any other contracts, made subject to the peculiar valid and reasonable usages of the trade, and rules of that institution, existing at the time of the formation of the contract. These usages and rules are very numerous, and the following cases are illustrations of what the courts have held to be valid and reasonable rules and customs, and what have been considered not to be, in transactions between non-members dealing with stock brokers. *{Contracts on the Stock Exchange made subject to the usages of the trade.}*

In Duncan v. Hill,[1] the broker had become insolvent, and, by a usage of the Exchange, his accounts were closed on the quotations of that day, and it was found that his principal was indebted to him, for which debt he brought suit. Blackburn, J., said, that " for " any loss incurred by the agent, by reason of his " having entered into such contracts, according to " such rules, unless they be wholly unreasonable, and *{Duncan v. Hill. Remarks of Blackburn, J.}*

[1] L. R., 8 Ex. 242, reversing case in L. R., 6 Ex. 255; and Nicholson v. Gooch, 5 Ellis & Blackburn, 999. See, also, Evans v. Wister, 1 Weekly Notes, 181.

"where the default is without any personal fault of
"his own, he is entitled to be indemnified by his prin-
"cipal upon an implied contract to that effect. But it
"is argued that where the agent, as in this case, is
"subjected to loss, not by reason of his having en-
"tered into contracts into which he was authorized
"to enter by his principal, but by reason of a default
"of his own,—that is to say, as in this case, by reason
"of his insolvency, brought on by want of means to
"meet his other pecuniary obligations,—it cannot be
"said that he has suffered loss by reason of his having
"entered into the contracts made by him on behalf of
"his principal; and consequently there can be no
"promise which can be implied on the part of his
"principal to indemnify him, and in the present case
"there certainly was no express promise to that effect.
"* * * The plaintiffs' insolvency was, so far as regards
"the defendant, entirely the result of their own default.
"We think there is no implication of law to force upon
"the defendant an obligation to indemnify the plaintiffs
"in such a case."

Sutton v. Tatham.

In Sutton *v.* Tatham,[1] a person employing a broker to sell shares, directed him, by mistake, to sell two hundred and fifty instead of fifty, and the broker contracted with another broker for the sale. Subsequently the shareholder, discovering his error, asked the broker if he could rectify it, but was told it was too late. By the rules of the Stock Exchange, in transactions of this kind no principal is named, and if the vendor does not complete his contract by a delivery, the purchaser may buy the requisite number of shares, and hold

[1] 10 Adolphus & Ellis, 27 [1839].

CHAP. VI.] EFFECT OF USAGE OF TRADE ON CONTRACT. 217

the vendor liable for the loss if he sustains any. The shareholder's broker paid the loss the purchaser had sustained, and sued the vendor for the loss. Held, that he could recover. Lord Denman, C. J., said that if a person employed one who was notoriously a broker, he must be taken to authorize his acting in obedience to the known usages of the Stock Exchange. Littledale, Patteson, and Coleridge, JJ., concurred.

In Johnston *v.* Usborne,[1] the defendant, a corn merchant in Ireland, instructed his factor and *del credere* agent in London to sell oats of a certain quality on the defendant's account, and the factor sold them in his own name, but, proving of an inferior quality, he was compelled to pay the difference to the vendee. In an action against the vendor to recover the difference, the defendant objecting to the broker's having sold in his own name, and so incurred the liability, it was held, that a custom of London, to show that a factor was warranted by such instructions to sell in his own name, was admissible in evidence.

Johnston v. Usborne.

In Stewart *v.* Cauty,[2] in an action for the non-acceptance of railway shares, which by the contract (made at Liverpool through brokers) were to be delivered in a reasonable time, a written rule of the Liverpool Stock Exchange, stated to be acted upon by all Liverpool brokers, to the effect that "the seller of "shares was in all cases entitled to seven days to com-"plete his contract by delivery, the time to be com-"puted from the day on which he was acquainted with "the name of his transferee," was held admissible, on an issue, whether the plaintiff within a reasonable time

Stewart v. Cauty.

[1] 11 Adolphus & Ellis, 549 [1841].   [2] 8 M. & W. 160.

was ready to make the transfer; though it was not in evidence that either of the principals or their brokers were members of the Liverpool Stock Exchange.

Mitchell v. Newhall.

In Mitchell *v.* Newhall,[1] the plaintiff, a broker on the Stock Exchange, received an order to purchase fifty shares in a foreign railway company. At the time no shares were in the market, it not being yet established, but letters of allotment for the shares being then on the market, which were commonly bought and sold on the market as shares, the plaintiff bought a letter of allotment for fifty shares; and it was held, that it was competent for the jury to find this a good execution of the order.

Bayley v. Wilkins.

In Bayley *v.* Wilkins,[2] A. employed a broker, a member of the Exchange, to buy shares for him. At the time of the purchase, a call had been made on the shares, but was not then payable. The seller paid the call to enable the transfer to be made, and the broker, who by the rules of the Stock Exchange was personally responsible for it, paid the money. Held, that the broker could recover from A. the sum so paid.

Hodgkinson v. Kelly.

In Hodgkinson *v.* Kelly,[3] A. bought through a broker, of a jobber, on the Stock Exchange, certain shares, and subsequently B. sold to another jobber, shares in the same company at a lower price for the same settling day. The company stopped payment in the mean time. On the name day, according to the usage of the Stock Exchange, the name of A. was given to B. as the purchaser of B.'s shares, and B. executed a transfer of the shares to A., and delivered it

---

[1] 15 Meeson & Wellsby, 308 [1848].
[2] 18 L. J., C. P. 273; 7 C. B. 886.
[3] L. R., 6 Eq. Cas. 496.

with the certificates to A.'s broker, who paid him the price for which B. purchased at, and A. subsequently repaid his broker and took the certificates and transfer, but did not execute the transfer, and never had it registered. Owing to the insolvency of the company, B. was compelled to pay calls, and brought an action against A. to recover the money so paid. On behalf of B. it was contended that he was not liable, as he had never accepted B. as his vendor, and had, therefore, no contractual relation with him, but that his name was given to B. by a custom of the Stock Exchange, which it was not proved he was aware of. The court, however, held, that the acceptance of the certificates of the shares and the transfers was an acceptance of the contract, and that A. was liable to indemnify B. against all the consequences springing from the ownership of the shares.

The opinion of the Master of the Rolls, Lord Romilly, in this case is an instructive statement of the law on this peculiar method of dealing at the Stock Exchange of London, and we shall quote certain passages.

"When a man," said he, "sells or buys shares "through his broker on the Stock Exchange, he enters "into an implied contract to sell or buy according to "the custom and usages prevalent in that body. For "instance, in this case, it was strongly argued that "there was no privity between the plaintiff and the de- "fendant, that they personally entered into no contract "with each other, and that neither authorized any agent "to enter into a contract with the other. The Stock "Exchange, with its ramifications, is the only body

Opinion of Lord Romilly, M.R.

"through which stock, shares, and the like, can be
"bought or sold by the public. No doubt A. may
"enter into a contract with B. to sell shares to him
"without the intervention of the Stock Exchange, but
"such transactions are of very rare occurrence, nor do
"I remember to have met with one which has been
"made the subject of any decision in any court of law
"or equity. The invariable, or almost invariable,
"practice is, to buy and sell through the medium of
"the Stock Exchange; and unless the shares can be
"so bought and sold, they are not considered to be in
"the market. The question, then, is, what is the nature
"of the contract, which a man enters into, when he
"directs shares to be bought or sold through the in-
"strumentality of the Stock Exchange? The answer,
"in my opinion, is a very plain and obvious one: he
"undertakes to buy and sell according to the practice
"and usage of the Stock Exchange, assuming of course
"such practice and usage not to be illegal. That prac-
"tice and usage may, I believe, be stated to be gener-
"ally to this effect: The broker instructed to buy shares
"enters into a contract with a jobber, who undertakes
"to deliver, on a particular day, a certain number of
"shares, at a specified price; the jobber then buys those
"shares at any price he pleases from another broker,
"who is instructed to sell shares, and this other broker
"contracts to deliver these on the day specified; when
"the day arrives, the names of the seller and purchaser
"are exchanged, an instrument of transfer is presented
"to the person who instructed the broker to buy, who
"accepts the shares, and thereupon the transaction, as
"between the seller and the buyer, is complete; while it

CHAP. VI.] EFFECT OF USAGE OF TRADE ON CONTRACT. 221

"is in progress the broker is liable to the seller to pay
"him the price at which the shares were sold to the
"jobber, the jobber is liable to pay that price to the
"broker, and, on the other hand, the broker instructed
"to buy the shares is liable to pay the jobber, and the
"person who instructed the broker to buy is liable to
"pay him the price for which he agreed to purchase
"the shares from the jobber; when the day arrives and
"the names are exchanged, all the prior steps and lia-
"bilities are overlooked, and the seller of the shares
"transfers them to the buyer, and the money is paid.
"I can see nothing illegal or immoral in the trans-
"action; it is the regular recognized course; it is what
"all persons who have recourse to the Stock Exchange
"submit to; they enter into a contract, not with a
"specified person, but with a person whose name is to
"be disclosed afterwards when the transaction is com-
"plete. It is not, as has been supposed, that the seller
"of the shares constitutes an agent to find out, and
"enter into a contract with, some particular buyer, or,
"on the other hand, that the buyer does the same as
"to the seller, but both parties agree to be bound by
"the usage of the Stock Exchange, which binds both
"parties from the beginning, but which leaves each of
"the parties to the eventual contract, ignorant of the
"other, till the day arrives, and the instrument of
"transfer is executed. It was put in the argument, as
"resembling a contract by which A. sells to B., B. to
"C., C. to D., and D. to E., and at the request of B.,
"C., and D., A. executes the transfer to E.; but, in
"truth, this does not appear to me to put the case suf-
"ficiently high; it is, in my opinion, an engagement

"entered into by A. on one side, and E. on the other, that through the instrumentality of certain other persons, whoever they may be, certain shares shall be sold and bought, and they undertake to complete the contract with the other person, whoever he may be, who buys on one hand and sells on the other. It is a transaction regulated by a particular practice, having reference to contracts of this description only, a practice long subsisting, recognized by courts of law, of which all parties are cognizant, and from which neither party can recede. It is obvious, also, that it is founded on common sense and common honesty, for it is of no sort of importance to A. to know, to whom his shares are transferred, nor is it to B., to know from whence the shares come. It is a machinery by which A. sells to B., and they are, in fact, in law and equity, the ultimate contracting parties. When, therefore, the transaction is complete, the necessary consequences flow from it, of which one is, that the buyer must indemnify the seller from all the consequences flowing from the ownership of the shares subsequent to the transfer." His lordship referred approvingly to Sheppard v. Murphy,[1] and Grissell v. Bristowe,[2] and Hawkins v. Maltby.[3]

Sheppard v. Murphy, Grissell v. Bristowe, Hawkins v. Maltby, approved.

Coles v. Bristowe.

In Coles v. Bristowe,[4] the plaintiff contracted by his broker, on the Stock Exchange, for the sale of shares in a company to the defendants, who were jobbers for a future day, called settling day. The jobbers, on name day, before the settling day, in ac-

---

[1] 1 Ir. Rep., Eq. 490; 16 W. R. 948.
[2] L. R., 3 C. P. 112.
[3] L. R., 3 Ch. App. 188.
[4] L. R., 4 Ch., App. 3.

CHAP. VI.] EFFECT OF USAGE OF TRADE ON CONTRACT. 223

cordance with a custom of the Stock Exchange, gave to the vendor's broker the names of several different persons, as ultimate purchasers, to whom the shares were transferred in different parcels. The brokers of the vendor had deeds of transfer executed by him, and on settling day handed them with the certificates to the jobbers, who then paid the price agreed upon. In the mean time the company had stopped payment. The several transferees had, through their brokers, paid up the purchase money to the jobbers, but had not yet received the deeds of transfer, and the plaintiff, whose name remained on the list of shareholders, was obliged to pay calls on the shares. On a bill filed against the jobbers for an indemnity, the court held, that the contract must be interpreted by the rules of the Stock Exchange, and that after the jobbers had paid to the vendor his purchase money, and given the names of the transferees to the vendor, who had executed transfers which the transferees' brokers had received, the liability of the jobbers was at an end.

In Maxted v. Paine,[1] the plaintiff sold through his brokers on the Stock Exchange, *inter alia*, ten shares in Overend, Gurney & Co., Limited, to the defendant, a jobber, who, on the "name day," passed a ticket to the plaintiff's broker having the name of one Goss as ultimate buyer. No objection being made to the name, the plaintiff executed a transfer to Goss of the shares, but the transfer was not registered, and the plaintiff's name remained on the books as shareholder. Subsequently, it was found that the brokers named on the ticket as Goss's brokers had been instructed to buy

Maxted v. Paine.

[1] L. R., 6 Ex. 132 [1871].

by one Spry, and had, in fact, largely bought for Spry, as undisclosed principal, and the ten shares had been delivered to them as part purchases, but Goss's name had been passed in pursuance of Spry's instructions, and by an arrangement through which Goss, who was a "straw man," allowed his name to be used. The purchasing brokers, as well as the defendant, were ignorant of the arrangement; but no objection was taken to the name within the time limited by the rules of the Exchange therefor. The plaintiff was compelled to pay calls, and, being unable to recover from Goss, he proceeded against the defendant. The court held the action not to be maintainable, it being obvious that everything had been done for completing the transfer, so far as the defendant was concerned, according to the rules of the Stock Exchange. Lord Blackburn said that in the present case, since the defendant had completely fulfilled his contract by passing a name in on the name day, really issued by a member of the Stock Exchange, he was not liable for any mistake or misconduct on the part of the issuers of the ticket, not having been applied to within the time limited by the rules therefor. Cockburn, C. J., thought that, as Goss was the ultimate purchaser within the meaning of that term as applied on the Stock Exchange, the question was no longer an open one.

Bayliffe v. Butterworth.

In Bayliffe v. Butterworth,[1] the defendant, who resided at some distance from Liverpool, authorized the plaintiff, a broker there, to sell for him certain scrip shares. The plaintiff sold them to C., another

[1] 1 Exch. 425.

CHAP. VI.] EFFECT OF USAGE OF TRADE ON CONTRACT. 225

Liverpool broker, who, the shares not being delivered on the day agreed on, bought others at the market price, and claimed the difference between the contract price and the market price. The plaintiff, having paid this difference, brought an action to recover it. On the trial it was proved to be the usage at Liverpool for the brokers to be responsible to each other on these contracts, and that the plaintiff knew of the usage. The court held the defendant was liable; and *semble* by Parke and Rolfe, BB., that it was immaterial whether the plaintiff was aware of the usage or not.[1] *Semble*, it is immaterial whether principal is aware of usage or not.

In Markham v. Jaudon,[2] plaintiff employed defendants to purchase stocks for him upon margin, he agreeing that all transactions in stocks should be in every way subject to the usages of defendants' office. In an action for a conversion by an alleged sale, without notice, of the stocks purchased, defendants offered to prove that it was the custom of their office to sell, on account of failure to furnish margin, at the Stock Exchange without giving notice to the customer of the time and place of sale, and the court on appeal held, overruling the court below, that such evidence was admissible, as such an agreement was not opposed to public policy. Markham v. Jaudon.

But if the rule of the Stock Exchange be not an existing one, at the time the contract is entered upon, it is not binding on non-members. Rule not binding if made after the contract.

Thus, in Westropp v. Solomon,[3] A. employed B., a broker and member of the Exchange, to sell for him certain paper purporting to be scrip in a projected Westropp v. Solomon.

---

[1] See Sutton v. Tatham, 10 A. & E. 549.
[2] 41 N. Y. 285.
[3] 8 C. B. 845.

15

railway company; subsequently B. sold these certificates of scrip to C. and handed over the proceeds to A. It was then found that the scrip was forged, and B. was called upon, pursuant to a resolution of the Stock Exchange, then passed, to pay C. on an agreed-upon value for the scrip. In an action against A. by B., the court held, *inter alia*, that A. was not bound by the terms of a resolution that was passed after the formation of the contract, however such a resolution might bind a member.

Distinction between rules binding on members and non-members.

The preceding case suggests the distinction between rules that may be binding on members alone, and those that may be binding on members and on non-members alike. A rule to be binding on a non-member must be such a one as is reasonable, though he might be bound, whether he was aware of its existence or not; but a rule can never be reasonable that violates any right the law gives him, or that in any way tends to violate the obligation of his contract. Thus, as was held in the preceding case, it is obvious that an after-made rule can never bind a non-member, for he can never know how he is contracting, though such a rule might very well bind a member, who must respect all the laws of the association he is a member of. The foregoing case is a good illustration of this principle, and the reader is also referred to the case of Tompkins *v.* Safferty, quoted on page 68, as another excellent example.

The following cases are examples of rules and customs which have been considered as violating the requirements of public policy and morality, and unreasonable with regard to a non-member.

CHAP. VI.]   EFFECT OF USAGE OF TRADE ON CONTRACT.   227

In Shaw *v.* Spencer,[1] a certificate of shares of stock standing in the name of A., as trustee, was pledged to secure his own debt, and the court held, that the pledgee was put on his inquiry by the notice of the trust, as the trustee had *prima facie* no right to pledge thus for his own debt. Evidence was offered of the existence of a custom that it was common to issue certificates of stock in the name of one as trustee, when there was in reality no trust, and that therefore the pledgee was not bound to take notice of the trust expressed on the transfer. But the court said that this had no legal bearing on the question. The circumstance that stock certificates issued in the name of one as trustee, and by him transferred in blank, are constantly bought and sold in the market without inquiry, is unavailing. A usage to disregard one's legal duty, to be ignorant of a rule of law, or to act as if it did not exist, can have no standing in the courts.

Shaw v. Spencer.

In Holmes *v.* Day,[2] it was held, that a usage among brokers to buy stock for their customer deliverable in sixty days at buyer's option, and then to purchase themselves stock at thirty days, and deliver it at the end of the sixty to the customer, at an increased price and interest, with commissions, was a bad custom, and the customer, in the absence of knowledge of it, was not bound.

Holmes v. Day.

Morton, J., said, "There are many forcible objections "to its validity; but a conclusive one is that it is "against sound policy and good morals. It authorizes "the broker, in his discretion, to disregard his instruc- "tions, and, instead of acting solely in the interest of

Remarks of Morton, J.

[1] 100 Mass. 382 [1866].   [2] 108 Mass. 306.

"his principal, to speculate upon the transaction for "his own benefit. It creates in the agent an interest "adverse to his principal, and is inconsistent with his "duty and the obligations which the law imposes upon "him when he enters into the contract of agency. "Such a usage, unknown to the principal, cannot be "supported."

Evans v. Waln.

In Evans *v.* Waln,[1] M. & Co., brokers in Philadelphia, sold certain stock for the plaintiffs, through the agency of W., another Philadelphia broker, by the defendants in New York. On W.'s failing, the defendants only remitted the stock after deducting the amount of W.'s own indebtedness to them. The defendants offered to prove that it was a custom among stock brokers, when dealing with stock brokers of other cities, to put all the transactions between them into one account, and to remit or draw for the general balance. This the court below refused to admit unless it was proved that the plaintiffs knew of the existence of such a custom, and charged the jury that if they believed that the stock sold by the defendant belonged to the plaintiffs, and that the defendants were aware of that, and knew that the order to sell was given by the broker, W., they could not credit W. with his own indebtedness to them and remit the balance, but must, after deducting their commission, remit the rest of the balance to the plaintiffs. Williams, J., in delivering the opinion of the court, affirming the court below,

Remarks of Williams, J.

said, "Nor was there any error in rejecting the offer. "* * * The defendants did not receive the stock from "him (W.), and they were not bound to account to

[1] 21 P. F. Sm. (Pa.) 69.

"him for the price for which it was sold. * * * But "if the defendants had received the stock from W., "knowing as they did that it belonged to the plaintiffs, "they would have no right to apply the proceeds "arising from its sale to the payment of W.'s indebt-"edness. If there is a custom among stock brokers, "when dealing with others, to appropriate money be-"longing to the principal to the payment of his "broker's indebtedness, the sooner it is abolished the "better: *malus usus est abolendus*. A custom so in-"iquitous can never obtain the force or sanction of the "law, and the marvel is that it should be set up as a "defence to this action."[1]

[1] See, also, the case of _____ ins v. Safferty, L. R., 3 App. Cas. 213.

CHAPTER VII.

RELATION OF THE VENDOR AND VENDEE AFTER THE CONTRACT.

	PAGE
SECTION I.—RELATION OF VENDOR AND VENDEE AFTER AN EXECUTED AND EXECUTORY CONTRACT OF SALE.	
Executed contracts	230
Executory contracts	231
Rule in Dixon v. Yates	232
Contracts sometimes for specific securities	233
SECTION II.—SPECIFIC PERFORMANCE.	
Duke of Somerset v. Cookson	234
Specific performance for executory contracts	235
§ 1. ENGLISH CASES.	
Rule deducible from the older cases	238
Duncuft v. Albrecht	239
Distinction between government bonds and shares of a private company	239
Sheffield Gas Co. v. Harrison	240
Hawkins v. Maltby	244
Principles deducible from the preceding cases	245
§ 2. AMERICAN CASES.	
Ross v. Union Pacific R. R. Co. Dictum of Miller, J.	251
Foll's Appeal, Pennsylvania	252
Remarks of Paxson, J.	252
Principles deducible from the cases on this subject	258

SECTION I.—RELATION OF VENDOR AND VENDEE AFTER AN EXECUTED AND EXECUTORY CONTRACT OF SALE.

IT is important to know what the relative position of vendor and vendee is after the contract of sale, but before any delivery of the securities is made. It is well known that contracts of sale are of two kinds, executed and executory.

Executed contract of sale. An executed contract of sale is where a man buys a specific thing, as an ear-marked bond, or share of stock, and nothing remains for the vendor but to deliver, whereby the vendee owns the thing sold absolutely after the contract; and if it be lost or stolen, the latter is the loser; or, if it be not delivered to him, he has several remedies for the failure to deliver;

as, for instance, he may bring an action of trover, or a bill for specific performance, etc.

An executory contract, on the other hand, is, where something remains for the vendor or vendee to do before delivery, and constitutes only an agreement to sell, and it does not become an executed contract of sale until something further is done by the parties. If in this condition of things the article contracted for be lost, or stolen, or destroyed, the loss falls, not upon the vendee, but upon the vendor; and if the vendor fails to make a delivery, the only remedy the vendee has, is an action for the breach of the contract. Thus, for instance, where a man contracts to sell fifty shares of stock, this is an executory contract, since any fifty shares of the stock in question will satisfy the terms of the sale. So, where one buys a certain quantity of grain in a field, uncut, this is also an executory contract; and in neither case will the contract become executed until the article or commodity stipulated for be separately ascertained, or ear-marked in some way; as if, in the former case, the stock broker should set apart a particular certificate for fifty shares of stock, or, in the latter, the grain should be cut and the stipulated quantity set apart and stored for delivery.

Thus, in Heseltine v. Siggers,[1] the court said that a contract for the sale of stock, exchequer bills, scrip, and securities, which pass by delivery, differs from a contract for the sale of a specific chattel, inasmuch as a contract for the sale of the former would be satisfied by the delivery of any securities of the same kind.

[1] 1 Exch. 856.

And it is to be observed, that it is not necessary, as formerly, to pay the money presently to make the contract complete, for the modern rule is, that the promise to pay constitutes the consideration.

Dixon v. Yates. Remarks of Parke, B.

The rule with regard to sales has been stated in Dixon v. Yates,[1] by Parke, B. "I take it to be "clear," said he, "that by the law of England the sale "of a specific chattel passes the property in it to the "vendee without delivery. * * * Where there is a "sale of goods generally, no property in them passes "till delivery, because until then the very goods sold "are not ascertained. But where by the contract itself "the latter thereby agrees to take that specific chattel, "and to pay the stipulated price, the parties are then "in the same situation as they would be after a de-"livery of goods in pursuance of a general contract. "The very appropriation of the chattel is equivalent to "delivery by the vendor, and the assent of the vendee "to take the specific chattel and to pay the price is "equivalent to his accepting possession. The effect of "the contract, therefore, is to vest the property in the "bargainee."

Gilmour v. Supple.

And again in Gilmour v. Supple[2] the rule was laid down in the same way. "By the law of England, by "a contract for the sale of specific, ascertained goods, "the property immediately vests in the buyer, and a "right to the price in the seller, unless it can be shown "that such was not the intention of the parties." This was pronounced by the present Lord Blackburn to be "a very accurate statement of the law."

With regard to the seller's rights, it is to be remem-

---

[1] 5 Barn. & Adol. 313.   [2] 11 Moore, P. C. C. 566.

bered that he may maintain an action in trover against the buyer until the latter fulfils all the conditions of the contract, even after delivery, as the title has not passed, and the loss by fire, etc., falls on the vendor. As where A. sells some Pennsylvania bonds to B. and delivers them at a certain price, B. to deliver to A. certain Reading bonds at a given price in three days, and B. fails to do so. Here no title in the latter bonds passes till B. performs his part of the contract, though A. has delivered the Pennsylvania bonds; and A. may maintain trover against B. for the bonds delivered by him.

There are also many sales of an executory character, such as conditional sales, where the buyer has the option of delivering or not, etc., and of course in such cases the sale does not become executed till the election is made, and the goods set aside, separated, or earmarked in some way. *Conditional sales execu-*

Having thus seen the distinction between these two kinds of contracts of sale, it will be observed that nearly all the sales at the Stock Exchange are of the latter character, and an illustration may be seen in the case of Heseltine *v.* Siggers,[1] quoted on a former page, it being extremely rare for a stock broker to buy or sell specific shares of stock, or scrip, or bonds. *Heseltine v. Siggers.*

It may, however, happen that under certain cases the sale may be for a specific security, and therefore executed; as where the stock broker contracts for all of the stock of a certain corporation. Here the property at once vests in the buyer, because, the vendee having a right to every share of that stock, the goods *Contracts sometimes for specific securities.*

[1] 1 Exch. 856.

are sufficiently ear-marked. So where the stock broker contracts for all those certain shares then in B.'s hands, it being ascertained how many he has, the goods may then be said to be ear-marked, because nothing remains for the seller to do but deliver, the setting apart being sufficiently made by the use of the word "all." It is true the seller may subsequently purchase more stock of the same kind, but his duty then is to separate, if necessary, the second lot from the first, on the principle that if goods once set apart become subsequently mixed, the loss, if any, falls upon the vendor.

Seeing then that in the vast majority of sales at the Stock Exchange the contract is an executory one for an article not at the time specifically determined, the question has arisen as to whether the buyer shall ever have a remedy against the seller other than the ordinary one by an action at law for damages. And this leads to the consideration of the doctrine of *specific performance* with relation to securities sold on the Stock Exchange.

SECTION II.—SPECIFIC PERFORMANCE.

Bill for specific performance lies for an executed contract of sale.

Before entering into the discussion of specific performance, it may be remarked that, in a sale of a chattel or thing, specified or ear-marked, a bill for specific performance will lie where there is not an equivalent or adequate remedy at law.

Duke of Somerset v. Cookson.

Thus, in Duke of Somerset *v.* Cookson,[1] where the Duke of Somerset, as lord of the manor of Corbridge, part of the estate of the late Earls of North-

[1] 3 P. Wm. 390.

umberland, was entitled to a remarkable altar-piece of silver, as treasure trove, which had been sold, by some one who got possession of it, to a goldsmith, it was held, that a bill of specific performance would lie, as it was not merely the *intrinsic value* of the chattel that Lord Somerset desired.

In analogy, then, to this case, though in the absence of direct authority on the subject, there can hardly be any reasonable doubt that a court of equity will decree specific performance in reference to a transfer of stock, when there is no adequate remedy at law. Though persons have doubted it, the courts have uniformly granted this equitable remedy where they thought there was not a sufficient remedy at law, making no distinction between this and any other species of personal property.[1]

With the assumption, then, that the rule is settled with regard to a bill lying for the specific delivery of things personal, we shall proceed to examine the decisions on the subject of specific performance relative to stocks and similar securities.

Specific performance of an executory contract of sale.

§ 1. *English Cases.*

In Cud *v.* Rutter,[2] the Lord Chancellor, Parker, afterwards Lord Macclesfield, overruling the lower court, refused to decree specific performance in relation to a transfer of South Sea stock. In this case the defendant, in consideration of two guineas paid down, had agreed to transfer one thousand pounds' worth of South Sea stock, at a fixed price, at the end

Cud v. Rutter.

---

[1] See following cases in text.   [2] 1 P. Wm. 571; better reported in 5 Viner, Abr. 538.

of three weeks. The plaintiff on that day demanded the stock and offered to pay the price, and on the defendant's declining to transfer the stock, but offering only to pay the difference in price, the plaintiff brought a bill to have the stock assigned. The court below ordered a specific performance, but the Lord Chancellor reversed this decree, on the ground that the agreement to buy was a purely executory one, for a thing not specific, and there was, in addition, a sufficient remedy at law. "This differs," he said, "very much from the case of a contract for land, "some lands being more valuable than others, or, at "least, more convenient than others, to the purchaser; "but there is no difference in stock. One man's stock "is of equal benefit and convenience as another's."

Colt v. Netterville.

In Colt *v.* Netterville,[1] Lord King overruled a demurrer to a bill for specific performance of stock, on the ground that something might turn up of peculiar hardship in the case.

Cappur v. Harris.

In Cappur *v.* Harris,[2] it was held in relation to contracts for South Sea stock, "First, that if a con- "tract be executed, a court of equity will not unravel "or break into it; secondly, if it is only executory, "and a man comes to have it carried into execution, "there a court of equity will not aid the plaintiff, but "leave him unto such remedy as he can have by law."

Gardener v. Pullen et al.

In Gardener *v.* Pullen *et* Phillips,[3] the defendant Pullen lent the defendant Phillips three shares of stock on a memorandum in writing to reassign such shares on demand. Phillips neglecting to do so, the plaintiff

---

[1] 2 P. Wm. 305.   [2] Bunbury, P. 135.
[3] 2 Vernon, 894.

CHAP. VII.]   RELATION OF VENDOR AND VENDEE.   237

and he executed a deed poll to Pullen, whereby Phillips and the plaintiff became bound in a penalty that Phillips should reassign the shares on a certain day. The shares were not retransferred, and Pullen brought an action against Gardener, Phillips being bankrupt. Gardener, losing the action, filed a bill, offering to pay the cost of the stocks at the time of the loan, they having risen in value, and the court decreed that Gardener should transfer the stock, and subsequent dividends, or have his bill dismissed with costs.

In Doloret v. Rothschild,[1] the defendant contracted to grant a loan to the Neapolitan government in consideration of a certain annual sum to be paid by that government, called Neapolitan Rentes, or Neapolitan stock. This stock was brought by the defendant into the market in the manner usual in cases of public loans; and the mode in which he disposed of it, was by selling scrip receipts, which were issued to the purchasers on their paying ten per cent. on the amount of the stock. In these scrip receipts it was expressed, that on payment of the balance, on or before the 1st of February, 1823, the bearer would be entitled to that amount of stock. The defendant purchased some of the scrip certificates, but failed to pay the balance in the proper time. A bill was filed to compel the defendants to issue the certificates on tender of the balance, but on a demurrer, the court thought it too late, time being of the essence of the contract; but Sir John Leach was of the opinion that a court of equity could decree specific performance, on the ground, that the bill asked for a delivery of certain certificates, and a

Doloret v. Rothschild.

[1] 1 Simon & Stuart, 590.

judgment in money, in such a case, might be of no value to the plaintiff, since the value of the judgment would depend only on the personal responsibility of the parties, while the actual certificates gave a claim on the government itself.

It is to be observed, here, that the bill asked for the delivery of certain certificates of stock in defendant's possession to confirm a title, and not for shares of stock; at all events, it was distinguishable from Cud *v.* Rutter, where no such particular case of hardship is reported.

<small>Rule deducible from the older cases.</small>

The rule, then, deducible from these cases, most of them early ones, seems to be that a decree for a specific performance of a purely executory contract will not lie where an action and judgment at law will put the plaintiff in substantially as good a position as the actual transfer of the stock. In Cud *v.* Rutter, the defendant offered to pay the difference in price, and an equivalent amount of stock could have thus been purchased at the Stock Exchange by the plaintiff without any loss to himself. But in Doloret *v.* Rothschild, the dictum of Sir John Leach indicates, that, where a mere money judgment would not practically put a buyer of shares in as good a position as their actual delivery, a bill in equity would lie. And it is obvious that wherever shares of stock, contracted for, cannot readily be purchased in the market, a case arises, where a mere judgment for damages is not the equivalent of the transfer of the shares, and does not put the purchaser in as good a position as their actual delivery. Hence, following the reasoning of these early decisions, we see, in the later ones, a tendency of courts of equity

CHAP. VII.]   RELATION OF VENDOR AND VENDEE.   239

to interpose to enforce a specific performance of a contract for the purchase of shares, on the ground, that when the shares of a company are limited in number, a party may suffer a great damage by a breach of the contract not capable of being compensated in damages alone. *Tendency of the later cases is to decree specific performance even in executory contracts.*

In Duncuft v. Albrecht,[1] where a bill was filed for specific performance in reference to shares, the court allowed it, the Vice-Chancellor saying, "I agree that "it has been long since decided that you cannot have "a bill for the specific performance of an agreement to "transfer a certain quantity of stock. But, in my "opinion, there is not any sort of analogy between a "quantity of 3 per cents., or any other stock of that "description (which is always to be had by any person "who chooses to apply for it in the market), and a "certain number of railway shares of a particular "description, which railway shares are limited in num- "ber, and which, as has been observed, are not always "to be had in the market; and as no decision has been "produced to the contrary, my opinion is that they are "a subject with respect to which an agreement may be "made which this court will enforce." *Duncuft v. Albrecht.*

Distinction made between stock (or bonds of the government) and shares.

Having seen now that a bill to enforce the specific performance of the stock contract, even though it be executory only, will lie, we shall proceed to examine some cases as illustrations of the general principles already indicated, which guide the courts in interfering to compel such specific performance, or in refusing to do so.

In Shaw v. Fisher,[2] the plaintiff employed a broker *Shaw v. Fisher.*

[1] 12 Simons, 189.   [2] 5 De G. M. & G. 596.

to sell railway shares, and the broker employed an auctioneer who sold them to the defendant. Subsequently the defendant employed the same auctioneer to resell the shares, and the vendee's name was handed in by the auctioneer to the plaintiff for a deed of transfer, which was thereupon executed, conveying the shares to the vendee, who, however, refused to get registered as a shareholder. A year after this, calls being made on the plaintiff, he brought a bill to force the defendant to fulfil his contract; but the court held, that it would not lie, as the plaintiff, having executed the transfer to the subsequent vendee, had put an end to the privity of contract between himself and the defendant.

Sheffield Gas Co. v. Harrison. In Sheffield Gas Company *v.* Harrison,[1] where there was a contract by the defendant to take shares in a joint stock company and to execute the deed of settlement under which it had been formed, and by which the person so executing it became a partner, it was objected that this was a bill to compel a person to become a partner, which could not be enforced specifically. The argument on the part of the plaintiff was that joint stock companies of this kind differed from ordinary partnerships, and that as the responsibility for calls was a personal one, which attached to the vendor of shares, so long as his name remained on the company's share register he was entitled in equity to compel a vendee to have his name substituted, and to sign the deed of settlement, even though he should afterwards sell and retransfer. The bill was, however, dismissed, on the ground that it sought to compel the defendant to become a partner.

[1] 17 Beavan, 294.

CHAP. VII.] RELATION OF VENDOR AND VENDEE. 241

The Master of the Rolls said, "It is a contract to become a partner in a partnership, of which, according to the terms of the deed, the defendant could cease to be a partner in fourteen days. * * * To specifically perform a contract of this description would be simply nugatory." Remarks of the Master of the Rolls.

How far the reasoning upon which the decision in this case proceeded, is applicable to the case of existing joint stock companies, especially in America, may admit of considerable doubt. Such companies may all be defined to be partnerships with limited liability, though differing in essential respects from such companies as the Sheffield Gas Company,—created under a deed of settlement,—which resemble more nearly the "limited partnerships" created and authorized by the statutes of several of our States.[1] In them, a partner cannot assign his shares unless the assignee becomes a party to the partnership articles, and is approved of by the remaining partners. But, if applied to the shareholders of all corporations, this reasoning would prevent a court's compelling, in any case, a specific transfer to, or acceptance of, shares by a vendee, and it will probably be necessary to restrict it in the manner just indicated. Effect of the principles decided in the foregoing case.

In Harris v. North Devon Railway Company,[2] the directors had the authority, on non-payment of calls, to sue for them, or forfeit, and sell out, the shares. They proposed to a shareholder, to relieve him from further liability, on his consenting to an absolute Harris v. North Devon Railway Co.

---

[1] See Act of June 2, 1874, and its Supplements, in Pennsylvania; Laws of Pennsylvania, 1874, p. 271.
[2] 20 Beavan, 384.

forfeiture, which he did, but, subsequently finding out that he was a person of means, before the final steps were taken, the directors refused to complete the contract. The court refused to compel them to do so, on the ground that they were trustees for all the shareholders, and were bound to use their discretion for all, and if they found, before the transaction was concluded, that it was not for the benefit of all that the man should be released, they could retract, and further there was no valuable consideration. This decision was by Sir John Romilly, and its reasoning proceeds, not so much on the contract itself, as on the power of the directors to make it, at least so as to exclude the subsequent exercise of the discretion by law vested in them.

Robinson v. Chartered Bank.

In Robinson *v.* Chartered Bank,[1] the question arose, as to whether a bill would lie, to compel the bank to approve of a transferee, who in all other respects was a fit person, excepting that he was the nominee of a rival bank, the directors having, under the bank's charter, to approve before the transferee could become a shareholder. The Master of the Rolls overruled the demurrer to the bill, thinking the directors were bound to use their discretion reasonably, but did not state whether there was in the case sufficient ground for them not to give it, but he said he would abide the result of the issue of the cause.

In re London Bank.

In *In re* London, etc., Bank,[2] A. contracted to buy shares in a company, after a petition had been presented for winding up, but before it had been ad-

[1] L. R., 1 Eq. Cas. 32. [2] L. R., 1 Ch. App. Cas. 433.

vertised, and in ignorance of the fact, and the Court of Appeals reversed the decision of Lord Romilly, M. R., who had placed the purchaser on the register. Turner, J., said, "These shares were not transferred "into the name of the purchaser. The transactions "were in this respect incomplete, and, under the cir- "cumstances of this case, I do not think a court of "equity could or would compel the purchaser to com- "plete them, and to register the shares in his name." *Remarks of Turner, J.*

In Poole v. Middleton,[1] by the deed of settlement of a joint stock company, it was provided that "no share- "holder should be at liberty to *transfer* his shares "except in such manner as a board of directors should "approve." A shareholder had contracted to sell his shares, and the court held, that he must specifically perform by executing the transfer, though the directors refused their consent. The Master of the Rolls said, "What then is there to deprive a shareholder of his "right to give another his power of receiving divi- "dends, or his liability to any debts which may be "incurred by the company? The clause does not say "that no shareholder shall be at liberty to enter into "any contract for the sale of his shares, except with "the consent of the directors. * * * But a transfer "necessarily infers that a prior contract had been "entered into, and then the clause says that the trans- "fer shall not take place, except in such manner as "the board of directors shall approve. I do not say "whether the plaintiff will become a shareholder, "unless they approve of the manner in which the "transfer is made, etc." *Poole v. Middleton.*

[1] 29 Beavan, 646.

Evans v. Wood.

In Evans *v.* Wood,[1] A. sold to N., a jobber, in the Exchange, and B. purchased from N., five shares in a company. N. gave A. the name of B. as purchaser, according to the usage of the Exchange, and B. got an executed transfer from A., and the purchase money was paid. B. was prevented by accident from having the registration made till the company had stopped payment. The company was wound up, and the liquidators registered all the transfers at the office, but refused to register B. It was held, that A. was entitled, on a bill in equity, to a decree against B. for calls, and indemnity against future calls, and also that where the directors had a discretionary power to refuse objectionable transferees, in the absence of evidence of an objection to him, it was to be presumed the directors would have registered him.

In re London, etc.

On comparing this case with *In re* London, etc., Bank, quoted above, it must be observed that in that case no steps had been taken to complete the contract to buy shares. It was a mere executory contract;

Evans v. Wood.

while in Evans *v.* Wood, all the steps necessary, so far as the parties to the contract were concerned, to make it an executed one, had been completed. The five shares contracted to be sold had been ascertained and ear-marked; the transfer was executed by the vendor, and the purchase money paid. The court, therefore, did not there interfere to compel specific performance of an executory contract. The contract had become an executed one, and the court merely compelled both parties to give full effect to it, as between each other.

[1] L. R., 5 Eq. Cas. 9.

In the same category falls the case of Hawkins *v.* Maltby.¹ Here the plaintiff sold forty shares on the Stock Exchange by his broker to a jobber, and the defendant subsequently bought from the jobber, by a broker, one hundred shares, and his name was given the plaintiff, as the purchaser of forty shares. The plaintiff executed a transfer, and gave a deed of transfer, the consideration being left blank, to the defendant. The brokers filled in the consideration, and the defendant got the transfers, which he never executed, but kept them, though without repudiating the transaction. An order was made for winding up, and the court held, there was a contract between A. and B., and decreed, that the defendant specifically perform the sale and register of the transfer.

Hawkins v. Maltby.

And in Oriental Steam Co. *v.* Briggs,² the court said, where there is a clear contract to accept shares, and the remedy is shown to be inadequate at law, the court will decree specific performance, but where, as in the case at bar, there was a doubt as to the contract to accept the shares, and the inadequacy of the legal remedy was not clearly made out, and there was an unexplained delay of two years, the court would allow the demurrer to the bill.

The principles deducible, therefore, from the English authorities, of which the cases above quoted are leading instances, are:

I. As a general rule, courts of equity will interfere to compel specific performance of contracts for the sale of shares of stock, or of other securities sold at the Stock Exchange, where there is no adequate

Principles deducible from preceding cases.

¹ L. R., 6 Eq. Cas. 505. ² 2 J. & H. 625.

remedy at law, or where such remedy will not put the party suing in as good a position.

II. That an apparent distinction has been drawn between contracts for the sale of public stock and for the sale of shares of a private corporation, to the effect that, in the latter class of cases, a specific performance of the contract might be ordered, because the shares are not always to be had in the market, while in the case of government securities they could always be purchased. But the reasoning in these cases shows that this distinction is only one of degree, and that it does not exist, in principle, between the two classes of securities; but that where public securities are not to be had in the market, or where, for any other equitable reason, an action at law would not put the party injured, in the same position, a court will grant relief of this character in the case of government securities, as well as of others, as in the case of Doloret *v.* Rothschild,[1] above quoted, where Sir John Leach, although he refused on other grounds the relief prayed for, intimated that in such case a bill would lie.

III. That with regard to contracts which, although originally executory, have been so far performed as to become executed, courts of equity will compel an entire specific performance of the contract so as to give full effect to it as between the parties to it.

It must be admitted that, in principle, no distinction has been drawn, in regard to specific performance, between those sales of securities which are simply executory and those executed. In either case, where there is no adequate remedy at law, the courts have inter-

---

[1] 1 Simon & Stuart, 590.

vened, or have held, that, in the absence of any other equitable objection, a bill would lie: while, where a specific security had been sold, and the remedy at law was entirely adequate, the reasoning adopted by the courts would leave the parties to it.

§ 2. *American Cases.*

We shall now proceed to examine the cases in the United States on the subject of the specific performance of contracts for the sale of stocks and securities which will illustrate the principles already laid down.

In Clark v. Flint,[1] a person had agreed, for a valuable consideration and in writing, to hold a chattel subject to the order of the plaintiff. But he subsequently assigned it to another, with notice of the agreement, and the court held, that the plaintiff could maintain a bill against the assignee for specific performance. Here the plaintiff only had a remedy at law against parties who were insolvent.

Clark v. Flint.

In Todd v. Taft[2] (1863), it was held, that a bill in equity would lie for the specific performance of an agreement to transfer certain shares of a corporation upon the maturing of a note, without days of grace, given for the price thereof, although, owing to a mistake in the phraseology of the agreement, payment had not been offered until the last day when it would have been due, had the note been drawn in the usual form. Time was not of the essence of the contract, as shown by the circumstances. The court here took a distinction between an executory and an executed contract. "It is true," said Dewey, J., "as contended in behalf

Todd v. Taft.

Remarks of Dewey, J.

[1] 22 Pick. (Mass.) 231.   [2] 7 Allen, 371.

"of the defendant, that no legal transfer of this stock to F. was effected by this contract, and the defendant remained the legal owner of it. It was only an executory contract by T. to convey the stock upon certain conditions. But, practically, as regards F., it created all the liability on his part to make the payment therefor that would have attended a purchase and transfer of the stock. It was to be his upon the payment of a certain promissory note, which he had given to the defendant. * * * It is to be dealt with in equity much like the case of a sale of stock, absolute on its face, but in fact designed to secure the payment of a certain sum of money upon a future day certain, where a bond or other paper writing is given by the vendee, undertaking to transfer the shares to the debtor upon payment at the day named of the sum stated."

Leach v. Fobes.

In Leach v. Fobes[1] (1858), owing to a compromise with reference to a will, there was an agreement to transfer shares, and the court held, a bill for specific performance would lie, as there was not an adequate remedy at law. Here the bill prayed for a conveyance of land as well as a transfer of stock, and the court, without deciding whether it would have lain, had it asked for the transfer of shares alone, said that the prayers of the bill would be granted when the same bill asked for both.

In New York, the subject is settled in the same way.

Pollock v. National Bank.

Thus, in Pollock v. The National Bank,[2] it was held, that where a bank had permitted a transfer of

[1] 11 Gray, 506. [2] 3 Selden, 274.

stock owned by a stockholder upon a forged power of attorney, and had cancelled the original certificates, it might be compelled to issue new certificates, and if it could not do so, to pay the value thereof.

In Purchase v. Bank,[1] the court held, that after an assignment of the bank stock, the bank, upon the application of the owner, was bound to permit a transfer to be made on its books, and issue new certificates, unless restrained by a court of competent jurisdiction.

Purchase v. Bank.

In White v. Schuyler,[2] it was held, that a specific performance of an agreement to transfer stock may be decreed, where the contract is clear, and the value of the stock very uncertain, so that a judgment at law will not compensate.

White v. Schuyler.

In Cushman v. Thayer Manf. etc. Co.,[3] P., the plaintiff's husband, executed without a consideration an assignment to the plaintiff, and delivered her the certificates. Subsequently P. for a valuable consideration executed a transfer of the same shares to B., and had a transfer made on the company's books to him, B., however, having notice of the prior assignment to the plaintiff. By the rules of the company, no transfer is good unless the old certificate is delivered up to be cancelled. The plaintiff subsequently presented the certificates and demanded a transfer, and the court held, that a bill would lie to compel a transfer to her.

Cushman v. Thayer Manf. Co.

In Cowles v. Whitman,[4] A. agreed with B., that A. in B.'s name should subscribe for five shares of stock, of a new bank, about to be distributed, and all

Cowles v. Whitman.

---

[1] 3 Robt. 164.
[2] 1 Abb. P., N. S. 300.
[3] 31 Sickles, N. Y. 365.
[4] 10 Conn. 121.

the shares allowed on such subscription beyond what B. could pay for, should be paid for by and belong to A. A. subscribed in B.'s name for five shares, which were accordingly allotted, the first instalment being paid by A. B. then declared her inability to pay for any, and A. paid the remaining instalments, and brought a bill against B.'s administrator for specific performance, and the court allowed the bill to lie, saying this was a trust for A., which it was the province of a court of equity to enforce.

Austin v. Gillaspie. In North Carolina, in Austin *v.* Gillaspie,[1] it appeared that A. had agreed, conditionally with others, to subscribe a certain amount to the stock of a company, and B. and C. had agreed with him, in writing, that, if he would do so unconditionally, they would each take one-fourth of the subscription off his hands, and A. accordingly made the subscription. The court held, that a bill for specific performance would lie to execute the sale in accordance with the agreement.

Ashe v. Johnson. In Ashe *v.* Johnson's administrators,[2] the court declared that in a question of the specific performance of a contract, shares in a recently chartered railway stood on a very different footing from government stocks in England.

Baldwin v. Commonwealth. In Kentucky, in Baldwin *v.* Commonwealth,[3] the Legislature by an act directed the commissioners of the sinking fund to sell the stock owned by the State in a turnpike company, and the latter, having advertised, made a conditional acceptance of a bid which

---

[1] 1 Jones, Eq. 261. [2] 2 Jones, Eq. 149.
[3] 11 Ky. Rep. 417.

CHAP. VII.]   RELATION OF VENDOR AND VENDEE.   251

was offered, and verbally directed their agent to notify the bidder of their action, which being done, the bidder accepted the terms, and so notified the company. On a bill filed by the latter, the court held, *inter alia*, that the contract was completed when the notice of acceptance was accepted by the board of commissioners, and that, although the act conferring on the commissioners the right to act had been repealed, yet a bill would lie to compel the specific performance of the contract; as the repealing act, if applied to the contract which had thus been called into existence, operated to violate its obligations, which was forbidden by the Federal Constitution.

In Ferguson *v.* Paschall *et al.*,[1] the bill was dismissed for multifariousness, but Scott, J., said, "It "seems to be now settled, though it was once held "otherwise, that in general a specific performance "of a contract for the transfer of stock will not be "decreed." *Ferguson v. Paschall. Dictum of Scott, J.*

In Treasurer *v.* Commercial Coal, etc. Co.,[2] a court of equity decreed the specific performance of a contract to transfer shares of mining stock, owing to their fluctuating value, and the difficulty of finding out what the proper measure of damage was. *Treasurer v. Commercial Coal Co.*

In Ross *v.* Union Pacific R. R. Co.,[3] there was a contract to build a railroad and furnish materials, etc., and the work was to be paid for in United States bonds, and in bonds and stock of the company. The plaintiff did a small amount of work, and, after making arrangements to do more, their contract was *Ross v. Union Pacific R. R. Co.*

[1] 11 Mo. 267.   [2] 28 Cal. 890.
[3] 1 Woolw. C. C. Rep. 26.

declared forfeited, and a new arrangement made by the defendants with regard to the bonds, in payment of the second contractors, which would of course interfere with any rights to them the plaintiffs might have. An injunction was asked to restrain the issue and delivery of these bonds to the second contractor and for specific performance. The court, Miller, J., said that in any view the contract was but an executory one, and that a bill would not lie, for this, as well as for other reasons. But speaking of the specific performance in reference to transfers of stocks, etc., he said that government bonds were like public funds in England, and might be bought in the market, and therefore a court of equity would not interfere to compel specific performance of a contract to transfer them; that as to railroad bonds and stock, he was in doubt as to whether the distinction drawn in England would prevail here, but that he thought it was not a just one, where they could easily be procured in the market, but the point was not necessary to be decided in the case.

Foll's Appeal.
Remarks of Paxson, J.

In Pennsylvania, there is no case exactly in point. In Foll's Appeal,[1] Paxson, J., said, where a bill was presented to enforce the specific performance of a transfer of stock, "The avowed object of the pur-
"chase of the stock and the filing of this bill, was to
"get the control of the bank for G. and his friends.
"* * * The general rule is that equity will not
"enforce specific execution of a contract relating to
"personal chattels. * * * This is especially true of
"stocks and public securities which have a known

[1] 86 Legal Int. 495.

"market value. The disappointed purchaser can go
"into the market and purchase a corresponding num-
"ber of shares of the same stock. * * * I know of
"no instance in this State, in which a court of equity
"has decreed specific performance of a sale of stocks.
"* * * But we need not pursue this subject further,
"as the case in hand turns upon a different principle.
"While the legal right of the complainant to buy up
"sufficient of the stock of this bank to control it in the
"interest of himself and friends may be conceded, it
"is by no means clear that a court of equity will lend
"its aid to help him. * * * This purchase has not
"even the merit of being an investment on the part
"of the plaintiff."

This review of these American cases seems to afford us the same general principles as the English cases. These cases, like the English, have drawn a distinction between the case of public, or government stocks, and the shares of private corporations, by *dicta*, though they have never positively decided that relief would not be granted in the case of public stock, for in Ross *v.* Northern Pacific R. R. Co. the case turned upon another point.

American cases afford the same general principles as the English.

Ross v. Northern Pacific R. R. Co.

It may also be added with regard to railroad shares that there is no difference in principle between them and shares in any other kind of company. It is true that Miller, J., in his remarks in Ross *v.* the Railroad Company,[1] might be supposed to intimate this; but this is but a *dictum*, and the question whether other similar shares could in that case have been had in the market was not discussed; while

---

[1] 1 Woolw. C. C. Rep. 26.

in North Carolina[1] relief in regard to such shares was granted.

It is true that, in Foll's Appeal, Paxson, J., did say that there was no case in Pennsylvania that had decreed a specific performance of stock; but that case went off on another question, the court refusing to enforce a man's agreement where it was avowed that the only object was to control the corporation, that being clearly a case for an action at law. That case, therefore, does not militate against the general rule.

Result of the review of the cases. A cursory examination of these decisions undoubtedly presents difficulties. In many cases there appears to be drawn, as in the early English cases, a distinction between an executed contract of sale, as where the vendor has delivered certificates of stock to the vendee, with a blank power of attorney, and nothing but the actual transfer of names to be registered, and where the vendee has no *indicia* of title, but prays the aid of a court of equity to carry out the contract. So the case, where the vendor has no more of the stock contracted to be sold by him than the actual amount covered by his contract, appears, as amounting to an executed contract, to differ, in the eyes of judges, from where the vendor, having more of the stock than that contracted to be sold, has yet not set aside any specific part to the vendee. In other cases, however, of merely executory contracts, where an action at law was obviously inadequate, the courts, as has been seen, have compelled the vendor to transfer the very shares which are the subject of his contract. It must be admitted that in all those cases

[1] 1 Jones, Eq. (N. C.) 261.

where the vendor, at the time of the contract, or at the time of the filing of the bill, possesses a sufficient number of shares of the stock in question to satisfy the terms of the contract, the distinction between an executory contract, where only so many shares are contracted to be sold, and an executed one, where the certificate is actually ear-marked and set apart by the vendee, appears to be an idle one. An analysis of the decisions shows that this is not the principle upon which they ultimately turn. And if, where a man possesses stock of the kind which he has agreed to sell, we apply the maxim that equity will consider as done that which should be done, and presume the vendor to have set apart for the vendee a proper portion of the stock to satisfy his contract, the contract will then fall into the category of an executed sale, where the courts have felt no difficulty in decreeing specific performance.

But where the person contracting to sell the stock does not at the time possess any such stock, as in the case, for example, of all short sales, there is no instance of a court's having entertained a bill for specific performance, which would amount to ordering the vendor to go into the market and buy the shares in question for the vendee,—a decree which in many cases would be nugatory. In such a case the only remedy is an action at law for damages. We may safely say, therefore, that a court of equity will not entertain a bill for the specific performance of a contract for the sale of stocks or securities, excepting where there actually exist, in the possession, or under the control, of the vendor, at the date of the contract, or, at all events, at the time fixed for its completion, securities of the kind in question to an adequate amount, which the court can properly assume to have been the actual subject-matter of the contract in question. Subject to this limitation, the distinction, on this question of specific performance, between executed and executory sales, though often alluded to, appears from a review of the authorities, both English and American, to be unsubstantial and to afford no criterion in arriving at a correct result.

We have thus reviewed the English and American cases upon this subject, which, if we regard only the *dicta* and expressions of opinion of individual judges, seem often to darken rather than enlighten the principles involved. And, undoubtedly, the attempt to draw general deductions from the peculiar circumstances of particular cases, has led many persons to suppose that equity, instead of differing merely in degree, differed arbitrarily in principle, in affording relief in regard to different kinds of personal property. But the real difference between a contract for the sale of a specific chattel and a contract to sell railway shares, or grain, or oil, is this. In the former case there is always a specific chattel which constitutes the subject-matter of the contract; in the latter there may or may not be any article or commodity under the vendor's control, or in his possession, the whole or any part of which a court can lay hold of as and for the subject-matter of the contract, as where a contractor sells short, without having any of the securities or of the commodity contracted to be sold, belonging to him. In such a case, of course, a court of equity cannot intervene. And, in dealing with those cases where the vendor has the stock or commodity in question, and the court therefore has a proper subject-matter to deal with, we have seen, that where the stock can readily be bought in the market, and the vendee's remedy at common law in damages is complete, equity will not interfere. But where a court of equity has within its reach a proper subject-matter, as to which specific performance can be decreed, and no adequate remedy at common law exists, then the decisions do not appear to disclose any difference between dealing with these securities and with any other kind of personal chattels.

CHAPTER VIII.

COMPLETION OF THE CONTRACT, OR THE DELIVERY OF THE THING SOLD.

	PAGE
Different meanings of the word "delivery"	258
Meaning employed here	260
SECTION I.—THE VENDOR.	
Division of the subject	261
§ 1. WHAT THE VENDOR MUST DELIVER.	
§ 2. IMPLIED CONDITION ATTACHED TO THE DELIVERY BY THE VENDOR.	
Cases discussed	263
Reclamations at the Stock Exchanges	264
Security delivered must be marketable	265
Implied warranty of vendor's title	266
§ 3. MANNER OF EFFECTING THE DELIVERY.	
Transfer	266
Registration	266
Vendor's duties, *prima facie*	267
Calls	267
No form of transfer legally necessary	268
Transfer usually under seal, so by by-laws of corporations	268
Transfers in blank	269
English and American cases discussed at length	270
Clearing House delivery	279
Time	280
Leap-year	280
Month	280
Day	280
Hour	280
Place of delivery	281
At common law	281
By rule of the Stock Exchange	281
SECTION II.—THE VENDEE.	
§ 1. ACCEPTANCE AND PAYMENT.	
Price	282
Registration	283

Different meanings of word "delivery."

AFTER all the terms of the contract of sale have been completed on both sides, or when the contract of sale has been executed, the duty of the vendor is then to deliver.

It is especially necessary to caution the reader against confusion by reason of the various senses in which the word "delivery" in this relation has been employed. Mr. Benjamin, in his excellent work on Sales, remarks, at page 629:

"*First.* The word delivery is sometimes used with "reference to the passing of the property in the "chattel,[1] sometimes to the change of the possession "of the chattel. In a word, it is used in turn to "denote transfer of title, or transfer of possession.

"*Secondly.* Even where 'delivery' is used to sig- *Its different* "nify the transfer of possession, it will be found that *plained by* "it is employed in two distinct classes of cases, one *Mr. Benjamin in his* "having reference to the formation of the contract, *work on Sales.* "the other to the performance of the contract. When "questions arise as to the 'actual receipt' which is "necessary to give validity to a parol contract for the "sale of chattels exceeding £10 in value, the judges "constantly use the word 'delivery' as the correlative "of that 'actual receipt.' After the sale had been "proven to exist, by delivery and actual receipt, "there may arise a second and distinct controversy "upon the point whether the vendor has performed "his completed bargain by delivery of possession of "the bulk to the purchaser.

" *Thirdly.* Even when the subject under con- "sideration is the vendor's delivery of possession in "performance of his contract, there arises a fresh "source of confusion in the different meanings at- "tached to the word 'possession.' In general it "would be perfectly proper, and even technical, to "speak of the buyer of goods on credit as being in "possession of them, although the actual custody "may have been left with the vendor. The buyer "owns the goods, has the right of possession, may

[1] As, for instance, in the opinion B. & Ald., at p. 340.
of Parke, B., in Dixon *v.* Yates, 5

"take them away, sell or dispose of them at his pleasure, and maintain trover for them; yet, if he become insolvent, the vendor is said to have retained possession. Again, if the vendor has delivered the goods to a carrier for conveyance to the purchaser, he is said to have lost his lien, because the goods are in the buyer's possession, the carrier being the agent of the buyer; but if the vendor claim to exercise the right of stoppage *in transitu*, while the carrier is conveying them, the goods are said to be only in the constructive, not in the actual, possession of the buyer."

Meaning of word "delivery" as employed here.

Having seen the various interpretations which have been given the word, it is intended here to treat the word as meaning such a transfer of the evidence of the *possession* of the thing sold at the Stock Exchange as will defeat an action for non-delivery brought by the vendee. The word as meaning the transfer of the evidence of the title of the thing sold from vendor to vendee only, has been considered in the discussion of executed and executory contracts. The word as meaning the transfer of the title or possession so as to defeat the creditors of the vendor, will be treated of later under the head of Avoidance of the Contract. The subject may be conveniently divided into two parts: the duties of the vendor in delivery, and the duties of the vendee in accepting the delivery.

SECTION I.—THE VENDOR.

Vendor's duty to deliver is only prima facie.

It is apparent that the duty of the vendor is only *prima facie* to deliver, since the vendee may become

CHAP. VIII.]   COMPLETION OF THE CONTRACT.   261

insolvent, or a creditor of the vendor or vendee may stop the goods *in transitu*, and the courts may enjoin the vendor from delivering. The subject of stoppage *in transitu* may be examined in any work on sales,[1] as the securities sold at the Stock Exchange do not differ from other chattels in the application of these rules of law, and cases rarely occur affecting the stock broker; and we confine ourselves here to the examination of what may constitute a valid delivery of the thing sold in the sense in which we use the term here.

In examining the vendor's duties, we shall consider,— *Division of subject.*

§ 1. What the vendor must deliver.

§ 2. The implied condition attached to the delivery by the vendor.

§ 3. The manner of effecting the delivery.

§ 1. *What the Vendor must Deliver.*

It has been more than once remarked that, in the sales effected at the Stock Exchange, it is very unusual for a contract to be made for a specific bond or share of stock, and consequently, as we have seen, a delivery of any share or bond of the kind contracted for will sufficiently fulfil the condition of the contract, so as to make it a valid execution of it. There must, however, always be a delivery of strictly the same kind of stock contracted for, for in no case will another kind make a valid delivery.

---

[1] *E.g.*, the very valuable work of Mr. Benjamin on Sales.

§ 2. *The Implied Condition attached to the Delivery by the Vendor.*

<small>Stock broker does not give an express warranty.</small>

A stock broker does not, as a rule, warrant the value of the thing sold as being either legally issued or of a pecuniary value; certainly not, unless expressly authorized to do so by his principal, for there is no usage of trade authorizing a stock broker to warrant the thing sold.[1] But although there is no express warranty of value given by the stock broker, there is always an implied warranty of *genuineness* in the thing sold; that is to say, that the thing sold is in truth and in fact what the contract calls for, and which may be conveniently called an implied warranty or condition of genuineness, which must always exist in all sales; or, in other words, the buyer in all sales has a right to get what he bargained for, whether it be totally valueless or not.

<small>Always an implied warranty of title.</small>

Thus, for example, if scrip or stock of a particular kind be dealt in at the Stock Exchange which turns out thereafter not to have been properly or legally issued by the corporation issuing it, the broker is not liable to a vendee to whom it has been delivered, even though it should prove valueless. Where, however, the broker delivers without his knowledge forged certificates, the vendee has a right to recover from him the value of genuine certificates of the same kind. Cases, of course, may be imagined, where the two classes thus indicated run into each other, as where an officer of the company issues a security without authority, and the company subsequently repudiates it. But in these cases the question is purely one of

---

[1] Pickering *v.* Busk, 15 East, 38; Smith *v.* Tracy, 36 N. Y. 79.

fact: "Was the intention of the parties, as interpreted "by their contract, to purchase the thing or security "in question, or not?" This, of course, is a question for the jury.

Thus, in Lambert v. Heath,[1] the plaintiff bought through a stock broker certain "Kentish Coast Rail-"way scrip," signed by the secretary of the railway company. This turned out to have been a fraudulent issue, the secretary signing without authority, and was repudiated. In an action to recover from the defendant the price paid him for the scrip and his commission, the court held, it was a question for the jury to say whether the plaintiff intended to buy this particular scrip. Alderson, B., said, "The question "is simply this: was what the parties bought in the "market 'Kentish Coast Railway scrip'? It appears "that it was signed by the secretary of the company; "and if this was the only Kentish Coast Railway "scrip in the market, as appears to have been the "case, and one person chooses to sell and the other to "buy, that then the latter has got all that he con-"tracted for. That was the question for the jury."

Lambert v. Heath.

Remarks of Alderson, B.

In Mitchell v. Newhall,[2] the defendant gave the plaintiff, a broker, an order to purchase fifty shares in a foreign railway company. At that time no shares were in the market, but there were letters of allotment, which were usually sold as such on the Stock Exchange. The plaintiff bought fifty of these allotments; and the court held, it was for the jury to say what the nature of the order was, and that they might hold this was a good execution of the order.

Mitchell v. Newhall.

[1] 15 M. & W. 486.   [2] 15 M. & W. 308.

Westropp v. Solomon.

In Westropp *v.* Solomon,[1] a stock broker employed by A. to sell stock in a projected railway company, handed the proceeds to A., and afterwards, the certificates turning out to be forged, was obliged by a rule of the Stock Exchange, subsequently made, to pay the value of genuine certificates to the purchaser. It was held, that the stock broker could, at least, recover from A. the proceeds so paid.

Young v. Cole.

In Young *v.* Cole,[2] plaintiff sold for the defendant four Guatemala bonds, which being unstamped were unmarketable; whereupon the plaintiff refunded the money and sued the defendant for the money, and the court held, that he could recover.

The principle deducible from these cases then is, that in all sales at the Stock Exchange there is an implied condition of genuineness, *i.e.*, that the article delivered must be what was contracted for, and that where the thing delivered is the only thing known on the Stock Exchange, and usually passes there as what the buyer named, it is for the jury to say whether he meant to buy it or not; but that when there are genuine and spurious shares on the market, the buyer will be supposed to have intended to buy the genuine, and a delivery of the spurious shares will not be good.

Implied condition of genuineness.

Reclamation of contract at the Stock Exchange.

Most of the Stock Exchanges have rules upon the subject of reclamations by their members for irregularities in the delivery of securities. These rules are all to the effect that such reclamations will not, where they do not affect the validity of the stock, but merely its currency, be considered after a limited

---

[1] 8 M. & G. & S. 345. [2] 3 Bingham's New Cases, 724.

CHAP. VIII.] COMPLETION OF THE CONTRACT. 265

period, usually from five to fifteen days. A rule of this kind is undoubtedly binding upon the members of the Exchange, and might probably bind their principals, as rules reasonable and proper under the circumstances. Subject, however, to such existing regulations, it may be said that where a broker buys a stock in the Exchange he is entitled to have delivered to him a certificate of stock or a security not merely legally valid, but one which at the time of delivery passes current, and is in all respects marketable. *Rules respecting reclamations, how far binding.*

Security delivered must be in all respects marketable.

For example, a company may begin, *bona fide*, to issue certain additional stock, the legality of which may be disputed by other shareholders. In such a case, recently,[1] an injunction was obtained at the instance of a shareholder, restraining the company from proceeding with the issue, and, the company having closed its transfer books, the question arose in several of the Stock Exchanges, whether certificates dated after the issue of the stock in question had begun, could be used in making deliveries of this stock in the Stock Exchange. No adjudicated case on the subject, it is believed, exists; but the views generally adopted by the Stock Exchanges were, that certificates whose currency was, by reason of their date, rendered questionable, could not be used to make a delivery, whether they were, in fact, actually valid or not, as that was a question that could only be passed on by a court of law; and that all persons making reclamations within the time allowed by the rules of the Exchange, could return such certificates *Illustration of principle.*

[1] Northern Pacific Railway Company.

and require the redelivery to them of certificates in all respects marketable.

Should certificates of stock turn out to be actually invalid, for any reason, there is no doubt that either the brokers or their principals could return them and demand the delivery of valid certificates or their value, whether the reclamation were made within the time allowed by the rules of the Stock Exchange or not. No rule, impairing such a right on the part of the vendee, would, it may be safely asserted, be upheld as a reasonable one, by a court.

Implied warranty of vendor's title.

There is also, of course, always an implied warranty of the vendor's title in the thing sold.

§ 3. *The Manner of Effecting the Delivery.*

The method employed to give complete and absolute title to the securities, registered or not negotiable, sold at the Stock Exchange, is by a transfer and registration.

Vendor must give vendee the usual evidence of title.

And though the courts have held that the owner of shares may really hold them without any certificate at all, and the company be bound to respect his rights,[1] still it is usually the duty of the vendor to deliver the certificates or evidences of ownership to the vendee.

Vendor need not have vendee's name on register.

But it does not follow that the vendor, to effect a delivery to the vendee, must cause the vendee's name to be put on the register of the corporation, as well as to make him a transfer of the stock, etc.

---

[1] Bank *v.* Burr, 24 Me. 256; Bank *v.* Wilson, 24 Me. 273; Ellis *v.* Bridge Co., 2 Pick. (Mass.) 243; Sargeant *v.* Ins. Co., 8 Pick. 90; Chester Glass Co. *v.* Dewey, 16 Mass. 94. See, also, the rules, as to delivery, of the New York and Philadelphia Stock Exchanges.

CHAP. VIII.] COMPLETION OF THE CONTRACT. 267

Prima facie, the vendor's duties are at an end when he offers,[1] and, if accepted, then actually transfers to the vendee, the legal evidence of the title to the securities he has sold him, there always being an implied warranty that the vendor's title to the thing sold is good, and the vendor can have his name put on the register when he likes. *Vendor's duties prima facie at an end when indicia of ownership are delivered to vendee.*

As, for instance, in Munn v. Barnum,[2] it was held, that mere readiness to transfer will be considered sufficient, and an actual transfer is not necessary, where the purchaser declines to pay the price. *Munn v. Barnum.*

The usual method of effecting the transfer is simply to hand the vendee the bond, or certificate of stock, sold, with a proper power of attorney to have it transferred to his name. But this is not necessary, for it is conceived that any other manner of showing a readiness to transfer would be sufficient. *What delivery necessary to make.*

But where there is any custom of the trade, of course that must be strictly followed; as, for instance, where the vendor's duty is, by a rule, to have the vendee's name put upon the register, he must do so.

The title to many kinds of stock renders the possessor of the shares liable to calls or assessments; and with regard to the delivery, it is a little embarrassing to see how far the vendor is bound to give the vendee a title clear from all existing calls. *Calls.*

It is, in the absence of express agreement, to be naturally presumed that the vendee is to get a delivery of the thing sold, freed from any liability to the company which did not actually exist at the time the

---

[1] See Humble *v.* Langston, 7 M. & W. 200; Hibblewhite *v.* Mc-Morine, 6 M. & W. 517; Hammic *v.* Goldner, 11 M. & W. 849.
[2] 24 Barb. (N. Y.) 288.

contract of sale was made; and in Shaw v. Rowley,[1] it was held to be a good offer of delivery, though the seller had not paid up intervening calls, as he might have done so at the moment of making the transfer. But with regard to calls made after the contract of sale and before the delivery, the case is not free from doubt. Perhaps the safer rule would be to allow the liability of either of the parties to be gathered generally from the agreement of the contract of sale, and to say that, in the absence of any stipulation to the contrary, the transferee is entitled to a transfer, freed from all liability to pay existing calls. With regard to the payment of calls after the transfer and before registration, see *infra*, under Registration.

No particular mode of transfer legally necessary.

We have said above that no particular mode of making the transfer is legally necessary, and a written order, or even verbal, would theoretically be sufficient from the principal to enable the stock broker to convey the certificates to the vendee, or even have them registered in the vendee's name at the office of the company. Generally, however, it is a by-law of the company that the transfer of names or registration must be made under seal, and then the stock broker is compelled to give a certificate of stock, etc., with a power of attorney to the purchaser to have it transferred to his name.

Transfer usually under seal by by-law of company.

It is very inconvenient to have a deed made out in full at each sale by the parties, as frequently shares pass through a dozen hands before they are registered again, and to hand them up after sale for registration would cause great loss to the owner, as they could not

[1] 5 Railway Cases, 47.

CHAP. VIII.] COMPLETION OF THE CONTRACT. 269

be used in trade during the time taken for registration; and, therefore, in several of the United States it has been found convenient by stock brokers within the last few years to effect the conveyance or transfer of shares from one party to the other by the broker's handing the certificate of shares to the buyer, together with an assignment in blank and power of attorney to transfer from his principal, usually on the back of the certificate. And the vendee, then, on handing this to the corporation, gets the shares transferred to his name. Where it is not necessary that the assignment should be under seal, as in certain cost book mining companies in England,[1] in which the shares are transferable without the intervention of any sealed instrument, but simply on the receipt of a letter signed by a shareholder directing the transfer, and leaving blanks to be filled up by the agent, and in Massachusetts, where under the general law no seal is necessary to the transfer,[2] and where the courts have held that a person could hold shares without any certificates,[3] and in fact anywhere, where the corporation does not demand that the transfer should be under seal, such a method is perfectly valid. But where it is a rule of the corporation that the transfers should be under seal, it has been objected that such transfers are invalid, because a deed signed in blank by the vendor cannot be legally filled up by the vendee.

In England, this strict common-law rule that an agent must receive his powers under seal to legally

Transfers by power of attorney, in blank.

---

[1] Walker v. Bartlett, 18 C. B. 845. See Humble v. Mitchell, 11 Ad. & El. 205.

[2] See Atkinson v. Ib., 8 Allen, 15; Quiner v. Marblehead Ins. Co., 10 Mass. 476.

[3] Chester Glass Co. v. Dewey, 16 Mass. 94; 8 Pick. 95.

execute an instrument under seal is now in full force, and therefore such transfers as these would be there considered not valid. It was, indeed, attempted by Lord Mansfield, in Texira *v.* Evans,[1] to relax this rigid rule of the common law, but it was unsuccessful, and, after holding its ground for over fifty years, was finally overruled by Parke, B., in Hibblewhite *v.* McMorine.[2]

Texira v. Evans.

Hibblewhite v. McMorine.

Davidson v. Cooper.

Again, in Davidson *v.* Cooper,[3] Texira *v.* Evans was declared bad law, and later, in Squire *v.* Whitton,[4] the House of Lords held, that a bond executed with the obligee's name in blank, and filled in by an implied authority, was void in law and equity.

Swan v. N. B. A. Co.

In Swan *v.* N. B. A. Co.,[5] Baron Parke held, that an instrument under seal executed in blank by the plaintiff and afterwards filled up by an agent, deriving his authority by parol, in fraud of third parties, was void, though the plaintiff had been guilty of culpable negligence.

In America, in the great Stock Exchanges,[6] the custom is to effect transfers of stock in this manner. But the law is by no means uniform in the United States on the subject of these transfers or deeds in blank, and it becomes, therefore, our duty to give a *résumé* of the cases of the various States on this subject.

A majority of the States[7] incline to the common-

---

[1] Cited in Master *v.* Miller, 4 T. R. 320.
[2] 6 M. & W. 216.
[3] 11 M. & W. 793.
[4] H. L. C. 333.
[5] 8 Jurist, N. S. 940; see, also, Humble *v.* Langston, 7 M. & W. 517; Eagleton *v.* Eagleridge, 11 M. & W. 465.

[6] New York, Philadelphia, and San Francisco.
[7] See, on this subject, the excellent note of Mr. Richard S. Hunter, to the case of Preston *v.* Hull, to be found in 12 Amer. Law. Reg., N. S. 711, from which the following cases and the text are in the main taken.

law rule, but by a large minority it is rejected. Hesitating between the mischiefs that might ensue from too bold an innovation upon the common law, and the evident injustice of allowing obligers to escape from the consequences of their acts, the courts in those States which reject the strict doctrine, have departed from it only so far as it was necessary in the premises. Distinctions have been taken between a bond and a conveyance; between a piece of paper signed and sealed, and a bond or deed in which some essential part was wanting; between express and implied authority; between authority to fill up a given name or a fixed sum, and authority to insert the name of any one at all, or for an amount to be determined by the agent. Nor have the decisions in individual States been consistent. The fluctuations of judicial opinion, as evinced in the number of cases doubted and overruled, are very noticeable. In such a chaos of conflicting authorities, perhaps it will be best to give the law of the different States *seriatim*, stating as far as necessary the law of each case.

Arkansas, Illinois, Georgia, Kentucky, Massachusetts, Mississippi, North Carolina, Tennessee, and Virginia follow the old English rule of the common law, and, while at periods the courts have been inclined to relax it, the later decisions have fully restored it.

In Arkansas, in the leading case of Cross *v.* The State Bank,[1] a bond was executed with a blank for the sum, and filled in without express authority, and the court held, that the writing was not, nor could be,

Cross v. State Bank.

[1] 5 Pike, 525.

a deed, except when made by an agent under seal, and here the American decisions were reviewed.

Maus v. Worthing.

In Illinois, in Maus *v.* Worthing,[1] written authority was given to sign a surety's name to an appeal bond; but, the court said, "the rule of law seems well "settled that an agent or attorney cannot bind his "principal by deed, unless he has authority by deed "to do so." Breese, J., said, in dissent, "The rule as "laid down appears to me destitute of any good "reason, and altogether too technical for this age."

Bragg v. Fessenden.

In Bragg *v.* Fessenden,[2] an agent, according to a written request, executed an appeal bond for his principal, and a regular power of attorney ratifying his action was afterwards filed, under seal; but the court held, that the original deed was void, and *quære* whether the ratification could date back.

Ingram v. Little.

In Georgia, in Ingram *v.* Little,[3] the court held, that a deed executed in blank and filled up by an agent appointed in writing not under seal, was void.

Remarks of Nisbet, J.

Nisbet, J., said, "We put our decision upon the "authority, conceding that the books in England "and in this country are in distressing conflict, and "with some misgivings whether reason and common "sense do not condemn it."

Cummins v. Cassily.

In Kentucky, in Cummins *v.* Cassily,[4] the court said, "Can an agent, without authority, under seal, "bind his principal by a sealed instrument? The "unbroken current of decisions is to the contrary."

Smith v. Crocker.

In Massachusetts, in Smith *v.* Crocker,[5] which was

---

[1] 3 Scammon, 26.
[2] 11 Ill. 544; see People *v.* Organ, 27 Ill. 27.
[3] 11 Georgia, 174.
[4] 5 B. Monroe, 75; see Southard *v.* Steele, 8 Monroe, 435.
[5] 5 Mass. 538.

followed in Hunt v. Adams,[1] the name of a surety, after he had executed a bond, was filled up in the body of the bond by an agent appointed by parol. The decision turned entirely upon the immateriality of the addition. But in Burns v. Lynde,[2] it was decided, that "filling up a blank form of a deed exe-"cuted by the parol authority of one who had signed "and sealed it, will not make it a valid convey-"ance, unless the instrument be redelivered." In this case the Massachusetts decisions are shown to be consistent, and in accordance with the common law. But in Day v. Holmes,[3] the practice of transferring stock by blank assignment seems to have been recognized. But the assignments of shares in a corporation under the Gen. Sts., c. 60, § 13, need not be under seal.[4]

In Mississippi, a blank bond sealed and afterwards filled up by a parol agent, was held void, in Williams v. Crutcher;[5] and in Dickson v. Hamer,[6] the Chancellor said he was constrained to follow Williams v. Crutcher.

In North Carolina, the law was settled in Graham v. Holt,[7] in which a sum left in blank in a bond was afterwards filled up by an agent, whose authority was not under seal, and the court, disapproving of Texira v. Evans, held it void.[8]

In Tennessee, a blank paper signed and sealed,

[1] 6 Mass. 519.
[2] 6 Allen, 305 [1863].
[3] 103 Mass. 306.
[4] Atkinson v. Ib., 8 Allen, 15; see, also, Quiner v. Marblehead Ins. Co., 10 Mass. Rep. 476; 8 Pick. 95.
[5] 5 Howard, 71.
[6] Freeman's Ch. 284.
[7] 3 Iredell's Law, 300.
[8] McKee v. Hicks, 2 Dev. 379; see, also, Davenport v. Sleight, 2 D. & B. 381; Van Hook v. Barnet, 4 Dev. Law, 272.

with verbal authority to fill up as a bond, was held void after the blanks were filled up.[1]

Preston v. Hull.

In Virginia, the authorities were carefully reviewed in Preston v. Hull,[2] where the court came to the conclusion that a bond executed by two persons in the bond, where the name of the obligee was to be inserted, and delivered, in this condition, to one of the persons by the other, with verbal authority to borrow money upon it, and to insert the name of the person from whom the money was obtained in the blank as obligee, was a mere nullity, and not the deed of the person delivering it, and Texira v. Evans was disapproved of.

The following States incline towards the English doctrine, without positively laying it down:

Upton v. Archer.

In California, in Upton v. Archer,[3] it was held, that a deed in due form, but with the grantee's name afterwards filled in by an agent, without an authority under seal to act, was void. In this case, though decided under the Statute of Frauds, the counsel relied upon the common-law doctrine, and the reasoning of the court would seem to imply that they upheld it.

In Ohio, a blank paper was signed and sealed, and a money bond written over it by an agent appointed verbally, and the court said, "an authority to fill one "particular blank falls far short of an authority to "make an entire deed."[4]

Byers v. McClanahan.

In Maryland, in Byers v. McClanahan,[5] a case similar to Ayres v. Harness, the court held the bond

---

[1] See Smith v. Dickinson, 6 Humph. 261; Turbeville v. Ryan, 1 Humph. 113; Mosby v. State, 4 Sneed, 324.
[2] 12 A. L. R., N. S. 699.
[3] 41 Cal. 85 [1871].
[4] Ayres v. Harness, 1 Ohio, 368.
[5] 6 G. & J. 250.

void, but decided that a subsequent acknowledgment by the grantor of his hand and seal constituted a re-delivery.

In Delaware, the distinction is taken between an implied and express authority, and in Clendaniel *v.* Hastings,[1] it was held, that an authority merely implied to fill in the blanks in a bond already executed did not bind the obliger.

Clendaniel v. Hastings.

In Pennsylvania, the decisions are conflicting, and the earlier decisions support Texira *v.* Evans.[2]

In Wiley *v.* Moor,[3] the obligers signed and sealed a piece of blank paper, and left it with a judge to be filled in as a bond, and it was held binding, and Texira *v.* Evans followed as good law; and to the same effect was Graham *v.* Ogle.[4] But in a later case, that of Wallace *v.* Harmstead,[5] the court held, that no authority to fill up a deed could be *implied*. Gilison, J., said, "There is no instance of an implied "agency to alter a deed. Texira *v.* Evans can be "supported, if at all, only upon the ground of an "estoppel by an act *in pais*."

Wiley v. Moor.

Graham v. Ogle.
Wallace v. Harmstead.

In Lyon *v.* Denny,[6] where the owner of stock executed and delivered to a friend a power of attorney, with the certificates authorizing the person therein named to transfer to ———, with the understanding it was to be used with reference to a particular creditor of the friend, whose name was afterwards inserted by him, the court held, that in any view the authority of the agent was exhausted by the insertion of the first

Lyon v. Denny.

---

[1] 5 Har. 408.
[2] See Sigfried *v.* Levan, 6 S. & R. 308; Stahl *v.* Berger, 10 S. & R. 170.
[3] 17 S. & R. 438.
[4] 2 Pa. 132.
[5] 3 Harris, 468; 2 Barr, 194.
[6] 38 Pa. 98.

name designated, that the creditor had paid his debt, and that the principal was entitled to a return of the stock, notwithstanding that the agent had transferred it to secure other debts, by erasing the first name and inserting another.

German Ass. Co. v. Sendmeyer. In the German Union Building, etc. Association *v.* Sendmeyer,[1] however, the court expressly held, that the delivery by an owner of stock of a power of attorney to transfer, executed in blank, with the certificates, is evidence of an implied authority to fill up the name of an attorney and make the transfer, where there is a valuable consideration.

In New York, the decisions are not harmonious.

Ex parte Kerwen. In *Ex parte* Kerwen,[2] a blank for the amount in an appeal bond was filled in, after execution, by an agent verbally appointed, and held valid.

Hanford v. McNair. But in Hanford *v.* McNair,[3] a very strong case, the agent was authorized in writing to enter into a contract for the purchase of lands, and, having made the contract under seal, and had it ratified by the principal, it was held void. The only exception to the strict rule "is where the agent affixes the seal of the prin-"cipal in his presence and by his direction."[4]

Bank of Buffalo v. Kortright. In Bank of Buffalo *v.* Kortright,[5] the Court of Errors declared this to be law in New York. Here the court held, that proof as to the usage of transferring stock with blank powers was admissible, and that a blank power of attorney to transfer was good, by usage and otherwise. It may be added, that Hibblewhite *v.* McMorine had not yet arisen. And in Wor-

Worrell v. Munn.

---

[1] 50 Pa. 67.
[2] 8 Cowen, 118.
[3] 9 Wend. 54.
[4] See, also, Blood *v.* Goodrich, 9 Wend. 68; 12 Wend. 525.
[5] 22 Wend. 348.

CHAP. VIII.] COMPLETION OF THE CONTRACT. 277

rell v. Munn,[1] it was held, that if the instrument executed by an agent derives its validity merely from the seal, it is void; but if good without seal, it will be binding as a parol contract.

In Chauncey v. Arnold,[2] where the blanks were never filled in, the deed was held void; but see the opinion of the court. The point may perhaps be considered as doubtful in New York. *Chauncey v. Arnold.*

In Iowa, there is a strong dictum by Dillon, J., in Simms v. Hervey,[3] against Texira v. Evans. But in Devin v. Himer,[4] an express authority to insert a grantee's name, followed by ratification, was held binding; and in Owen v. Perry,[5] the court held, that a written authority would be sufficient, though the deed was to be filled up to any one. *Simms v. Hervey. Devin v. Hiner. Owen v. Perry.*

In Connecticut, the point does not seem to be directly ruled, but the inclination of the courts is towards Texira v. Evans.

In Bridgeport Bank v. R. R. Co.,[6] a blank power of attorney accompanying stock was filled up, and the court held it valid under the New York law; but Ellsworth, J., intimated the Connecticut law would be the same. *Bridgeport Bank v. R. R. Co.*

In New Jersey, the case of Camden Bank v. Hall[7] does not seem decisive, as the circumstances of the case might amount to a redelivery. *Camden Bank v. Hall.*

In Maine, parol authority to fill in any instrument under seal is sufficient. See Inhabitants of South Berwick v. Huntress.[8] *Inhabitants, etc., v. Huntress.*

---

[1] 1 Selden, 239.
[2] 24 N. Y. 330.
[3] 19 Iowa, 273.
[4] 29 Iowa, 298.
[5] 25 Iowa, 412 [1868].
[6] 30 Conn. 281.
[7] 2 Green, 383.
[8] 53 Maine, 89.

Boardman v. Gore.

In Alabama, in Boardman v. Gore,[1] there was a case of implied authority to fill in the obligee's name, but the bond was payable to "———, or bearer," and the insertion was hardly material.

Gibbs v. Frost.

In Gibbs v. Frost,[2] an express authority was held sufficient, and Texira v. Evans is quoted as authority.

In Texas and Indiana, the statutes abolishing seal, and in Louisiana, the peculiar system of the State, would be probably fatal to the common-law rule. In the latter State, appeal bonds filled in, after execution by the sureties, have always been held binding.[3]

In South Carolina, the courts explicitly sustain Texira v. Evans. All the cases appear to be those of express authority; but the reasoning of the judges goes the full length.[4]

Finally, the Federal courts now lean towards Texira v. Evans.

Speake v. United States.

In Speake v. The United States,[5] it was settled that an express parol authority to alter a sealed instrument could be shown; but in United States v. Nelson,[6] it was held, by Marshall, C. J., "with much doubt," that no implied authority will be sufficient.

United States v. Nelson.

Drury v. Foster.

In Drury v. Foster,[7] although the decision turned upon a personal incapacity, the court intimated that otherwise a deed filled in by a parol agent would be valid, adding that, "Although it was at one time

---

[1] 1 Stew. 517.
[2] 4 Ala., N. S. 720.
[3] Breedlove v. Johnson, 2 Martin, N. S. 517; State v. The Judges, 19 La. 179; Charlaron v. McFarlane, 9 La. 230.
[4] Bank v. Hammond, 1 Rich. 281; Gourdin v. Commander, 6 Rich. 497; Duncan v. Hodges, 4 McC. 239. It was intimated that in the last case a blank piece of paper signed and sealed is utterly nugatory.
[5] 9 Cranch, 28.
[6] 2 Brock. 64.
[7] 2 Wallace, 24.

CHAP. VIII.] COMPLETION OF THE CONTRACT. 279

"doubted whether parol authority was adequate to "authorize an alteration or addition to a sealed instru- "ment, the better opinion at this day is that the power "is sufficient."

It may be added, that all the cases agree that if the instrument under seal be filled up *in the presence* of the grantor and with his consent, it will be binding upon him.

Hitherto we have examined those modes of delivery of transfers which are made directly by the stock broker, but, as has already been stated in a former part of this work, the larger proportion of the daily deliveries of stock at some of the Stock Exchanges in this country are made through the Clearing House, which is an office or bureau where the amount of shares of stock to be delivered to and by each broker in the transactions of each day is ascertained by ex- amining and balancing the several accounts of each one. This is a direct delivery through the interven- tion of a third agency, and the method by which it is effected is fully described in detail in Part I., Chap- ter II., Section II.[1] *The Clearing House deliv- ery.*

The vendor must also be ready to deliver the docu- ments of title at the time stipulated for, or in the absence of any stipulation, according to the custom of the trade or the rules of the Exchange in such cases; and it is always a question for the courts to determine upon, the usage being a reasonable one. *Time.*

Where the time is fixed in the contract itself, its construction is, of course, a matter of law for the courts.

[1] Page 55.

With regard to "leap-year," in England, see the first volume of the English Revised Statutes, page 4.

"Month" in mercantile transactions. The word "month" in mercantile transactions is generally understood to mean a calendar month, and the court will look into the transaction to see if that was not the intent.[1]

"Month" in stock transactions. In stock transactions, generally, the word "month" would probably be interpreted as meaning calendar month,[2] though perhaps in England, where there are account days of a fortnight each, the word "month" might mean a lunar month, or twenty-eight days, when equivalent to two accounts.[3]

Days. Where days are counted to ascertain the time for delivery on a time contract, they are counted as consecutive days, and include Sundays,[4] unless the contrary be expressed. A usage of the trade or rule of the Stock Exchange is, however, always admissible in evidence to show a different rule,[5] and probably where there are several days allowed for the delivery, the count must be made exclusive of the day of contract.

Coddington v. Paleologo. Thus, in Coddington v. Paleologo,[6] on a "delivering on April 17th, complete 18th May," the court was divided whether the vendor was bound to commence on April 17th.

Hour. The hour up to which one can deliver on the last day agreed upon by the contractor, is discussed in

---

[1] See Simpson v. Margitson, 11 Q. B. 23; Webb v. Fairmaner, 3 M. & W. 473; see also 13 Vict. c. 21, s. 4.

[2] See Hart v. Middleton, 2 C. & K. 9.

[3] Jocelyn v. Hawkins, 1 Strange, 446.

[4] Brown v. Johnson, 10 M. & W. 331.

[5] Cochran v. Retberg, 3 Esp. 121; Webb v. Fairmaner, 3 M. & W. 473; Young v. Higgin, 6 M. & W. 49; Isaacs v. Ins. Co., L. R., 5 Ex. 296.

[6] L. R., 2 Ex. 193.

Startup v. McDonald.[1] Respecting the place of delivery, probably that usual in like cases is the proper place; certainly in the absence of agreement.

Startup v. McDonald. Place.

It is, however, to be observed that the foregoing remarks, as well as the cases quoted to illustrate them, are applicable only where the usage in reference to these subjects is not expressly defined by the regulations of the Stock Exchange where the transaction takes place. Most of these particulars are specifically fixed by the rules of the London Stock Exchange, as well as of the chief American Exchanges; and in the latter every member is required to have a place of business in the vicinity of the Stock Exchange, where all notices required by the rules of the Exchange can be served, and where, probably, deliveries to a member, not effected through the Clearing House, would, *prima facie*, have to be made.[2]

Regulations of Stock Exchange on deliveries.

SECTION II.—THE VENDEE.

The duty of the vendee is to pay the price agreed upon and accept the thing sold, and, where it is necessary, he must have his name placed upon the register.

§ 1. *Acceptance and Payment.*

The vendee, by accepting one mode of delivery without objection, as by receiving a certificate of stock accompanied by a power of attorney to transfer, executed in blank, thereby waives his right to insist upon another, as, for example, an actual transfer.

---

[1] 6 M. & G. 593.
[2] See Rules of New York Stock Exchange, pp. 20–45, etc.; and of Philadelphia Stock Exchange, Art. vi. § 4, p. 43; of San Francisco Board, p. 25, etc.

Price.

With regard to the price, the vendee's duties resemble those in any case of sales of personal chattels. We shall, then, merely lay down a few principles. As we have already seen, this is *prima facie* an absolute cash payment, or sometimes may be a conditional payment by checks or notes. In sales of this kind credit is very unusually given, and never without express stipulation.

Tender.

There are certain rules in some of the Stock Exchanges regulating the method of payment, but, in the absence of such, the payment must always be cash, or a tender of cash made, equal to the price, though the actual money need not be produced. But there should be an opportunity for the seller to count the money,[1] which will be sufficient. The tender for more than enough is good,[2] but a tender will not be valid for less than the amount;[3] and the tender must be unconditional.[4] Where, however, a peculiar mode of payment is agreed to by the vendor, as, for instance, where the agency of the post is employed, the vendee has sufficiently complied, even though the money never reach the vendor. Ordinary caution should be used, and perhaps it would be requisite for the vendee to have the letter placed in the post-office itself,[5] or even registered; certainly if he were in the habit of ordinarily doing so.

Medium of payment.

The proper medium of payment is, in England, either in pursuance to the statute of 3 & 4 Will. IV.

---

[1] Isherwood *v.* Whitmore, 11 M. & W. 347.

[2] Dean *v.* James, 4 B. & A. 546; see Betterbee *v.* Davis, 3 Campb. 70.

[3] Dixon *v.* Clarke, 5 C. B. 365.

[4] Eckstein *v.* Reynolds, 7 Ad. & E. 85.

[5] Hawkins *v.* Rutt, Peake, 186; see, also, Gordon *v.* Strange, 1 Ex. 477; Eyles *v.* Ellis, 4 Bing. 112.

ch. 98, in notes of the Bank of England, payable to bearer, so long as the bank is solvent, for sums in excess of five pounds,[1] or in silver for certain sums, and over that in gold,[2] and in the United States there are three media—United States paper made legal tender, gold coin for certain amounts, and silver for smaller, for which the reader is referred to the acts of Congress. At the common law, the tender was required to be made in foreign coin legally current, or in current money.[3]

Frequently the medium of payment is regulated by the rules of the Stock Exchange, which then govern members, and, unless held by a court to be unreasonable in their character, those acting through them. Thus, payment in current bank notes, or in due bills of banks belonging to the Bank Clearing House, is allowed.[4] And, perhaps, if any papers are to be prepared, it would be the duty of the vendee to have them ready.[5]

Papers.

§ 2. *Registration.*

The *prima facie* duty of the vendee is to have his name placed on the register by himself or attorney, and in England there is a stamp duty on a power of attorney for this purpose,[6] though if a rule of the Stock Exchange existed to the effect, the vendor would have to have it accomplished for him.

---

[1] Warwick *v.* Noakes, Peake, 68.
[2] Coinage Act, 1870, sec. 4.
[3] See Bac. Abr., Tender, B. 2; 5 Reports, 114.
[4] See rules of N. Y. Stock Exchange, and of Philadelphia Stock Exchange, Article xiii. § 2, p. 47.
[5] See Lawrence *v.* Knowles, 5 Bing. (N. C.) 399; Bowlby *v.* Bell, 3 C. B. 692; Stephens *v.* De Medina, 4 Ad. & El., N. S. 422.
[6] 27 Vict. c. 18.

It is, however, optional with the vendee when he will have it done; but, after a valid tender of the securities and acceptance, if he negligently or wilfully do not have his name placed upon the register, he is responsible for any loss that may occur to the vendor in consequence of his failure to do so. In other words, he makes an implied warranty to save the vendor harmless for any fault of his in not registering when he should have done so after the transfer.

<small>Implied warranty to save vendor harmless.</small>

Thus, by the Act of 8 & 9 Victoria, c. 16, § 15, the vendor remains liable for calls until the registry of the vendee's name is made.

<small>Walker v. Bartlett.</small>

In Walker v. Bartlett,[1] the owner of five hundred shares in a cost book mine, in which the person registered is liable to calls, sold his shares to the defendant, and delivered him a paper addressed to the secretary of the mine, requesting a transfer to the transferee, but leaving his name in blank, and with a blank acceptance on the part of the transferee. The defendant did not get registered, and, in an action brought by the plaintiff for money spent to his use in the payment of calls, the court held, that the defendant was not bound, as it appeared clearly by the terms of the contract, it was not necessary to fill up the blank and get registered unless he liked; but that if, for his convenience, he did not, he was bound to indemnify the plaintiff for the calls he had paid.

<small>Humble v. Langston.</small>

In Humble v. Langston,[2] the facts were as follows. The plaintiff contracted with the defendant, through their respective brokers, for the sale of thirty shares in a railway company. There was no time mentioned for

---

[1] 18 C. B. 844.   [2] 7 M. & W. 517.

the completion of the contract. On the 3d of March, the defendant wrote requesting the plaintiff's brokers to "dispatch the thirty shares forthwith," and they replied, "We send you the transfer of thirty * * * shares in *blank*," and the purchase money was paid. Calls were subsequently made, and the plaintiff, being still registered, was compelled to pay. In an action against the defendant for an indemnity against *present* and all *future* calls, it was held, however, that under the circumstances there was no implied obligation to indemnify against all subsequent calls. This decision was, however, based upon the fact, that the conveyance or transfer in blank was not a valid one; and that the plaintiff might have insisted on a valid deed of conveyance, if he had desired, but that he was content with what he got; and the law raised no implied promise to indemnify. It is to be noted in this case that the plaintiff asked to be indemnified against *all future* calls, that is, longer than he might be beneficially interested.

In Sayles *v.* Blane,[1] Coleridge, J., followed the opinion of the Court of Exchequer in Humble *v.* Langston. Here, also, the transfer was in blank.

It is difficult to distinguish, in principle, the preceding case of Walker *v.* Bartlett, from the case of Humble *v.* Langston, and this the court, in the former case, admitted. Still, the facts did differ, since in Humble *v.* Langston a *deed* of transfer was necessary, though not in Walker *v.* Bartlett; and, besides, the plaintiff in Humble *v.* Langston asked to be indemnified longer than he was beneficially interested, and this

Sayles v. Blane.

[1] 14 Q. B. 205.

is a very important distinction. It may be added, under this general head, that by the common law it is a mooted question whether the buyer could demand a receipt for money;[1] where, however, the buyer gives one, it is not necessarily an acceptance of the transfer, but will perhaps become so if he do nothing further within a proper time.[2] With regard to where there is a usage of the trade on this subject, see *supra*, page 215.

---

[1] Cole *v.* Blake, Peake, 179; Richardson *v.* Jackson, 8 M. & W. 298; Wood *v.* Hitchcock, 20 Wend. 47.

[2] Parker *v.* Palmer, 4 B. & A. 387; Chapman *v.* Morton, 11 M. & W. 534; Fitzsimmons *v.* Woodruff, 1 N. Y. S. C. 34; Treadwell *v.* Reynolds, 39 Conn. 31; Bianchi *v.* Nash, 1 M. & W. 545.

CHAPTER IX.

AVOIDANCE OF THE CONTRACT.

	PAGE
Division of chapter	287
SECTION I.—AVOIDANCE OF THE CONTRACT BY FRAUD, ETC.	
§ 1. FRAUD	288
§ 2. MISTAKE	288
§ 3. FAILURE OF CONSIDERATION	289
SECTION II.—AVOIDANCE OF THE CONTRACT BY ILLEGALITY.	
§ 1. CONTRACTS ILLEGAL AT COMMON LAW, BECAUSE IN RESTRAINT OF TRADE	290
Cases discussed	291
Corners illegal	294
Restraint in respect to time	295
§ 2. CONTRACTS ILLEGAL BECAUSE IN THE NATURE OF WAGERS	296
Wagers at common law	297
Wagers by statute	298
Act of Sir John Barnard	298
Act of 23 & 24 Vict.	298
Act of 8 & 9 Vict.	299
Wagers in the United States	299
Divisions of subject	299
I. Where the vendor, at the formation of the contract, has not the goods in his possession, nor a reasonable expectation of getting them, but contemplates an actual unconditional delivery	302
Cases discussed	302
II. Where the vendor, at the formation of the contract, contemplates a symbolical, but not a manual, unconditional delivery of the goods	302
Cases discussed	303
Pennsylvania cases	305
Pennsylvania cases doubtful	308
III. Where the parties, at the formation of the contract, contemplate an actual delivery, but conditional as to time	309
Cases discussed	309
IV. Where the parties, at the formation of the contract, contemplate no actual delivery, but reserve the option to do so or not	310
Cases discussed	310
V. Where the parties, at the formation of the contract, contemplate no delivery at all, but only a settlement of the difference in price	313
Cases discussed	314
Principles deducible from the foregoing cases	318

CONTRACTS for the sale of securities made at the Stock Exchange may be avoided—first, by fraud, mistake, or failure of consideration; and, secondly, where the contract is tainted by illegality, and therefore voidable as being against the law.

Division of chapter.

SECTION I.—AVOIDANCE OF THE CONTRACT BY FRAUD, ETC.

Fraud.

With regard to the first of these heads, the same law that is applicable to sales of any other chattels, is applicable to the securities sold at the Stock Exchange; and therefore this part of the subject will require but brief notice, as few cases have arisen under it relating especially to these securities.

§ 1. *Fraud.*

Fraud defined.

Fraud is difficult to define, and perhaps the word may be best understood by looking at its legal effect on the contract; and it may then be defined to be some ground for setting aside the contract, upon the discovery, and in consequence, of an intentional and successful artifice causing an injury, practised by one of the parties without the knowledge of the other, and which was essential to the formation of the contract.

Fraud makes contract only voidable.

It will be seen that the presence of fraud does not make the contract void, but only voidable at the election of either the vendor or the vendee, as the case may be, who shall be discovered to have been injured.

In order to render fraud an efficacious means of avoiding the contract of sale, it is obvious that the party must have been deceived, and that the party deceiving must have done so intentionally, and that there must be evidence of injury resulting from the fraud, otherwise it is of no avail. We have come across no cases of fraud under the statute of Elizabeth which turned on the avoidance of the sale of these securities.

§ 2. *Mistake.*

It is obvious that, in order to make a valid contract of sale, the minds of the contracting parties must meet,

CHAP. IX.] AVOIDANCE OF THE CONTRACT. 289

and contract certainly with reference to the thing to be sold. If there has been a wrong impression on the part of one of the parties at the formation of the contract, it frequently may be set aside, for this reason. The common maxim of the law is that a mistake of law is not a ground for avoiding a contract, though this must be somewhat modified, and it is now settled that some mistakes of law as well as of fact are grounds for avoidance. It is difficult, perhaps, to distinguish exactly between the kinds of mistakes of law which will constitute a ground for rescinding a contract and those which do not. Perhaps the best explanation is that of Lord Westbury, in Cooper *v.* Phibbs.[1] "It is said," he remarked, "*ignorantia juris haud excusat*, but in "that maxim the word *jus* is used in the sense of "denoting general law, the ordinary of the country. "But when the word *jus* is used in the sense of de-"noting a private right, that maxim has no appli-"cation. Private right of ownership is a matter of "fact; it may also be the result of matter of law; but "if parties contract under a mutual mistake and mis-"apprehension as to their relative and respective rights, "the result is, that the agreement is liable to be set "aside as having proceeded upon a common mistake."

<small>Mistake of fact, and, in certain cases, mistake of law, avoids the contract.</small>

<small>Remarks of Lord Westbury in Cooper v. Phibbs.</small>

§ 3. *Failure of Consideration.*

Another ground for setting aside the contract is where the thing sold is not what the buyer desired to purchase.

Thus, as has been above remarked, on the subject of the guaranty of genuineness, the buyer is entitled

[1] L. R., 2 Eng. & Ir. App. 148.

19

to receive valid certificates of stock, and not forged ones,[1] and he is also entitled to get back his money, where he has subscribed in a projected railway, which is abandoned;[2] though, as has been observed under the condition of genuineness, there is no failure of consideration,[3] when he gets what he contracted for, but it proves to be worthless.

SECTION II.—AVOIDANCE OF THE CONTRACT BY ILLEGALITY.

The most numerous class of decisions certainly, and probably the most conflicting that have been given, with reference to the securities dealt in at the Stock Exchange, are those relating to the avoidance of the contract of sale in consequence of its being tainted by some kind of illegality.

Contracts usually illegal because "in restraint of trade," or wagering transactions.

The cases on this subject have all arisen upon the question, first, as to when, and how far, contracts are void because they tend in some way to hamper or restrict or otherwise injure trade and commerce, in which case they are termed contracts "in restraint of trade;" and, secondly, whether particular contracts do not institute wagers, which, though not originally voidable at the common law, are now made so by statute in England, as well as in most of the American States.

§ 1. *Contracts Illegal at Common Law because in Restraint of Trade.*

As just stated, a contract is said to be in restraint of trade when, in the opinion of a court, it will, if carried

---

[1] Westropp v. Solomon, 8 C. B. 345.
[2] Kempson v. Saunders, 4 Bingham, 5.
[3] Lambert v. Heath, 15 M. & W. 487.

CHAP. IX.] AVOIDANCE OF THE CONTRACT. 291

out, be of detriment to the material well-being of the county or community, or it is in any other way against public policy.

In the leading English case of Mitchell v. Reynolds,[1] the following rules were laid down by Parker, C. J., which, with some modifications, have been frequently upheld: that voluntary restraints of trade by agreement by parties were either—first, general, and in such cases void, whether by bond, covenant, or promise; whether with or without consideration, and whether of the parties' own trade or not; or, secondly, particular, and these latter were either without consideration, in which case they are void by what sort soever of contract created; or with consideration; in this latter class they are valid when made upon a good and adequate consideration,[2] so as to make them proper and useful contracts.[3] *Mitchell v. Reynolds. Rules of Parker, C. J.*

In Morris Run Coal Co. v. The Barclay Coal Co.,[4] several coal companies of Pennsylvania entered, in New York, into an agreement to divide two coal regions of which they had the control; to appoint a committee to take charge of their interests, and to decide upon all questions, and to appoint an agent at Wilkesbarre. The coal mined was to be delivered through him, and each corporation to deliver its proportionate share at its own cost in the different markets at such time and to such persons as the committee might direct, the committee to adjust the prices, rates, *Morris Run Coal Co. v. Barclay Coal Co.*

---

[1] 1 P. Wm. 181.
[2] Overruled in Hitchcock v. Coker, 6 Ad. & El. 438, as to adequacy of consideration.
[3] See Stuart v. Nicholson, 3 Bing. N. C. 118; Gale v. Reed, 8 East, 83.
[4] See 68 Pa. 173.

etc. It was also agreed that each of the five companies could only sell coal to the extent of its own proportionate share, and they agreed to be governed by the rules and regulations of the committee in their sales. It was held by the court, that this agreement was against public policy and void, and also within a statute in New York making it a misdemeanor for "persons to "conspire to commit any act injurious to trade or com-"merce."

Remarks of Agnew, J.

In delivering the opinion of the court, Agnew, J., said, quoting Parker, C. J., that to obtain "the sole "exercise of any known trade in England is a com-"plete monopoly and against the policy of the law. A "reason given is 'the great abuses the voluntary re-"straints are liable to, as, for instance, from corpora-"tions, who were perpetually laboring for exclusive "advantage in trade and to reduce it into as few hands "as possible.' In reference to a contract not to trade "in any part of England, it is said there is something "more than a presumption against it, because it never "can be useful to any man to restrain another from "trading in all places, though it may be to restrain "him from trading in some, unless he intends a mo-"nopoly, which is a crime. * * * The result of those" cases "in which particular restraints in trade have been "held to be valid between individuals is that the re-"straint must be partial only, the consideration ade-"quate and not colorable, and the restriction reasonable "upon the last requisite. Tindal, C. J., remarks in

Tindal, C. J., in Horner v. Graves, quoted.

"Horner v. Graves,[1] 'We do not see how a better test "can be applied to the question, whether reasonable or

[1] 7 Bingham, 743.

CHAP. IX.] AVOIDANCE OF THE CONTRACT. 293

"not, than by considering whether the restraint is such
"only as to afford a fair protection as to the interests
"of the party in favor of whom it is given, and not so
"large as to interfere with the interests of the public.
"Whatsoever restraint is larger than the necessary
"protection of the party can be of no benefit to either.
"It can only be oppressive, and, if oppressive, it is in
"the eye of the law unreasonable. What is injurious
"to the public interest is void upon the ground of pub-
"lic policy."

Many cases have been decided as to what is a reasonable restriction and what is not, and is therefore void, but two only may be referred to as illustrations.

In Mallan v. May,[1] a covenant not to practise as a dentist in London, or in any of the places in England or Scotland where the plaintiff might have been practising before the expiration of the term of service with them, was held to be reasonable as to the limit of London, but unreasonable and void as to the remainder of the restriction. *Mallan v. May.*

So, in Green v. Price,[2] a covenant not to follow the perfumery business in the cities of London and Westminster, or within the distance of six hundred miles therefrom, was good as to the cities, and void as to the limit of six hundred miles. *Green v. Price.*

The reader is also referred to the cases of Pierce v. Fuller,[3] and Chappel v. Brockway.[4] An important principle stated in these cases is, as to contracts for a limited restraint, the courts start with the presumption that they are illegal unless shown to have been *Pierce v. Fuller. Chappel v. Brockway.*

[1] 11 M. & W. 653.
[2] 13 M. & W. 695.
[3] 8 Mass. 223.
[4] 21 Wend. 158.

made upon adequate consideration and upon circumstances both reasonable and useful.

Keeler v. Taylor.

In Keeler *v.* Taylor,¹ Woodward, C. J., said, the general rule is, that all restraints of trade, if nothing more appear, are bad.

Commonwealth v. Carlisle. Remarks of Gibson, J.

In Commonwealth *v.* Carlisle,² Gibson, J., said, "I "take it, a combination is criminal whenever the act "to be done has a necessary tendency to prejudice the "public or to oppress individuals by unjustly subject- "ing them to the power of the confederates, and "giving effect to the purpose of the latter, whether "of extortion or of mischief."

The principles of law enunciated in these cases are of general application, and embrace contracts made at the Stock Exchange, as well as others. Whenever, therefore, the performance of such contracts may affect, or tend to affect, injuriously the general or commercial interests of the community, they have been held to be illegal.

Sampson v. Shaw. Agreement to make a "corner" illegal.

In Sampson *v.* Shaw,³ it was held, that an agreement to make "a corner" in stock, by buying it up so as to control the market, and then purchasing for future deliveries, is illegal, and the parties thereto are not partners; and any one of said parties who has authorized the others to use his funds already in their hands to carry out the agreement, cannot recover any amount actually appropriated according to its terms, but can recover, in an action for money had and received, any balance not so expended.

Raymond v. Levitt.

In the recent case of Raymond *v.* Levitt,⁴ decided

---

¹ 3 Sm. (Pa.) 468.
² Brightley's Rep. 40.
³ 101 Mass. 145.
⁴ 13 Cent. Law Jour. 110 [1881].

CHAP. IX.] AVOIDANCE OF THE CONTRACT. 295

in the Supreme Court in Michigan, a contract was entered into between different parties for the purpose of controlling the wheat market, for what is called the "May deal," with a view of forcing up prices, and producing what is understood as "a corner," and thereby compelling parties, who had contracts to fulfil, to purchase the wheat at a higher price in order to do so. Campbell, J., said, "The object of the ar- "rangement between these parties was to force the "fictitious and unnatural rise in the wheat market for "the express purpose of getting the advantage of "dealers and purchasers whose necessities compelled "them to buy, and necessarily to create a similar "difficulty, as to all persons who had to obtain or "use that commodity. * * * That such transactions "are hazardous to the comfort of the community is "universally recognized. This, alone, may not be "enough to make them illegal. But it is enough to "make them so questionable that very little further "is required to bring them within distinct prohibi- "tion." He held, on the authority of the Morris Run Coal Co. v. Barclay,[1] Arnott v. Pittston, etc.,[2] and People v. Fisher,[3] that the contract was illegal.

Remarks of Campbell, J.

Morris Run, etc. Co. v. Barclay; Arnott v. Pittston; and People v. Fisher, followed.

Reverting for a moment to the general principles already laid down, it does not appear clear, whether restrictions upon trade in regard to time have been pronounced illegal or not. Such restrictions may be either general or limited.

Restraint in respect to time.

As, for instance, in the case of Ward v. Byrne,[4] where a person covenanted not to follow a particular

Ward v. Byrne.

[1] 68 Pa. 173.
[2] 68 N. Y. 558.
[3] 14 Wend. 9.
[4] 5 M. & W. 548.

trade for nine months, Parke, B., said, "When a general restriction, limited only as to time, is imposed, the public are altogether losers for that time of the services of the individual, and do not derive any benefit whatever in return; and, looking at the authorities cited upon this subject, it does not appear that there is one clear authority in favor of a total restriction in trade only as to time. But when the restriction is otherwise reasonable, it is unimportant whether the restriction be general or not; in fact, the restriction might extend through the whole lifetime of the party, and, if otherwise reasonable, be good."[1]

In Rex *v.* De Berenger,[2] it was held to be a conspiracy to combine to raise the funds on a particular day by false rumors. "The purpose itself," said Lord Ellenborough, "is mischievous; it strikes at the price of a valuable commodity in the market, and if it gives a fictitious price by means of false rumors, it is a fraud levelled against the public, for it is against all such as may possibly have anything to do with the funds on that particular day."

§ 2. *Contracts Illegal because in the Nature of Wagers.*

Certain kinds of contracts of sale at the Stock Exchange have, in England and in some of the United States, been made illegal by statute, because considered to partake of the nature of wagering contracts.

---

[1] Mumford *v.* Gething, 7 C. B., N. S. 305.

[2] 3 M. & S. 67; see, also, Hitchcock *v.* Coker, 6 Ad. & El. 438; Hinde *v.* Gray, 1 M. & G. 195; Home *v.* Ashford, 3 Bingham, 322; 1 Sm. Lead. Cas. 172; Commonwealth *v.* Hunt, 4 Metcalf, 111.

CHAP. IX.] AVOIDANCE OF THE CONTRACT. 297

At the common law, wagers were not *per se* regarded as illegal, and an action lay to recover the money won on a wager, except where the courts considered them to be opposed in some way to public policy. *Wagers at the common law.*

Thus, in Good *v.* Elliott,[1] a wager that A. had purchased a wagon of B. was held not to be an illegal contract. *Good v. Elliott.*

And so, in Walpole *v.* Saunders,[2] it was held, that where a judge had chosen to try a case on a wager for a cricket-match, the court in banc would not grant a rule for a new trial. *Walpole v. Saunders.*

But in Da Costa *v.* Jones,[3] it was held, that an action would not lie upon a voluntary wager, between two indifferent persons, as to the sex of a third person, who was acting apparently as a man in a public capacity, on the ground that it tended to disturb the peace of an individual, and that of society, and also because the evidence necessitated an indecent exposure in court. *Da Costa v. Jones.*

And so, in Brown *v.* Leeson,[4] no action lay on a wager to determine the method of playing an illegal game. Nor in Hartley *v.* Rice,[5] on a wager that a person would not marry in six years, because in restraint of marriage. Nor in Phillips *v.* Ives,[6] where the subject of the wager was the possible duration of the life of an individual. *Brown v. Leeson.* *Hartley v. Rice.* *Phillips v. Ives.*

In America, some of the States have followed the rule of the common law, as, for example, California,[7] Delaware,[8] Texas,[9] etc., while in New Hampshire[10] and

[1] 3 T. R. 693.
[2] 16 E. C., L. R. 276.
[3] 2 Cowper, 729.   [4] 2 H. Bl. 43.
[5] 10 East, 22.   [6] 1 Rawle, 36.
[7] Johnson *v.* Fall, 6 Cal. 359.
[8] Dewees *v.* Miller, 5 Harrington (Del.), 347.
[9] Wheeler *v.* Friend, 22 Texas, 683.
[10] Winchester *v.* Nutter, 52 N. H. 507; Clark *v.* Gibson, 12 *ib.* 386.

Maine,[1] the courts have decided that a wager was not a valid contract in those States. In Massachusetts, the judicial opinions have been adverse to wagers;[2] and all wagers are void in Pennsylvania courts,[3] as well as in those of Vermont.[4]

Wagers by statute in England.

From the middle of the eighteenth century, however, there have been passed a series of statutes in England, directed against gambling contracts, and particularly those in stocks. In 1834, the well-known

Act of Sir John Barnard.

Act of Sir John Barnard was passed, to prevent the "Infamous Practice of Stock Jobbing" (see statutes 7 George II. c. 8, and 10 George II. c. 8), and related to all bargains for the sale and purchase of the public stock of the British government.[5] The act was, how-

Act of 23 & 24 Victoria.

ever, repealed by 23 & 24 Vict. c. 28. These were the only statutes that were passed with reference especially to contracts in stocks or bonds. But the Act of 8 & 9 Vict. c. 109, § 108, which embraces all wagering contracts, applies to transactions in stocks, etc., where the contract savors of wagering.

---

[1] Lewis v. Littlefield, 15 Maine, 233.

[2] Ball v. Gilbert, 12 Metc. 399; Sampson v. Shaw, 101 Mass. 150; Babcock v. Thompson, 3 Pick. 446.

[3] Phillips v. Ives, 1 Rawle, 36; see Brua's Appeal, 5 Sm. 294.

[4] Collamer v. Day, 2 Vt. 144; Tarlton v. Baker, 18 Vt. 9. See, also, on this subject, Perkins v. Eaton, 3 N. H. 152; Hoit v. Hodge, 6 N. H. 104; Bunn v. Riker, 4 John. 426; Hasket v. Wootan, 1 Nott & McC. 180; Martin v. Terrell, 12 Sm. & M. 571; Doxey v. Miller, 2 Bradw. (Ill.) 30; Ryerson v. Derby,

1 Russell & Chesley (N. S.), 13; Whitwell v. Carter, 4 Mich. 329; Wilkinson v. Tousley, 16 Minn. 299; Petillon v. Hipple, 90 Ill. 420; Brown v. Thompson, 14 Bush. 538; Gilmore v. Woodcock, 69 Maine, 118; Digglev. Higgs, L. R., 2 Exch., D. 422; Alvord v. Smith, 63 Ind. 58; Allen v. Hearn, 1 T. R. 56; Robinson v. Mearns, 16 E. C., L. R. 253.

[5] Nicholson v. Gooch, 5 E. & B. 999; Williams v. Trye, 18 Beavan, 366; Olivierson v. Cole, 1 Starkie, 405; Brown v. Turner, 2 Espinasse, 631.

The wording of the Act of 8 & 9 Vict. c. 109, § 108, is, that "all contracts or agreements, whether by "parol or in writing, by way of gaming or wagering, "shall be null and void, and no suit shall be brought "in any court of law or equity for recovering any sum "of money or valuable thing alleged to be won upon "any wager;" and this is still in force. *Act of 8 & 9 Vict.*

In the United States, but few statutes directed against wagering in stocks or commodities have been passed, and most of the cases have been decided either on general principles of public policy, or else in the older States, where, prior to the Revolution, the statute of George II. was in force. *Wagers in the United States.*

In the cases upon the subject under consideration, the first test generally applied to distinguish between a valid sale, or agreement to sell, and a mere gambling contract, is, whether, from the terms of the contract, it appears that the parties contemplated a delivery of the thing sold, as a fulfilment of it, or a mere payment of damages in lieu of a delivery. In the earlier cases, as will be seen, the additional question whether or not at the formation of the contract the vendor had possession of the thing agreed to be sold, or had a reasonable expectation of getting it, was treated as decisive. The first question therefore arises as to those cases where the vendor sells without having the thing sold in his possession, but where both parties contemplate delivery. But, as has already been seen, delivery may be manual, or it may be symbolical, as where a vendee resells before any actual delivery to him. Here he never has possession, and all he can transfer by the resale is his title under his original purchase. Here a *Division of subject.*

second class of cases has arisen, where a resale, or the possibility of it, was contemplated, and therefore no manual, but only a symbolical, delivery.

The next general category into which the decisions on wagering contracts fall, is where, by the terms of the contract, an option is given to either party, either as to time of delivery, or as to the fact of delivery itself. Where the option is merely as to time, the real nature of the contract does not greatly vary from the preceding classes. But where the option is given as to whether there shall or shall not be a delivery of the subject of the contract at all, it is obvious that the contract is of a radically different nature. It is not, in its inception, a sale of a commodity at all, but an agreement for a consideration to do, or not to do, a specified thing upon certain terms, at the will of a third party, expressed within a given time. It may, at the election of the party having the option, become by its terms a contract of sale of the commodity, when, of course, a delivery comes to be contemplated; but it is in regard to its binding effect upon the parties to it, in its original form, that questions have arisen.

It is obvious, also, that the contract "to settle by "payment of differences," so often spoken of and so frequently confused with cases under the first general head, where a delivery, manual or symbolical, is contemplated, really falls under this category; for such a contract is a direct agreement to pay the difference between the market price of the article sold at the time of the formation of the contract, and of its fulfilment; and, of course, no delivery is ever contemplated. But such a contract is not a contract of sale

CHAP. IX.] AVOIDANCE OF THE CONTRACT. 301

at all. The legal measure of damages for its breach would be the same as that for the breach of a contract of sale; but the subject-matter of the one is an actual commodity, while the other is a wager on price.

We may therefore divide the cases which have arisen in States where the common law is opposed to any recovery on wagering contracts, and, in this connection, those which have arisen in England under the statute, into the following classes, the first three of which comprehend sales, properly so called, where a delivery of the thing sold is contemplated; the last two, contracts of a different character, one of which, options, may eventuate in a sale of a commodity and a delivery, but which do not, at the time of their formation, necessarily contemplate any delivery of the commodity sold at all.

I. Where the vendor, at the formation of the contract, has not the goods in his possession, nor a reasonable expectation of getting them, but contemplates an actual unconditional delivery.

II. Where the vendor, at the formation of the contract, contemplates a symbolical, but not a manual, unconditional delivery of the goods.

III. Where the parties, at the formation of the contract, contemplate an actual delivery, but conditional as to time.

IV. Where the parties, at the formation of the contract, contemplate no actual delivery, but reserve the option to do so or not.

V. Where the parties, at the formation of the contract, contemplate no delivery at all, but only a settlement of the difference in prices.

We shall proceed to consider these several categories in their order.

First class of contracts of § 2.

I. Where the vendor, at the formation of the contract, has not the goods in his possession, nor a reasonable expectation of getting them, but contemplates an actual unconditional delivery.

Bryan v. Lewis.

With regard to executory contracts for the sale of goods not yet belonging to the vendor, it was held by Lord Tenterden, in Bryan *v.* Lewis,[1] at *nisi prius*, that if the goods be sold, to be delivered at a future day, and the seller have not the goods, nor any contract for them, nor any reasonable expectation of receiving them on consignment, but intends to go into the market and buy them, it is not a valid contract, but a mere wager as to the price of such commodity.[2] This doctrine, however, was doubted in a case[3] somewhat later, in the Common Pleas, and finally overruled in Hibblewhite *v.* McMorine,[4] and Mortimer *v.* McCallan,[5] and the principle completely exploded; and the rule is established generally in the United States,[6] that where there is an intention to deliver, the contract is never considered a gaming one.

Bryan v. Lewis, overruled in Hibblewhite v. McMorine, and Mortimer v. McCallan.

Second class of contracts of § 2.

II. Where the vendor, at the formation of the contract, contemplates a symbolical, but not a manual, unconditional delivery of the goods.

It has been objected that a contract, where the pur-

---

[1] Req. & Moody, 386 [1826].

[2] See, also, Lorymer *v.* Smith, 1 B. & C. 1.

[3] Wells *v.* Porter, 3 Scot. 141.

[4] 5 M. & W. 462.

[5] 6 M. & W. 58.

[6] See Clark *v.* Foss, 7 Bissell, 540; Cole *v.* Milmine, 88 Ill. 349; Phillips *v.* Ocmulgee Mills, 55 Ga. 633; Bank *v.* McDougall, 28 U. C. C. P. 345; Smith *v.* Bouvier, 20 Sm. (Pa.) 325; McIlvaine *v.* Egerton, 2 Robertson, 422; Stanton *v.* Small, 3 Sandford, 230; Brown *v.* Speyers, 20 Grattan (Va.) 296; Cassard *v.* Hinman, 1 Bosworth, 207.

chaser does not intend to take a manual delivery, but resells again before such a delivery takes place, is a gaming contract, and void. But such a view is not tenable, for the instant the goods are ear-marked, the contract of sale is, as we have seen, completed *qua* the vendor and the vendee, and the former can sue for the price, and the latter bring trover for the goods, and there is, therefore, always a symbolical or theoretical delivery at the execution of the contract of sale between the parties, the vendor being then only an ordinary bailee. In fact, were there not one, the vendee, when selling in his turn, could not deliver at all to a third party, because he would not have the title in himself. And this, then, is now held to be the law in England and the United States.

In Ashton *v.* Dakin,[1] the plaintiff, a stock broker, was directed to buy railway stock for the account, by the defendant, who had no intention of taking a *transfer* thereof. The stock was bought by the plaintiff's agent, and the bought notes sent to the defendant, who before settling day directed plaintiff to resell. On the plaintiff's demanding payment, defendant said, he was not compelled to do so, but would do so at a future time. In an action against the defendant for commission and disbursements, the court held the transaction to be perfectly valid, and not a gambling one. In this, Pollock, C. B., and Channell and Martin, BB., concurred.

Ashton v. Dakin.

In Sawyer and Hamilton *v.* Taggart,[2] one of the questions was, whether a contract for the sale of goods to be delivered at a future time, in which the buyer

Sawyer et al. v. Taggart.

[1] 4 Hurlston & Norman, 867.   [2] 14 Bush. Ky. 727.

intends to resell before a manual or physical delivery, was gaming. The court held such a contract valid. Cofer, J., said, "That no *actual* delivery was ever "made directly to Hamilton, or to the appellants for "them, proves nothing. This was not expected or "intended, and was not essential to the validity of the "contracts. No case has been found, in which it has "been held, that the fact that no delivery was made or "intended was of any importance, where it also ap- "peared that the purchaser intended and had resold "before the time for delivery, and thereby procured "another to become bound to receive and pay for the "goods in his stead."

Remarks of Cofer, J.

In Cameron *v.* Durkheim,[1] the defendants sold a large quantity of gold "short" for the plaintiff (*i.e.*, executed a contract of sale for the plaintiff, the latter contemplating buying the gold later at a different price), and, in accordance with the custom, borrowed gold to make the delivery; an extraordinary rise in gold taking place, the plaintiff was called upon by the defendant to furnish collateral security or "margin." It was testified to, that the plaintiff replied and told the defendants to take care of themselves, he could furnish none. It further appeared, that one of the usual methods of closing the transaction in such a case, was to effect a settlement with the finder of the gold, and such a settlement was made. The court held, that such statement, if made, and such a custom, author- ized such a settlement, and that the contract was valid.

Cameron v. Durkheim.

In fact, if the law were held to be otherwise, nearly every contract for the sale of stock on the London

[1] 55 N. Y. 425.

CHAP. IX.] AVOIDANCE OF THE CONTRACT. 305

Stock Exchange would be gambling; for in almost every instance the jobber buys, intending to resell before a delivery is made to him, and giving up the name of a third party as the purchaser.

In Pennsylvania, however, the courts have held, in the later cases, that a contract for the sale of stock for a future delivery, where the vendor has not the shares in his possession, nor a reasonable expectation of getting them, but has to borrow or purchase them to make good his delivery, and depositing a sum of money with his agent in the sale, to save him harmless, as collateral security, is void, and gambling, as being a mere payment of differences; and so also of a contract to buy goods, where the vendee intends reselling before he has a physical delivery, and therefore takes only a theoretical one, depositing in the same way a sum of money with his agent as a margin. *Pennsylvania cases.*

Thus, in Brua's Appeal,[1] A., having no stock at the time, sold short to B., or order, two hundred and fifty shares of railroad stock, deliverable in twenty-five days, and gave B. notes as collateral security for the fulfilment of the contract of sale. On a suit, by the assignee of A., it was found by the auditor that the contract was a gambling one, and, being a gambling one, the Supreme Court held, there was no consideration to support the notes. *Brua's Appeal.*

In North *v.* Phillips,[2] N. purchased one thousand shares of railway stock for Phillips, buyer's option, of thirty or sixty days, Phillips agreeing to deposit as collateral security, or "margin," ten per cent. of the value of the shares, and Phillips failing to comply with *North v. Phillips.*

[1] 5 Sm. (Pa.) 294.   [2] 89 (Pa.) 250.

20

his agreement to deposit the collateral security, his thousand shares were sold out, without notice, by North & Co. to reimburse themselves, a fall having taken place in the stock. In an action against North to recover the value of his stock sold without his authority, the court held, that the transaction was gambling, that Phillips *never owned any stock,* and that he could not recover. Gordon, J., said, "From the above testimony "one would naturally conclude that Phillips was the "actual owner of one thousand shares of stock which "his brokers had without authority disposed of. But "there was nothing of the kind. *These stock shares* "*belonged to the defendants.* Phillips neither had "paid for, nor intended to pay for, any of them. * * * "In other words, they agreed to hold this stock in "his name for thirty or sixty days, as the case might "be, in order that he might have the advantage of "any rise in price that might happen in the mean "time, it being also understood that he must make "good any fall in such price. Thus, the dealings of "the parties were in '*differences*' and '*margins,*' and "the purchase and sale of the stock was a pretence," and the court held, Phillips could not recover.

Remarks of Gordon, J.

In Dickson's Executor *v.* Thomas,[1] D. directed T. to sell five hundred shares of stock for him, D. not having at the time any shares of his own, and T. borrowed the shares to make the delivery. Subsequently T. purchased five hundred shares to make good the loan, the deliveries being made, as usual, through the instrumentality of the Clearing House attached to the Phila-

Dickson's Executor v. Thomas.

---

[1] 10 Weekly Notes of Cases, 112. is perhaps likely to mislead.
N.B.—The syllabus of the report

delphia Stock Exchange. In an action against D. to recover disbursements and commissions, the Court of Common Pleas, Briggs, J., left the question to the jury, who found the sales and deliveries *bona fide*. But the court above, reversing the rulings of the judge below, and the finding on the facts by the jury, held the sales to be fictitious and void. Gordon, J., said, "Thomas *Remarks of Gordon, J.* "swears that he sold for Dickson five hundred shares "* * * short, fifteen days, buyer's option. This "means, of course, that Dickson had no such stock, "and so further on Thomas explains, by saying that "at the time he professed to sell this stock he had no "such stock in his hands to sell. Nevertheless, he "says, when he sold these five hundred shares he "delivered them. This anomalous kind of testimony "he explains by saying that this delivery was made "on the Clearing House sheet, which means a mere "settlement of differences. It appears, also, * * * "that in order to keep up appearances, when the time "came for delivery, he had to borrow five hundred "shares of stock from somebody whose name does not "appear, and of these there was no actual delivery, "but, as the witness says, it came through the Clear-"ing House sheet."

In Ruchizky *v.* De Haven *et al.*,[1] R., an infant, *Ruchizky v. De Haven et al.* directed the defendants to buy and sell shares of stock, depositing collateral security with them in the event of their losing by the fall or rise of stock. The sales resulted in a heavy loss to the plaintiff, and he sued for the money advanced by him as collateral, etc., the defendants having sold the collateral security to

[1] 10 W. N. C. 109.

reimburse themselves. The court held, that the action lay, Gordon, J., saying, "When, under the case stated, "the court below assumed the defendants must be re-"garded as the agents of Ruchizky (the minor) in "the buying and selling of stocks, in other words, as "the mere hand or medium through which he acted in "transactions with other parties, it committed an error. "* * * The parties were *dealing not in* STOCKS, *but* "MARGINS, *and Ruchizky knew no* PRINCIPALS but "De Haven & Townsend. It was with them and no "one else."

<small>*Remarks of Gordon, J.*</small>

In Fareira *v.* Gabell,[1] the same principles were substantially laid down, the court holding, that where a broker had advanced money to his principal, who had employed him in the purchase and sales of stock, to pay for his principal's losses, he could not recover.

<small>*Fareira v. Gabell.*</small>

Though these cases are sufficient in number to settle a question of law, it is doubtful if they will be recognized as of authority outside of Pennsylvania, or any length of time in that State, being opposed, in principle, to all the decisions both of the English courts, and of every court of every State in the Union.

<small>*The Pennsylvania cases of doubtful authority, and opposed to all others.*</small>

The cases of Dickson's Executor *v.* Thomas, and Ruchizky *v.* De Haven *et al.*, are particularly remarkable, as the finding of the jury in the court below was reversed, and the decision rendered by the Supreme Court on an assumed state of facts, that did not appear from any evidence in the cause to have existed. The language of the opinions, also, in speaking of, dealing in collateral security or "margins," in holding, an agent in a sale of stocks to be a principal to his customer, and

<small>*Dickson's Exec. v. Thomas. Ruchizky v. De Haven.*</small>

[1] 89 Pa. 89.

CHAP. IX.] AVOIDANCE OF THE CONTRACT. 309

declaring, a settlement of sales of stocks made through a Clearing House to be an illegal method of settling differences to avoid delivery, all seems to indicate a slight misapprehension of the character of the actual transactions under discussion.

III. "*Bona fide* time contracts about the subjects of "actual purchase and sale of stocks and other property, "seem from custom necessary in our country, and when "they are so, although they may be greatly affected by "the rise and fall of the market, they are not illegal."[1] Third class of contracts of § 2.

Nor are contracts, where there is an option allowed as to the time of delivery, void.

Thus, in Gilbert *v.* Gauger *et al.*,[2] plaintiff was requested to sell, for Gauger and another, 10,000 bushels of wheat to H., the seller to have the option of delivering at any time during September. The day of delivery was afterwards changed to October, and in September, plaintiff by order of defendants sold to another party, F., 10,000 bushels, deliverable in October. The transaction was closed, as the prices varied, by rebuying from H. 10,000 bushels and executing the contract to F., with this wheat. The court held, that these transactions did not come within the purview of the statute of Illinois to prohibit options to sell or buy, and that if the defendants directed plaintiff to settle, before the maturity of the contract, it did not render it void, as there had been an intention to deliver. Gilbert *v.* Gauger.

So, in Logan *v.* Musick *et al.*,[3] with reference to the same statute, the court said, "The statute does not prohibit a party from selling or buying grain for future Logan *v.* Musick. Remarks of the court.

---

[1] *Per* Thompson, J., in Brua's Appeal, 5 Sm. (Pa.) 299.
[2] 10 Chicago Legal News, 340.
[3] 81 Ill. 415.

"delivery; such was not the purpose of the statute, nor
"can it make any difference as to the legality of the
"contract, whether the party, who sells for future de-
"livery at the time the sale was made, has on hand
"the grain; a party may sell to-day a certain quantity
"of grain for delivery in a week or month hence, and
"then go upon the market and buy the grain to fill
"the contract. It is true, the defendant had the
"option, under the contract, to select a day within a
"limited time on which he would receive the grain;
"but such an option does not fall within the statute, for
"the reason that it does not render the sale optional."

<small>Fourth class of contracts of § 2.</small>

IV. Where the option is to deliver or not deliver, as the purchaser chooses, the sale is not necessarily void, or gambling.

<small>Chicago, etc. R. R. Co. v. Dane.</small>

Thus, in Chicago & G. E. R. R. Co. v. Dane,[1] the defendant *offered* by letter to *receive* from the plaintiff, and to *transport* to Chicago, iron not to exceed a certain amount, at a specified rate, and the plaintiff answered, merely assenting to the proposal, but did not agree to deliver iron for the transportation; and the court held this not to be a binding contract, as there was no agreement to furnish iron, and there was no consideration passed.

<small>Remarks of Grove, J.</small>

But Grove, J., said, "This amounted to "nothing more than the acceptance of an option by "the plaintiff for the transportation of such quantity "of iron by the defendants as it chose; and had there "been a consideration given to the defendants for such "option, the defendants would have been bound to "transport for the plaintiff such iron as it required "within the time and quantity specified, *the plaintiff*

[1] 43 N. Y. 240.

CHAP. IX.] AVOIDANCE OF THE CONTRACT. 311

"*having its election* not to require the transportation "of any."

In Bigelow *v*. Benedict,[1] the defendant, in consideration of two hundred and fifty dollars, acknowledged to have been paid him by B., agreed to receive from B., at any time within six months from the date of the contract, two thousand five hundred dollars in *gold coin* of the United States, and to pay him therefor, in good current funds, at the rate of one hundred and ninety-five dollars in currency for every *one hundred dollars in coin*, and B. to deliver the *gold coin* or not, at his option, and the court held this not to be an invalid or gambling contract.

Bigelow v. Benedict.

Andrews, J., said, "By this contract the defendant "bound himself, at the price named, and he ran the "hazard of loss in case the market price of gold should "be more than ten per cent. less, at the time specified "for the delivery, than the price he agreed to pay. "This hazard he was willing to assume for the consideration paid by the other party. The seller paid "the two hundred and fifty dollars for the right to "deliver it, and he could in no event lose anything "beyond that sum, for he assumed no obligation to the "defendant, and he might gain by a fall in the market. "That there was an element of hazard in the contract "is plain. But the same hazard is incurred in every "optional contract for the sale of any marketable commodity, when, for a consideration paid, one of the "parties binds himself to sell or receive the property "at a future time, at a specified price, at the election of "the other.

Remarks of Andrews, J.

[1] 70 N. Y. 202.

"Mercantile contracts of this character are not infrequent, and with a *bona fide* intention on the part of both parties to perform them. The vendor of goods may expect to produce or acquire them in time for a future delivery, and, while wishing to make a market for them, is unwilling to enter into an absolute obligation to deliver, and therefore bargains for an option which, while it relieves him from liability, assures him of a sale, in case he is able to deliver; and the purchaser may in the same way guard himself against loss beyond the consideration paid for the option, in case of his inability to take the goods. There is no inherent vice in such a contract. * * * If the contract in question was a mere device to evade the statute, it was, as has been said, illegal; but the question here is, does the contract, on its face, disclose an illegal transaction, and we are of the opinion, that it does not. * * * The burden was upon the defendant to show the illegality of the contract, and this he did not do."

Cooke v. Davis.

In Cooke v. Davis,[1] defendant contracted to deliver "*current funds of the United States*" (*i.e.*, coin, or legal tender notes of the United States), at "fifteen cents on the dollar, in ten months from date." The court said that such a contract was for either notes or coin, and that one was to be paid for, in the other, or else the contract would be insensible, and that here an intelligent meaning was, $10,000 in paper, for $1500 in gold.

Kirkpatrick v. Bonsall.

In Kirkpatrick v. Bonsall,[2] defendants, in consideration of $1000, agreed to deliver to the plaintiff 5000

---

[1] 53 N. Y. 318. [2] 22 Sm. (Pa.) 155.

barrels of oil at any time within the first six months of 1871, and "if this oil is called for, and this call "becomes a contract, ten days' notice shall be given, "and the plaintiff or his assigns agree to receive, and "pay for the same, cash on delivery, at 10½ cents per "gallon." Held, not to be on its face a gambling contract.

V. All the courts in England and the great majority in the several States of the United States confederation hold, that where it is clear that no delivery of the thing sold was ever intended, but only a mere settlement of differences, then the contract of sale is mere gambling, and the one party cannot recover the consideration, nor the other enforce on his side the execution of the contract. The question of intention to deliver is a question for the jury.

Fifth class of contracts of § 2.

The difference between contracts of this nature and sales proper, where a delivery of the thing sold is contemplated, has already been pointed out; and where the contract to pay the difference in prices is made expressly in so many words, there is no difficulty in ascertaining its precise nature. But in many cases, options, or contracts, which, on their face, import intention to deliver, have been, from surrounding circumstances, held to be, in fact, mere agreements to pay differences in price; and, as the legal measure of damages is the same in both cases, it becomes necessary, to distinguish the real character of a contract, to look not merely at its terms, but to the action of the parties to it, in fulfilling it; that is, to regard not merely the agreement, but the transaction. We shall give a few cases, as illustrations of what has been held to be a settlement of differences, and what were considered valid contracts.

Grizewood v. Blane.
In Grizewood *v.* Blane,[1] the declaration averred that the plaintiff bargained for, and bought of the defendant, four hundred and fifty shares of railway stock, to be deliverable at a certain future date, and then to be paid for by the plaintiff; that the defendant was not at the day of the making of the contract possessed of any of the shares, but must have purchased them or otherwise acquired them to make the delivery; that the shares had risen greatly in value; and that in order to fulfil the contract the defendant would be obliged to purchase them at a greatly enhanced value in the market, and therefore, in consideration of the aforesaid bargain and sale, the parties agreed to annul the contract of sale, while it was yet unexecuted, and before the day of delivery, and instead the defendant should buy of the plaintiff, at the then enhanced market prices, an equivalent number of shares in the same companies; that the defendant should pay the plaintiff the difference in price of the shares; and that none of the shares should be delivered by the defendant to the plaintiff or the plaintiff to the defendant in either transaction, but that there should be a set-off, the one against the other. Jervis, C. J., left the question to the jury to say whether this was a gambling transaction, and they held it to be so.

Ex parte Marnham.
In *Ex parte* Marnham,[2] etc., X., a member of the Stock Exchange, then having certain railway shares, agreed to sell them to M., another member, for the next settling day. By the rules of the Stock Ex-

[1] 11 C. B. 528.   [2] 2 De G. F. & J. 634.

change, if the sale is not taken up on the appointed day, the vendor is entitled to hold the shares, the differences in price of the shares being paid by the lender or borrower according to the market, until the next settling day, and so on. M. did not take up the shares, and the transaction was carried on for several settling days, the dividends being paid to M. Subsequently X. bought back some of the shares, and accounted to M. for the price of these. On M.'s being declared a defaulter, X. took the rest of the shares, which were worth less than formerly, and sought to prove for the difference. The court, Turner, L. J., held the contract to be valid, and in this Knight Bruce, S. J., concurred.

In Porter v. Viets,[1] the parties entered into a written agreement to purchase and sell grain for a future delivery, to be paid for on the delivery. On a suit brought for non-delivery, the pleas set forth, that at the formation of the contract the vendor was not possessed of the grain, nor had he any reasonable expectation of obtaining it, and that it was simply a contract to pay the differences between the price mentioned in the contract, and the value of the grain at the day of delivery. The court sustained a demurrer to the plea. Drummond, J., said, "The defendant now insists that he "did not make such a contract as is presented to the "court by the pleadings in the case, but that it was an "agreement to pay the difference between the price of "corn, as stated, and the price at a future day; in "other words, he wishes to prove what the law deter- "mines is ordinarily the measure of damages for the

Porter v. Viets.

Remarks of Drummond, J.

[1] 1 Biss. 177.

"non-performance of his contract. The rule is well settled, that when two men make a contract, and reduce it to writing, and sign it, that it is the *contract* between them. It cannot be shown verbally that something different was intended at the time, from what appears in the writing. * * * The defendant says he wishes to show, that the intention of the parties at the time was to make a wager as to the price of corn during the last half of June, and that the amount of the wager, and the party that was to win or lose, was to depend upon the market price of the corn. Now, it may be true, that the result is precisely the same; that is, the one party loses and the other gains, the same amount as in a wager. So it is in any case of this kind, when a party does not perform his contract, the same. In the case of a wager on the price, when a man pays the 'difference,' he performs his contract, but he does not fulfil this contract by paying the difference. He meets the penalty of the law for a breach of it. * * * No doubt all contracts, which are illegal, may be attacked, but no case has been shown, which authorizes a party to prove verbally, that another contract (in itself illegal) existed, and so get rid of a written contract on its face unexceptionable."

Ex parte Young.

In *Ex parte* Young,[1] C., desiring to make a "corner" in grain, purchased all the oats he could get for cash, and took all the "options" offered him for the June delivery. It appeared that C. was endeavoring to keep the price up, while the owners of the options were trying to keep it down, and all the parties knew

[1] 6 Biss. 53.

of the attempted "corner," and that in nearly all the cases no delivery was intended, unless they could break the market. The market broke, and the owners of the "puts" sold grain to the amount of the "puts," and claimed the difference from C.'s assignee. The court held, that the transaction was void; and Blodgett, J., said, "I do not mean to be understood as holding, that "every option contract for the delivery of grain or "stock, or that every 'put,' is necessarily void, but "only that all these contracts, in the light of the testi-"mony before the court, were in their essential features "gambling contracts." *Remarks of Blodgett, J.*

The Pennsylvania cases seem to lay down different principles on this subject from that of England and any other State in the Union, and the courts have held in Brua's Appeal,[1] North v. Phillips,[2] Fareira v. Gabell,[3] Ruchizky v. De Haven,[4] and Dickson's Executor v. Thomas,[5] that the sale of goods for a future delivery, where the vendor neither has the goods, nor possesses a reasonable expectation of acquiring them, but expects to go into the market to purchase them, and deposits collateral security to protect his agent, in case of a change in the value of the goods, is void, being a mere settlement of differences. *Pennsylvania cases opposed to the other authorities. Brua's Appeal, North v. Phillips, Fareira v. Gabell, Ruchizky v. De Haven, Dickson's Exec. v. Thomas.*

Several of these decisions, however, are, as has already been stated, open to the criticism of an apparent misapprehension of the transactions they attempt to discuss. In one of them, Dickson's Executor v. Thomas,[6] the court profess to follow the English au- *Dickson's Exec. v. Thomas.*

---

[1] 5 Sm. (Pa.) 294.
[2] 89 Pa. 250.
[3] 6 W. N. C. (Pa.) 490.
[4] 10 W. N. C. 109.
[5] 10 W. N. C. (Pa.) 112.
[6] Exec. of Dickson v. Thomas, 10 W. N. C. (Pa.) 182.

thorities, in adopting a contrary view, which would render invalid almost all the transactions through jobbers on the London Stock Exchange,—transactions which, it is needless to say, have been repeatedly upheld by the English courts.[1]

Principles deducible from the above cases with respect to evidence of intention.

From a review of these cases it will be seen that a contract of sale of stock is valid, wherever it can be inferred from the whole transaction arising out of it, that a delivery, either physical or symbolical, is contemplated by the parties; even in those cases where the delivery is made conditional, as in the case of options. *Prima facie*, the transaction is valid where from the terms of the contract itself an intention to make a delivery may be gathered, though, as in *Ex parte* Young,[2] such a presumption arising from the language alone of the contract, may be overturned by an examination of the general character of the whole transaction, by the light of which the contract must be interpreted. Where the contract is by its terms an agreement not to deliver stock, but to pay the difference in its price between specified periods, it is, as a matter of law, a gaming one, which it is the province of the court to pronounce illegal. But where, on its face, it contemplates a delivery of the thing sold, and the question arises whether it is in truth a contract to sell stock or a mere cover for a gaming transaction, such a question is obviously one of fact, and has always been left to the decision of a jury; unless we except

Ex parte Young.

---

[1] See Mewburn *v.* Eaton, 20 L. T. 449, and the cases referring to Jobbers' Transactions, in Part I., Chap. IV. See also the American cases, Sawyer *v.* Taggart, 14 Bush. (Ky.), 727; Pickering *v.* Cease, 79 Ill. 328; Bigelow *v.* Benedict, 70 N. Y. 202; Clark *v.* Foss, 10 Chicago Legal News, 211.

[2] 6 Biss. 53.

the Pennsylvania cases already adverted to,[1] where an appellate court seems to have undertaken to reverse the finding of a jury on a question of fact, and enter a final judgment without granting a new trial.

On the question of evidence the Federal courts seem to have held in some of the foregoing cases[2] that parol testimony will not be admitted to invalidate the terms of a written contract by proving that there was, at the time of its formation, an illegal understanding between the parties. Undoubtedly the law of evidence in the Federal courts, and in many of the States, renders inadmissible parol testimony to contradict the terms of a contract in writing, or to vary them. But the Federal as well as the English courts have admitted evidence to show that the written instrument delivered, constitutes only a portion of the whole contract made between the parties, and to supplement it, holding this to be neither a contradiction nor a variation of the writing.[3] Subject to this exception, no doubt, the Federal courts would refuse to admit parol testimony to prove that the real contract between the parties was an illegal or gaming one, and different wholly or in part from the written one. But where evidence, parol or otherwise, is offered to show what the whole transaction between the parties was, of which the written contract was but a part, such evidence, it is submitted, is always admissible, not merely on the authority of the cases above referred to, but as evidence of facts which constitute part of the *res gestæ*. For the *res*, in

Parol and written evidence in Federal and other courts.

---

[1] See Porter *v.* Viets, p. 315.
[2] See Porter *v.* Viets, 1 Biss. 177.
[3] McCulloch *v.* Girard, 4 Washington, C. C. Rep. 289; compare Kemmil *v.* Wilson, *ibid.* 308; see, also, Pym *v.* Campbell, 6 El. & Black. 370; Wallis *v.* Littell, 11 C. B., N. S. 369.

these cases, it is to be observed, is not the mere written contract, nor what occurred only at the time of its execution, but the transaction as a whole between the parties. If that be shown to be a mere wager on prices, or a gambling one, the contract out of which it grew cannot, whatever its terms, legalize it.

PART III.

THE PLEDGE.

INTRODUCTION.

In the daily transactions of the stockholder in the securities we have been treating of, the pledge forms almost as prominent a feature as the sale itself, and it is intended here to examine the nature and the law of pledges of securities of the character we have been speaking of.

The subject may be conveniently considered under the following heads, viz.:

Chapter I. The Formation of the Pledge.
Chapter II. The Effect of the Pledge.
Chapter III. The Avoidance of the Pledge.

CHAPTER I.

FORMATION OF THE PLEDGE.

	PAGE		PAGE
Pledge defined	322	Trustee, *prima facie*, cannot pledge	331
Division of chapter	322	Trustees must act jointly	333
SECTION I.—WHO MAY PLEDGE.		Trustee cannot delegate his authority for a judicial act	333
Who may pledge	322	Powers of executors and trustees to sell or buy	334
Persons whose powers are restricted	322	Lowry v. Commercial Bank	335
Corporations	323	General rules	335
Executors, administrators, trustees, etc.	323	SECTION II.—THE SUBJECT-MATTER OF THE PLEDGE.	
Powers of executors to pledge	324		
Sub-pledgees	326	SECTION III.—MANNER OF EFFECTING THE PLEDGE.	
Wood's Appeal	326		
Limitation as to time	328		
Co-executors	329		
Powers of trustees to pledge	331	Pledge of negotiable securities	338
Shaw v. Spencer	331	Pledge of non-negotiable securities	338
Cases discussed	331		

Pledge defined. A PLEDGE is a bailment of personal property, whereby the bailee contracts with the bailor to hold the thing deposited as security for some debt or engagement, and to return it again to the bailor, in an unchanged state, when the debt or engagement has been paid or fulfilled.[1] We shall see, first, who may pledge; secondly, the subject-matter of the pledge; and, thirdly, the manner of effecting it.

Division of chapter.

SECTION I.—WHO MAY PLEDGE.

Who may pledge. As a general rule, any one capable of contracting may make a valid pledge, just as he can make a valid contract of sale.

Persons whose powers to pledge are restricted. There are, however, persons, both artificial and natural, whose general powers of contracting are

---
[1] See 2 Kent, Com. p. 578.

CHAP. I.] FORMATION OF THE PLEDGE. 323

restricted, and whose right to pledge property owned or controlled by them often depends upon the circumstances of each case. With respect to pledges made by the first class, corporations, acting in excess of their authority, the reader is referred to a former page of this work[1] to see what the effect of such a contract would be, which would be governed by laws similar to those respecting sales.[2] Corporations.

There is also another class of persons, namely, executors, administrators, trustees, guardians, and others acting in fiduciary relations, whose power of pledging and selling securities held by them in their representative capacity is limited; and such property is now held by them to such an extent that a full discussion of their powers of dealing with it, and of the liabilities of persons contracting with them in reference to it, is necessary in any treatise on the law affecting stock brokers, or other financial agents. Executors, administrators, trustees, guardians.

First, as to their power to hypothecate securities held by them.

There is a broad distinction between executors or administrators, and other trustees. "There is a marked "difference," says Judge Strong, in Bayard *v.* The Bank,[3] "between the powers of an administrator or "executor, and those of an ordinary trustee. * * * No "purchaser either of land or personalty would be safe "in buying from a known trustee without looking at "the nature and extent of his trust. It is true a trus- "tee may have power to sell, but the power is not a Remarks of Strong, J., in Bayard v. Bank.

---

[1] Page 182, also page 82.
[2] And see, also, 2 Kent, Com. p. 300, n. 1 (a), and p. 492, n. 1 (12th Amer. ed.).
[3] 52 Penna. Rep. 233.

"necessary incident to his trust, as it is to the office of "executor. He may have the legal title, and yet have "no authority to sell. His sale may be entirely un- "authorized by the instrument that created the trust; "it may have been forbidden." It is one of the chief duties of executors, as such,[1] or administrators, to collect the assets of the testator, pay his debts, and fulfil or settle other obligations binding upon his estate. In order to do this, they must have power to sell, and, often, to pledge the assets. Executors, therefore, apart from any power contained in the will, as well as administrators, have implied authority, not only to dispose of, but to pledge, the assets of the decedent, to raise the money for the purposes of the estate.[2] "For "the purpose of selling the estate of a testator," says Sir John Romilly, "the executor is considered as the "absolute owner, and has all the powers incidental to "that character. On what principle can it be maintained that he is not to be regarded in the same light "and to have the same power for the purpose of effect- "ing a mortgage, which may be the most beneficial "course to be adopted for a *cestui que trust*, and of "which benefit the executor is constituted the sole "judge?"[3] A banker or broker, therefore, is safe in loaning to an executor or administrator, on securities registered in his name, money borrowed by him ostensibly for the purposes of the estate, where no circum-

Remarks of Sir John Romilly.

Powers of executors to pledge.

---

[1] That is, when not also acting as trustees under the same will, in which case the law regards them as acting in two entirely distinct capacities.

[2] Russell *v.* Plaice, 18 Beav. 21.

[3] See, also, on this point, Cruikshank *v.* Duffin, L. R., 13 Eq. 555; Tyrrell *v.* Morris, 1 Dev. & Bat., Eq. 559; Williamson *v.* Morton, 2 Maryland, Ch. 94, 100; Ashton *v.* The Atlantic Bank, 2 Allen Mass. 217.

stances exist to lead to the inference that the money is borrowed by the executor for his own purposes.

But as it is a fraud for an executor to pledge the assets of the estate as security for his own debt, or to deal with them otherwise for his individual benefit, a court of equity, or probate court, will follow such assets in the hands of the pawnee, and compel their return, without a repayment of the advances on them, wherever fraud on the part of the latter can be inferred. And it will be inferred in many instances.[1]

Thus, a pledge of securities belonging to an estate to secure a pre-existing debt of the executor, is a fraud on its face.[2]

Pledge of securities to secure a pre-existing debt of the executor is a fraud.

In Ellis's Appeal,[3] the court held, that where an executor, in fraud of the trust under which he held the stock, and as collateral security for his own debt, transferred the stock to one having notice of the fact that the stock was the property of the borrower's testator, and actual knowledge of the fact that there were other executors who did not join in the transaction, the pledgee was possessed of sufficient to put him upon inquiry, and in the event of his omitting to do so, he could not be deemed a *bona fide* holder for value, and would be decreed to return the stock discharged of the lien of his advances. And, generally, where either the pawnee has actual notice that the executor is not acting in good faith, or has notice of facts which would put a reasonable man on inquiry, as, for instance, from the course of his dealings with the executor, the law will presume knowledge on his part of the fraud, so far, at

Ellis's Appeal.

---

[1] See Hill *v.* Simpson, 7 Vesey, 152. Hare, 93; Wilson *v.* Moore, 1 Mylne & Keen, 337.
[2] See Haines *v.* Forshaw, 11
[3] 8 Weekly Notes, Phila. 538.

least, as to found a civil proceeding to fix the pawnee with the amount of the advances. The power of the executor, however, over the assets, if he be acting in good faith, is plenary, and extends to stock or securities which have been specifically bequeathed to a legatee, though in this case it is usually safer to have the assent of the legatee to the hypothecation given, as the executor may have done some act amounting to an assent to the bequest.[1]

Sub-pledgees. How far affected by pledgee's actual notice. If, then, an executor may pledge the securities of an estate, and a mortgagee is safe in advancing money on them, provided he has no notice of fraud, how far is a sub-pledgee safe in advancing on stocks registered in the name of an executor? Of course where the original pledgee's title is good there is no difficulty. But where the first pledgee is affected with actual notice of fraud, the question has arisen how far the title of a sub-pledgee, without notice, is affected by the character of the transaction between the executor and the first lender.

It has been argued, strenuously, that in all such cases the original pledgee can transfer no better title to any one than he himself possessed; and that if his title was bad, every subsequent bailee or transferee must take subject to the equities of those interested in the estate.

Wood's Appeal. In Wood's Appeal,[2] however, this view has been overruled; and it was held, that where one of four executors had pledged certain certificates of stock, registered in his name as executor, with a firm of

---

[1] See 1 Amer. Lead. Cas. in Eq. 95. [2] 92 Penna. Rep. 379.

brokers, as security for his own personal debt, accompanied by a blank power of attorney executed by him as acting executor,—and these brokers, in turn, sub-pledged the stock to persons who advanced money on them, without notice of the fraud,—the title of the sub-pledgee was good, and that the remaining executors could not recover the stock until the advances made thereon were paid. " An executor," said Judge Trunkey, " holds under a trust; he is the minister or " dispenser of the goods of the defendant. He has " the same property in the personal effects as the de-" ceased had when living. * * * Co-executors are " regarded in law as an individual person; and the " act of any one of them, in respect to the adminis-" tration of the effects, is deemed to be the act of all. " * * * An exception to this general power will be " found in those cases only when collusion exists be-" tween the executor and the purchaser. That the ex-" ecutor may waste the money is not alone sufficient to " invalidate the sale: it must further appear that the " purchaser participated in the devastavit or breach of " duty in the executor. Thus, when the person to " whom the executor passes the property knows that " the executor is acting in violation of his trust and in " fraud of those interested in the due administration of " the assets, the fraud vitiates the transaction, and the " attempted transfer is void. * * * The fact that the " legal title to the stock was known to have previously " been in the executor, and that the title of the holder " purported on its face to have been derived from him " in his representative capacity, will not raise a sus-" picion, nor put a purchaser on inquiry, for the reason

Remarks of Trunkey, J.

Prall v. Tilt quoted.

"that it is the executor's primary duty to dispose of the assets and settle the estate (quoting, also, Prall *v.* Tilt[1]). We think the Master was right in holding that the same principle which prevails in the case of an absolute owner applies in the case of an executor who invests the owner with entire ownership.

"The defendants had a right to infer that McDowell & Wilkins (the first pledgees) were owners of the stock, although the certificates showed title in Charles S. Wood (the testator), and the blank powers and assignments were signed by George R. Wood as acting executor. They found McDowell & Wilkins clothed with an apparent ownership. The testator had given George R. Wood the strongest confidence in making him the executor of his will, thereby investing absolute power in him to sell and transfer the stock in the line of his duty."

A broker may generally loan to third parties upon a pledge of securities registered in an executor's name, where he has no notice of any fraud.

An executor, who is also a trustee, has no implied power to pledge, after a certain period after testator's death.

The doctrine enunciated in this case makes it safe, generally, for a banker or broker to loan to third parties, upon a pledge of securities registered in the names of executors, where he has no notice of any circumstance which would put him on notice of fraud. But this doctrine is subject to another important limitation, that although an executor has *prima facie* a right to transfer, yet where he is made by the will a *trustee*, as well as an executor, no implied power on his part to transfer exists, after a sufficient period since the death of the testator has elapsed to raise a presumption of the payment of all debts.

Lowry v. Commercial and Farmers' Bank.

In Lowry *v.* The Commercial and Farmers' Bank,[2] decided by Chief Justice Taney, stock stood in the

---

[1] 28 New Jersey, Eq. 70.   [2] 3 Amer. Law Journal, 111.

name of an executor. The bank allowed him to transfer it and receive the proceeds. The stock had been bequeathed by the will to the executor, in trust, to pay over the dividends, etc., to certain *cestuis que trustent*, and the transfer was made eight years after the testator's death. The court held, that after a lapse of eight years, the bank was bound to presume payment of the debts of the testator, and that no implied power to sell, therefore, existed. The bank was compelled to make good to the *cestuis que trustent* the stock transferred.

It is obvious, then, that even since the decisions in Wood's estate and the other cases referred to in connection with it, a person lending on stocks or securities held by executors ought to make inquiry as to the date of the testator's death. If a comparatively short time has elapsed,—less, for instance, than two years,—an implied power exists to sell and to pledge for the purposes of the estate. And so long as the lender has no reason to suppose that the money is borrowed for any other purpose, he is safe in loaning on such securities, either directly to the executor, or to third parties. But if the testator has been dead for several years, or there are any other circumstances which would lead to the belief that the loan is effected for other than the legitimate purposes of the estate,[1] the loaner lends at his peril.

It must be added, that co-executors are regarded in law as one individual, and in most transactions any of

Co-executors usually regarded in law as one individual.

[1] Miller *v.* Ege, 8 Barr (Pa.), 352; Bellas *v.* McCarty, 10 Watts, 13; Collinson *v.* Lister, 7 De G. M. & J. 634; Elliot *v.* Merryman, 1 Lead. Cas., Eq., 4th Am. ed. 59; Garrard *v.* P. & C. R. R. Co., 5 Casey (Pa.), 154.

them can act for all. "It is well settled, in general, "that the act of one co-executor binds all the others, by "reason of the confidence reposed in them individually, "in consequence of which each has full power over the "assets."[1] But where both executors *join* in the administration of the assets, it has been held, that each is responsible for their safe keeping; as, for instance, where a deposit of money with a banker is made in the name of two executors, a release by one cannot discharge the banker.[2]

<small>Langford v. Gascoyne. Remarks of Sir William Grant.</small>

In Langford v. Gascoyne,[3] Sir William Grant laid down the rule as being, "in all cases, that if an exec- "utor does any act by which money gets into the pos- "session of another executor, the former is equally "answerable with the other; not where an executor "is merely passive by not obstructing in receiving it."

<small>Remarks of Lord Cottenham in Clough v. Bond.</small>

And in Clough v. Bond,[4] Lord Cottenham, following this case, said, that a co-executor, if without necessity "he be instrumental in giving to the person failing "possession of any part of the property, he will be "liable, although the person possessing it be a co-ex- "ecutor or co-administrator." Where therefore several executors have joined in a deposit, or pledge, it is very doubtful whether the pawnee can safely return it without a receipt or release from all at least of the acting executors. The proper rule would be, on the return of the securities hypothecated by several executors, for an advance, to retransfer or redeliver to all, or else to require a joint receipt or acknowledgment from all.

---

[1] Beltzhoover v. Darragh, 16 Serg. & Rawle (Pa.), 329.
[2] See De Haven v. Williams, 2 Weekly Notes, 295.
[3] See 11 Vesey, 833.
[4] 3 My. & Craig, 496.

CHAP. I.] FORMATION OF THE PLEDGE. 331

We now pass to the case of trustees. The power of trustees to hypothecate, or otherwise deal in, trust securities held by them, differs, as has already been stated, from that of executors. The duty of a trustee is, primarily, to hold. No power, therefore, to sell, still less to hypothecate, is *implied* in a trustee, excepting in the case of assignees for the benefit of creditors, or in bankruptcy, whose duty is, of course, to distribute. Consequently he has no power to sell, except where expressly authorized by the instrument creating the trust.[1] The stock broker, therefore, or other pledgee, becomes the pledgee at his own risk, if there is anything to put him upon notice that the subject of the pledge is property held in trust, and he is bound to make inquiries of a trustee always in dealing with trust funds.

Power of trustees to pledge.

Trustee has no implied power to sell or pledge.

Thus, in Shaw *v.* Spencer,[2] where a certificate of stock standing in the name of "A. B., as trustee for C. D.," is by him pledged to secure his own debt, it was held, that the pledgee was put upon notice and received the pledge at his own risk. In this case it was objected, upon the argument, that there was no one of whom the pledgee could inquire with regard to the right of the pledgeor to effect the pledge, but the fraudulent trustee. Foster, J., said, "The objection "that in the present case the only persons of whom "inquiry could have been made were 'the trustees "who committed the breach of trust,' is sufficiently "answered by the words of Sir John Romilly, Master "of the Rolls, in a recent and leading case. 'With

Shaw v. Spencer.

Remarks of Foster, J.

Sir John Romilly quoted.

[1] Bayard *v.* The Bank, 52 Penna. Rep. 232. [2] 100 Mass. 382.

"respect to the argument that it was unnecessary to "make any inquiry, because it must have led to no "results,' he says, 'I think it impossible to admit the "validity of this excuse. I concur in the doctrine of "Jones v. Smith,[1] that a false answer, or a reasonable "answer, given to an inquiry made, may dispense with "the necessity of further inquiry,' but I think it im- "possible beforehand to come to any conclusion that a "false answer would have been given, which would "have precluded the necessity of further inquiry. A "more dangerous doctrine could not be laid down, "nor one involving a more unsatisfactory inquiry, "namely, a hypothetical inquiry, as to what A. would "have said if B. had said something other than what "he did say."[2]

Jones v. Smith.

So, in Duncan v. Jaudon,[3] the court held, that a person lending money to a trustee on a pledge of a trust consisting of stocks, etc., and selling the same for the repayment of the loan, is responsible to the *cestui que trust*, where the certificates of stock show on their face that the stocks are held in trust, and the loan is apparently for the trustee's benefit. If, however, the stock broker or pledgee makes inquiry and is deceived by the trustee, the former will not be held responsible to the *cestui que trust*.[4]

Duncan v. Jaudon.

Any one therefore advancing on a security registered in the name of a person as trustee, takes it with notice of everything he could have ascertained by examining the trust deed. Knowledge or assent on the part of

A broker taking a pledge from a trustee, as such, is affected with notice.

---

[1] 1 Hare, 43.
[2] Jones v. Williams, 24 Beavan, 62.
[3] 15 Wallace, 165.
[4] See Buttrick v. Holden, 13 Metcalf, 355; Calais Steamboat Co. v. Van Pelt, 2 Black, 372.

CHAP. I.] FORMATION OF THE PLEDGE. 333

the *cestui que trust* in most cases is insufficient to render the advance safe, as many trusts are created to exclude discretion on the part of the *cestui que trust*, as, for example, those for married women, and "Spendthrift Son Trusts,"[1] as they are sometimes called, and others, where the object of the trust would be defeated if the assent of the *cestui que trust* could authorize a pledging or dealing with the security.

Where power to hypothecate is expressly given, as, for instance, where trustees are empowered to carry on a business, all the trustees must join, unless otherwise directed by the deed of trust. While one executor may bind his co-executor, there is no such thing recognized as an *acting* trustee. A person therefore advancing to trustees must take the obligation, or at least act with the assent, of every trustee,[2] or he may become a pledgee at his own risk.

Where several trustees have power to pledge, all must join therein.

Nor can one of several trustees delegate, by power of attorney or any other instrument, to his co-trustees, or any of them, or to an agent, power to act for him in the trust in any matter involving discretion, which a pledge of security, of course, always does.[3]

A trustee cannot delegate his authority except for a ministerial act.

Delegatus non potest delegare, is the rule applicable

---

[1] These trusts are peculiar to some States, and have not generally been sustained in England. See Fisher v. Taylor, 2 Rawle, 33; Holdship v. Patterson, 7 Watts, 547; Ashhurst v. Given, 5 Watts & Serg. 323; Vaux v. Parke, 7 *ibid.* 19; Brown v. Williamson's Ex'rs, 12 Casey, 338; Shankland's Appeal, 11 Wright, 113; Keyser's Appeal, 57 Penna. 236.

[2] Vandever's Appeal, 8 Watts & Serg. 405; Sinclair v. Jackson, 8 Cowen (N. Y.), 544; Sloo v. Law, 3 Blatch. C. C. 471; Chapin v. First Universalist Society, 8 Gray, 575; Holcomb v. Holcomb, 3 Stockton (N. J.), 281; Lewin on Trusts, p. 298.

[3] For the proposition that a power of sale necessarily involves discretion, see argument of Sir Edward Sugden, in Bradford v. Belfield, 2 Simons, 264.

to trustees in all, excepting mere ministerial acts, such as pledging a specific security for a specific advance, which has been determined upon beforehand. Where this *appears* in the letter of attorney, the mere duty of depositing the securities mentioned, with the pledgee, upon receiving the amount named, may be delegated to a co-trustee or an attorney in fact. But where the power of attorney on its face assumes to delegate any discretion to the agent, it is *ipso facto* void.[1] A person therefore advancing to trustees who have power to borrow money should see that they all join individually in executing the power of attorney to transfer, or, if any one act through an attorney in fact, the letter of attorney should purport to contain no delegation of discretion, but merely authorize the agent to perform the ministerial act of executing the transfer.

Power of executors and trustees to sell or buy.

We proceed, in this connection, to say a few words about the power of executors and trustees to sell assets held by them, as securities of this description are continually the subject of purchase and sale.

Executor, prima facie, may sell.

The power of executors to sell is implied by law, apart from any express power in the will, because, as already stated, it is their duty to collect the assets for payment of creditors and distribution among those entitled. A purchaser therefore is safe in receiving securities registered in the name of an executor or administrator, unless some special instance should exist

---

[1] See Hawkins *v.* Kemp, 3 East, 410; Bulteel *v.* Abinger, 6 Jurist, 410; Sugden on Powers, vol. i. * p. 222; Berger *v.* Duff, 4 Johnson's Ch. (N. Y.) 369; Sinclair *v.* Jackson, 8 Cowen, 575; Hawley *v.* James, 5 Paige, 487; Pearson *v.* Jamison, 1 McLean, C. C. 197, and other authorities, *infra*, on power of trustee to delegate a discretion to sell.

to lead him to infer fraud, or unless such a long period has elapsed since the death of the decedent as to lead to the inference that his debts have been paid. But in Lowry *v.* The Commercial Bank,[1] the court held, that where eight years had elapsed since the death of a testator, a bank was negligent in allowing the executor, who it appeared from the terms of the will was also appointed a trustee, to allow a transfer of stock standing in his name. Judge Taney, who delivered the opinion of the court, held, that after the lapse of such a time the bank was bound to presume that all the testator's debts had been paid, and that even an executor after that period had no implied power to sell.

Lowry v. Commercial Bank.

The powers of a trustee to sell depend, as his power to pledge, upon the instrument creating the trust. If it contains no express power, the trustee cannot deal with the assets, excepting under an order of court. And, where such an express power does exist, all the existing trustees must join in the sale.

Trustee, *prima facie*, cannot sell.

The trustees, moreover, must act jointly. It is not sufficient for them to act separately,[2] if the separate instruments executed by each do not show an intention on the part of each to concur in the joint act of all.

Trustees must act jointly.

Failure on the part of all to join may be fatal to the title of the purchaser.[3] And it is not competent for one trustee to delegate to an agent, or even to his co-trustees, power to act in the sale, unless it appear, on the face of the letter of attorney, that the sale, and *the terms of it*, have been decided upon by the former, and

---

[1] 3 Am. Law Jour. 111.
[2] See Vandever's Appeal, 8 Watts & Serg. 405.
[3] Sinclair *v.* Jackson, 8 Cowen, 543; Chapin *v.* First Universalist Society, 8 Gray, 583.

the agent is clothed with the authority only to perform the mere ministerial duty of carrying it out.

Indeed, it is a safe rule for the purchaser to refuse taking any transfer unless executed by the trustees individually.[1]

In regard to the delegation of discretion by trustees, it has been argued that a difference exists between those cases where the trustee's power is coupled with an interest, and where the trustee is by the trust deed given a mere naked power to sell.

Delegation of trustee's authority where there is a power coupled with an interest. In the case of a power coupled with an interest, it has been said that the trustee may delegate his discretion by reason of the interest vested in him. But unless this rule be restricted to those cases where the donee of the power is, in fact, the beneficial owner, so that his interest and power, combined, invest him with complete control over the property, the cases do not bear out this distinction. A delegation of discretion has been pronounced void in many instances, where the power of discretion in the trustee has been coupled with an interest.[2]

---

[1] Bulteel v. Abinger, 6 Jurist, 410, and authorities *infra*, under following note.

[2] In the following cases, where a power was coupled with an interest, a delegation of discretion by the trustee to an attorney or agent was held void. See Combe's Case, 9 Rep. 75 b (A.D. 1612); Bulteel v. Abinger, 6 Jurist, 410; Hawkins v. Kemp, 3 East, 410; Sinclair v. Jackson, 8 Cowen, 575; Hawley v. James, 5 Paige, 487; Greenough v. Wells, 10 Cush. 571; Budd v. Hiler, 3 Dutcher, 43; Belote v. White, 2 Head (Tenn.), 703; Whittlesay v. Hughes, 39 Missouri, 20; Saunders v. Weber, 39 California, 287; Bohlen's Estate, 75 Penna. 304. For cases of naked power, see Wilson v. Denison, 1 Ambler, 86; Heger v. Deares, 2 Johnson's Ch. 154 (Ch. Kent); Berger v. Duff, 4 Johnson's Ch. 369; Tainter v. Clark, 13 Metcalf, 226; Pearson v. Jamison, 1 McLean, C. C. 197; Hunt v. Douglass, 22 Vt. 130; Newton v. Bronson's Ex'rs, 13 N. Y. 587; Wilson v. Pennock, 3 Ca. Pa. 239; Piatt v. McCullough, 1 McLean, C. C. 69.

CHAP. I.] FORMA N OF THE PLEDGE.   337

The power of a trustee, or other person acting in a fiduciary relation, to purchase securities, can, so far as the stock broker is concerned, only practically come in question where a person presents a check or draft drawn by him in his character of trustee, etc., for payment of securities purchased by him. In such a case the broker has direct notice that the money belongs to the *cestui que trust*, and there is little doubt, if the securities purchased were not directed to be registered in the name of the person buying them in his fiduciary capacity, that the broker might be held liable for the money, thus misapplied. Where, however, the securities purchased are directed to be registered in the name of the trust estate, it is conceived that the broker could not be held responsible for receiving payment in this manner, even should it turn out that trust funds had been misapplied. It is the safer rule for the broker to decline receiving payment in any way which necessarily puts him upon notice that the moneys paid do not belong to the customer.

SECTION II.—THE SUBJECT-MATTER OF THE PLEDGE.

Nearly all personal property may be the subject of a pledge by the owner, or by one by him duly authorized to do so; and it may be said that bonds, scrip, mortgages, debentures, shares of stock, and nearly all choses in action capable of assignment, may be pledged by one authorized to do so.

What may be pledged.

SECTION III.—MANNER OF EFFECTING THE PLEDGE.

Delivery of pledge.

The thing pledged must always be delivered[1] either manually[2] or symbolically[3] by the pledgeor to the pledgee.

Pledge of negotiable securities.

Where the property passes merely by delivery, as coupon bonds, scrip, and a few peculiar kinds of shares, the pledge is effected by simply handing the thing to the pledgee, since, as these are negotiable, the holder is *prima facie* the owner.

Pledge of non-negotiable securities.

With regard, however, to other choses in action which do not pass by mere delivery, the title to them must be transferred to the pledgee in the mode required by law to pass title to the particular property, in each case, made the subject of pledge. As regards registered bonds,—*i.e.*, bonds registered in the names of the holders on the books of the company issuing them,—and shares of stock, the title is in the former case ordinarily transferred by the pledgeor having the bonds registered in the pledgee's name at the transfer agency, and in the latter, by the pledgeor handing the certificates of stock to the pledgee, with a power of attorney executed in blank, to transfer; and the pledgee may or may not have them registered in his name: as indeed also, in the case of bonds, the same thing may be done, and frequently when no actual transfer is made the company is notified of the intended pledge.[4]

---

[1] Murray v. Lardner, 2 Wallace, 110.
[2] Brewster v. Hartley, 37 Cal. 15.
[3] Markham v. Jaudon, 41 N. Y. 235.
[4] See 2 Kent, Com. p. 578, note *d* (12th ed.); Bank v. Cook, 4 Pick. (Mass.) 405.

CHAPTER II.

EFFECT OF THE PLEDGE.

	PAGE
Division of chapter	339
SECTION I.—PLEDGEE'S TITLE IN THE PLEDGE.	
Pledgee registered as shareholder in joint stock company	340
Pledgee liable as ordinary bailee for care, etc.	341
SECTION II.—PLEDGEE'S RIGHT TO ENJOY THE USE OF THE THING PLEDGED.	
§ 1. PLEDGEE'S RIGHT TO VOTE, COLLECT DIVIDENDS, COUPONS, ETC.	
Pledgee may collect dividends, coupons, vote, etc.	342
§ 2. PLEDGEE'S RIGHT TO SELL THE PLEDGE.	
When and how pledgee may sell	343
Pledge of commercial paper	344
Sale by judicial process	344
Sale without the aid of a court	344
Public sale	345
Cases discussed	345
Right of pledgee to bid at sale	347
Special agreement	348
Example of, in note	349
Demand and notice	350
Cases discussed	350
Sufficient notice	351
Cases discussed	352
§ 3. PLEDGEE'S RIGHT TO REHYPOTHECATE.	
Subject divided into two heads	353
I. Cases under first head, in England and America, discussed	354
II. Cases under second head, in England, discussed	864
Donald v. Suckling	864
Review of the principles on pledgee's right to sub-pledge	868

In this chapter we shall examine,— *Division of chapter.*

Section I. The pledgee's title in the pledge.

Section II. The pledgee's right to enjoy the use of the pledge.

§ 1. The pledgee's right to vote, collect dividends, coupons, etc.

§ 2. To sell the pledge.

§ 3. To sub-pledge or rehypothecate.

SECTION I.—THE PLEDGEE'S TITLE IN THE PLEDGE.

Pledgee's title.

As we have seen, a pledge of negotiable instruments, like coupon bonds, scrip certificates passing by delivery, and the like, is effected by handing the pledgee the instruments, and he becomes then, as regards third parties, the legal owner of them, if nothing more be done.[1] In the case of registered bonds and shares of stock, the pledgee gets the legal title only when a transfer into his own name is made properly on the books of the company;[2] and, while he merely holds the certificates of stock with a power of attorney to transfer executed in blank, his title is only an equitable one.[3]

Title of pledgees registered as shareholders in a joint stock company.

When the pledgee holds the legal title in his own name, there is little doubt that in the United States, as well as in England, he is liable to the company for calls, or any other obligations of a stockholder, and continues so liable until his name is properly taken off the register of shareholders. There are, moreover, in many of the States of the Union, peculiar personal liabilities, of a more or less onerous character, which a shareholder in a joint stock company, especially manufacturing or improvement companies, may incur, such as back wages of operatives, or corporate debts contracted without compliance with certain statutory regulations. These liabilities attach to the ownership of the stock, and, generally, irrespective of the capacity in which the person holding the legal title owns it.

---

[1] Morris Canal & Bank Co. *v.* Lewis, 12 N. J., Eq. 323.

[2] Telegraph Co. *v.* Davenport, 7 Otto, 369; Roberts's Appeal, 4 Norris (Pa.), 84.

[3] Lightner's Appeal, 1 Norris (Pa.), 301.

For the theory on which these joint stock companies are organized is, that the shareholders are all partners in the common enterprise, whose liability for debts is limited by statute only, either to the par value of the shares held by them, or to some further ascertained sum. And, as a trustee or other person acting in a fiduciary capacity, who carries on business for his *cestuis que trustent*, either by himself or in partnership with others, cannot do so without becoming personally liable for debts contracted in the course of business, so the only limit of his liability as shareholder in a company is the statutory one of the par value of the shares held by him. This reasoning, of course, extends to pledgees, whenever they allow themselves to be registered as shareholders, since they hold themselves out to the world as partners, although, as between themselves and the pledgeor, the latter may be liable for calls, etc., just as the trustee may look to the trust estate for indemnity against loss incurred by him in the course of his duty. A pledgee, therefore, by registering stock hypothecated with him in his own name, incurs all the liabilities of a shareholder. He obtains, on the other hand, a recognition by the company of his title as a shareholder, which they are thereafter estopped from disputing, even if it turn out that the certificate of stock was forged, or that the transferor, if a trustee, or agent, etc., had no authority to transfer off the register of shareholders.[1]

The pawnee is bound to take ordinary care, and is responsible only for gross neglect; for the bailment is beneficial both to the debtor and creditor. The

---

[1] Johnson *v.* Underhill, 52 N. Y. 203; Wheeler *v.* Kost, 77 Ill. 296.

pawnee, upon delivery to him, has a special property in the thing pawned, and if it be not injured by use he may use it.¹

SECTION II.—THE PLEDGEE'S RIGHT TO ENJOY THE USE OF THE THING PLEDGED.

§ 1. *Pledgee's Right to Vote, Collect Dividends, Coupons, etc.*

<small>Pledgee, when legal owner, may exercise all rights of owner consistent with the terms of the pledge.</small>

When the pledgee has the registered bonds or certificates standing in his name on the books of the company, absolutely, without any notice to its officers that he is not the actual owner, or when he holds negotiable securities, he may, being the legal owner, exercise all the rights of such an owner, consistent with the terms of the pledge.

<small>*Ex parte* Willcocks.</small>

Thus, in *Ex parte* Willcocks,² the court allowed the pledgee to vote on the pledged stock only so long as it stood in the pledgor's name in the books of the company.

<small>Merchants' Bank *v.* Cook.</small>

And in Merchants' Bank *v.* Cook,³ the court did not allow the pledgee to vote, because notice was left with the company stating the existence of the pledge.

<small>Pledgee of stock may vote, collect dividends, etc.</small>

The pledgee may, moreover, in the absence of any express or implied condition to the contrary, collect coupons⁴ or interest, and draw dividends,⁵ accruing in money on the security pledged, accounting for them on the final settlement of accounts between himself and the pledgeor, and, in short, exercise all the privileges

---

¹ 2 Kent, Com. 579 (12th ed.).
² 7 Cowen, 402.
³ 4 Pick. 405.
⁴ See Androscoggin R. R. Co. *v.* Bank, 48 Maine, 335.
⁵ Hasbrook *v.* Vanderoort, 4 Sandford, 74.

of a real owner, not inconsistent with the terms of the pledge.[1] He would not, however, without special authority from the pledgeor, be entitled to convert into money, scrip of stock, dividends, or any other increment in the security pledged not accruing in money, since this would amount to a sale of a chose in action made the subject of pledge, which, except on nonpayment of the advance, is contrary to the terms of the contract.

§ 2. *Pledgee's Right to Sell the Pledge.*

In the event of the debt not being paid at the time designated in the agreement, the pledgee may either sell the pledge by a judicial foreclosure and sale, which involves a proceeding at law, and notice (by service of legal process) to the pledgeor, or at least what is in law deemed the equivalent of notice; or, without proceeding at law, he may, on demand and reasonable notice, sell the pledge at a public sale, not judicial; or if there be a special arrangement between the parties, the pledgee may sell according to its terms.

Or, finally, he may proceed in an action at law against the debtor personally, and not sell the pledge at all; as in Robinson *v.* Hurley,[2] where it was stipulated that should the note pledged as collateral "not be promptly met at maturity," the pledgee reserves "the right and privilege of" disposing of the pledge at private sale, the proceeds to be applied to the satisfaction of the debt, and the balance to be paid the

---

[1] See Butterworth *v.* Kennedy, 5 Bosw. 143; see, also, McDaniels *v.* Manf. Co., 22 Vt. 274; Heath *v.* Silverthorn, 39 Wisc. 147; Rev. Stat. N. Y., 5th ed.

[2] 11 Iowa, 410.

pledgeor, and the court held, that it did not require a sale at the maturity of the note.

Pledge of commercial paper. In the case of commercial paper, held as collateral security, it has, for obvious reasons, been held, that the pledgee cannot sell, but must collect at maturity.[1]

Sale by judicial process. Where the pledge is sold by a judicial sale, with the aid of a court of equity, the transaction is simple,

Sale without the aid of a court. and no cases need be cited for illustration. But where the sale is effected without the aid of a court, either publicly or privately, the questions arising as to the rights of the parties become somewhat more complicated, and will require consideration.

In all cases, however, where it is possible to make a sale of the pledge without the aid of the court of law, it must be remembered that the securities pledged must, if negotiable, have been actually delivered, or, where not negotiable, the certificates, or other muniments of title, with a power of attorney to transfer, have been handed to the pledgee when the hypothecation was effected; for in those cases where the certificates are handed over to the pledgee without being accompanied by a proper power of attorney, the aid of a court must, in every instance, be invoked to effect a sale.

Johnson v. Dexter. As, for instance, in Johnson v. Dexter et al.,[2] where, when the loan fell due, it was discovered that the power of attorney to transfer had been severed from the certificate without the knowledge of the pledgeors, who, however, on being informed of the fact by the

---

[1] See Fletcher v. Dickenson, 7 Allen, 28; Nelson v. Wellington, 5 Bosw. 178; Wheeler v. Newbould, 16 N. Y. 392; Lamberton v. Windom, 12 Minn. 232.

[2] 2 McArthur, 530, Supreme Court District of Columbia.

CHAP. II.] EFFECT OF THE PLEDGE. 345

complainant, refused to re-execute another power; on a bill and answer filed, the court decreed the sale of the stock to be made, and the proceeds applied to liquidate the defendant.

Humphreys, J., remarked, that the machinery of a court of equity was the only method possible to enforce such a transaction; the defendant could repossess himself of the certificates, it was true, but not without paying the debt. It was the defendant's duty to endorse the collateral security properly when passed to raise the money; and, when informed of the mistake, he should have corrected it; and if he would not do so, the court, considering that to be done which ought to have been done, would decree a sale. *Remarks of Humphreys, J.*

The sale, when made without the aid of a court, must be public, and a question has arisen as to what constitutes a public sale. The Stock Exchange usually constitutes the best mart for the sale of any security there dealt in, and is now practically the only one for many securities. It is not, however, public, in the strict sense of the word,—only its members, and not the general public, being admitted to its sittings. A sale at auction, on the other hand, constitutes, in a literal sense, a public sale. *Sale without judicial process must be public, ordinarily.*

Public sale.

In Rankin v. McCullough,[1] Edmonds, P. J., said, "But the objection as to the place where the stock "was sold was well taken. The sale at the Board of "Brokers has often been held not to be such a public "sale as is required in such cases." *Rankin v. McCullough. Remarks of Edmonds, P. J.*

In Brass v. Worth,[2] Brown, J., said, "The sale, which the defendants made of the plaintiff's stocks, *Brass v. Worth. Remarks of Brown, J.*

[1] 12 Barb. (N. Y.) 103.   [2] 40 Barb. (N. Y.) 648.

was not public. It was essentially private. The Board of Brokers is an association of dealers in stocks, and is not open to the public. None but members are allowed to be present at the meetings, except upon invitation."

Brown v. Ward.

In Brown *v.* Ward,¹ Hoffman, J., held, that a public sale in New York may be held at the Merchants' Exchange, as a custom has grown up which is sanctioned by the courts, on demand and notice of the place of sale, and that any other mode of sale must rest upon express agreement.

Willoughby v. Comstock.

Although in Willoughby *v.* Comstock,² Nelson, C. J., held, that inasmuch as there were no restrictions as to the place of sale, and the pledgeor had been notified of the place of sale, and made no objections, he was estopped from afterwards setting up that the Board of Brokers was not a proper place of sale, there being no usage to the contrary.

Fire Ins. Co. v. Dalrymple. Remarks of Bartol, J.

But in the State of Maryland a contrary doctrine has been established, and in Maryland Fire Ins. Co. *v.* Dalrymple,³ Bartol, J., said, "It was contended "* * * that the sale must in all cases be made at "public auction, and that a sale at the Brokers' Board "would not be legal; and some decisions in New York

Brown v. Ward quoted.

"were cited in support of this view. In Brown *v.* "Ward,⁴ it was said that 'a custom has grown up (in "New York), and been sanctioned by the courts, of "selling stock at the Merchants' Exchange.' There "is no evidence of any such custom in Baltimore, and, "considering the requirements of the law, and the

---

¹ 8 Duer (N. Y.), 660.
² 3 Hill (N. Y.), 389.
³ 25 Md. 265.
⁴ *Supra.*

"reason and nature of the transaction, we are of the
"opinion that the most proper and suitable place for
"a sale of stock is at the Board of Brokers. There is
"the stock market,—the mart to which vendors and
"purchasers resort, by their agents, to buy and sell
"stock, where competition among bidders is most apt
"to be found; such sales are public, and unless there
"be, in the particular case, some ground for impeach-
"ing their fairness, we are of opinion they are reason-
"able and ought to be supported."[1]

In Maryland, sale at Board of Brokers held to be a public sale.

At a judicial sale, at a time and place and with the notice ordered by a court, there exists no reason why the pledgee should not bid at the sale with the public. But it has been decided in the case of a sale, even though public, made by the pledgee on his own responsibility, that he cannot, in the absence of a special stipulation to that effect, become the purchaser of the security pledged with him, on the ground of his interest as a prospective buyer being inconsistent with his duty as a pledgee.

Right of pledgee to bid at sale.

Thus, in Maryland Fire Ins. Co. v. Dalrymple,[2] Bartol, J., said, " But, as we have seen, the defendant
"became itself the purchaser of the stock, and the
"question arises, what was the legal effect of the pro-
"ceeding? Did it amount to a valid and effectual sale
"so as either to vest in the defendant as purchaser an
"absolute title, or to operate as a conversion of the
"property, break up the bailment, and the relation of
"bailor and bailee between the parties? The doctrine
"that trustees, executors, administrators, and others

Md. Fire Ins. Co. v. Dalrymple.

Remarks of Bartol, J.

---

[1] See, also, Robinson v. Hurley, 11 Iowa, 413.   [2] 25 Md. 265.

"holding fiduciary relations are incompetent to pur-
"chase the property held by them in trust, is well
"settled.[1] * * * The sale of the pledge by the de-
"fendant to itself was contrary to the faith of the
"bailment, forbidden, as we have shown by the citation
"from Story, by the common law, and might be treated
"by the bailor, at his election, as a tortious conversion
"of the property. In this case, no such election was
"made by the plaintiff. There was no transmutation
"of title or change of possession, and the sale being
"inoperative to work a conversion, the relation of the
"parties remained unchanged thereby. The defend-
"ant remained in possession of the stock as before, in
"the same manner as if the sale had been attempted,
"and both in fact and in contemplation of law the
"bailment continued. This point was decided in
"Middlesex Bank v. Minot.[2] That decision was fol-
"lowed by the Supreme Court of Iowa in The Bank
"v. Dubuque R. R. Co."[3]

Middlesex Bank v. Minot.

Bank v. Dubuque R. R. Co.

Special agreement.

Hence it has become usual, in most cases of advances on collaterals, to make an express stipulation[4] that, in case of failure to pay the advance at the time specified, the pledgee may sell the securities pledged at public sale, and may, at such sale, become the purchaser himself. It is obvious that, in the case of securities not well known or current on the market, such a power is essential in order to enable the pledgeor to protect his loan.

Private sale.

Where the parties agree to a private sale, in case

---

[1] Story, Eq. §§ 321-323; Story, Bail., § 819; Greenlow v. King, 5 Lond. Jur. 18, cited in Torrey v. Bank, 9 Paige, 663; 12 Md. 384; 16 Md. 456; 20 Md. 117.
[2] 4 Metc. 325.
[3] 8 Clarke, 277.
[4] See example, next page.

CHAP. II.]   EFFECT OF THE PLEDGE.   349

of failure to pay the advance, that is of course sufficient to enable the pledgee to sell privately; though in case of any circumstances showing fraud, a court of equity would not hesitate to give the pledgeor an equity of redemption on proper terms, provided a bill were filed within a reasonable time, and no laches could be imputed to the plaintiff.

In order to effect a valid sale of a pledge, since the pledgeor may always redeem the pledge on payment of the debt in full, with the broker's disbursements,

---

$............   *Philadelphia,*...............*188*

.... *promise to pay to the*

Order of..

....*Dollars,*
                                                         100

with interest at the rate of.............*per cent. per annum,*

FOR VALUE RECEIVED, WITHOUT DEFALCATION, hereby waiving all right to stay of execution and exemption of property in any suit on this note. As collateral security

   have delivered ....

....

which   hereby authorize and empower the holder hereof, on default in payment at maturity, with a view to its liquidation, and of all interests and costs thereon, to sell and transfer, in whole or in part, without any previous demand upon or notice to either at Brokers' Board or at public or private sale, with the right of becoming the purchaser and absolute owner thereof, free of all trusts and claims, should such sale be made at Brokers' Board, or be public.   Furthermore,   agree, that so often as the market price of these and subsequently-deposited securities shall, before maturity of this note, fall to a price insufficient to cover its amount, with   per cent. margin added thereto,   will, on demand, within two hours thereafter, deposit with the holder additional security, to be approved by said holder, sufficient to cover said amount, and margin; and that, in default thereof, this note shall become instantly due and payable precisely as though it had actually matured, and all the foregoing rights to sell and transfer collaterals shall at once be exercisable, at   risk, in case of any deficiency in realizing proceeds.

....

Example of special agreement.

350   THE PLEDGE.   [PART III.

Demand and notice of sale. commission, etc.,[1] there must always be a demand made by the pledgee upon the pledgeor to redeem, and a notice given within a reasonable time of the place and time of sale,[2] and a demand may be given at the same time as the notice of the sale.[3]

What is reasonable notice. What constitutes a reasonable notice depends, in all cases of the pledge of personal property, upon the character of the transaction, the currency on the market of the property pledged, and the time requisite to bring it to the knowledge of purchasers, and, more especially, upon whether the notice actually given was, under the circumstances, sufficient to have enabled the owner to protect himself by returning the loan or bidding at the sale; and it is difficult to lay down any legal rule upon the subject. It is, in most cases, a matter of common sense, upon which a court will only be guided in every case by its own judgment, assisted by evidence as to the circumstances, the salability of the property, its value, etc.

Maryland Fire Ins. Co. v. Dalrymple. In Maryland Fire Ins. Co. v. Dalrymple,[4] by the terms of the contract, the loan was made payable on one day's notice, and if not paid according to the agreement, the defendant was authorized, *without further notice,* to sell the stock pledged for the purpose of satisfying the same. In the case a week's notice was given, which was naturally held to be ample.

Willoughby v. Comstock. In Willoughby v. Comstock,[5] Nelson, C. J., held,

---

[1] See Neiler v. Kelly, 69 Pa. 403; Stearns v. Marsh, 4 Denio, 227; Cushman v. Hayes, 46 Ill. 145.
[2] Wilson v. Little, 2 N. Y. 443; Howe v. Bemis, 2 Gray, 205; 25 Md. 364.
[3] Howe v. Bemis, 2 Gray (Mass.), 205.
[4] 25 Md. 264.
[5] 3 Hill (N. Y.), 389.

CHAP. II.]   EFFECT OF THE PLEDGE.   351

that where the pledgee had received two days' notice, and had not objected to it, that was sufficient.

In Bryan *v.* Baldwin,[1] the evidence showed that a formal written notice of the sale, with a copy of the advertisement thereof annexed, signed by the auctioneer by whom the sale was made, was left at the defendant's place of business, with the person in charge, two days before the sale, and, though the defendant did not appear to have recollected receiving any, the court held this to be sufficient.

<small>Bryan *v.* Baldwin.</small>

In Stevens *v.* Bank,[2] certain securities were held by a bank as collateral security, with the right to sell them in a reasonable time. The bank made a conditional sale of them without previous notice to the pledgeor, and notified him then, that if his debt was not satisfactorily paid or secured, on that day, the stocks would be sold. The pledgeor asked one day more, and, in fact, would have been ready to pay a large portion of the debt, but the bank refused, and sold the securities, and the court held the notice not a reasonable one. The court said, "We think, "therefore, that the conduct of the officer of the "bank, in completing the sale under these circum- "stances, ought not to be regarded as standing upon "any higher ground than it would have done had he "made an entirely secret sale, without any notice to "the plaintiff."

<small>Stevens *v.* Bank.</small>

<small>Remarks of the court.</small>

It is obvious from the foregoing remarks, and these illustrations, that there are many cases where, from the nature of the security pledged, the situation of the parties, and the character of the transaction itself,

<small>Sufficient notice.</small>

---

[1] 7 Lansing (N. Y.), 174.   [2] 31 Conn. 146.

as in the case of demand loans, one day's notice might, and probably would, be considered sufficient, in the absence of any usage to the contrary; and, *a fortiori*, where such is the time given by general usage of the business in which the parties are engaged. Indeed, wherever there is a time ordained by usage, that would probably be held to be a reasonable one by the courts, in the absence of a special agreement, and certainly where the pledgee, having had the opportunity, had not objected to the time.[1] In a waiver of notice, the sale may take place without, according to the terms of the private agreement, and, consequently, it has been held, that if there is any agreement to abandon the right to notice made or acquiesced in by the parties, the court will give effect to it.

Davis v. Funk. Thus, in Davis v. Funk,[2] Thompson, J., said that notice was only necessary in the absence of any agreement to sell *ex mero motu*.

Wicks v. Hatch. So, in Wicks v. Hatch,[3] the plaintiff executed to W. a power of attorney to sell, etc., and to do whatever in his discretion might be necessary in the business, with power of substitution. W. employed defendants as stock brokers, depositing with them a margin, with authority to sell at public or private sale, in their discretion, without notice, the stocks they were carrying for plaintiff, whenever the margins should fall below five per cent. The court held, that defendants might sell at the Board of Brokers without notice, when they exercised a sound discretion, and they believed the state of the market justified it.

---

[1] See Willoughby v. Comstock, *supra*, p. 346.

[2] 39 Pa. 243.

[3] 62 N. Y. 535.

CHAP. II.] EFFECT OF THE PLEDGE. 353

In Hyatt *v.* Argenti,[1] it was likewise held, that when securities are deposited as a pledge, the pledgeor may agree with the pledgee to waive a notice of the time and place of the sale, and the courts will be governed by the conditions of the agreement.[2]

Hyatt *v.* Argenti.

In accordance with this rule, it has, recently, been usual to insert in notes given for advances on the pledge of collaterals, a stipulation that, on failure to pay, the pledgeor may sell without notice, as will be seen in the form given *supra* on page 349.

The legal expenses are borne by the pledgeor, and deducted from the amount returned him.[3]

§ 3. *Pledgee's Right to Sub-pledge or Rehypothecate.*

The question, whether a party, with whom an article has been pledged as security for the payment of money, has a right to transfer his interest in the thing pledged, subject to the right of redemption in the pawnor, to a third party, is of considerable importance; and, in order to give a complete answer to it, it will be necessary to consider two categories under which it will be seen that it necessarily falls.

I. When securities have been deposited as collateral for the payment of a debt, with the right on the part of the pawnee to sell or otherwise dispose of the same in the event of non-payment of the debt, and the pawnee repledges the securities to a third party for an advance to himself, can the original pawnor, the debt

---

[1] 3 Cal. 151.
[2] See Baker *v.* Drake, 66 N. Y. 518; Markham *v.* Jaudon, *supra;* Rozet *v.* McClellan, 48 Ill. 345; Fisher *v.* Fisher, 98 Mass. 303; Cushman *v.* Jewelry Co., 76 N. Y. 365; Fancourt *v.* Thorne, 9 Q. B. 312.
[3] See 2 Kent, Com. 578 (12th Am. ed.); 29 Leg. Int. (Pa.) 366.

23

remaining unpaid, treat the contract of pawn between himself and the first pawnee as at an end, so as to bring an action of detinue or trover against the second pawnee, without tendering the amount of the debt, for which the security has been given?

II. If the contract of pawn between the first pawnee and the original pawnor is not at an end, in the event of the former thus rehypothecating the security deposited with him for a debt of his own, is it, at all events, such a breach of the contract of pawn that an action for damages will lie against the first pawnee, at the hands of the first pawnor, and can the original pawnor, on tendering the amount of his own debt to the second pawnee, obtain possession of the subject of the pawn?

Donald v. Suckling.

I. In considering this question, it must be borne in mind, as remarked by Cockburn, C. J., in Donald *v.* Suckling,[1] that we are not dealing with the case of a lien, which is merely the right to retain possession of the chattel, and which right is immediately lost on the possession being parted with, unless to a person who may be considered as the agent of the party having the lien for the purpose of its custody. There is a great difference in this respect between a pledge and a lien.

Distinction between lien and pledge.

The authorities are clear that a right of lien, properly so called, is a mere personal right of detention, and that an unauthorized transfer of the thing does not transfer that personal right. The cases which established, before the Factors' Acts,[2] that a pledge by a

---

[1] L. R., 1 Q. B. C. 618.

[2] See the English Factors' Act of 6 Geo. IV. ch. 94, s. 2, and the amendment of 5 & 6 Vict. c. 39, as well as the acts in the several States of the Union, which have been moulded on this act, as in New York, Pennsylvania, Massa-

factor gave his pledgee no right to retain the goods, even to the extent to which the factor was in advance, proceed on this ground.

In Daubigny v. Duval,[1] Buller, J., puts the case on the ground that "a lien is a personal right and cannot be transferred to another." In McCombie v. Davies,[2] Lord Ellenborough puts the decision of the court on the same ground, saying that "nothing could "be clearer than that liens were personal and could "not be transferred to third persons by any tortious "pledge of the principal's goods."

Daubigny v. Duval.

McCombie v. Davies.

Remarks of Lord Ellenborough.

In Legg v. Evans,[3] an action of trover was brought against a sheriff of Middlesex to recover some pictures, who justified under an execution, to which plaintiff replied by setting up a lien on the goods, and the replication was held good on demurrer. Parke, B., is reported to have said, "If we consider "the nature of a lien, and *the right* which it confers, "it will be evident that it cannot form the subject- "matter of a sale. A lien is a *personal right* which "cannot be parted with, and continues only so long "as the possessor holds the goods. It is clear, there- "fore, that the sheriff cannot sell an interest of this "description, which is a personal interest in the "goods."

Legg v. Evans.

Remarks of Parke, B.

The effect of the civil law is thus stated by Story in his Treatise on Bailments, s. 328: "It enabled the "pawnee to assign over or to pledge the goods again,

Remarks of Story, J.

chusetts, Ohio, Rhode Island, etc.; see, also, a discussion as to what agents are within the meaning of these acts, in Benjamin on Sales, 3d Amer. ed., with American notes,
p. 17, and succeeding pages.
[1] 5 T. R. 606.
[2] 7 East, 6.
[3] 6 M. & W. 36.

"to the extent of his interest or lien on them; and "in either case the transferee was entitled to hold the "pawn until the original owner discharged the debt "for which it was pledged. But beyond this the "second pledge was inoperative and conveyed no title, "according to the known maxim, *nemo plus juris ad* "*alium transferre potest quam ipse haberet.*"

In England, it is held, that the contract of pledge, when perfected by possession, creates an interest in the pledge which may be assigned, and the original pawnor cannot claim the thing pawned from the transferee without a tender of the payment of the debt to the pawnee.

Coggs v. Bernard. Remarks of Lord Holt.

In the celebrated case of Coggs *v.* Bernard,[1] Lord Holt said that a pawnee "has a special property, for "the pawn is a securing to the pawnee that he shall "be repaid his debt, and to compel the pawnor to pay "him."

Mores v. Conham.

In Mores *v.* Conham,[2] the court said, the pawnee will be responsible if he misuseth the pawn; "also "he hath such interest in the pawn as he may assign "over, and the assignee shall be subject to detinue if "he detains it upon payment of the money by the "owner."

Johnson v. Stear.

In Johnson *v.* Stear,[3] one Cumming, a bankrupt, had deposited with the defendant two hundred and forty-three cases of brandy, to be held by him as a security for the payment of an acceptance of the bankrupt, discounted by the defendant, and which would become due on January 29, and in case such

---

[1] 2 Ld. Raymond, 916. [3] 15 C. B. (N. S.) 330.
[2] Owen, 123.

acceptance was not paid at maturity, he was to be at liberty to sell the brandy and apply the proceeds to the payment of the acceptance. On the 28th January the defendant contracted to sell the brandy to a third person, and delivered him the dock warrant on the 29th, and on the 30th the third person got possession of the brandy. In an action of trover, brought by the assignee of the bankrupt, the majority of the court held (Erle, C. J., Byles and Keating, JJ.), that the plaintiff was only entitled to nominal damages, on the ground "that the deposit of the goods in ques- "tion with the defendant to secure repayment of a "loan to him on a given day, with a power to sell in "case of default on that day, created an interest and "a right of property in the goods which was more "than a mere lien; and the wrongful act of the pawnee "did not annihilate the contract between the parties, "nor the interest of the pawnee in the goods under "the contract." From this view Williams, J., dissented.

In the late case of Donald *v.* Suckling,[1] after very elaborate argument, it was held by the court (Mellor, Blackburn, JJ., and Cockburn, C. J., Shee, J., *dissentiente*), that, when debentures had been deposited as security for the payment of a bill of exchange, with a right on the part of the depositee to dispose of them on the non-payment of the bill when due, and the pawnee pledged it to a third party for an advance of money, the original pawnor, the bill still remaining unpaid, could not, without having first tendered the amount of the bill to the second bailee, maintain

Donald *v.* Suckling.

[1] L. R., 1 Q. B. C. 585.

an action of detinue against the latter for the recovery of the debentures.

<small>Remarks of Blackburn, J.</small>

"Story," said Blackburn, J., "in his Treatise on "Bailments, s. 327, says, 'But, whatever doubt may "be indulged as to the case of a factor, it has been "decided, that is in America, that in case of a strict "pledge, if the pledgee transfers the same to his "own creditor, the latter may hold the pledge until "the debt of the original owner is discharged.' In "Whitaker on Lien, published in 1812, p. 140, the "law is laid down to be that the pawnee has a special "property beyond a lien. I do not cite this as an "authority of great weight, but as showing that this "was an existing opinion in England before Story "wrote his treatise. * * * Now, I think that the sub-"pledging of goods held in security for money, before "the money is due, is not in general so inconsistent "with the contract as to amount to a renunciation of "that contract. There may be cases in which the "pledgeor has a special personal confidence in the "pawnee, and therefore stipulates that the pledge "shall be kept by him alone; but no such terms are "stated here, and I do not think that any such term "is implied by law. In general, all that the pledgeor "requires is the personal contract of the pledgee that "on bringing the money the pawn shall be given up "to him, and that in the mean time the pledgee shall "be responsible for due care being taken for its safe "custody. This may very well be done though there "has been a sub-pledge."

In the United States, the point has not often arisen, as in nearly all the cases relating to stocks, etc., the security pawned was either negotiable, and passed by delivery, or the pledgee, in the case of non-negotiable securities, held a bill of sale of the goods, and all the necessary *indicia* of ownership, sufficient to give a good title, so that the point in the cases has been, not whether the sub-pledge terminated the contract of pledge between the original parties to it, or was a breach of it for which an action for damages lay, but whether a party, who places in the hands of another all the necessary *indicia* of ownership over property, will not be estopped from setting up his title, when it has passed into the hands of a *bona fide* purchaser for value; and whether such a *bona fide* purchaser does not, on the doctrine of estoppel, get an absolute title, in the case of a sale, or at least a good title, in the case of a pledge, till a tender of his own debt is made. And the courts have held that, when a pledgee has the power of giving a good title to a vendee or pledgee, the original pledgeor cannot dispute an innocent vendee's title, and that he can in no case get back the securities from an innocent pledgee, without tendering the amount of the debt.

Thus, in McNeil *v.* Tenth National Bank,[1] where the pledgeor had deposited certificates of shares with a bill of sale, Rapallo, J., said, "The true point of "inquiry in this case is, whether the plaintiff did "confer upon his brokers such an apparent title to, "or power of disposition over, the shares in question, "as will thus estop him from asserting his own title, "as against parties who took *bona fide* through the "brokers. Simply entrusting the possession of a

McNeil v. Tenth National Bank.

Remarks of Rapallo, J.

[1] 46 N. Y. 325.

"chattel to another as depositary, pledgee, or other
"bailee, or even under a conditional executory con-
"tract of sale, is clearly insufficient to preclude the
"real owner from reclaiming his property, in case of
"an unauthorized disposition of it by the person so

Ballard v. Burgett cited.

"entrusted (Ballard v. Burgett[1]). The mere posses-
"sion of chattels, by whatever means acquired, *if there
"be no other evidence of property or authority to sell
"from the true owner*, will not enable the possessor to

Remarks of Denio, J., in Covill v. Hill, quoted.

"give a good title. *Per* Denio, J., in Covill v. Hill.[2]
"But if the owner entrusts to another, not merely the
"possession of the property, but also written evidence,
"over his own signature, of title thereto, and of an
"unconditional power of disposition over it, the case
"is vastly different;" and it was held, that the innocent pledgee for value was protected.

Jarvis v. Rogers.

In Jarvis v. Rogers,[3] the certificates of the stock of a company had, by a vote of the company, been made transferable by endorsing the name of the person to whom they were issued on the back, and one of the company, holding such certificates, endorsed his name on it and pledged it as collateral security for a debt. The debt was paid by his friend, who secured the cer- tificates, and subsequently repledged them, as security for his own debt; and the court held, that a *bona fide* creditor might lawfully hold them against the original owner, until the debt for which they were pledged should be paid.

Lewis v. Mott.

In Lewis v. Mott,[4] one Brown placed certain securi- ties in the hands of Howe as collateral to two prom-

---

[1] 40 N. Y. Rep. 314.
[2] 4 Denio, 323.
[3] 13 Mass. 105.
[4] 36 N. Y. 395.

CHAP. II.]   EFFECT OF THE PLEDGE.   361

issory notes. The notes not being paid in proper time, Howe assigned them with the securities to Varnum, who subsequently without notice, the debt still not being paid, had them sold at public sale, and bid them in himself. Brown offered to pay the debt, but made no tender, and the court said, "It must be conceded "that Varnum, by the purchase of these securities "from Howe, acquired the lien and interest of Howe, "whatever that may have been; and the plaintiff's "assignee, to have entitled himself to a redelivery of "these securities, must have tendered the amount of "the lien. There was simply an offer to pay Var-"num the amount due upon those notes. It was "unattended with any tender of the amount due, and "was insufficient to extinguish the lien and thus en-"title Brown to the return of the notes." *Remarks of the court.*

In Talty v. Freedman's Savings & Trust Company,[1] the court held, that a *bona fide* purchaser of securities held by a stock broker as collateral, would not be compelled to give them up without a tender of the amount due on the pledge. The court approved the ruling in Lewis v. Mott, Jarvis v. Rogers, and Donald v. Suckling, *supra;* and Swayne, J., suggested that there was a question as to whether the *bona fide* purchaser for value did not hold the security absolutely; but expressed no opinion on that point. *Talty v. Freedman's Savings & Trust Co.*

Lewis v. Mott, Jarvis v. Rogers, Donald v. Suckling, approved.

In Wood's Appeal,[2] already discussed, it was held, that one who had placed all the *indicia* of ownership in a bailee's hands would be estopped from setting up any title against an innocent third party, who had *Wood's Appeal.*

[1] 3 Otto (U. S.), 321.   [2] 8 W. N. C. 441; 92 Penna. 379, quoted and discussed, *supra*.

purchased from the bailee for a valuable consideration. We may conclude, then, that a *bona fide* holder or depositee, for value, will in no event be compelled to render the pledged property back to the original pawnor without a tender or payment of the amount of the money which the pledge was given to secure.[1]

Wood v. Hayes et al.

In Wood *v.* Hayes *et al.*,[2] it was held, that where a broker has bought stock for another with money advanced by himself, and holds it in his own name, he may pledge it to a third party to secure his own debt, so long as the advances made by him have not been paid or tendered, without subjecting himself to an action. Shaw, C. J., said, "The doctrine of trover "does not apply. A. advanced the money to buy the "shares for account of B., and held the shares in his "own name. It stood on the footing of contract. The "contract was strictly conditional, to deliver so many "shares on payment of so much money. The money "was never paid, and the title to have performance "never accrued."

Remarks of Shaw, C. J.

Work v. Bennett.

In Work *v.* Bennett,[3] however, stock and bonds were delivered by the plaintiff to the defendant as collateral security, which the latter sub-pledged for a debt of his own, and the sub-pawnee sold it without notice to the original pledgeor. Here the court held, that the pledgeor need not make a tender before the bringing of an action of trover for damages, as there had been a wrongful conversion by the defendants in sub-pledging to the sub-pawnee, and by the latter in selling them without notice. The court, however, said expressly,

---

[1] See McNeil *v.* Tenth National Bank, 46 N. Y. 325.
[2] 15 Mass. 375.
[3] 70 Penna. 484.

"Had the stock and bonds, which were the subject of "this action of trover, remained unconverted in the "hands of the defendants, the plaintiff could not have "recovered without a tender of the amount of the debt "for which they were then pledged, or proof of pay-"ment of such debt."

And they allowed the pledgee to set off against the damages the balance due them for their advance, with interest.

In New York, however, in Allen *v.* Dykers *et al.*,[1] a stock broker borrowed some money of B. on a promissory note, the note stating that there had been "deposited with them" (the brokers making the advance), "as collateral security, with authority to "sell the same on the non-performance of this "promise, two hundred and fifty shares North Amer-"ica Trust and Banking Company's stock. Sale to "be made at the Board of Brokers. Notice waived, "if not paid at maturity." The pledgee rehypothecated the stock, and in an action of trover against the pledgee by the original pledgeor, after the note fell due, Wilson, C. J., said, "The defendants being "stock brokers and dealers in stock, their counsel "offered to prove on the trial that it was the usage, "when stock was transferred to such dealers by way "of collateral security, not to hold it specifically, but "to transfer it by hypothecation or otherwise, at "pleasure, and, on payment or tender of the money "advanced, to return an equal quantity of the same "kind of stock; also, that this usage was general, "and known to the agent who made the loan in

[1] 3 Hill (N. Y.), 593.

"question. The object of the offer was, to lay the "foundation that the usage should be regarded as "incorporated in, and forming part and parcel of, "the agreement; thus making the latter import a "consent on the part of the plaintiff, that the de-"fendants might use the stock during the running "of the loan the same as if they were the absolute "owners. It is not necessary to determine what effect "would be due to such proof in the case of a simple "pledge as collateral security, without any further "agreement. Possibly the known usage in like cases "might be considered as attaching itself to the trans-"action, and constituting a part of it. But where "the parties have chosen to prescribe for themselves "the terms and conditions of the loan, they must be "held to abide by them; and we are especially bound "to refuse effect to any general or particular usage "when in direct contradiction to the fair and legal "import of a written contract."

Merchants' Bank v. Trenholm.

In Merchants' Bank v. Trenholm,[2] it was held, that trover would lie against a pledgee, being a factor, or his sub-pledgee, without notice, though he pledged but up to his lien.

II. We now pass on to the consideration of the second category, which the question of the right to sub-pledge may be considered under: namely, conceding that the contract of pawn is not broken by the pledgee's sub-pledging, is this such a breach of the contract as to permit an action for damages to lie by the pawnor against the original pawnee?

Donald v. Suckling.

In Donald v. Suckling,[2] this point was not decided,

---

[1] 12 Heisk. (Tenn.) 520. [2] See L. R., 1 Q. B. C. 585.

the court confining itself to the question, as to whether the sub-pledge was such a total termination of the contract between the pawnor and pawnee as to allow an action of detinue to lie against the sub-pawnee, the debt still being unpaid, and the pawnor making no tender of the amount to the sub-pawnee. Cockburn, C. J., however, said, " I think it unnecessary "to the decision in the present case to determine " whether a party, with whom an article has been " pledged as a security for the payment of money, " has a right to transfer his interest in the thing " pledged (subject to the right of redemption in the " pawnor) to a third party. I should certainly hesitate " to lay down the affirmative of that proposition. " Such a right in the pawnee seems quite inconsistent " with the undoubted right of the pledgeor to have " the thing pledged returned to him immediately on " the tender of the amount for which the pledge was " given. In some instances it may well be inferred " from the nature of the thing pledged—as in the " case of a valuable work of art—that the pawnor, " though perfectly willing that the article should be " entrusted to the custody of the pawnee, would not " have parted with it on the terms that it should be " passed on to others and committed to the custody of " strangers. * * * I am of opinion that the transfer " of the pledge does not put an end to the contract, " but amounts only to a breach of contract, upon " which the owner may bring an action,—for nominal " damages if he has sustained no substantial damage ; " for substantial damages if the thing pledged is " damaged in the hands of the third party, or the

Remarks of Cockburn, C. J.

"owner is prejudiced by delay in not having the
"thing delivered to him on tendering the amount for
"which it was pledged."

Remarks of Mellor, J.

In the same case, Mellor, J., said, "I think that
"when the true distinction between the case of a de-
"posit by way of pledge of goods, for securing the
"payment of money and all cases of *lien*, correctly so
"described, is considered, it will be seen that in the
"former there is no implication, in general, of a con-
"tract by the pledgee to retain the personal possession
"of the goods deposited; and I think that although he
"(the pawnee) cannot confer upon any third person
"a better title or a greater interest than he possesses,
"yet if, nevertheless, he does pledge the goods to a
"third person for a greater interest than he possesses,
"such an act does not annihilate the contract of
"pledge between himself and the pawnor; but that
"the transaction is simply inoperative as against the
"original pawnor, who, upon tender of the sum se-
"cured, immediately becomes entitled to the posses-
"sion of the goods, and can recover in an action for
"any special damage which he may have sustained
"by reason of the act of the pawnee in repledging
"the goods."

Remarks of Blackburn, J.

And Blackburn, J., said that in England there
were *strong authorities* that the contract of pledge,
when perfected by delivery of possession, created an
interest in the pledge, which might be assigned.

Halliday v. Holgate.

In Halliday *v.* Holgate[1] (1868), A. deposited scrip
certificates with the defendant as collateral security
for a loan, and, on his becoming bankrupt, the de-

[1] L. R., 3 Exch. 299.

fendant sold out the scrip, without demand or notice, to repay to himself the debt. The creditor's assignee, without making a tender, brought an action of trover against the defendant, and the court held, that the action would not lie. Willes, J., said, "It has been *Remarks of Willes, J.* "argued that the plaintiff is at any rate entitled to "nominal damages, for that a conversion was com- "mitted by the sale of the certificates. That sale, it "is contended, had the effect of putting an end to the "bailment of pledge; the property of the pledgee was "thereby determined, so as to enable the assignee to "say that at the moment when the sale took place he "became entitled to the certificates by virtue of the "general property which was then revested in him. "This reasoning proceeds upon a somewhat subtle and "narrow ground, for it is admitted that the assignee "could only claim nominal damages. But we cannot "arrive at the conclusion that he is so entitled with- "out getting rid of the case of Donald *v.* Suckling, "*supra.* * * * There are three kinds of security:— "the first, a simple lien; the second, a mortgage, "passing the property out and out; the third, a se- "curity intermediate between a lien and a mortgage, "viz., a pledge, where by the contract a deposit of "goods is made a security for a debt, and the right to "the property vests in the pledgee so far as is neces- "sary to secure the debt. It is true, the pledgeor has "such a property in the article pledged as he can "convey to a third person, but he has no right to the "goods without paying off the debt, and until the "debt is paid off the pledgee has the whole present "interest. If he deals with it in a manner other than "is allowed by law for the payment of his debt, then, "in so far as by disposing of the reversionary interest "of the pledgeor he causes to the pledgeor any diffi- "culty in obtaining possession of the pledge on pay- "ment of the sum due, and thereby does him any "real damage, he commits a legal wrong against the "pledgeor. But it is a contradiction in fact, and "would be to call a thing that which it is not, to say "that the pledgee consents by his act to revest in the "pledgeor the immediate interest or right in the "pledge, which by the bargain is out of the pledgeor "and in the pledgee. Therefore, for any such wrong "an action of trover or of detinue, each of which "assumes an immediate right to possession in the "plaintiff, is not maintainable, for that right clearly "is not in the plaintiff."

Review of the principles on the pledgee's right to sub-pledge. We are now in a position to consider the principles upon the subject of the right of the pawnee to sub-pledge. And while it is obvious from the foregoing cases that the sub-pledge by the pawnee to a third party of a pledge of collateral security does not, certainly in England, *ipso facto* terminate the contract between himself and the original pawnor, so that the latter cannot bring an action of trover or detinue for the goods, without first tendering a payment of the debt which they were originally pawned to secure, yet the right of the pawnee to rehypothecate, without a special contract to that effect, has not, either here or abroad, been recognized or sanctioned by law. If on payment or tender of the debt the goods or securities be not returned, an action of trover or detinue will lie. And in those cases in which in Eng-

CHAP. II.]   EFFECT OF THE PLEDGE.   369

land it has been held, that trover or detinue will not lie against the pledgee for having parted with the possession of the goods pawned, unless a tender of the advance on them be first made, it will be observed that the court nowhere justify, as legally proper, the action of the pledgee, but merely decide that for technical legal reasons an action of this character will not lie unless at the time of bringing suit the plaintiff has an immediate right to possession; which, of course, the pawnor never has without a tender of the debt. It is, on the contrary, treated as a breach of the contract of pledge for which the original pawnor " can " recover in an action,[1] for any special damage which " he may have sustained by reason of the act of the " pawnee in repledging the goods." In most of the States of the Union, this technical rule has not been followed, and in Pennsylvania, as we have seen,[2] an action of trover has been held to lie against a pledgee, presently on his parting with possession of the securities pledged, for the actual damage sustained by the pawnor, the debt and interest due the pledgee being first deducted. The authorities in New York, and in Tennessee, also, regard rehypothecation as illegal.

In certain States there may be statutory regulations on the subject, and in that case the above can have no application. Thus, in Pennsylvania there is a penal statute on the subject of rehypothecation, and forbidding it, though no cases have as yet arisen on the construction of this statute, and it is impossible to state its effect.

[1] See opinion of Mellor, J., in Donald v. Suckling, *supra*, p. 366.
[2] In Work v. Bennett, 70 Penna. 484, *supra*.

CHAPTER III.

AVOIDANCE OF THE CONTRACT OF PLEDGE.

	PAGE		PAGE
Various ways of avoiding the contract of pledge	370	Contract of pledge avoided by pledgee doing some act inconsistent with the contract.	376
Contracts made on Sunday	371	Contract avoided by the pledgeor	376
Contracts made by one not having authority to do so	371	Markham v. Jaudon	376
Contracts avoided by failure of consideration	371	Remarks of Hunt, J.	379
Pledge for a pre-existing debt.	371	Law in Pennsylvania	383
England	372	Return of identical shares pledged	384
America	373	Cases discussed	384
Fraud	373	Mortgage of stock	387
Security transferred as pledge not according to the rules of the company issuing it	374	Peculiar loans secured by bonds	387

Various ways of avoiding the contract of pledge. THE contract of pledge may be avoided in various ways, as, for example, by the contract being made on Sunday; by the fact of the parties making it having no authority to do so; by there being no consideration to support it, or an illegal consideration; by the pledgeor retaining such a possession of it as to make it void under the Statutes of Elizabeth; by the pledgee doing some act in respect to the pledge inconsistent with his interest in it; by the sale of the pledge on the part of the pledgee, after proper demand and notice; by the pledgeor's not fulfilling the conditions of the contract of pledge, for a breach of which it was agreed the contract was to be at an end; by the pledgee paying the debt, which the pledge is given to secure; and by the pledgee returning the pledge to the pledgeor.

CHAP. III.] AVOIDANCE OF CONTRACT OF PLEDGE. 371

The rule as to contracts made on a Sunday now generally is, that, if executory, they cannot be enforced; but that, if executed, they cannot be ripped up by the parties, but remain binding, so that if the pledge be made on a Sunday and executed, the parties will usually be bound by the contract of pledge. The reader is referred on this subject to the elaborate article in the 19th American Law Register, page 137, for the effect of legal acts performed on Sunday. *Contracts of pledge made on Sunday.*

Pledges are voidable when the parties have no right to make them. With regard to the case where the parties making the pledge do so in excess of their authority to act, the reader is referred to page 322 of this work, where he may find discussed the subject of, who may legally pledge; and with respect to the case of a corporation acting in excess of its authority in effecting a pledge, he is referred to page 82, upon the subject of *ultra vires*. *Contract of pledge made by one having no authority to do so.*

The case of pledges effected by persons having no title has already been discussed in relation to rehypothecation, and the character of the title taken by the pledgee, whether innocent, or affected with notice.[1]

Pledges are also avoided when given for a bad consideration. Where the security is given to secure an illegal or void contract, the same rule will apply as we have stated before on page 287, under Avoidance of the Contract of Sale. *Contract of pledge avoided because of a bad consideration.*

The question has also very frequently arisen, as to whether a pledge of securities is voidable for a want of consideration, on the ground that it was created *Pledge of securities given to secure a pre-existing debt.*

---
[1] *Supra*, p. 358.

only to secure a pre-existing debt owed by the pawnor to the pawnee.

English cases.

In England, it is difficult to find any authorities directly on the subject.

Percival v. Frampton.

In Percival *v.* Frampton,[1] Baron Parke, though he thought there was consideration in the case, said that

Remarks of Parke, B.

the "replication would be sustained if that were not "so; for if the note were given to the plaintiffs as "a security for a previous debt, and they held it "as such, they might properly be stated to be the "holders for valuable consideration." Alderson, B., concurred.

Poirier v. Morris.

In Poirier *v.* Morris,[2] Lord Campbell, C. J., said, that the Poirier Frères were holders for value, and that the debt due from certain parties to them was

Remarks of Lord Campbell, C. J.

ample consideration to make them so. "I can see "nothing in this part of the case to vary it from the "ordinary rule where a bill is received by a creditor "as a security for an antecedent debt."

American cases.

In America, the cases are conflicting.

Rule of the Federal courts.

In the Federal courts, the question is finally settled, that a deposit of security for an antecedent debt constitutes the holder, a holder for value.[3]

The States that adopt the rule of the Federal courts.

The following States adopt the ruling of the Federal courts: Massachusetts,[4] Rhode Island,[5] Connec-

---

[1] 2 C. M. & R. 180.
[2] 2 E. & B. 89.
[3] National Bank *v.* R. R. Co., 14 Blatch. 242; *In re* Huddell & Seitzinger, 14 Amer. Law Rev. 503, overruling Mack *v.* Baker, 5 Weekly Notes (Phila.), 212; Railroad Company *v.* National Bank, 12 Otto, 14; Swift *v.* Tyson, 16 Peters, 1.

[4] Blanchard *v.* Stevens, 3 Cush. 162; Breton *v.* Pierce, 2 Allen, 14; Paine *v.* Furness, 117 Mass. 290.
[5] Bank *v.* Carrington, 5 R. I. 515; Cobb *v.* Doyle, 7 R. I. 550.

CHAP. III.] AVOIDANCE OF CONTRACT OF PLEDGE. 373

ticut,[1] probably Vermont,[2] New Jersey,[3] Illinois,[4] Missouri,[5] Indiana,[6] California,[7] Texas,[8] Georgia,[9] probably Mississippi,[10] South Carolina.[11]

The following States adopt a contrary view, and hold a holder of securities, pledged for an antecedent debt, is not a holder for value: New York,[12] Pennsylvania,[13] Maine,[14] probably New Hampshire,[15] Arkansas,[16] Ohio,[17] Wisconsin,[18] Kentucky,[19] Alabama,[20] probably North Carolina,[21] Tennessee.[22] *The States that adopt a contrary rule.*

The authorities on the foregoing principle are reviewed elaborately in the American Law Review,[23] in a note to *In re* Huddell & Seitzinger, by one of the authors of the present work.

The contract of pledge may also be avoided, *qua* third parties, by the fraud of the parties in effecting *Avoidance of the contract of pledge, by fraud.*

---

[1] Bridgeport Bank *v.* Welch, 29 Conn. 475; Roberts *v.* Hall, 37 Conn. 213.
[2] Atkinson *v.* Brooks, 26 Vt. 569; Austin *v.* Curtis, 31 Vt. 64; Bank *v.* Leavenworth, 28 Vt. 209.
[3] Allaire *v.* Hartshorne, 1 Zab. 665.
[4] Manning *v.* McClure, 36 Ill. 490.
[5] Savings Institution *v.* Holland, 38 Mo. 49.
[6] Valette *v.* Mason, 1 Sm. 89.
[7] Robinson *v.* Smith, 14 Cal. 94; Naglee *v.* Lyman, 14 Cal. 410.
[8] Grenaux *v.* Wheeler, 6 Texas, 515.
[9] Gibson *v.* Conner, 3 Ga. 47; Meadows *v.* Bird, 22 Ga. 246.
[10] Fellows *v.* Harris, 12 S. & M. 462.
[11] Bank *v.* Chambers, 11 Rich. 657.
[12] Coddington *v.* Bay, 20 Johns. 636; Stalker *v.* McDonald, 6 Hill, 93.
[13] Petrie *v.* Clark, 11 S. & R. 377; Walker *v.* Geisse, 4 Whart. 258; Royer *v.* Bank, 4 W. N. C. (Phila.) 86.
[14] Nutter *v.* Stover, 48 Me. 163.
[15] Williams *v.* Little, 11 N. H. 66; Jenners *v.* Bean, 10 N. H. 266.
[16] Bertrand *v.* Barkman, 6 Eng. 159.
[17] Roxborough *v.* Messick, 11 Ohio St. 172.
[18] Cook *v.* Helms, 5 Wisc. 111.
[19] Lee *v.* Smead, 1 Metc. 628; May *v.* Quimby, 8 Head, 96.
[20] Fenouille *v.* Hamilton, 35 Ala. 319.
[21] Reddick *v.* Jones, 6 Ired. 107.
[22] King *v.* Doolittle, 1 Head, 77; see, also, Prentice *v.* Zane, 2 Gratt. (Va.) 262.
[23] Vol. 14, page 503.

it, as where it is only created to confer upon the pledgee an apparent right, while in reality the pledgeor retains the use and entire control of the pledge, and thus hinders or defeats the rights of creditors, though the contract is never voidable between the parties. As a general rule, the question of fraudulent intent is always a question for the jury.[1]

Question of fraud usually for the jury.

Again, in transferring stocks, as we have seen, in the United States, all that is necessary to effect the transfer is to deliver the certificates, with a power of transfer, to the transferee. The by-laws, however, of many corporations point out a particular mode of transfer, and the question has arisen, how far a transfer, not effected according to the rules thus established by the corporation, is good as against attaching creditors of the transferor.

Effect of transfer, not made according to the rules of the company, on attaching creditors.

In New York and New Jersey, in cases where corporate by-laws declare that no transfer is valid unless made upon the books of the company, the courts have held, that this only means that the corporation is not itself bound to recognize any one unless standing on its books, but a transfer by delivery of a power of attorney with the certificates of stock is valid against attaching creditors, though the attachment has been served before a transfer upon the books of the company.[2]

---

[1] The cases on this subject may be found in Benjamin on Sales, under the head of "Sales," page 390.

[2] See Broadway Bank v. McElrath, 13 N. J., Eq. 24; Bank v. Bank, 17 N. J., Eq. 496; McNeil v. Bank, 46 N. Y. 325; Rogers v. Ins. Co., 8 N. J., Eq. 167; Bank v. R. R. Co., 30 Conn. 231; Lee v. Bank, 2 Cin. (Ohio) 298; N. Y. & N. H. R. R. Co. v. Schuyler, 34 N. Y. 30; State Ins. Co. v. Gennett, 2 Tenn. Ch. 100; Newberry v. Iron Co., 17 Mich. 141.

CHAP. III.] AVOIDANCE OF CONTRACT OF PLEDGE. 375

In other States, however, as in Pennsylvania, California, Massachusetts, and some others, a similar provision has been construed by the courts, to indicate the only method of giving a legal title to the stock, valid against an attaching creditor.

Thus, in Fisher *v.* Essex Bank,[1] the charter of the bank provided that they should "be transferable only at its banking hours and on its books," and it was held, that they could not be effectually transferred as against a creditor of the transferor, who had attached them without notice of a previous delivery of the certificates, together with an assignment and blank power of attorney from the vendor to the vendee, by which a transfer had been attempted, even if notice of such previous delivery had been given to the bank before the attachment.

Fisher v. Essex Bank.

So, in The Bank of Commerce's Appeal,[2] where the members of a building association were entitled to a loan on each share, a member assigned his stock in the association and delivered the certificate to a bank for a loan, with the usual power of attorney to transfer. Subsequently he borrowed all he was entitled to from the association, transferring his stock to it on its books, the bank still holding the certificate. In this instance the stock was not transferred to the bank on the books of the association, as there was no provision or by-law requiring that to be done. The association finally wound up, and the assets were distributed among the stockholders appearing on their transfer books, without any notice from the bank. Subsequently the bank presented the certificate, and the

Bank of Commerce's Appeal.

[1] 5 Gray, Mass. 378.   [2] 73 Pa. 59.

officers of the association refused to pay the distribution share, to which the stock represented by it would have been entitled, because these moneys had been already appropriated to meet the advance made by the society on this stock, which had been transferred to itself on its own books. The court held, that, as between a corporation and a corporator, the stock book was evidence of their relation, the certificate being but secondary evidence, and that therefore the officers of the association were not liable to the bank for the certificates held by it.[1]

Avoidance of the pledge by the pledgee doing an act inconsistent with the contract.

We have already treated of acts by the pledgee inconsistent with the interest he has in the thing pledged, such as rehypothecating or foreclosing without notice, or by a private instead of a public sale, and the effect such a course of proceeding has on the contract of pledge.[2]

Contract avoided by the pledgeor.

The contract of pledge is also avoided or concluded when the pledgeor does not execute his part of the contract. This happens where the security is sold because the pledgeor does not pay the debt to secure which the security in question was given; and then, upon sufficient notice and demand, the pledgee may, as we have seen, terminate the pledge by a sale of the security. In the business of stock brokers this very frequently occurs in connection with what is commonly known as "carrying stock." As was said by Judge Woodruff in Northrup v. Shook,[3] and pointed out in the beginning of this work, it would not be a

Northrup v. Shook.

---

[1] See, also, Shipman v. Ætna Ins. Co., 29 Conn. 245; Naglee v. Wharf Co., 20 Cal. 529; Brown v. Adams, 5 Biss. 181; Dutton v. Connecticut Bank, 13 Conn. 493; Williams v. Bank, 5 Blatchford, 59.
[2] See pages 342–369, *supra*.
[3] 10 Blatchford, C. C. R. 243.

CHAP. III.] AVOIDANCE OF CONTRACT OF PLEDGE. 377

part of the business of a broker, strictly as such, to purchase stock or other securities for his customer until the latter furnishes him with the money to do so. Under existing commercial usage, however, both in this country and in England, the broker frequently obtains the money by rehypothecating with third parties the stock purchased for the customer, charging the amount thus obtained to complete the purchase, as a loan by himself to his customer, and the customer appears on his books as his debtor for that amount. The stock is entered to the credit of the customer, and this is done whether the stock is actually transferred on the books of the corporation into the customer's name, or not. The customer then owns the stock; so that if the broker resells it at a higher price the customer gets the profit. But as the broker is obliged, by the rules of all the Stock Exchanges, to become personally responsible to the person in the Exchange from whom he buys or to whom he sells the stock, he requires, before executing an order of this kind for a customer, that the latter should deposit with him, either in money or other securities, a certain amount, usually a certain percentage of the market value of the stock bought on the customer's account. Should the market value of the stock change, as if, for instance, in the case of a purchase the market price should fall, the broker on a resale would primarily lose the difference in price. This loss, being, as between himself and his principal, charged to the latter, is deducted from the deposit with the broker. If, after a fall in the value of the stock, the customer still desires the broker to hold it on his account, he is usually requested by the broker to deposit an additional margin to secure the latter against possible loss by a still further fall. When the customer makes these successive deposits of money or securities, he is said to keep his margin good. And on a resale of the stock, a loss or gain in the price is debited or credited to the principal, and after this is settled the margin is then returned to him; the usual transaction in the case of loss being to deduct it from the margin and return the customer the balance.

Now, it is very obvious in the case just put, that the stock itself, purchased on the account of the customer, as well as the margin, is his property, and that they are both held by the broker as a pawnee to secure his advances, which he, the broker, has made to the customer in order to purchase the stock. If the stock itself should rise greatly in price, and its value exceed the advance made by the broker to the customer to purchase it, it would constitute itself a sufficient collateral security without any other margin. Consequently, in all transactions of this kind, the customer, or principal, is to be regarded as the owner and pledgeor of the stock purchased for his account, as well as of such additional securities as he may deposit as collateral for the advances made to him by his broker to purchase the stock in question. And it is a consequence of this contract of pledge between the principal and his broker, that the broker may demand payment of his advance. Usually, of course, the broker only demands additional margin to secure himself against possible loss, but his right is to demand the whole advance; and unless this is paid or secured to the broker's satisfaction, he may, upon a sufficient notice and demand, terminate the pledge by selling the stocks purchased, as well as any additional collateral securities hypothecated with him.

The case of Markham v. Jaudon[1] is an excellent illustration of this kind of transaction, and of the relation of the parties in it to each other. The plaintiff instructed the defendants, stock brokers, to purchase certain stocks, he depositing a margin equal to ten per cent. on the value of the stocks to be kept good by him, and the defendants to hold or carry the stocks in their own name for him, and subject to his order. The defendants, on a change in the market value of the stock, requested the deposit of a further margin, and, on the plaintiff's failure to supply it, sold the stock without notice, and he brought suit to recover for this conversion of his stock. It was contended, that there was not a relation of pledgeor and pledgee established between the parties, but that the agreement to carry stock existed by force of a mutual and dependent contract: the defendants' agreement to hold the stock being dependent on the plaintiff's agreement to supply the margin; and that when the plaintiff failed to do so, the defendants' contract was at an end, and they were at liberty to sell the stock without notice. But the court held, that the relation of pledgeor and pledgee did exist, and refused to admit evidence, that it was a custom of the trade so to sell

Markham v. Jaudon.

[1] 41 N. Y. 235.

without notice, as such a custom was unreasonable, and thus contrary to law.

Remarks of Hunt, C. J.

Hunt, C. J., in an elaborate opinion, analyzing the relation of the parties to each other in such a contract, said, "An analysis of the contract in question, "and a separation of the powers and obligations of "the parties thereto, will enable us the better to de-"termine its character. The customer employs the "broker to buy certain railroad stocks for his account, "and to pay for them, and to hold them subject to his "order as to the time of sale. The customer advances "ten per cent. of their market value, and agrees to "keep good such proportionate advance, according to "the fluctuations of the market. * * * I state the "following, as the result of the agreement:

"The broker undertakes and agrees—

"1. At once to buy for the customer the stocks "indicated.

"2. To advance all the money required for the "purchase beyond the ten per cent. furnished by the "customer.

"3. To carry or hold such stocks for the benefit "of the customer so long as the margin of ten per "cent. is kept good, or until notice is given by either "party that the transaction must be closed. An ap-"preciation in the value of the stocks is the gain of "the customer, and not that of the broker.

"4. At all times to have in his name or under his "control, ready for delivery, the shares purchased, "or an equal amount of other shares of the same "stock.

"5. To deliver such shares to the customer when

CHAP. III.] AVOIDANCE OF CONTRACT OF PLEDGE. 381

"required by him, upon the receipt of the advances
"and commissions accruing to the broker; or,

"6. To sell such shares upon the order of the cus-
"tomer, upon payment of the like sums to him, and
"account to the customer for the proceeds of such
"sale.

"Under this contract the customer undertakes—

"1. To pay a margin of ten per cent. on the cur-
"rent market value of the shares.

"2. To keep good such margin, according to the
"fluctuations of the market.

"3. To take the shares so purchased on his order,
"whenever required by the broker, and to pay the
"difference between the percentage advanced by him
"and the amount paid therefor by the broker.

"The position of the broker is twofold. Upon the
"order of the customer he purchases the shares of
"stocks desired by him. This is a clear case of
"agency. To complete the purchase, he advances
"from his own funds, for the benefit of the customer,
"ninety per cent. of the purchase money. Quite as
"clearly, he does not, in this, act as an agent, but as-
"sumes a new position. He also holds, or carries, the
"stock for the benefit of the purchaser, until a sale is
"made by the order of the purchaser, or upon his own
"action. In thus holding or carrying, he stands, also,
"upon a different ground from that of a broker or
"agent, whose office is simply to buy and sell. * * *
"In so doing, he enters upon a new duty, obtains
"other rights, and is subject to additional responsi-
"bilities. * * * The substance of the first branch of
"the transaction is this: The plaintiff calls upon the

"defendants, who are brokers, to purchase for him certain shares of railroad stock, and furnishes them with $1000 for that purpose, agreeing to pay interest on advances they shall make in the purchase and commissions. The defendants make the purchase, having themselves advanced ninety per cent. of the purchase money. They bring to the plaintiff the certificates of the stock thus purchased by him, and for him, and deliver them to him as the owner thereof. He thereupon hands them back to the defendants, to hold as security for their advance on the purchase, with interest and commissions. If these precise forms had been observed, no one would deny that the redelivery of the certificates would have constituted a strict formal pledge. In my opinion, the transaction, as it took place, amounted to the same thing. To have delivered the certificates to the plaintiff, and that the plaintiff should then have returned them to the defendants, to be held by them as security for the advance in their purchase, would leave the parties in precisely the same situation as if the defendants had returned them for that purpose; the form of a delivery to the plaintiff being waived by agreement of the parties. * * * In my judgment, the contract between the parties to this action was, in spirit and in effect, if not technically and in form, a contract of pledge."

Work v. Bennett.

Upon a similar state of facts, the Pennsylvania courts, in Work v. Bennett,[1] held the transaction to be a pledge, which had, however, been broken by the pledgee's parting with the possession; though in an

[1] 70 Pa. 484.

action of trover, against him, for the stock pledged, he was allowed to deduct the amount of his advances and interest; but in later cases, they have decided similar transactions, as a whole, to be gambling ones, on grounds which have already been discussed at length, and the reader is referred for them to North v. Phillips,[1] Fareira v. Gabell,[2] Dickson's Executor v. Thomas,[3] and Ruchizky v. De Haven,[4] and the remarks upon them.[5] *Later cases in Pennsylvania opposed to the earlier decisions of that State.*

When the pledgeor tenders the amount of the debt in full with interest, this ends the pledge, *ipso facto*, and he can bring an action against the pledgeor for its return in the modes already pointed out.[6] *Tender of payment, with interest, by pledgeor ends the contract.*

And so, finally, when the pledgee returns the pledge to the pledgeor, this usually terminates or avoids the contract of pledge, as, for example, in the cases of Day v. Swift,[7] Kimball v. Hildreth,[8] or Bodenhammer v. Newsom;[9] though sometimes the pledgeor is made the custodian of the property as a servant only of the pledgee,[10] or the pledge is given back for a special purpose to the pledgee; as where a bond was given back, at the pledgeor's request, to get it exchanged for some stock.[11] *Day v. Swift, Kimball v. Hildreth, Bodenhammer v. Newsom.*

At the avoidance or termination of the hypothecation, the security pledged, as above stated, must, if not sold, be returned to the pledgeor. The question then arises as to whether the pledgee is obliged to return

---

[1] 8 Norris (Pa.), 250.
[2] 8 Norris, 89.
[3] 10 Weekly Notes of Cases (Phila.), 112.
[4] 10 *ibid.*, 109.
[5] See pp. 302–318.
[6] See *supra*, page 376.
[7] 48 Maine, 368.
[8] 8 Allen, 167.
[9] 5 Jones (N. C.), 107.
[10] Way v. Davidson, 12 Gray, 465; Reeves v. Capper, 5 Bing., N. C. 54.
[11] Hayes v. Riddle, 1 Sanford (N. Y.), 248; see, also, Thayer v. Dwight, 104 Mass. 254; Cooper v. Ray, 47 Ill. 53.

the identical security pledged. As most securities are not ear-marked or otherwise distinguished from others of like kind, it would seem that the return of any shares of the same kind as those pledged, to the pledgeor, is sufficient.

Langton v. Waite. — In Langton *v.* Waite,[1] A. & B., stock brokers, borrowed, on behalf of the plaintiff, a sum of money for a term of three months, from the defendants, also stock brokers, upon the security of certain shares of stock, which were transferred to the name of one of the defendants' firm. Before the end of the term, the plaintiff, having contracted to sell the stock, applied to the defendants for a retransfer of it, tendering the amount of the debt in full, with interest. The defendants, having sold the stock, refused to return it, or similar shares, alleging that the loan was made for the full term, and the plaintiff, in consequence of the refusal of the defendants, was obliged to go into the market and buy other shares, at a loss to himself, to complete his contract of sale. At the expiration of the term, the defendants, having bought other similar shares at a lower figure, tendered the amount of the security to the plaintiff. A rule of the Stock Exchange, to the effect that, "In all cases of loans on the deposit of security, "the lender is bound to return the identical securities "deposited, unless it be otherwise stipulated at the time "of making the loan. But this liability does not apply "to a member who has taken in stock or shares, upon "continuation at the market price," was offered in evidence in an action by the plaintiff to recover the amount of profit realized by the defendants from the

[1] L. R., 6 Eq. C. 165.

CHAP. III.] AVOIDANCE OF CONTRACT OF PLEDGE. 385

use they had made of his stock; and the court held, that the rule was conclusive on the subject; that the pledgee was bound to return the identical shares pledged, and that, the sale of the pledge being a wrongful conversion, the plaintiff was entitled to recover. The court said further, that an alleged custom for a pledgee to sell pledged stock was in direct opposition to the express rule, and also, that the pledgee had no right at law to sell the stock, citing *Ex parte* Dennison.[1] *Ex parte Dennison.*

In Gilpin *v.* Howell,[2] Bell, J., who delivered the opinion of the court, was of the opinion that a pledgee of stock, transferred to his name, was not obliged to return the identical shares, but had a right to do what he pleased with them, provided he always kept an amount of the same stock on hand equivalent to the pledge, and was always ready, on demand and payment in full of the loan, to retransfer it to the pledgeor. *Gilpin v. Howell.*

In Neiler *v.* Kelly,[3] in an action of trover by the pledgeor of stock to recover for a wrongful conversion by the pledgee in selling the same without notice to the pledgeor, the debt being due and unpaid, Sharswood, J., said, "The defendants below were at no "time under any obligation to deliver these stocks "and bonds *specifically* to the plaintiff. He never "had put himself in a position to demand them before "the bringing the suit, or up to the time of trial, by "tendering or offering to pay the amount of his in- "debtedness to the defendants. Had the action been "detinue or replevin, he must have failed entirely. "* * * Where a plaintiff seeks to fasten a responsi- *Neiler v. Kelly. Remarks of Sharswood, J.*

[1] 3 Vesey, 552.   [2] 5 Pa. 41.
[3] 69 Pa. 409.

25

"bility for more than the usual measure of damages, he must also fasten upon the defendants the duty or obligation to deliver, *specifically*, the stock or securities at some particular time, and their refusal to fulfil that duty, *non constat*, that upon a demand and tender the defendants would not have been able to deliver to the plaintiff similar stocks and securities, as, according to Gilpin *v.* Howell,[1] they might well do."

Gilpin v. Howell approved.

Boylan v. Huguet.

In Boylan *v.* Huguet,[2] it was held, that, in the ordinary transactions between principals and brokers, the former were not entitled to receive the identical shares purchased on their account by the brokers, and that the brokers were acting within the terms of their contracts with their principals so long as they were ready to deliver, on demand and payment, certificates representing the requisite number of shares. Whitman, J., said, "So long as he (the broker) held a certificate or certificates representing the requisite number of shares and was prepared to deliver them on payment and demand, so long was he within the terms of his contract; and though he might have used and re-used the identical certificates received on filling Boylan's (the principal's) orders, mixed them with others, destroyed them even, there was no conversion until he, or, as in this case, his voluntary assignees, refused to deliver upon demand."

Remarks of Whitman, J.

Langton v. Waite not necessarily inharmonious with the

The case of Langton *v.* Waite, it will be observed, really turned on the express rule of the Stock Exchange, but it must, according to the principles of the

[1] *Supra,* p. 385.   [2] 8 Nevada, 345.

foregoing cases, have been decided the same way, had there been no such rule, as the pledgees evidently did not keep on hand a sufficient number of shares to satisfy the amount of security deposited on demand and payment of the loan. So that, notwithstanding the *dictum* of Malins, V. C., this case cannot be taken to militate against the other foregoing cases.

In England, and in those States of America, where mortgages may be made of personal property, mortgages may also be made of shares of stock and bonds, by making an absolute transfer to the mortgagee.[1] In this case it may possibly be that the mortgagee would be obliged to return the identical shares mortgaged. But we confess we do not see any imperative reason for that, any more than in the case of a pledge of stock, nor why the mortgagee should be held liable for not returning the identical shares of stock, provided he return stock, equally good, of the same character as that mortgaged, and always keep enough of such stock on hand to satisfy the amount mortgaged.[2]

Sometimes loans are secured by a bond, conditioned to replace the amount of stock at the date agreed upon, and for the payment of interest, and here the creditor would only be entitled to the same amount of stock as that borrowed, with interest, etc., and not necessarily the market value on the day the loan expires.[3]

---

[1] Pbené v. Gillan, 5 Hare, Rep. 1.
[2] See Gilpin v. Howell, 5 Pa. 41; Neiler v. Kelly, 69 Pa. 409; Boylan v. Huguet, 8 Nevada, 345.
[3] See Blyth v. Carpenter, L. R., 2 Eq. 501.

PART IV.

REMEDIES OF THE PARTIES FOR A BREACH OF THE CONTRACT OF SALE.

INTRODUCTION.

THE general law as to remedies for a breach of the contract of sale, in relation to the securities sold at the Stock Exchange, is not different from that as to any other kinds of chattels or choses in action.[1] There are, however, a few principles of law that relate particularly to daily transactions in these securities, and the results arising from them, and with a review of the cases relating to these we shall close this treatise.

<small>Division of Part IV.</small> We shall consider first the remedies of the parties against each other for a breach of the contract of sale or pledge, as well as the remedies of creditors against the security itself; and also the remedies of the parties against a corporation for refusing to transfer stocks on its transfer books. And, secondly, we shall treat of the proper measure of damage in these cases.

---

[1] The subject of remedies for breach of contracts of sale is discussed in Benjamin on Sales, pp. 616-755.

CHAPTER I.

REMEDIES OF THE PARTIES AGAINST EACH OTHER, OF CREDITORS AGAINST THE THING ITSELF, AND OF THE PARTIES AGAINST THE CORPORATION FOR REFUSING TO TRANSFER STOCK ON ITS TRANSFER BOOKS.

	PAGE
SECTION I.—REMEDIES OF THE PARTIES AGAINST EACH OTHER.	
Relief in equity	389
Relief at law	390
The actions	391
SECTION II.—REMEDIES OF CREDITORS AGAINST THE THING ITSELF.	
Cases discussed	391
SECTION III.—REMEDIES OF THE PARTIES AGAINST THE CORPORATION FOR REFUSING TO TRANSFER STOCK ON ITS TRANSFER BOOKS.	
Transferor and transferee	393
Restriction by corporation on transfer	893
Effect of certificate issued by corporation, ordinarily	394
Effect of certificate issued by agent, fraudulently, for his own benefit	394
Cases discussed	395
Certificate only secondary evidence in Pennsylvania	401
Bank of Commerce's Appeal	401
Effect of certificate issued by	

	PAGE
agent acting fraudulently for benefit of company	402
Cases discussed	403
Negligence	403
Questions arising on forged powers of attorney	404
Division of subject	405
1. Where the company acts on a forged transfer, and issues a certificate which a *bona fide* purchaser subsequently buys	405
2. Where the transferee purchases stock, and takes a forged power to transfer to the company, and gets certificates issued to him by reason of the forged power	407
3. Where the transferee bargains for stock, and refuses to take the certificates till registered in his name, and the company issues certificates on the faith of a forged power of attorney presented by the seller	410
Principles deducible from the cases cited under the foregoing heads	410

SECTION I.—REMEDIES OF THE PARTIES AGAINST EACH OTHER.

Formerly, in the case of both executed and executory contracts as to chattels, the only remedy through the intervention of the courts for a breach of the con- *Relief in equity.*

389

tract, was an action at law, but, as we have seen,[1] the courts will now frequently, in the case of executed contracts, grant relief by compelling a specific performance, where there is no adequate remedy at law.

In regard to executory contracts, however, relating to this species of property, that is, where only so many shares of a given stock are contracted to be sold, but no specific shares are set apart or ascertained as the very property sold, then, as we have pointed out on a former page, the courts have usually declined to compel an actual fulfilment of the contract, unless at the date of the contract, or, at all events, of the filing of the bill, shares of the same description can be shown to be in the actual possession of the vendor, which, from the evidence or the circumstances, the court may fairly infer to have been the actual property intended by the parties to be dealt with. Excepting in such cases, the parties to a contract purely executory are usually left to their remedy at law. In London, under the peculiar system of that Stock Exchange, where a name is passed by the first taker of the shares as that of the ultimate purchaser, the courts, as we have seen, have held, that a contract arises between the seller and the person whose name is passed. And this contract is one for a breach of which an action at law will lie, though two judges, Channell and Cleasby, expressed the view that the only remedy, if any, lay in equity;[2] but the right to the equitable remedy seems free from doubt.[3]

Relief at law. The question then remains as to what action lies

---

[1] *Supra*, p. 284.
[2] Davis v. Haycock, L. R., Ex. 4, 878.
[3] Musgrove & Hart's case, L. R., Eq. 5, 193; see Wilson v. Keating, 7 W. R. 484.

CHAP. I.]   REMEDIES OF THE PARTIES.   391

for a breach of a contract of sale or pledge of this species of property, by the buyer against the seller, or *vice versa;* and what other remedies a creditor of the owner or holder of securities possesses.

For bonds and debentures, an action of detinue, or of trover, will of course lie;[1] but, shares, and probably scrip, being a kind of ideal and incorporeal property, trover or detinue will not lie,[2] though they would, probably, in all cases lie for the certificates. In some States of the Union, however, the courts have held, that trover does lie for a share of stock.[3]

Actions.

It has always, also, been held, that stock is not *money;* so that a declaration so describing it is demurrable.[4] An action of covenant lies, as in other cases, for a breach of contract under seal, relating to these securities, and assumpsit, when it is by parol.

SECTION II.—REMEDIES OF CREDITORS AGAINST THE THING ITSELF.

Shares of stock were thought to be of such an intangible nature that it was formerly considered there could be no change of possession, and it could not be known whether they could be attached or not, and, therefore, there could be no sale of them on execution.[5]

Thus, in Denton *v.* Livingston,[6] where the sheriff had levied upon and sold one share of bank, and three

Denton *v.* Livingston.

---

[1] Neiler *v.* Kelly, 69 Pa. 403; Acraman *v.* Cooper, 10 M. & W. 585.
[2] Neiler *v.* Kelly, 69 Pa. 408.
[3] See Payne *v.* Elliott, 9 Reporter, 678; Kuhn *v.* McAllister, 1 Utah, 273; Boylan *v.* Huguet, 8 Nevada, 345.
[4] See *supra*, p. 140.
[5] See Denny *v.* Hamilton, 16 Mass. 402; Howe *v.* Starkweather, 17 Mass. 240.
[6] 9 Johns. 96.

shares of library stock, Kent, C. J., said, "The bank "and library shares were levied on by mistake; "for these were mere choses in action, and not the "subject of a levy and sale by a *fieri facias*, any "more than bonds and notes."

Remarks of Kent, C. J.

And so in Howe *v.* Starkweather,[1] Parker, C. J., said, "Shares in a turnpike or other incorporated "company have more resemblance to choses in action "than to real estate, being merely evidence of prop-"erty, the sale of them upon execution not being jus-"tifiable at the common law." And also in Ammant *v.* New Alexandria Turnpike Company,[2] the court held, that a turnpike road could not be levied upon, under a judgment against the company, because the company had no tangible interest, and nothing but a right to receive tolls; though in Connecticut it has been held, that shares in such a company are real property.[3]

Howe v. Starkweather.
Remarks of Parker, C. J.

Ammant v. New Alexandria Turnpike Co.

This has, however, been altered by statute in England,[4] and in many of the United States,[5] and now there are statutory processes established everywhere for issuing execution on shares of stock.

With regard to bonds and debentures being choses in action, the same rule would apply to them as to shares of stock or promissory notes. But in respect to coupon bonds, or bonds payable to bearer, they would, as their title passes by delivery, perhaps be liable to execution at the common law.

---

[1] 17 Mass. 243.
[2] 13 S. & R. 210.
[3] 2 Conn. 567.
[4] 192 Vict. c. 110, s. 14, 15, & s.
12; also see Nicholls *v.* Rosewarne, 6 C. B. (N. S.) 480.
[5] See Angell & Ames on Corporations, § 589.

SECTION III.—REMEDIES OF THE PARTIES AGAINST A CORPORATION FOR NOT TRANSFERRING STOCK ON ITS TRANSFER BOOKS.

An action will lie either by the transferee or transferor against a corporation for not allowing the registration of a transfer on the books of the company, or for a refusal to pay dividends.[1] Where the company improperly refuses to register, the remedy is by an action on the case, or by assumpsit;[2] but an action for money had and received will not, as we have seen, lie against the corporation for merely refusing to issue certificates.[3]

Actions by transferor or transferee against corporation.

In Rex v. Bank,[4] the court refused a mandamus to compel a transfer, because there was a remedy by action on the case at law.

Rex v. Bank.

If the purchaser is ready and willing to be registered, it is then *prima facie* the duty of the company to place his name upon the register. Sometimes, it is true, the company has a right to impose certain restrictions with regard to registration, and it may be said that these are to be interpreted by the terms of the charter or deed of settlement of the company allowing it to do so. This has been, as far as practicable, discussed, *supra*, on page 176.[5]

Restrictions corporation may impose on transfer.

Where a stock certificate has been duly issued by

---

[1] Stracy v. Bank, 6 Bing. 754; Foster v. Bank, 8 Q. B. 689; Coles v. Bank, 10 Ad. & El. 487; Davis v. Bank, 2 Bing. 393.

[2] Kortright v. Bank, 20 Wend. 91.

[3] Arnold v. Bank, 27 Barb. 424.

[4] 2 Douglass, 523.

[5] See, also, *In re* Hall, 17 Q. B. 645; Hubbersty v. Ry. Co., 8 B. & S. 425; Railway v. Dalbiac, 6 Ry. Cases, 753; Rudolph v. Ins. Co., 8 L. T., N. S. 551; Ry. Co. v. Mount, 4 M. & G. 651; N. A. Col. Ass. Co. v. Bentley, 19 L. T., Q. B. 427.

Effect of certificate issued by corporation, ordinarily.

a corporation having power to do so, it has been held in the United States to be a continuing affirmation of the ownership of the specified amount of stock, by the person therein designated, until it is in some legal manner withdrawn; and in England to be so as regards third parties, so that a purchaser buying, in good faith, from a vendor who holds a certificate in his own name, under the seal of the company, for its stock, has a right to rely thereon, and to claim the benefit of an estoppel in his favor against the corporation, should the latter attempt subsequently to deny the vendor's title; and of course a person making advances upon the faith of the ownership by the borrower of such a certificate, ranks, up to the amount of his loan, as a purchaser.

Holbrook v. N. J. Zinc Co.

Thus, where, in Holbrook *v.* New Jersey Zinc Co.,[1] the plaintiff brought an action against the company for a refusal to deliver certificates of stock, the court held, that he was not bound to show affirmatively the title of his immediate transferor, and that the corporation could not defeat his title as a *bona fide* purchaser without actual notice, by affirmative proof, of the pendency of an action in a competent court of that State, to determine the title of the original holder to the stock, since its own positive statements in the certificate could not be overcome by such a constructive theoretical notice.

Effect of certificate issued by agent, acting fraudulently for his own benefit.

Where, however, the officers of a company act fraudulently, not as agents, but as individuals; that is to say, where the fraud is committed by them upon the company, the company not pocketing the benefits of the fraud,—as where the transfer agent forges a cer-

[1] 57 N. Y. 616.

tificate in the name of himself or of an accomplice, and fraudulently affixes the seal of the company to it,—a more difficult question is presented. As the fraudulent transferee himself could have no right of action against the company, it has been argued that his vendee, even though buying *bona fide*, cannot assert any greater rights against it, so that a certificate so created could not bind it. Here, the act of affixing the seal is not, properly speaking, that of the company, and the question is removed one step further back, to the general authority conferred upon its officers to affix the seal. In the Bank of Ireland *v.* The Evans Charities,[1] the trustees of a charity gave the custody of their corporate seal to the secretary, who affixed it fraudulently to an order, transferring stock, in a bank belonging to the charity. The signatures to the order were genuine, the secretary having obtained them fraudulently. The bank having transferred the stock according to the order, the trustees sued the bank. It was held, that the trustees were guilty of no negligence in giving the custody of the seal into the keeping of the secretary.

Bank of Ireland v. Evans Charities.

"We all concur in the opinion," said Baron Parke, in delivering the opinion of the law judges, which was requested by the House of Lords, "that the evidence " given, which was only of a supposed negligent cus- " tody of their corporate seal by the trustees, in leaving " it in the hands of Mr. Grace, whereby he was en- " abled to commit the forgery, is not sufficient evidence " of that species of negligence which alone would war- " rant a jury in finding that the plaintiffs were dis- " entitled to insist upon the transfer being void. * * *

Remarks of Parke, B.

[1] 5 H. L. C. 389.

"If there was negligence in the custody of the seal, it was very remotely connected with the act of transfer. The transfer was not a necessary or ordinary or likely result of that negligence. It never would have been, but for the occurrence of an extraordinary event, that persons should be found either so dishonest or so careless as to testify on the face of the instrument that they had seen the seal duly affixed. It is quite impossible that the bankers could have maintained an action for the negligence of the trustees, and recovered the damages they had sustained by reason of their having made the transfer."

This case, which is useful, however, only by way of analogy, was decided on the ground of negligence; and it more nearly resembles the case of a transfer by a corporation of stock really owned by a stockholder on a forged power of attorney from him. It only goes to show that where a fraud is committed on a corporation by the officer having the custody of its seal, and *prima facie* authority to use it in proper cases, it does not thereby bind the corporation when he fraudulently affixes it to an instrument for his individual benefit.

Mechanics' Bank v. N. Y. & N. H. R. R. Co.

In The Mechanics' Bank *v.* The New York & New Haven R. R. Co.,[1] however, Robert Schuyler, the transfer agent of the defendants, fraudulently issued to one Kyle a certificate for eighty-five shares of stock, when in fact the latter owned none; and the bank advanced to Kyle, *bona fide*, $12,000 on the certificate as collateral. Kyle had paid nothing for the certificate, and was treated as a party to the fraud.

[1] 3 Kernan, 599.

In an action by the bank against the railway company, it was held by the court, that the certificate was void as against the corporation, because it had been fraudulently issued, and because, moreover, all the stock authorized by the company's charter had been already issued, and that the transferees by purchasing Kyle's certificate, with a power of attorney executed in blank by Kyle, took thereby no better title than Kyle himself. The by-laws of the railroad company provided[1] that transfers might be made by the stockholders by executing an instrument in writing on the transfer books, and only in case of a surrender of the outstanding certificate for the same stock prior to the transfers being made. Comstock, J., who delivered the opinion of the court, said, "By the charter of this corporation the shares of its capital stock were made transferable in such manner and in such places as the by-laws should direct; and the by-laws declared that all transfers should be made in the transfer books kept at the proper office, and where a certificate of stock had been issued that the same should be surrendered prior to the transfers being made. The certificate now in question, as all others, declared on its face the same conditions. This certificate has in fact never been surrendered, and no such transfer has ever been made. The plaintiffs, on making their loan to Kyle, took from him an assignment and power of attorney in blank, but paid no regard to the fundamental conditions on which alone a legal title to the stock could be transferred. Of these conditions of course they had notice. * * * If extreme

Remarks of Comstock, J.

[1] See Report, p. 605.

"caution is exercised, the purchaser will inquire of the "maker of the obligation, and procure his admission "of its validity and his assent to the transfer; and, "having done so, an estoppel will arise in his favor, not "because he has invested his money in the purchase, "but because he purchased after procuring such ad- "mission or consent, and upon the face thereof."

This case, which was one of the earliest cases upon this subject, was followed by the New York & New Haven R. R. Co. v. Schuyler.[1] In this case, which arose out of the same frauds as in the last, the facts appeared somewhat differently. It was shown in this subsequent litigation that in addition to the powers which were stated in the former case to have been delegated to the transfer agent, Schuyler, he really had authority to issue certificates in precisely the same form to the original subscribers, and did so; that he had further authority to dispose of the stock of the company not taken by original subscribers, and of which there was a large amount, and had issued certificates in the same form to the purchasers; that he was the general financial agent of the company, and had raised money on its behalf by the issue of fictitious stock; and, further, that the transfers had been entered on the transfer book of the company of stock which never existed, and for which the fraudulent certificates were issued, and that the transfer books themselves would, if examined, have shown the over-issue of the stock. The same court, under these circumstances, held the railroad company liable to purchasers of this fraudulently issued stock, on the ground that Schuyler

[1] 7 Tiffany's Reports (34 N. Y.), 61.

CHAP. I.] REMEDIES OF THE PARTIES. 399

had power to sell the original stock of the company, and that transfers of the stock had been made in the transfer book to some person, generally to Schuyler himself, before the fictitious certificates had been issued. "We may," said Mr. Justice Davis, "with con- *Remarks of Davis, J.* "fidence declare the true doctrine on this branch of "the law of agency to be, that, where the principal has "clothed the agent with power to do an act upon the "existence of some extrinsic fact, necessarily and pecu- "liarly within the knowledge of the agent, and of the "existence of which the act of executing the power is "itself a representation, a third person dealing with "such agent in entire good faith, pursuant to the ap- "parent power, may rely upon the representation, and "the principal is estopped from asserting the truth to "his prejudice." But the court, in delivering their opinion, stated[1] that the inquiries in this case were not involved in the case of the Mechanics' Bank *v.* the New York & New Haven R. R. Co.

In Pennsylvania, the earliest case on this subject is *Bank of Kentucky v. Schuylkill Bank.* the Bank of Kentucky *v.* the Schuylkill Bank,[2] where the controversy was between the principal and his agent. The defendants, who were the agents of the Bank of Kentucky for the purpose of transferring its stock in Philadelphia, over-issued the stock to *bona fide* purchasers for value. The Bank of Kentucky sued their agent, and recovered the amount of loss sustained. It appears, however, from the report of the case, that the moneys, or part of them, thus fraudulently raised, had been used by the defendants in their corporate capacity; and, as they must have

[1] On page 58 of the Report.   [2] 1 Parsons, Reports, 180.

been held liable in any case, the remarks made by the court as to the rights of *bona fide* purchasers must be considered rather as *dicta*.

Willis v. Darby R. R. Co.

But in the recent case of Willis v. The Darby Railroad Company,[1] Fry, the president of the defendant corporation and its transfer agent, fraudulently issued fictitious certificates of stock in his own name, and borrowed money on them from various banks and individuals, executing the usual blank power of attorney to transfer in all cases. In some instances, the borrower sent the certificates, with the power of attorney thus executed by Fry, the transfer agent, back to the company, and obtained for it a new certificate in their own name; while, in others, the original certificate only, in Fry's name, was preserved. When the frauds were found out, suits were brought against the company by those who had advanced on the certificates, and it was held, by the Court of Common Pleas, that the company was liable to all the plaintiffs alike.

Remarks of Hare, J.

"It is well settled," said Judge Hare, "that one, who, as a purchaser or lender, gives value "on the face of a certificate of stock, authenticated by "a receiver of the corporation, and the signatures of "the proper officers, acquires an equitable title, and "may require the corporation to transfer the stock to "him or respond in damages for the default. It is not "a sufficient answer to such a demand that the certifi- "cate was fraudulently issued, because corporations are "not less than actual persons answerable for the con- "duct of their agents in the business entrusted to their "care, nor is it necessarily concluded that the party

[1] 6 Weekly Notes, Phila., 461.

"from whom he bought was cognizant of or par-
"ticipated in the fraud. If a certificate of stock is
"not a negotiable instrument, it is a written declara-
"tion that the holder has a definite share in the capital
"or profits of the concern, which, though delivered to
"him, is intended for circulation, and virtually ad-
"dressed to all the world, and third persons who are
"misled by such an instrument may justly require
"that the loss shall fall on the corporation, and not on
"them." And Railroad Company *v.* Schuyler, and
Bank of Kentucky *v.* the Schuylkill Bank, were cited.
This case was never appealed; and no decision by
the Supreme Court of Pennsylvania, on the subject,
exists.

<small>R. R. Co. *v.* Schuyler, Bank of Ky. *v.* Schuylkill Bank, cited.</small>

But in the Bank of Commerce's Appeal,[1] that court
held, that as between the corporator and the corporation the record of the corporation or its stock book was
the evidence of their relation. "The certificate," said
the court, "is but secondary evidence, and is never de-
"manded except when the stockholder deals with the
"corporation in a contract relation. * * * The assign-
"ment of the certificate is only an equitable transfer of
"the stock, and to be made available must be produced
"to the corporation and a transfer demanded. * * *
"When the corporation itself is not dealing with its
"stockholders on the security of its stock, and is merely
"performing a corporate duty, its own record is the
"only authority it need consult," etc. In this case,
which has already been referred to, a stockholder in
a building association transferred to the Bank of Commerce his certificate, with the usual power of attorney,

<small>Bank of Commerce's Appeal.

Certificate of stock only secondary evidence of ownership.</small>

[1] 73 Pa. 64.

executed in blank, as collateral security for an advance. He subsequently borrowed from the association itself on the same stock, without being required to produce the certificate. The association was wound up by trustees, who, finding the stockholder's name still on their books, paid him over the balance due on the shares after deducting the loan due the association. Subsequently the Bank of Commerce presented the certificates with the power of attorney, and demanded payment. The court declined to hold the association liable, on the grounds just mentioned.

Effect of certificate when issued by agent, acting fraudulently for benefit of company.

There can, of course, be no doubt that where the fraud is committed by the officer, not for his individual benefit, but for the corporation, the latter pocketing the proceeds, it will be liable at all events to the extent of the money that it has received through the fraud. But where the fraud is committed by the agent for his own benefit, he, and not the company, obtaining the fruits of it, the later cases seem still to show that the company is estopped by its seal, although affixed without authority, from disputing the title of any *bona fide* holder, on the ground that it is within the apparent authority of the transfer agent to affix the corporate seal to the stock certificate. This doctrine is a necessary corollary of that of the negotiability of stock, accompanied by the power of attorney executed in blank; a doctrine which is undoubtedly in accord with existing commercial usage both in this country and in England, and which has of late years influenced, more and more, judicial decisions. The question is further complicated in that the powers of the transfer agent depend, in almost every case, upon the charter of the company; so that one case is not necessarily a precedent for another.

Apart from the doctrine of the *quasi* negotiability of the certificate accompanied by a power of attorney, which has not, as yet, been actually decided, the real question in these cases is, whether the case is brought within the doctrine of Pickard v. Sears,[1] and Freeman v. Cooke,[2] that if a person makes a representation with the intention that it shall be acted upon by another, and he does so, that person is estopped from denying the truth of what he has represented to be the fact. And as the act which here constitutes the alleged representation, is not the corporate act of the company, but, in reality, a fraud upon it, the question reverts to the corporate powers of the officers to make such a representation in its behalf, so as to bind it.

Pickard v. Sears, Freeman v. Cooke.

In Willis v. The Darby Railroad Company,[3] the charter declared that the certificates should be transferable at the pleasure of the holder, in the presence of the president or treasurer, on the books of the company, but conferred no authority upon the transfer agent to issue certificates, which he did only by virtue of the custom to issue a fresh certificate on the surrender of the old one.

Willis v. Darby R. R. Co.

A strict construction of such a corporate power would lead to the result announced in The Mechanics' Bank against the Railroad,[4] namely, that the purchaser took no better title than his transferor.

The ground of negligence, on which many of these cases have been argued, depends upon whether the

Negligence.

[1] 6 Adol. & Ellis, 469.
[2] 2 Exch. 654.
[3] *Supra*, p. 400.
[4] *Supra*, p. 396.

transfer books, which are made by most charters the direct and only evidence of title to their stock, disclose transfers or attempted transfers of the fictitious stock for which the forged certificates were issued. If they do, a purchaser of such a certificate would, if he examined the transfer book, see an apparently valid title to the shares bought by him; and, as the directors are bound to examine the books, they would be negligent in not discovering fraudulent entries upon them. But if no such entries appear in the transfer books, no diligence on the part of the directors could ascertain the fact that their transfer agent was tearing blank certificates out of one of the certificate books, and affixing the corporate seal to them, and issuing them, as the book out of which the blanks were taken could be concealed, or new blank certificates printed. Nor are directors guilty of negligence in leaving the custody of their seal to a transfer agent, for they must, in the very nature of the case, leave it to some one.[1] And if they be not negligent in selecting him, no neglect can be imputed to them because they so leave the seal with him.

Questions arising on forged powers of attorney. We have hitherto discussed the case where the company or its officers are at fault. But it not unfrequently happens that corporations make transfers on their books of stock, standing in the name of some stockholder, upon the presentation to them of a forged power of attorney purporting to be from him; and important questions arise as to their liability to the transferee in such cases, which for convenience may be considered under the following categories:

[1] See Bank v. The Evans Charities, 5 House of Lords Cases, 389, above referred to.

CHAP. I.] REMEDIES OF THE PARTIES. 405

1. Where the company acts on a forged transfer, and *Division of subject.* issues a certificate which a *bona fide* purchaser subsequently buys.

2. Where the transferee purchases stock, and takes a forged power to transfer to the company, and gets certificates issued to him by reason of the forged power.

3. Where the transferee bargains for stock, and refuses to take the certificates till registered in his name, and the company issues certificates on the faith of a forged power of transfer presented by the seller.

1. In the first case, it has been held, that the company is liable to the transferor; for he acts, not on the faith of the forged transfer, but on the faith of the certificate issued by the company; and the negligence is on its part in permitting the certificate, and consequently the company will be estopped from afterwards denying his title.

Thus, In the matter of the Bahia and San Francisco, etc. Railway Company,[1] Miss Trittin, being the registered owner of five shares in a registered joint stock company, left the certificates in the hands of her broker. A transfer of the shares to S. & G., purporting to be executed by her, together with the certificates, was left with the secretary for registration. The secretary, in the usual course, wrote to her, notifying her that the transfer had been so left, and, receiving no answer, after ten days, registered the transfer and removed her name, placing that of S. & G. on the register, and giving them fresh certificates certifying that they were the registered owners. A. *In the matter of the Bahia and San Francisco, etc. Ry. Co.*

[1] L. R., 3 Q. B. C. 584.

bargained for five shares, through a broker, on the Stock Exchange, and paid the value of them, and took a transfer from S. & G. of these specific five shares, and A.'s name was placed upon the register and share certificates were given him. It was afterwards discovered that the transfer to S. & G. was a forgery, and the company was ordered to restore Miss Trittin's name upon the register. On a case stated, the court held, that the giving the certificate to S. & G. amounted to a statement by the company, intended by the company to be acted upon by purchasers of shares in the market, that S. & G. were entitled to the shares, and that A. having acted on that statement, the company was estopped from denying its truth, and that A. was consequently entitled to recover from the company the value of the shares.

Hart v. Frontino, etc. Gold Co.

On the same principle, in the case of Hart *v.* Frontino, etc. Gold Co.,[1] plaintiff purchased shares in the defendants' company, and received duly executed share certificates, but was not registered on their books. The seller, being compelled to pay a call upon them, demanded repayment of the plaintiff, who required to have transfer of the shares registered in his name. Plaintiff's name was thereupon entered on the registry, and he received from the company a certificate certifying that he was the owner of the shares. On the faith of this certificate and registration he paid the call to the seller. The company subsequently discovered that, before the plaintiff had purchased the shares, they had been bought by a Mr. Fitzgerald, and

[1] L. R., 5 Ex. 111.

transferred to him by a duly executed transfer. The plaintiff's name was then removed from the register, and that of Fitzgerald substituted. The plaintiff sued the company for removing his name, and it was held that, by the registration of plaintiff's name and the delivery to him of the certificates, followed by a payment by him of the call, the defendants were estopped from denying his title, and were liable to him for the value of the shares.

2. An excellent illustration of the second class is the recent case of Simm v. Anglo-American Telegraph Company.[1] In this case Burge & Co. purchased upon the Stock Exchange £5000 of stock in the defendant company. Before the transfer was effected, Burge & Co., desiring to borrow money on the stock, requested to have the transfer made in the name of Spurling & Co., and a transfer of the stock purporting to be executed by C., the true owner, was lodged with the company by Spurling & Co., who had agreed to make the advances. The company, after sending the usual notice to C., registered Spurling & Co. as holders. Spurling & Co. again repledged the stock with Simm & Co., who were in like manner registered as owners, a certificate being issued to them by the company. The advances, however, were subsequently all paid off, so that the plaintiffs, Simm & Co., continued to hold the stock merely as trustees for Burge & Co. It was discovered, meanwhile, that the transfer from C. was a forgery, and the company thereupon replaced C. upon the register, and refused to pay dividends to the plaintiffs or to acknowledge their title to the stock. The court below held,

Simm v. Anglo-American Telegraph Co.

[1] 20 American Law Register, p. 159.

that Spurling & Co. and Simm & Co. had, by having fresh certificates issued to them, acquired a title by estoppel against the company, and that, having so acquired it, the benefit of that estoppel enured to Burge & Co., who had, though innocently, originally presented a forged power of attorney to the company by which they had obtained the certificates to their nominees. This, however, was held by the Court of Appeals to be erroneous. "Mr. Benjamin contended," said Bramwell, L. J., "that it was the duty of the de-"fendants to make inquiries, and that by putting the "plaintiffs on the register and giving them the certifi-"cate, they affirm that the transfer is correct. I en-"tirely dissent from that proposition. This system of "companies making inquiries before putting the names "of purchasers of stock on the register is comparatively "modern, and is a very reasonable one, but it is for "their own benefit only; for, as between themselves and "the transferees of the company, having given a certifi-"cate, they would be estopped from denying their title "to the stock, and therefore for their own protection "they ought to make inquiry; but I do not see why, "because they do so, they should be precluded in this "action from saying that the transfer presented by "Burge & Co. is a forgery. * * * In my opinion, it "is unnecessary to consider in this case whether any "damage has accrued to the plaintiffs. Even if it "could be shown that Burge & Co. have suffered dam-"age in consequence of what the company have done, "it would not, I think, make any difference. It would "be their misfortune." Brett, L. J., said, "The com-"pany are not bound to make inquiries, and indeed if

"the transferee does not put credit in the broker he
"can himself make inquiry of the transferor. All the
"facts which caused Burge & Co. to be put upon the
"register and entitled them to a certificate are as much
"known to them as to the defendants, and some of
"them are more within their knowledge than the com-
"pany's. They know, for instance, what the contract
"with the broker was, and it is quite as much their
"duty to make inquiries as it is the company's. All
"the company do is to put the names on the register,
"which act of the transferor, if valid, makes Burge &
"Co. holders of the stock, but the company do this on
"the statement of Burge & Co. The certificate is
"merely a statement that the company have accepted
"Burge & Co. as holders, but does not allege any fact
"known to the company and not known to Burge &
"Co. The only use of it is for the purpose of making a
"transfer, or to show the title to the stock. The issuing
"of it, therefore, does raise an estoppel against the com-
"pany as between them and a subsequent purchaser,
"as it is given with the intent that he may act upon it,
"and is a representation by the company of facts not
"within his knowledge. There is, then, no representa-
"tion made by the defendants to Burge & Co. sufficient
"to raise the estoppel, and I doubt whether Burge &
"Co. have made any representation which might estop
"them as against the company. Even if the company
"had made such a representation to Burge & Co. they
"would not be estopped, because the legal position of
"Burge & Co. has not been altered by it. If ever
"they had a remedy against the broker at law, they
"have it still; and I think any remedies they may

"have had under the rules of the Stock Exchange, "they have still."[1]

3. The case, where a person bargains for stock, but does not pay the price until a certificate is procured for him from the company, on the faith of a forged transfer by the forger, is well illustrated by the case of Pratt v. Machinists' National Bank.[2] There, certificates of stock were stolen from the plaintiff, Miss Pratt, and given by the thief to F. & Co. to sell, together with a forged power to transfer. They employed H. to sell the stock at auction, who sold them to D. The certificates, with the transfer filled up to H., were sent after the sale to the company to issue new certificates to H., and the new certificates then sent with a transfer to D., the buyer, to the company, who issued fresh certificates to him. All the parties acted *bona fide*. On the discovery of the forgery, the plaintiff filed her bill against D. and against the company, asking for a decree of new certificates from the latter, and that the former be ordered to give his up. The court held, that the bill lay against the company, and cited the authorities in the notes,[3] but refused in that proceeding to order the purchaser to surrender his certificates, though without prejudice to any future proceeding as between these two co-defendants.[4]

Principles derived from the foregoing cases. A review of these cases will satisfy any one that the proper course for the broker to pursue, whenever he

---

[1] See Hilyard v. South Sea Co., 2 P. Wm. 76; Ward v. R. R. Co., 37 Georgia, 515.
[2] 123 Mass. 110.
[3] Ashby v. Blackwell, 2 Eden, 299; Sewall v. Boston Water-Power Co., 4 Allen, 277; Pollock v. Bank, 3 Seld. 274.
[4] See note by Mr. Bennett in 20 Amer. Law Register, p. 168, to the case of Simm v. Anglo-American Telegraph Co.

becomes either a purchaser of stock, or a holder as bailee for an advance, is to register it in his own name and get a fresh certificate from the corporation. In this case he is, according to all the decisions excepting that in Simm v. Anglo-American Telegraph Company,[1] just noticed, protected against mistake in the issue of the stock by the officers of the company or fraud in the execution of the transfer from the original owner. Under the last-mentioned case, a new certificate in the name of the purchaser would be no protection where it was issued on a forged transfer presented by an innocent purchaser, at least after his purchase. It did not, however, appear there that Burge and Co. had purchased expressly on the faith of the issue of the new certificate; as, if they had done so, the company might then have been estopped from setting up their defence. But the decision certainly seems to be at variance with the *dicta* of the court in Hart v. The Frontino, etc. Gold Company.[2] There, Bramwell, B., said, "If they" (the company) "elect to do it, and "acts are done by him" (the purchaser) "in conse- "quence, he cannot afterwards undo it. The plaintiff "has a right to say, 'I made you a tender of myself as "shareholder, and you accepted me, and I acted upon "that acceptance.' This is no novelty; as against a "*bona fide* holder for value a banker paying a forged "check or a drawee paying a forged bill cannot after- "wards recover back the money, nor can an acceptor "deny a drawer's signature. Suppose the plaintiff had "sold the shares and handed over the certificate, it is "admitted that the purchaser would have a good title

Simm v. Anglo-Amer. Tel. Co.

Remarks of Bramwell, B., in Hart v. Frontino, etc. Gold Co.

---

[1] *Supra*, p. 410.   [2] L. R., 5 Exch. 111.

"by estoppel against the defendants, who could not have denied his right to compel him to enter his name. That would show, if the defendant's contention is sound, that the plaintiff *would have been better off if he had sold the shares than if he had continued a shareholder;* but why should that be?"

Under this view, Burge & Co.,[1] after having received a certificate in their own name as purchasers, would clearly have been entitled to rely upon it as against the company; and it can hardly be that they were in a worse position because, when purchased, the stock was actually registered and certificates issued in the names of Spurling & Co. and Simm & Co., whose title as purchasers or lenders was confessedly valid. But, even under the reasoning of this case, a broker who refused to complete the purchase until a new certificate was issued at the transfer office, in his own name or that of his nominee, would acquire a good title as against the company by estoppel. This course would always protect the purchaser or lender from litigation and delay, which alone may involve great loss, in cases where the title to the stock sold or hypothecated is put in doubt by reason of some fraud, or on account of the capacity in which the seller is acting, as in the case of executors, trustees, etc.

---

[1] The real parties in interest in Simm *v.* The Anglo-American Telegraph Co., *supra*, p. 407.

CHAPTER II.

MEASURE OF DAMAGE FOR THE BREACH OF THE CONTRACT OF SALE AND PLEDGE.

	PAGE		PAGE
Preliminary remarks	413	SECTION II.—1, 2. MEASURE OF DAMAGES WHERE THE CONSIDERATION HAS PASSED.	
Division of chapter	414		
SECTION I.—MEASURE OF DAMAGES WHERE NO CONSIDERATION HAS PASSED.		Rule in England	416
		Rule in different States in America	416
Rule in England	414	Reader referred to cases involving other species of personal property	424
Rule in different States in America	415		

IN the business of a stock broker, the two contracts, of hypothecation and of sale, are those by means of which the great part of his daily transactions are executed. For a breach of either of these the remedy is usually by an action at law against the offending party. It becomes, therefore, requisite to consider the measure of damage which the injured party is entitled to as compensation for the breach of either of these contracts.

Preliminary remarks.

The breach of the contract of sale occurs when there is a refusal to deliver or transfer stock. The breach of the contract of pledge occurs when there is a refusal to return borrowed stock.

The breach of the contract of sale falls obviously under two heads:—*first*, where the vendee has actually paid the consideration money; *secondly*, where no consideration money, or at all events but a small portion of it, has passed.

413

Law in the United States conflicting.

Unfortunately, the law respecting the measure of damage is, in the United States, in great confusion; and in discussing this subject, we shall be compelled, generally, to examine the rules laid down in different States. We shall, however, classify decisions of the several States as far as is possible.

We shall consider in Section I.—

Division of chapter.

The measure of damages, where there is a failure to fulfil a contract to deliver stock, but where no consideration has passed; and in Section II.—

1. The measure of damages, where there is a failure to fulfil a contract to deliver or transfer stock where the consideration has been actually paid.

2. The measure of damages, where there is a failure on the part of the bailee to return borrowed stock.

SECTION I.—MEASURE OF DAMAGES WHERE NO CONSIDERATION HAS PASSED.

Rule in England.

The measure of damages, where there is a breach of a contract to deliver stock, and no consideration has passed, is, in England, the difference between the contract price and the market price at the time the contract was broken. Thus, in Shaw *v.* Holland,[1] Parke, B., said that he "was at first disposed to think this "was like the case of an action for not replacing "stock, in which the measure of damages is the dif- "ference of price on the day on which it ought to "have been replaced, and on the day of trial, but "upon consideration," he thought, "it more resembled "the case of an action for the non-delivery of goods."

Shaw v. Holland.

Remarks of Parke, B.

Gainsford v. Carroll.

In the case of Gainsford *v.* Carroll,[2] which was an

[1] 15 M. & W. 136.   [2] 2 Barn. & Cr. 624.

action for not delivering goods on a given day, the court held, that it was not like the case of a loan of stock, where the borrower holds in his hands the money of the lender, and thereby prevents him from using it altogether; but that the plaintiff, having his money in his possession, might purchase the like goods the very day after the contract was broken; and, therefore, that the true measure of damages was the difference between the price agreed upon and the market price of the goods at the time the contract was broken. Here the plaintiff had his money in his own possession, and might have gone into the market and bought other shares as soon as the contract was broken.

In Pennsylvania, the rule, laid down by the more recent cases with regard to stocks, where the consideration had actually passed, was the same as that of any ordinary commodity.[1] Where, therefore, the consideration has not passed, it would probably also be in analogy to the case of any other commodity, and would be the difference between the contract price and the market value at the time the contract was broken.[2]

Rule in America.

So, in New York, where no case precisely analogous exists, probably the ordinary rule of measure of damages would apply, as in the case of other chattels, which was discussed in Clark v. Pinney,[3] on the breach of a contract to deliver salt.

Clark v. Pinney.

In Kansas,[4] in executory contracts, the court said, that the measure of damages was the difference between

---

[1] Huntington, etc., R. R. Co. v. English, 86 Pa. 247; North v. Phillips, 89 Pa. 250.
[2] See Wilson v. Whitaker, 49 Pa. 114.
[3] 7 N. Y. 681.
[4] Field v. Kinnear, 4 Kan. 476.

the stipulated value and the market value at the time the contract was broken.

In Louisiana,[1] the court has held, that the proper measure of damages was the value at the breach of contract, or the conversion.

SECTION II.—MEASURE OF DAMAGES WHERE THE CONSIDERATION HAS PASSED.

1. 2. The principle in respect to the measure of damages, (1) where the consideration has been paid, and there is a failure to deliver stock, and (2) in the case where there is a failure to replace borrowed stock, is obviously the same, as in each case the offending party is, in effect, a bailee, and the stock held in bailment.

Rule in England. In England, the measure of damages is, in these two cases, the value at the time the contract was broken, with interest, where there has been a fall in the price of the stock;[2] and where the price has risen, it is the value at the day of trial.[3]

It was at one time supposed that the highest intermediate value, between the time the contract was broken and the day of trial, constituted the true measure of the damage suffered; but this idea has been repudiated.[4]

Rule in America. In Pennsylvania, the later cases hold, where the consideration has passed, and there is a failure to deliver, or where there is a failure to replace borrowed

---

[1] Vance v. Tourne, 13 Louisiana, 225.

[2] Forrest v. Elwes, 4 Vesey, Jr., 492; Sanders v. Kentish, 8 T. R. 162; In the matter of the Bahia, etc., Ry. Co., L. R., 3 Q. B. C. 584.

[3] Shepherd v. Johnson, 2 East, 211; Harrison v. Harrison, 1 C. & P. 412; Owen v. Routh, 78 E. C., L. R. 326.

[4] McArthur v. Seaforth, 2 Taunton, 257; see Greening v. Wilkinson, 1 C. & P. 625.

stock, that the proper measure is the value at the time of the breach of the contract, with interest to the day of trial,[1] unless, it is said, some peculiar relation exists between the parties, as in the case of a *cestui que trust* and a *trustee*.

It is true, that in Bank of Montgomery v. Reese,[2] where bank stock had been wrongfully withheld from a party entitled to it, the consideration of the stock having been paid, the measure of damage was held to be the highest value between the breach of the contract and the trial, together with the bonus and dividends which had been received in the mean time; but where the consideration had not been paid, the plaintiff, it was said, would be allowed the difference between it and the value of the stock, together with the difference between the interest on the consideration money and the dividends on the stock. The highest intermediate value was, in this case, allowed. But this has been frequently said, by the Supreme Court of Pennsylvania, to have been done here, because the corporation was considered as a trustee for the stockholders. The reasoning, however, adopted, in the opinion of the court, does not support this explanation, but proceeds upon the broad principle of giving due compensation to the injured party under the circumstances of the case. Lewis, C. J., in delivering the opinion of the court, said, "The case of stock is an exception to the "general rule applicable to chattels. It is made an "exception in obedience to the paramount obligation

[1] Neiler v. Kelly, 69 Pa. 403; Huntington, etc. R. R. Co. v. English, 86 Pa. 247; Work v. Bennett, 70 Pa. 484; North v. Phillips, 89 Pa. 250.
[2] 26 Pa. 143.

"to indemnify the party for his loss. The rule of
"convenience gives place to the rule of justice. The
"moment we proceed, on this ground, to take it out of
"the general rule, we are obliged to substitute one that
"will do complete justice to the party injured. The
"question is, what did the plaintiff lose? * * * He is
"entitled to all the advantages he could have derived
"from the stock if it had been delivered at the speci-
"fied time. * * * Those advantages are the highest
"market value between the breach and the trial, to-
"gether with the *bonus* and dividends which have
"been received in the mean time. * * * This is the
"rule where the consideration has been paid. * * *
"Nothing short of this will do justice, because nothing
"short of it will give the plaintiff the benefits he could
"have enjoyed if he had not been deprived of his
"rights."

Neiler v. Kelly.

In the subsequent case of Neiler *v.* Kelly,[1] Sharswood, J., remarking that the rule regarding the measure of damages had been somewhat modified in respect

Remarks of Sharswood, J.

to stocks from that of ordinary chattels, said, "The
"rule, however, is not changed, but only modified to
"this extent, that wherever there is a duty or obligation
"devolved upon a defendant to deliver such stocks or
"securities at a particular time, and that duty or obli-
"gation has not been fulfilled, then the plaintiff is
"entitled to recover the highest price in the market
"between that time and the time of the trial." And
in all the subsequent cases where the highest intermediate value has been allowed in Pennsylvania, there has been some peculiar relation existing be-

[1] 69 Pa. 403.

CHAP. II.]   MEASURE OF DAMAGE.   419

tween the parties other than mere bailor and bailee, or vendor and vendee.[1] The rule apparently laid down, therefore, in Bank of Montgomery *v.* Reese, can hardly be regarded, except with this important qualification, as the law of Pennsylvania.

In New York, the courts have from an early period favored the highest intermediate value between the conversion and the trial, and the rule with regard to that State is that, where there is a failure to replace borrowed stock, or to deliver stock, when the consideration has passed, the measure of damages is the highest intermediate value between the conversion, or breach of contract, and the trial.[2]

In Romaine *v.* Van Allen,[3] where the trial had been protracted, and the stock risen in the mean time, the measure of damages was the highest value between the conversion and the last day of the trial.

Romaine v. Van Allen.

The courts in New York, however, have taken a distinction between the case of a failure to deliver stock which has been paid for by the agent of the vendor, and by the vendor himself; and where the former has advanced the purchase money, and the latter has not advanced any, the later decisions lay down as the measure of damage, the value of the stock at the time of the demand by the vendee, or within a reasonable time

---

[1] See Persh *v.* Quiggle, 7 Sm. (Pa.) 247; Reitenbaugh *v.* Ludwick, 7 Casey (Pa.), 131; Musgrave *v.* Beckendorff, 53 Pa. 310; Wagner *v.* Peterson, 83 Pa. 238.

[2] See Cortelyou *v.* Lansing, 2 Caines's Cases, 216; Nauman *v.* Caldwell, 2 Sweeney, 212; West *v.* Wentworth, 3 Cowen, 82; Bank *v.* Kortright, 22 Wend. 348; Burt *v.* Dutcher, 34 N. Y. 493; Allen *v.* Dykers, 3 Hill, 593; Markham *v.* Jaudon, 41 N. Y. 235; Lobdell *v.* Stowell, 51 N. Y. 70; Baker *v.* Drake, 53 N. Y. 211; same case, 66 N. Y. 518; Thayer *v.* Manly, 73 N. Y. 305; Morgan *v.* Gregg, 46 Barb. 183.

[3] 26 N. Y. 309.

afterwards, where there has been a failure to replace a deposit made as security.

Markham v. Jaudon.

A different rule was laid down in Markham v. Jaudon,[1] where the highest intermediate value was allowed.

Baker v. Drake.

But in Baker v. Drake,[2] the court said that the highest intermediate value was not invariably the correct measure of damage, and that where shares of stock were purchased by stock brokers for their principal, with the funds of the former, and carried in their name merely for speculative purposes, and not for investment, which had been converted by the brokers, the proper measure of damages was what it would have cost the plaintiff to replace the stocks on some day within a reasonable time after the wrongful sale, deducting the sum due the defendants for commissions,

Remarks of Rapallo, J.

etc. Rapallo, J., said, in delivering the opinion, "More than two-thirds of this supposed damage arose "after the bringing of this suit. This enormous "amount of profit, given under the name of damages, "could not have been arrived at except under the un- "reasonable supposition, unsupported by any evidence, "that the plaintiff would not only have supplied the "necessary margin and caused the stock to be carried "through all its fluctuations until it reached its high- "est point, but that he would have been so fortunate "as to seize upon that precise moment to sell, thus "avoiding the subsequent decline, and realizing the "highest profit which could have possibly been derived "from the transaction by one endowed with the super- "natural power of prescience. In a case where the "loss of probable profits is claimed as an element of

[1] 41 N. Y. 235.   [2] 53 N. Y. 211; 66 ib. 518.

CHAP. II.]   MEASURE OF DAMAGE.   421

"damage, if it be ever allowable to mulct a defendant
"for such a conjectural loss, its amount is a question
"of fact, and a finding in respect to it should be based
"upon some evidence. In respect to a dealing which,
"at the time of its termination, was as likely to result
"in further loss as in profit, to lay down as an inflex-
"ible rule of law that as damages for its wrongful
"interruption the largest amount of profit which sub-
"sequent developments disclose might, under the most
"favorable circumstances, have been possibly obtained
"from it, must be awarded to the fortunate individual
"who occupies the position of plaintiff, without regard
"to the probabilities of his realizing such profits,
"seems to me a wide departure from the elementary
"principles upon which damages have hitherto been
"awarded. * * * The plaintiff did not hold the stocks
"as an investment, but the object of the transaction
"was to have the chance of realizing a profit by their
"sale. He had not paid for them. The defendants
"had supplied all the capital embarked in the specu-
"lation, except the comparatively trifling sum which
"remained in their hands as margin. Assuming that
"the sale was in violation of the rights of the plaintiff,
"what was the extent of the injury inflicted upon
"him? He was deprived of the chance of a subse-
"quent rise in price, but this was accompanied with
"the corresponding chance of a decline, or, in case of
"a rise, of his not availing himself of it at the proper
"moment; a continuance of the speculation also re-
"quired him to supply further margin, and involved
"a risk of ultimate loss. If, upon becoming informed
"of the sale, he desired further to prosecute the adven-

"ture and take the chances of a future market, he had the right to disaffirm the sale and require the defendants to replace the stock. If they failed or refused to do this, his remedy was to do it himself and charge them with the loss reasonably sustained in doing so. The advance in the market price of the stock from the time of the sale up to a reasonable time to replace it, after the plaintiff received notice of the sale, would afford a complete indemnity." And the case of Markham v. Jaudon was overruled so far as it conflicted with the principles thus laid down.

_{Rule in Markham v. Jaudon modified.}

_{Moody v. Caulk.}

In Florida, in Moody v. Caulk,[1] the measure of damage was held to be the value at the time of the conversion with interest, but Randall, C. J., said, "In the case of *public stocks* held as an investment, of rare pictures, jewels, and like articles, held otherwise than for purposes of immediate commerce, it would be equitable and proper that the highest value after conversion should prevail, if the jury should be satisfied from the evidence the plaintiff would have held the property up to the time of the advance in value, for the defendant should make good the actual loss sustained by reason of his act. But this suggestion is probably not applicable to the present case." This, therefore, was merely an *obiter dictum*.

_{Remarks of Randall, C.}

_{Kent v. Ginter.}

_{Remarks of Perkins, J.}

In Indiana, in Kent *et al.* v. Ginter,[2] Perkins, J., said, "Generally, the value of the property at the time and place of delivery is taken as the datum for measuring damages. * * * But one exception to this rule is quite well established, and that is where stocks

---

[1] 14 Fla. 50.   [2] 23 Indiana, 1.

"are the subject-matter of the sale. Romaine v. Allen.[1]"

In Maine[2] and Massachusetts,[3] in the case of stocks, where the consideration has passed, or in the case of loaned stock, the measure of damage was the market value with interest; and in Pinkerton v. R. R. Co.,[4] in New Hampshire, the court especially stated that the above was the proper measure of damages, and that the value at the trial, and not any intermediate value, was to be considered by the jury.

Pinkerton v. R. R. Co.

In Maryland,[5] where stocks and bonds were deposited in a bank, and by them lost, as well as in a case in Virginia,[6] the measure of damage was held to be, in the former case, the value at the time of the theft or conversion, and in the latter, the value at the day when they should have been delivered; and in Arkansas the same rule seems to have been adopted.[7]

In Ohio, in Bates v. Wiles,[8] an action of trover was brought to recover the certificates wrongfully converted; and the court held, that the highest value intermediate between the conversion and the trial was a fair compensation to the injured party.

Bates v. Wiles.

In Nevada, in Boylan v. Huguet,[9] the court held, that the highest intermediate value between the conversion and the trial was not the true measure of damage, but the value at the conversion with interest to judgment, and generally any damage which legitimately might arise out of the transaction.

Boylan v. Huguet.

[1] 26 N. Y. Rep. 309.
[2] McKenney v. Haines, 63 Me. 74.
[3] Fisher v. Brown, 104 Mass. 259.
[4] 42 N. H. 463.
[5] Bank v. Boyd, 44 Md. 47.
[6] O. & H. R. R. Co. v. Fulvey, 17 Grattan, 366.
[7] Jefferson v. Hale, 31 Arkansas, 286.
[8] 1 Handy (Ohio), 532.
[9] 8 Nevada, 345.

Bercich v. Marye.

In Bercich v. Marye,[1] the court said that in the statutory action of claim and delivery of personal property, in case a return cannot be had, the value of the stock at the day of trial, with the dividends that have been paid upon it as damages for detention, is the only complete indemnity.

The courts sometimes, in deciding the proper measure of damages for the breach of contracts of sale, have drawn a distinction between those cases, where shares of stock, and those, where other kinds of property, constituted the subject-matter of the contract. We have therefore deemed it inadvisable to consider the decisions in those States where no cases apply the rule as to the measure of damages, either directly or indirectly, to the case of shares of stock, or bonds.

Reader referred to cases involving other kinds of personal property.

The reader is, however, referred to the following cases, where the subject has been discussed in States, other than those we have already quoted, in reference to other kinds of personal property.[2]

[1] 9 Nevada, 312.

[2] Dryer v. Lewis, 57 Ala. 552; Hamer v. Hathaway, 33 Cal. 117; Cofield v. Clark, 2 Col. 101; C. R. & B. Co. v. A. & G. R. R. Co., 50 Ga. 444; Deere v. Lewis, 51 Ill. 254; Stapleton v. King, 40 Iowa, 278; Derby v. Gullup, 5 Minn. 119; Allen v. Kinyon, 41 Mich. 281; Storm v. Green, 51 Miss. 103; Rickey v. Ten-Broeck, 63 Mo. 563; French v. Ramge, 2 Neb. 254; Woolcott v. Mount, 7 Vroom (N. J.), 262; Kid v. Mitchell, 1 N. & McC. (S. C.) 334; Cartwright v. McCook, 33 Texas, 612.

INDEX.

"ABOUT"
    meaning of, as applied to amount of stock or commodity, construed at law, 87, 88.
    meaning usually a question for jury, 89.
    construed by New York Stock Exchange, 87.

ACCOUNT
    sale for the, 69.

ACCOUNT DAY, 45, 69.

ACTION
    in rem, 391.
    for breach of contract, 390, 391.
        See, also, CONTRACT.
    by *feme sole trader*, husband joined, 78.
    against corporation refusing to transfer, 393.

ADMINISTRATORS, see EXECUTORS.

ADVANCES
    to executors and administrators, 323–331.
    by factor, give no right to repledge, 354, 355.
    to executor for his own purposes, fraudulent, 325.
    to trustees, 331–335.
    on collaterals, pledgee should protect himself by special agreement, 348, 349.
    usual form of collateral note, 349.

AGENCY, }
AGENT, } see PRINCIPAL AND AGENT.

ALLOTMENT, 70.

AMBIGUOUS INSTRUCTIONS, 87–90.
    See "ABOUT."

ANTECEDENT DEBT
    how far consideration for pledge, 371–373.
    See PLEDGE.

ATTACHMENT
    by creditors against stock, 374.
    See CREDITORS, and EXECUTION.

BACKWARDATION, 48, 70.

BAILEE
    broker, when, bound to use reasonable care, 100.
    See PLEDGE.

INDEX.

BANKRUPT ACT
    vests right to proceeds of sale of seat in assignee, subject to claims of Board creditors, 51.

BANKRUPTCY
    revokes broker's agency, 124.
    of member of Stock Exchange, 51.
    effect of, on proceeds of seat, see SEAT.

BARNARD'S ACT, 298.

BARTER
    stock broker has no authority to, 193.

BEAR
    definition of, 70.

BLIND POOL, see POOL, 73.

BONA FIDE PURCHASER
    of stock certificate, rights of, against company, 151.
    of stock for value, rights of, against real owner, 153.

BONDS, 147.
    how far negotiable, 157.
    foreign government, passing by delivery, held negotiable in England, 159, 171.
    of East India Company, made negotiable in England by statute, 158.
    in America, drawn to bearer or order, negotiable, 164.
    municipal bonds in America negotiable, 167.
    how pledged, see PLEDGE.
    as to coupon bonds, see COUPON BONDS.

BONUS
    defined, 70.

BOUGHT AND SOLD NOTE
    exchanged on sale of securities, 54.

BROKER, see STOCK BROKER.

BULL
    defined, 70.

BUYER'S OPTION, see OPTION.

BUYING IN
    shares at Stock Exchange, 48, 70.

CALLS, 70.
    liability of transferee to, 175.
    recoverable from customer by broker paying them, 218.
    due on shares, must be paid before making delivery, 268.

CALL LOAN, 66.

CANAL SHARES
    held by earlier cases to be within Mortmain Act, 207.
    but not by later ones, 208, 209.

CARRYING STOCK, 70, 376–378.
    See PLEDGE.

CERTIFICATE OF STOCK
    effect of, issued by corporation, 393, 394.
    held to be only secondary proof of ownership in Pennsylvania, 401.
    forged, how far binding, see FORGED CERTIFICATE.

INDEX. 427

CLEARING HOUSE
  definition and description of, 55–65.
  modus operandi of, 56.
  of stock, peculiar to Philadelphia, 59.
  example of account of broker with, 57.
  agent of buyer and seller, 61.
  transactions effected through, valid, 65.
  merely accomplishes what principals themselves may do, 62.
  customers of brokers not affected by, 64.
  sheet, decisions relating to, in Pennsylvania, 307.
  delivery through, see DELIVERY.

COLLATERAL NOTE
  form of, 349.

COMMISSIONS
  broker may sue for, 116.
  not recoverable in England by broker, unless sworn, 118.
  not recoverable by broker if guilty of negligence or misconduct, 116.
  fraud towards principal forfeits all right to, 118.
  where contract only partly performed through fault of principal, commission on whole may be recovered, 116, 117.
  not recoverable where contract illegal, 117.
  amount of, *prima facie* fixed by usage of Stock Exchange, 116.

CONSIDERATION
  failure of, what constitutes, 289, 290.

CONTANGO, 48, 71.

CONTANGO DAY, 71.

CONTINUATION, 71.

CONTINUING SHARES, 48.

CONTRACT
  at Stock Exchange, always of a thing *in esse*, 188.
  there must be mutual assent as to subject of, 192.
  effected by letter, 190, 191.
  by telegraph, 191, 192.
  by married women, 78.
  validity of, by *feme sole* trader, depends upon business carried on by her, 78, 80.
  for stock, how far must be in writing, 197–204.
  distinction between executed and executory, 230, 231.
  breach of, remedies for, 389.
  specific performance of executory contract, 234–257, 390.
  partly executed, cannot be countermanded to detriment of broker, 117.
  avoidance of, 287–318.
    by mistake, 288.
    because in restraint of trade, 290–295.
    because of wager, 297–318.
    because of fraud, 288.
  for sale of goods not owned by vendor, held illegal in earlier cases, legal by later ones, 302.
  where delivery is contemplated, not illegal, 301–304, 309.
  where delivery is not contemplated, how far illegal, 300, 301, 310, 313, 318.
  where no delivery is intended, but merely settlement by differences, illegal, 300, 313.
  intention to deliver, question for jury, 313, 314, 318.
  whether cover for gambling transaction, question for jury, 313.
  for options, see OPTIONS.
  of pledge, see PLEDGE.
  of sale, see SALE.

INDEX.

CONSOLS
    special account day for, in London, 46.

CORNER
    agreement to make, illegal, 294.
    combination to create by false rumors, held a conspiracy, 296.
    persons advancing funds for, cannot recover back amounts actually expended, 294.

CORPORATION
    acting within scope of authority, liable as natural persons, 83.
    power to contract to buy securities depends upon charter, 84.
    may contract to sell securities owned by it, 84.
    appointment of agent by, 82.
    if acting *ultra vires* in appointment of agent, not liable, 83.
    may ratify acts of agent by implication, 82.
    municipal, cannot ratify acts of agent when *ultra vires*, 88.

COUPONS
    dissevered from bonds may be sued on, 168.
    bear interest from demand and refusal to pay, 174.
    dissevered, have same qualities, as commercial paper, as instruments to which they were attached, 168.
    lien of, when detached from bonds, 174.

COUPON BONDS
    how far negotiable, 158.
    not negotiable at common law, 158.
    but in America held negotiable, 164, 167.

COVENANT, see RESTRAINT OF TRADE, and CONTRACT.

CREDITOR
    outside of Stock Exchange not affected by rules of, as to his rights against debtor's property, 68.
    otherwise as to seat of member, 68; see SEAT.
    attachment by, how far binding on stock not transferred in form prescribed by corporation by-law, 374.
    fraud as against, see FRAUD.

DAMAGES
    measure of, see MEASURE OF DAMAGES.

DAYS
    how counted in stock transactions, 280.

DEALERS, 46.
    See JOBBERS.

DEATH
    generally revokes agency, 124.
    See PRINCIPAL AND AGENT.

DEBENTURES
    definition of, 147.
    of private company to bearer, how far negotiable, 161–163.

DELEGATION
    of authority, by trustees, not permissible, 333.
    though authority to perform mere ministerial acts may be delegated, 334.
    no distinction as to, between naked power and power coupled with an interest, 336.

DELIVERY
definition of, as applied to transactions on Stock Exchange, 260.
remarks of Mr. Benjamin on, 259.
duty of vendor to deliver, 260.
vendor bound to deliver shares free of liability for pre-existing calls, 267.
manner of effecting, 49, 55, 266.
usual mode, by giving certificate and power of attorney, 266, 267.
by transfer and registration, 266, 283.
regulated by custom of trade, 267.
rules as to, in various Stock Exchanges, 266, note.
must be of stock of exact kind contracted for, 261.
must be with warranty of genuineness, 262.
must be of certificates marketable at time of delivery, 265.
broker may loan his own stock to customer to make delivery, 65.
usage as to time of, 280, 281.
through Clearing House, 55, 279.
through Clearing House constitutes actual delivery, 61.
through Clearing House hitherto not held good in Pennsylvania, 61, 307.
contract for future delivery, 183, 301-309.
unaccompanied by transfer, how far good against attaching creditors, 374, 375.

DEPOSITS, see PLEDGE.

DETINUE
will not lie against pledgee unless tender of advance first be made, 369.
will lie for bonds and debentures, 391.

DIFFERENCES
settlements by, see WAGER.

DIVIDENDS, 176.
discretionary with directors, 176, 181.
after declaration of, are individual property of stockholder, 180.
assumpsit lies for, by stockholder, 180.
improperly declared, may be recovered back, 179.

EQUITY OF REDEMPTION
pledgeor's right to, on fraudulent sale of pledge, 349.

ESTOPPEL
pledgeor estopped as against *bona fide* transferee of stock, 153-155.
how far company estopped by fraudulent use of its seal, 395.
corporation bound by certificate of shares under its seal, 402-404.
how far company bound by issue of certificate to person holding forged transfer, 404-412.
innocent transferee of certificate protected, 412.
how far company bound by entering name of person as stockholder on register, 406-408.

EVIDENCE
parol evidence not admissible to overturn written contract by showing illegal intent, 319.
but admissible to show writing only part of real contract, 319.
of *res gestæ* admissible to show whether or not transaction a gaming one, 819.

EXECUTION
on shares of stock, 391, 392.

EXECUTORS
power to sell or pledge securities of estate, 323-329.
prima facie power to sell, 334.
but not where long time has elapsed since decedent's death, 335.
advances to, on securities of their estate, 324.
advances on stocks, etc., in name of, 326-329.

FEME SOLE TRADER
how far she may contract, 78.
may act as agent, if within line of her business, 77.
power to contract limited by nature of her business, 80.
competent to carry on business of broker, 77.
in action by or against, husband generally joined, 78.

FLAT, 71.

FORGED CERTIFICATES
authority of officers of company to affix seal wrongfully, 395.
how far company estopped by forgery of transfer agent, 396–400.
when agent armed with authority to issue certificates, his forgery binding on company, 398.
where issued by agent, fraudulently, for benefit of company, the latter liable in any case, 398, 402.
where issued by agent without authority, how far binding on company, 403.
effect of forgery on parties acting *bona fide*, 403–412.
duty of purchaser to examine transfer book, 404.

FORGED TRANSFER
title of *bona fide* transferee, 405.
title of transferee purchasing on faith of new certificate, 407.

FRAUD
defined, 288.
avoidance by reason of, 288.
renders contract voidable only, 288.
in pledgee's sale of pledge, 349.
against creditors, by fictitious pledge, 373, 374.,
against creditors, pledge voidable for, under statute of 13 & 27 Elizabeth, 373, 374.
in over-issue of stock, see FORGED CERTIFICATE.

FRAUDS, STATUTE OF, 194–206, 214.
how far stock contracts in America are within, 200–204.
how far parol sales of securities in America held to be within, 196, 197.
held to embrace executory contracts, 196.
what is a sufficient memorandum in writing, 205.
agent duly authorized within, 206.
how far 4th section, relating to interests in land, includes sales of stock, 214.

GAMING CONTRACTS
advances in, not recoverable, 112, 113, 115.
advances in, distinction between void contracts and contracts voidable only, 115.
8 & 9 Vict. c. 109 against gaming contracts not pleadable in action for money paid at principal's request, 113.
See, also, WAGER.

HYPOTHECATION.
See PLEDGE.
measure of damages for breach of contract of, see MEASURE OF DAMAGES.

ILLEGAL CONSIDERATION
pledge by vendor voidable for, 370.

ILLEGAL CONTRACTS.
See CONTRACTS, GAMING CONTRACTS, and WAGER.

INDEX. 431

INFANT
 cannot be stock broker, 76.
INSOLVENCY
 of member of Stock Exchange, 50–52.
  See SEAT.
INSURANCE FUND
 for members of Stock Exchange in America, 53.

JOBBER
 definition of, 71, 132.
 not liable after transferee's name accepted by seller, 133–136.
 mode of dealing as member of Stock Exchange, 46.
 method of fulfilling his contract, 47.
 liability continues until acceptance of transfers by buyer, 134, 135.
 released from liability when name passed, 48.
 released, even though "man of straw" put forward as transferee, 136.
 not liable to vendor of shares for allowing the latter's name to remain on register, 223, 224.
 not responsible for passing name of "straw man" as ultimate purchaser, 223–4.
 may sue principal when circumstances show credit not given to broker, 136.

LAME DUCK, 71.
LAND COMPANIES
 not within Mortmain Act, 212.
LEAP-YEAR
 meaning of, 280.
LETTER
 contracts effected by, 190, 191.
LIEN
 definition of, 118.
 generally attaches only on liquidated demands, 122.
 differs from pledge, 121, 354–357, 366.
 generally gives no right to sell, 119.
 is not transferable by person holding, 354–357.
 of broker, for advances, governed by law regulating banker's lien, 119, 120, 122.
 of broker cannot arise, where inconsistent with his contract with customer, 121.
 of corporation on its own stock, 176.
 right to, by a corporation under its charter, must be clear, 177, 178.
 no implied lien by a corporation in its own shares, unless proviso in charter, 176–178.
 of corporation on dividends, 179.
LISTING STOCKS OR SECURITIES, 54.
LONG, TO BE, 71.

MAKING A PRICE, 71.
MANDAMUS
 when it lies to compel transfer, 393.
  See SPECIFIC PERFORMANCE.
"MAN OF STRAW"
 defined, 71, 72.
 after acceptance of, vendor cannot except to, 223.
  See JOBBER, and VENDOR AND PURCHASER.

432   INDEX.

MARGIN, 71.
    deposit of, 377, 378.
    keeping it good, 378.

MARRIED WOMAN
    contract of, at common law, void, and incapable ot ratification, 78.
    cannot be stock broker, 76.
    cannot bind herself through agent to carry out executory contract, 79.
    may invest or sell her own securities through broker, 79.
    may become principal in stock transactions to a limited extent with consent of husband, 79.
    may authorize agent, with consent of husband, to perform administrative act, 79.
    authorized by statute to transfer personal property, 79.
    may complete executed sale, 79.
    power to contract and carry on business if constituted *feme sole* trader, 78.
    See FEME SOLE TRADER.

MEASURE OF DAMAGES
    for breach of stock contract, 413-424.
    Where consideration has passed, value of stock at day of trial, 416, 417.
    highest intermediate value formerly favored in New York, 419.
    but lately qualified in that State, 420.
    highest intermediate value, distinction taken in New York, where consideration paid by agent of vendor and by vendor himself, 419.
    where consideration has passed, in other States in the Union, 422, 423.
    rule giving highest intermediate price generally abandoned, except where relation of trustee and *cestui que trust* exists, 416-419.
    Where no consideration has passed, difference between contract and market price, 414-416.
    distinction between sales of stock and other kinds of personal property, 424.
    for breach of contract of pledge, 413-424.

MEDIUM OF PAYMENT
    regulated by Stock Exchange, 283.

MEMBERS
    of Stock Exchange, 50. See STOCK EXCHANGE, and SEAT.

MEMORANDUM
    of sale made by broker with jobber, 46.
    what is a sufficient, see FRAUDS, STATUTE OF.

MINING SHARES
    how far within Mortmain Act, 211.
    See MORTMAIN ACT.

MISTAKE
    as to subject of sale, 192, 193.
    of customer, makes him responsible, 216.
    avoidance of contract by reason of, 288.
    of law, what constitutes, 289.

MONEY
    selling for, 71.

MONTH
    meaning of, 280.

"MORE OR LESS"
    construed in special cases, 87-89.
    See AMBIGUOUS INSTRUCTIONS.

MORTGAGE
of stock, 387.
difference between, and pledge, 367, 387.

MORTGAGE BONDS
of railway and canal companies within Mortmain Act, 210.

MORTGAGEE
of stock, how far obliged to return identical shares, 387.

MORTMAIN ACT
test of its application to stock, 209.
land companies not within, 212.
applies to shares only where representing aliquot portion of land, 211.
mortgages of railway and canal companies, how far within, 210.
shares and securities not within, under later decisions, 208–210.
how far the act applies to mining shares, 211.

NAME DAY, 47, 72.

NAME, PASSING A, 72.

NEGLIGENCE
in custody of seal by company, 395–400.
company liable for, in issue of forged stock, 403, 404.
   See FORGED CERTIFICATE.

NEGOTIABILITY
of securities generally, 148.
   See NEGOTIABLE INSTRUMENT.

NEGOTIABLE INSTRUMENT
can be sued on by holder, 148.
negotiability in England held to depend on usage, 163.
how far stock is negotiable, 156.
stock held in America to approximate to a negotiable instrument, 155.
scrip generally negotiable, 169, 170.
scrip certificates for shares, how far negotiable, 171, 172.
scrip exchangeable for government bonds held negotiable in England, 169.
distinction between government bonds and those of public companies as to negotiability, 159, 170.
as to specific performance, in contracts as to, distinction between government securities and bonds or stock of public companies, 239, 246, 252, 253.

NEW YORK
special account day for government securities, 55.

NOTE, 54.
   See BOUGHT AND SOLD NOTE.

NOTICE
what constitutes reasonable notice, 350.
determined by usage, 352.

NOTICES
under rules of Exchange, 281.

NOVATION, 72.

OMNIUM, 72.

OPTION, 72.
contracts for, legal, 309.
to deliver gold coin and money, 311.

OPTION—*continued.*
    held legal, 312.
    to deliver, not illegal, 300.
    to deliver or not to deliver, not necessarily illegal, 811.

OPTION ACCOUNT DAY, 72.

OPTION MONEY, 72.

OVER-ISSUE
    liability of company for, see FORGED CERTIFICATE.

PAROL CONTRACT
    within Statute of Frauds, in England, 194.
    See FRAUDS, STATUTE OF.

PASSING A NAME, 47, 72.

PAWNEE. See PLEDGEE.

PAYMENT
    of price, 282.
    medium of, 282.
    how it must be tendered, 282.
    See SALE.

PLEDGE, 322–400.
    defined, 322.
    distinction between, and lien, 854, 367.
    distinction between, and mortgage, 367, 387.
    right to make, 176, 323–330.
    avoidance of, 370.
    voidable from illegal consideration, 370.
    void for bad consideration, 371.
    made to secure pre-existing debt, how far good, 372, 373.
    voidable from fraud under statutes of Elizabeth, 370.
    void when made by one not having authority, 371.
  Who may pledge, 322–335.
    persons whose powers are restricted, 322.
    power of corporations to, 82–84, 323.
    powers of executor to, 322.
    executor or administrator may usually pledge for purposes of estate only, 323–325.
    bailee with notice of fraud compelled to return security, 325.
    executor or administrator has no implied power to, when a long period has elapsed after decedent's death, 328.
    how far co-executors pledging must join, 329, 330.
    trustees primarily have no power to, unless expressly authorized by instrument, 331.
    by trustees, where several, must act jointly, 333.
    trustees cannot delegate authority to agent to pledge, 335, 336.
    stock broker cannot pledge principal's property to secure his own debt, 91.
  Formation of, 322–328.
    manner of effecting, 338.
    subject-matter of, 337.
    what may be pledged, 337.
    of negotiable securities, how effected, 338.
    must always be delivered to pledgee, 338.
    if non-negotiable securities, how effected, 338.
  Effect of, 339–368.
    pledgee, how far bound to return identical shares deposited, 100, 384–387.
    under rules of London Stock Exchange, 101, 104.

INDEX. 435

PLEDGE—*continued.*
  Effect of—continued.
    in America, 102-105.
    sale of, on failure to pay demand loan, legal, 66.
    of stock carried by broker, broken by pledgeor's failure to perform his contract, 876.
  Rehypothecation by bailee illegal, 91, 853-869.
    rehypothecation made penal in Pennsylvania by statute, 104.
    rights of sub-pledgees without actual notice, 326-328.
    assignment of, see PLEDGEE.

PLEDGEE
  Powers and duties of.
    responsible for use of pledge, 841.
    responsible as ordinary bailee, 341.
    of shares of joint stock companies, liabilities of, 340, 341.
    holding legal title of shares, liable for calls, 340.
    holding legal title, liable for all obligations of stockholder, 340.
    may collect dividends and coupons and vote, 342.
    bound to account for dividend, 343.
  Rehypothecation by.
    how far bound to return identical security pledged, 100-104, 384, 385.
    return of identical securities, Langton *v.* Waite considered, 886, 387.
    termination of pledge by return of article pledged, 383.
    wrongful conversion by, terminates pledge, 362.
    may in England assign pledge, 356.
    right to sub-pledge, 353.
    review of general principles, 368.
    right to rehypothecate considered, 369.
    right to sub-pledge, how far upheld in America, 360-364.
    rights of sub-pledgee without notice, 326, 360-362.
  Sale by.
    right to sell the pledge, 343.
    bound to make demand on pledgeor to redeem, 350.
    bound to give reasonable notice of time and place of sale, 350.
    broker bound to notify customer of sale of stock carried for him, 379.
    reasonable notice of sale, 350.
    sale by, without the aid of court, 344.
    bound to sell publicly, 845.
    how far he may sell at Stock Exchange, 345.
    right of, to bid at sale of pledge, 847.
    sale by judicial process, 344.
    without entire possession of thing pledged, must always invoke court's aid to sell, 344.
    may stipulate for sale of pledge without notice, 353.
    safer to make special agreement to sell securities and purchase at sale, 348, 349.
    of commercial paper cannot sell, but must collect at maturity, 344.
    may proceed against debtor personally, 343.
  Advances by.
    what constitutes notice to, 350, 351.
    how far safe in loaning to executors, 325.
    advancing to executor for pre-existing debt of latter, party to fraud, 325.
    how far safe in advancing to trustees, 331, 332.
    bound to make inquiries of trustee, 331.
    taking certificates registered in name of trustee, put on notice, 332.
    of trustees should return deposit to both, 330.

PLEDGEOR
    bound to convey good title to pledgee, 844.

436 INDEX.

PLEDGEOR—*continued.*
    terminates pledge by tender of payment, 383.
    right to reasonable notice of sale, 346–350.
    entitled to notice of sale of stock carried for him, 379.
    bound to bear legal expenses of sale of pledge, 358.
    when pledge sold privately, how far equity to redeem exists, 349.
    may avoid sale of pledge, when bought in by pledgee, 347, 348.
    may maintain trover against pledgee for wrongful conversion of pledge by him, 362.
    can recover for special damage sustained by reason of rehypothecation, 369.
    rights of, as against sub-pledgee, 356.
    method of effecting pledge, see PLEDGE.
    powers of, when acting in a fiduciary capacity, see EXECUTORS, and TRUSTEES.
    powers of corporations pledging, see CORPORATION, and PLEDGE.

POOL, 73.

POST
    contracts effected through agency of, 190, 191.

POWER OF ATTORNEY
    to execute specialty, must be under seal, 269, 270.
  Executed in blank, how far good, 270–278.
    executed in blank, bad in England, 269, 270.
    in blank, usual method of transferring stocks in America, 81.
    executed in blank, valid in some American States, 274–277.
    invalid in others, 271.
    upheld by many later decisions in America, 276–278.
    executed in blank and filled up in presence of grantor, binding, 279.
    revoked by death of principal, 124–128.
    to transfer Bank of England stock, not revocable by death, 128.
    forged power of attorney, 404.
    See FORGED TRANSFER.

PRICE
    of securities sold at Exchange must be money, 193, 282, 283.

PRINCIPAL AND AGENT
    who may become principal, 78.
    married woman, in certain cases, may become principal, with husband's consent, in stock transactions, 79.
  Agency, how created.
    authority may be given by parol, 81.
    how agency of stock broker created, 81.
    duly authorized within Statute of Frauds, 206.
    agency to execute unsealed instruments may be created verbally, 82.
    to authorize agent to bind principal by contract under seal, his agency must be created by seal, 81.
    otherwise, may be created verbally, 81.
    but when principal present when agent executes sealed instrument, authority from principal implied, 82, 279.
    corporation may appoint agent under seal or by implication, 82.
  Broker's relation to principal, when carrying stock, considered, 380, 381.
    customer principal of stock broker, 75, 76.
    regulations of Stock Exchange binding on principal without actual notice, 42.
    principal usually not disclosed by broker, 46.
    agent cannot act for both buyer and seller as principal, 90.
    broker can only bind principal within scope of authority, 96.
    pledge by factor of principal's goods held to be void, 105.

PRINCIPAL AND AGENT—*continued.*
Obligations of agent.
    agent must follow principal's instructions, 85.
    agent bound to act wholly in principal's interest, 227.
    broker liable to principal for violation of duty, 106.
    brokers or agents acting as government agents not personally responsible, 97–99.
    broker cannot delegate authority unless purely ministerial, 94.
    delegation of power where ordered to be executed abroad, 95.
    principal liable to broker for advances and disbursements on his behalf, 110.
    broker may recover differences he has been forced to pay by principal's default, 111.
    sub-agent cannot retain debt due by agent employing him from sale of principal's securities, 91, 228.
    broker cannot recover advances in illegal transaction, 112.
    where broker guilty of negligence, cannot recover expenses, 111.
    principal making mistake liable to agent, 216.
    ambiguous instructions construed favorably to agent, 87.
Dissolution of agency, 122.
    dissolution of agency by parties, 122, 123.
    dissolution of agency by operation of law, 123.
    agency not *ipso facto* revoked by death, where there is a power coupled with an interest, 128.
    generally revoked by death of either party, 124.
    acts of agents performed in ignorance of principal's death, 125.
    acts *bona fide* after principal's death valid in certain States, 126.
    lien of agent on principal's securities, see LIEN.

PRIVILEGED COMMUNICATIONS
    broker's communications with principal not privileged, 105.

PURCHASE MONEY
    paid in London by broker to original seller, 47.

PURCHASER
    liable for calls paid by broker, 218.

PUT, 73.

PUT AND CALL, 73.

REASONABLE
    tests of what is, as applied to usages and rules of the Stock Exchange, 41, 42, 66.
    reasonable notice of sale, see PLEDGE, and PLEDGEE.

RECEIPT
    how far demandable by purchaser, 286.

RECLAMATIONS
    for irregularities in delivery governed by rules of various Stock Exchanges, 264, 265.

REGISTRATION
    duty of parties to sale to effect, 282, 283.
    duty of buyer to make, 49.
    vendee responsible to vendor for failure to effect, 284.
    vendee not registering liable for future calls during his ownership, 285.

REGULAR WAY
    defined, 73.

REHYPOTHECATION, 353–370.
 of stock carried for customer, 377.
 held illegal in several of the American States, 369.
 statute forbidding, in Pennsylvania, 91, 369.
  See PLEDGE.

REMEDIES
 for breach of contract of sale, 389, 390.
 against corporations for refusal to transfer, 393, 394.
 of creditors *in rem*, 391, 392.
  See ACTION.

RESTRAINT OF TRADE
 how far contracts bad for, 290.
 limited as to time, 296.
  See CONTRACT.

SALE
 subject, how considered, 138.
 who can make, 183.
 contract of, 182.
 assent of parties as to subject of, 192.
 when recorded in books of Stock Exchange, 54.
 At Stock Exchange, 139.
 of stock at Exchange, really a contract to sell, 184.
 method of executing, 54.
 always of a thing *in esse*, 188, 189.
 by jobbers, 133–135.
 by broker, must be for money, 91, 193, 282, 283.
 and for cash, unless otherwise instructed, 92.
 for money, 45.
 for the account, 45, 55.
 for cash, 54.
 regular way, 54.
 where, in London, no time mentioned, account day understood, 46.
 usually executory, 184, 234.
 executory, described, 187, 189, 230, 231.
 executory, vests no property in goods, until ear-marked, 233.
 executed contract of, vests property in buyer, 232.
 implied condition that article sold is genuine, but no warranty of value, 92.
 at future day, how far legal, 185.
  See, also, GAMING CONTRACT, and WAGER.
 of goods not owned by seller, legal, 187.
 how far sales of securities embraced in Statute of Frauds, 196, 197.
 of shares not within Statute of Frauds in England, 197, 199, 200.
 of stock, in America, how far within Statute of Frauds, 200, 201.
 public, what constitutes, 345–347.
 at Stock Exchange, how far public, 345.
 acceptance of offer by mail, 190, 191.
 as to powers of executors and trustees to sell, see EXECUTORS, and TRUSTEES.
 by pledgee, see PLEDGEE.
 measure of damages for breach, see MEASURE OF DAMAGES.

SCRIP, 73, 147.

SCRIP CERTIFICATES
 how far negotiable, 168.
 of foreign bonds transferable by delivery by usage of brokers, negotiable, 169.

SEAL
 effect of corporate seal on certificate of stock, see FORGED CERTIFICATE.

INDEX.

SEAT IN STOCK EXCHANGE
    assignment of, not good as against fellow-member of Exchange, 52.
    held subject to restrictions created by Stock Exchange, 53.
    subject to owner's debts to members of Stock Exchange, 50.
    may be sold on insolvency of member, 50.
    application of proceeds of insolvent's seat, 50.
    not subject to attachment, 68.
    of bankrupt member, proceeds of, distributed first among his creditors in Exchange, 51.
    distribution of proceeds among members only, legal, 67.
    by-laws of Exchange regulating distribution of proceeds of seat in case of insolvency, not a preference under Bankrupt Act, 51, 68.
    See, also, STOCK EXCHANGE, *Seat in*.

SECURITIES
    when delivered, carry rights incident to them, 49.
    list of, kept at Exchange, 45.
    how called at Stock Exchange, 54.
    rules governing listing of new securities, 45.
    special account days for new securities, in London, 46.
    account days for, in London, 46.
    government, special account day for, in London and New York, 46, 55.
    non-current securities, 48.
    how far negotiable, see NEGOTIABLE INSTRUMENT.
    how far parol sales of, governed by Statute of Frauds, see FRAUDS, STATUTE OF.

SELLER'S OPTION, see OPTION.

SELLING FOR MONEY, see SALE.

SELLING OUT, 48, 73.

SETTLING DAY, 45, 73.
    stock transferred on, 48.

SET-OFF
    sub-broker cannot retain debt due by broker employing him from sale of principal's securities, 91, 228.

SHARES, 73.
    See STOCK.

SHARE WARRANTS, 73.

SHAVE, 74.

SHORT SALES, 74.
    not illegal, 304.
    generally held illegal in Pennsylvania, 306, 307.

SPECIFIC PERFORMANCE
    general principles regulating, 234-257.
    enforced as to specific chattels, 235.
    of stock contracts, enforced, where shares limited in number, 239.
    of executory contracts, 239, 390.
    distinction between government securities and shares of private corporations, as to, 239, 246.
    distinction drawn in America between government bonds and other securities, 251-253.
    not enforced as to executory contracts, in early cases, 236.
    rule deducible from earlier authorities, 238.
    where executory contract has become executed, courts will award, 246.

SPECIFIC PERFORMANCE—*continued*.
    to enforce executory contract, awarded in America, where remedy at law not entirely adequate, 250, 251.
    American cases as to, 246, 255.
    remarks on decisions on, 254.
    granted to compel issue of certificates to stockholder, 249.
    awarded to compel transfer to be permitted, and certificates to be issued, 249.
    bill for, will not lie against directors in a discretionary matter, 241, 242.
    how far directors compellable to approve of a transferee, 242.

SPREAD EAGLE, 74.

STATUTE OF FRAUDS, see FRAUDS, STATUTE OF.

STATUTE OF MORTMAIN, see MORTMAIN.

STOCK
   Defined, 140.
    shares of, are choses in action, 145.
    is not money, 391.
    though bequest of money sometimes passes, 141.
    generally personalty, unless made otherwise by statute, 142.
    where land in a company owned individually by shareholder, shares constitute real property, 144, 145.
    held to be "goods, wares, and merchandise" under Statute of Frauds in the United States, 146, 197–204.
    subject of larceny and felony, 146.
    subject to judgment debts and execution, 146, 181.
    holders of, no right to profits until dividends actually declared, 179.
    owner of, entitled on registration to vote, 175.
    preferred shares, 146.
   How far negotiable.
    shares of, in England, not negotiable, 149.
    shares of, in America, how far negotiable, 149, 154.
    approximates to negotiable paper, 155.
   Transferability of, 174.
    transfer of, usually under seal, 268.
    usual mode of transfer in America is by power of attorney in blank executed by principal, 81.
    how far transferee affected by fraud of transferor, 150, 151.
    agency to purchase, may be given by parol, 81.
    certificate of, see CERTIFICATE.
    corner in, see CORNER.
    standing in name of executor or trustee, see EXECUTOR, and TRUSTEE.
    of canal, treated as real estate within Mortmain Act, 207; see MORTMAIN ACT.
    shares of, how pledged, see PLEDGE.
    obligation to return identical shares, when pledged, see PLEDGEE.
    carrying, 380–81; see PLEDGE.
    salability of, see SALE.
      See, also, SECURITIES.

STOCK BOOK
    register held only evidence as regards company, 375, 401.

STOCK BROKER
    definition of stock broker, 33.
    who may be, 39, 41, 76.
    women may be, 76.
    married woman cannot be, 76.
    but *feme sole* trader may be, 77.
    originally agent for both parties, 34.
    and incurred no liability, 37.

STOCK BROKER—*continued.*
   licensed vocation, open to all, 39.
   remarks of Justice Brett on functions and liabilities of brokers in general, 35.
   difference between, and ordinary broker, 34, 35.
   remarks of Woodruff, J., on, 37.
   additional functions of stock broker in England and America, 84.
   of London, 39.
   effect of London Relief Act, 40.
   unless sworn, cannot in England recover commissions, but may recover advances, though unlicensed, 118.
   in the United States, governed by statutes in the different States, 40.
   not necessarily member of Stock Exchange, 41, 76.
   admission to Stock Exchange, 45.
   if member of Exchange, affected by rules of, 41.
 Duties of, towards customer.
   liability to customer, 106.
   how far he may act as agent for married woman, 80.
   acting for *feme sole* trader, does so *prima facie* at his own risk, 80.
   in transactions for principal, all profits belong to latter, 90.
   bound to use reasonable skill and diligence, 100.
   bound to avoid unnecessary expense, 100.
   bound to keep accounts, 100.
   liable for deviating from principal's instructions even if done with intent to benefit principal, 85, 86.
   where misled by ambiguous instructions, excused, 86, 87.
     See AMBIGUOUS INSTRUCTIONS.
   when authorized to employ sub-agent, not responsible for latter's mistakes, 95.
   not liable for refusing to commit illegal transaction, 100, 106.
   cannot act for both buyer and seller without notifying parties, 34, 65, 90.
   when employed to sell, cannot buy from principal, 90.
   cannot act as both jobber and broker, 46.
   cannot have interest adverse to principal, 89, 227.
   entrusted with the possession of principal's property, 34.
   stock broker may receive property purchased and deliver property sold, 35.
 Right to make sale, 183.
   must sell for cash unless otherwise instructed, 91.
   no authority to sell, except for money, 193, 282, 283.
   with general authority to sell, may bind principal by sale at reasonable price, 92.
   may receive payment on behalf of principal, 91.
   principal may sue on contract made by agent, 131.
 Liability of principal to, 107.
   may recover loss incurred by principal's default, 111.
   cannot recover advances made in illegal transaction, 112.
   carrying stock, relations of, to customer considered, 380, 381.
   may loan shares or purchase money to customer, 65.
 Dealing with trustee, 84, 323–335.
   taking check or draft drawn by trustee, 337.
   not safe in receiving trust moneys in payment, 337.
 Relation to third parties, 129.
   stock broker a principal as to third parties, 35.
   brokers primarily liable to each other on Stock Exchange contracts, 96, 130.
   when making contract in his own name, may sue, 35, 37.
   may recover disbursements and advances made on principal's behalf, 110.
   no right to hypothecate principal's securities, 90, 91, 353–368.
   but may rehypothecate stock bought for a customer on margin, 362.
     See, also, PLEDGE.
   how far bound to return identical shares hypothecated with him, see PLEDGEE.

STOCK BROKER—*continued.*
  Relation to third parties—continued.
    should register stock whether as purchaser or as bailee in his own name, 411.
    deals with jobber as principal, 46.
    defaulting in delivery, compelled to pay increase in price on shares bought in, 48.
    creditors of, affected by rules of Stock Exchange, 66.
    dissolution of agency for customer, 122.
      See PRINCIPAL AND AGENT.
    in relation to Stock Exchange, 45; see STOCK EXCHANGE.
    right to commissions, see COMMISSIONS.
    for delivery by, see DELIVERY.

STOCK EXCHANGE
    definition of, 40, 43.
    history of, 44.
    character of principal Stock Exchanges, 49.
    who may become member of, 41, 76.
    of London, 44.
    of London, constitution of, 44.
    method of dealing in, in London, 46.
    definition of, in America, 49.
    origin of, in America, 49.
    origin of, in Philadelphia, 49.
    in America, method of dealing in, 53.
  Seat in.
    admission of members of, regulated by rules of, 53.
    purchase of seat, 50.
    vested interest in seat, 50.
    proceeds of seat in, in America, pass to executor, 50.
    member must be elected, 50.
    admission of members to, in England, 45.
    conditions of election of member, in England, 45.
    member has no vested interest in, in London, 45.
      See, also, SEAT IN STOCK EXCHANGE.
  By-laws and usages of.
    by-laws of, validity of, 51.
    by-laws of, binding without notice on each member, 67.
    members how far legally bound by, 65.
    usages of, binding on members, 41.
    rules of, how far binding on non-members, 66.
    rules of, binding on outsider employing member of, 66.
    non-member dealing through member, affected by usages of, 41.
    rules of, must be reasonable, 66.
    rules of, cannot give creditor in Stock Exchange general priority, against Bankrupt Act, 69.
    rules of, cannot vary broker's relation to outside creditors, 132.
    customs of, often evidence of commercial usage, 41.
    how far sale at, constitutes a public sale, 345.
    sales at, see SALE.
    insolvency of members, 50–52; see SEAT IN STOCK EXCHANGE.

STOPPAGE IN TRANSITU, 261.

STRADDLE, 74.

SUB-PLEDGE, see PLEDGE.

SUNDAY
    when delivery falls on, made on preceding day, 55.
    pledge made on, voidable, 370, 371.

INDEX. 443

TELEGRAPH
    contracts effected by, 191, 192; see CONTRACT.

TENDER, 282; see PAYMENT.

TICKET, 74.
    how passed to selling broker, 47.

TICKET DAY, 47, 74.
    See NAME DAY.

TIME
    days, how counted, 280.
    last hour for delivery, 280.
    in stock transactions, generally fixed by regulations of different Stock Exchanges, 281.
    construction of word "month," 280.
    of "leap-year," 280.
    when fixed by a contract, usually binding in stock transactions, 279.

TRADE
    restraint of, see RESTRAINT OF TRADE, and CONTRACT.

TRANSFER
    must, in England, be registered by buyer, 49.
    acceptance of, in one mode, by broker, waives right to insist on transfer in any other, 281.
    of negotiable instruments, 148.
    made without surrender of certificate, held good, 153, 375, 401.
    how far production of stock and certificate necessary to, 153, 375, 401.
    of stock usually under seal, 268.
    when not effected under by-laws of corporation, how far good against attaching creditors, 374.
    remedy for refusal to, by corporation, 393.
    right of company to impose restrictions as to, 393.
    right of owner of stock to, 174.
    under seal, executed in blank, how far good, 269–278; see POWER OF ATTORNEY.
    of forged certificates, 396; see FORGED CERTIFICATE.

TRANSFEREE
    when passed by jobber, must be *sui juris*, 136.
    name of ultimate transferee delivered to jobber with price, 47.
    selling broker, how far bound to accept, 47.
    not bound to show title of transferor in order to effect transfer, 394.
    of scrip certificates of bonds, 169–172.
    of stock, as to title of, see NEGOTIABLE INSTRUMENT.
    of stock, by forged transfer, see FORGED TRANSFER.

TROVER
    held in some States to lie for shares, 391.
    held to lie against pledgee on rehypothecation to latter, 369.
    will not lie against pledgee unless tender of advance first be made, 362, 369.

TRUSTEES
    no implied power to pledge, 331.
    cannot delegate power to pledge, 333.
    when authorized to pledge, must act jointly, 333.
    no implied power to sell, 331, 332, 335.
    person making advances to, is affected with notice of contents of instrument creating trust, 332, 333.
    in selling, all must join, 335, 336.
    cheque by persons acting as, how far broker safe in receiving, 337.
    power to buy securities other than those authorized by statute depends upon trust deed, 84.

ULTIMATE BUYER, 74.
ULTIMATE PURCHASER, 74.
ULTIMATE TRANSFEREE, 47.
  See TRANSFEREE.
USAGE
  of Stock Exchange, how far binding on persons dealing with and through stock brokers, 215, 219, 220.
  generally binding on person dealing on Stock Exchange even if ignorant of it, 225.
  what constitutes unreasonable, 226, 227.
  of sub-broker to deduct debt due him by broker from sale of his principal's securities, bad, 91, 228.
  evidence of, admissible, unless opposed to public policy, 225.
  distinction between rules binding on members and third parties, 226.
  new rules made by Stock Exchange after contract, not binding on third parties, 225.
  of trade as to payment, 91.
  of Stock Exchange, as to time, binding on outside parties dealing through it, 217, 218.
  regulates mode of making delivery, 267.
  as to notice, see NOTICE.
  See, also, STOCK EXCHANGE.

VENDOR AND PURCHASER, 230.
  vendor need not have possession of goods contracted to be sold, 187.
  what vendor must deliver, 260, 261.
  what parties contracted to buy and sell, question for jury, 263, 264.
  vendor's duties in making delivery, 267.
  how delivery effected, 55, 266.
  vendor must transfer usual evidence of title, 266.
  vendor warrants title, but not intrinsic value, 262.
  buyer may demand certificates of 100 shares each, 55.
  where "man of straw" put forward by jobber, vendor bound, unless he object at time, 136.
  duties of vendee as to registration, 283.
  vendor need not place vendee's name on register unless required, 266.
  either party may demand transfer by registration, in Philadelphia Stock Exchange, 55.
  vendee bound to register if required, 283.
  vendor may deliver power of attorney to transfer with certificate, 55, 266-269.
  vendee may demand actual transfer, in New York or Philadelphia Stock Exchange, 55.
  purchaser bound to accept and register name if required, 283.
  vendor, when bound to guarantee power of attorney, 55.
  vendor liable for delivering forged certificate, 262.
  how far vendor bound to give receipt, 286.
  purchaser may buy from executor, unless a long time has elapsed since decedent's death, 328-335.
  See EXECUTORS.
  effect of failure to register upon delivery, see DELIVERY.
  trustee has no implied power to sell, 331-333; see TRUSTEES.
VOTING
  privilege of, passes to transferee, 175.

WAGER
  not bad at common law, 297.
  statutes relating to, in England, 298.

WAGER—*continued.*
    Sir John Barnard's Act, 298.
    held void in America, 297, 298.
    cases on, in the United States, 299-318.
    Pennsylvania cases on, 305-308.
    general principles as to validity of stock contracts, 318.
    where contract mere cover for gaming transaction, illegal, 318.
    whether contract merely cover for gaming transaction, question for jury, 313, 318.
    test of what constitutes, applied in early cases, 299.
    how far sale for future delivery is, 185, 303.
    contract of sale held valid where delivery contemplated, 318.
    contract not illegal because no manual delivery intended, 303.
    short sale, where actual delivery not contemplated, not illegal, 304.
    question of intention to deliver, for jury, 313.
        See, also, GAMING CONTRACTS.

WARRANTY
    of genuineness of things sold by broker, 262.
    no warranty on sale of stocks on Stock Exchange, but condition that article sold is genuine, 94.
    vendor does not warrant that securities are properly or legally issued, 262.
    vendor liable for delivery of forged certificates, 262, 263.
    question of genuineness, one of fact for jury, 263.

WASH, 74.

WASHING
    illegal, 90.

WOMEN
    may be stock brokers, but never yet admitted as members of Stock Exchange, 76.
    See MARRIED WOMAN, and FEME SOLE TRADER.

THE END.

www.ingramcontent.com/pod-product-compliance
Lightning Source LLC
Chambersburg PA
CBHW020527300426
44111CB00008B/566